CRAFT AND CONCEPT
THE REMATERIALIZATION OF THE ART OBJECT

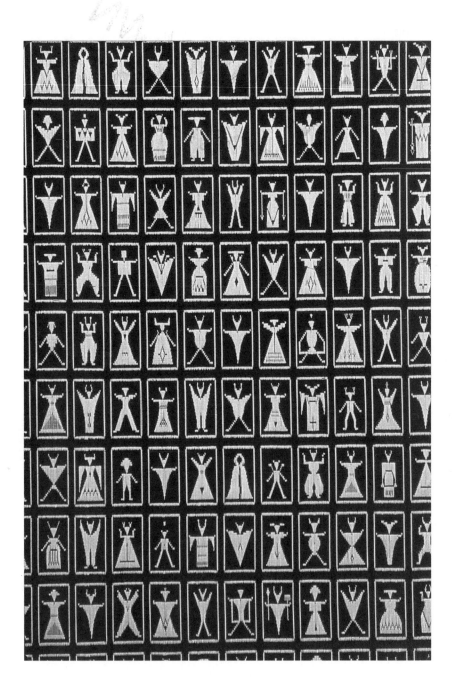

Thomasin Grim: *Characters* (detail), 1991–93, 96 x 60 x 1 ½".
Photo: Braunstein/Quay Gallery, San Francisco

CRAFT AND CONCEPT
THE REMATERIALIZATION OF THE ART OBJECT

BY

MATTHEW KANGAS

Midmarch Arts Press
New York City

The author and publisher wish to thank the following individual and institutions for their generous support of this publication:

Dale and Doug Anderson; Becky and Jack A. Benaroya; Karen Johnson Boyd; The Chazen Foundation; Stephen and Pamela Hootkin; Drs. R. Joseph and Elaine Monsen; George and Dorothy Saxe; The Jon and Mary Shirley Foundation; and Ronald and Anita Wornick.

Library of Congress Control Number 2006921487
ISBN 1-877675-56-3 (paper)
ISBN 1-877675-58-x (cloth)

Copyright © 2006 by Matthew Kangas and Midmarch Arts Press, Seattle and New York

Printed in the United States of America

Published in 2006 by
Midmarch Arts Press
New York, NY 10025

CONTENTS

In Memoriam

Lee Nordness

1922–1995

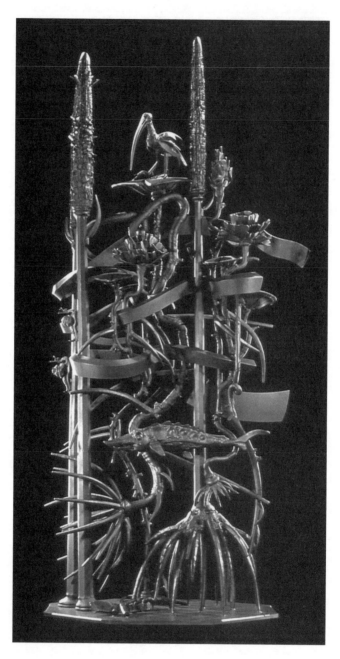

Albert Paley: *Gate Section for Central Park Zoo (Prototype)*, forged and fabricated
Cor Ten steel, 14 x 5 ½ x 5 ½". Courtesy of the artist, Rochester, New York.
Photo: Bruce Miller

PREFACE

If one has any doubt about the value of art criticism, this selection
of the craft-centered essays of Matthew Kangas should put those
misgivings to rest. Jargon-free and generous, the results of Kangas's
decade-long scouring—and liming—of the aesthetic minefields of contemporary crafts will prove invaluable to craft aficionados, artists, art
historians (present and future) and to other critics. Kangas is Seattle-
based and has written long and well about paintings and sculpture,
but this current collection of his writings will still be an eye-opener.
Yes, there is art criticism outside of New York. Yes, one can write
seriously about craft as art. Craft is art; rather, a kind of art. It may
have a slightly different history and a slightly different context than
painting and sculpture, but as these essays prove, it can be just as
aesthetically challenging and, on some levels, just as rewarding.

Comprised primarily of catalogue essays and magazines pieces for
such national venues as *American Ceramics, Sculpture* and *GLASS*,
this is a critical survey that may act as a craft overview, presenting
issues—some of them perennial—and touchstones. Kangas's long essay on glass master—and Seattle kingpin—Dale Chihuly is in itself
essential and full of insights as well as information. His "Toward a
Bicameral Esthetic of Clay" is an important critical contribution to
craft theory.

Seattle, of course, is now one of the American craft capitals, not because of its craft history—which, compared to such former meccas as
Cincinnati and Detroit, is thin—but because of the post-World War
II flowering of clay, wood, metal, fiber and, above all, the centrality,
glamour, and high visibility of the region's Studio Glass Movement.

If one counts glass art as real art (which one should do), then since
1972, when the now-renowned Pilchuck Glass School was founded,
Seattle has produced more nationally and internationally acclaimed
artists than any city of its size. A number of them make star appearances here. Besides the in-depth examination of Pilchuck mastermind
Chihuly, we are offered essays on Buster Simpson, William Morris,
Therman Statom, Ginny Ruffner, Paul Marioni, and Benjamin Moore.
Others who have taught and/or worked in Seattle have been included,
such as Marvin Lipofsky, Bertil Vallien, Toots Zynsky and Lynda
Benglis. To read these essays is to learn how glass moved from factory
floor to the studio and the atelier, from the gift shop to the art gallery.

Less Seattle-centered but almost as strong is the ceramic front as described by Kangas. Seattle is indeed the nation's glass capital; but despite such solid elders as Robert Sperry and Richard Fairbanks, it is much like other U.S. cities when it comes to clay. The colleges and universities own ceramics, freeing it, for better or worse, from production pottery. Seattle's Howard Kottler, surely a major ceramic artist, can be said to have embodied in his work both Funk and what might be called Concept Clay. Michael Lucero, who became more an East Village artist than a Seattle one, is also well represented.

But Kangas gets around. The local purview is not local at all. "American Figurative Ceramics" will be an important component of any broader view of ceramics. Kangas also has valuable insights about Picasso's ceramics, thanks to a 1999 exhibition of unique pieces that came to the Tacoma Art Museum outside Seattle, but strangely traveled nowhere else in the U.S.

To round out the traditional Big Five of crafts, Kangas covers wood, fiber, and metals. His discussion of the Ellensburg Funky school of avant-garde jewelry (tied forever to Central Washington University)—like his "Pacific Northwest Crafts in the 1950s" and "Shattered Self: Northwest Figurative Ceramics"—will need to be consulted over and over again for any historical survey of American craft.

These essays are important in another regard. Although Kangas has been fortunate that his home base is so crafts-rich, his response has been exemplary. Critics in other crafts regions could profit from his example. His essays on craft are templates of high seriousness. Over the years he has set about to document local accomplishments in a national context, indicating their larger import. Seattle has been lucky to have him and his persuasive writings. And so are all those who love craft.

—John Perreault

—John Perreault is a past president of the American section of the International Association of Art Critics and founder of Artopia (www. artsjournal.com / artopia).

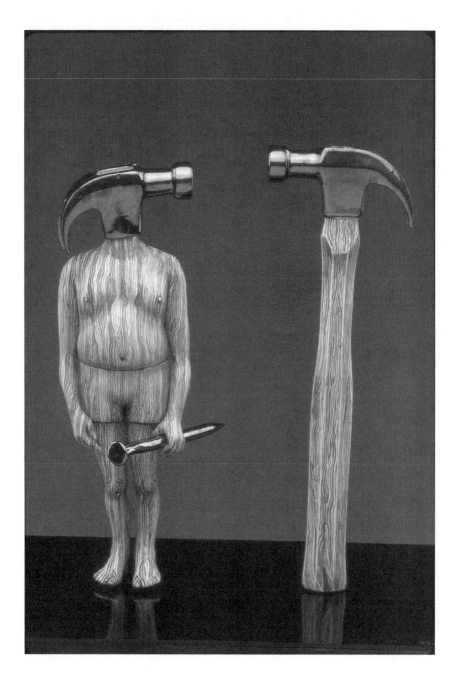

Patti Warashina: *The Imposter,* 1987, porcelain and glazes, 21 x 17 x 10".
Courtesy of Howard House, Seattle. Photo: Roger Schreiber

INTRODUCTION

American craft is like a large umbrella covering a multitude of artistic practices. From functional objects made by hand to sculptural constructions made of clay, glass, wood, fiber or metals, American craft is, in turn, part of a broader, global phenomenon. Every society or culture on earth has a craft tradition, one that unites American artisans with those of the past, as well as with people of other nations.

The essays collected here cover a 25-year period and represent the growth of my thought and opinions on craft art. As John Perreault points out in his generous preface, "craft is art; rather, a kind of art." If not all craft is art, conversely, not all objects using paint or bronze are automatically art either. Sometimes craft overlaps with art in a vector of aesthetic meaning; sometimes art overlaps with craft in its stressing of the readily evident appearance of handmade construction. As Donald Kuspit wrote, "there can be craft without art but there cannot be art without craft."

Like intertwined, mutually dependent siblings who do not always get along but who have much in common, craft and art come together only in the presence of concept and meaning. The skilled construction or craft in an artwork becomes the vehicle or conveyor of concept.

Rereading the essays here, I realize that the presence of theory or concepts in my own writing has been carried by the interpretations I have applied to the objects under discussion. The will or need to interpret has always coexisted in my writing with the appreciation and understanding of formal properties that are granted validity for their own sake. Developing as an art critic at a time when abstraction and representation seemed at odds with one another at times, I realize this was a critical dialectic that I benefited from as a working art critic. Narrative became as important as shape or pattern because both were reflected in the arts being analyzed. Growing up during the Cold War, I felt an acute longing for the reconciliation of seeming opposites. As modernism waned with its primacy of nonrepresentational imagery, I was frequently confronted with rising or resurging alternative concepts: politics; historicism; feminism; ornamentalism; ethnic revivalism and others. All these exposures and their attendant analyses confirmed my underlying conclusion about craft art, that without the obvious excellence of execution, any story, idea or narrative cannot be successfully carried forth.

What may appear evident to many today, that art and craft are fusing together and that craft practices are an alternative, constant influence on contemporary art, is outlined in many of the essays. The initial section, "Part I: On the Crafts," is both a collective theoretical position statement and a brief historical backgrounder from 1750 to the present. But instead of approaching such objects as would a decorative arts historian (the history of styles) or an anthropologist (the material culture approach), I have projected meaning onto objects of the past from the present and interpreted meaning in the present as a manifestation of individual, often idiosyncratic, artistic visions. Readers may sample a survey of storytelling in American craft; a case study of one decade, the 1950s, in one region, the Pacific Northwest; an omnibus overview of three separate historical periods in American craft; and two more polemical studies. "The Rematerialization of the Art Object" is my riposte to Lucy R. Lippard and John Chandler's 1968 essay, "The De-materialization of Art." I take conceptual art to task and defend the necessity of the art object over the stand-alone idea claiming aesthetic status. "The Myth of the Neglected Ceramics Artist" is the outgrowth of a Smithsonian Institution-funded research project on the role art critics played since 1945 in elevating American ceramics to fine arts status.

The next three sections concentrate on clay, glass, wood, fiber and metals. Ceramic art from the U.S., Canada, Finland, Japan, Nigeria and France is discussed in "Part II." Until it was supplanted by glass as the most visible and celebrated craft material in the art world, ceramic sculpture paved the way for all the other craft media: serious analysis; substantial individual achievements; and a startling variety of approaches that led to reciprocal influe3nces between the U.S. and other countries.

My bias toward figurative ceramic sculpture is clear in these essays, but the attentive reader or student will notice how American ceramics in general both paralleled contemporary art movements (Surrealism, Abstract Expressionism, Pop Art and Funk Art) and added a few of its own, like the pseudo-archaeological conceits of artists like Clayton S. Bailey and the family of artists in Colorado, life in general.

Unlike ceramics, which had a healthy balance of functional vessels and sculptural figures, glass art has long privileged the container shape over the figure. In "Part III: Glass," I trace this evolution in an opening essay so readers can place the rise of glass in the context of clay, metals, wood and fiber. Though glass artists' emphasis on the vessel may seem more conservative than the ceramists', they have succeeded in doing something few clay artists achieved: combining their chosen material in assemblages with other materials. Several of the essays, like those on Nancy Mee, Buster Simpson, Therman Statom and Ginny Ruffner, explore this development.

The concepts embodied in the art of the other glassmakers mentioned may center on the vessel but, in the case of a few like William Morris, Robert Willson, Bertil Vallien, Preston Singletary and Susan Point, they allude to ancient or prehistoric cultures in ways that put sculpture first. Whether with references to hunter-gatherer cultures, the Mayan civilization, Swedish maritime history or Native American rituals, these artists have advanced glass as a medium that can carry complex layers of meaning.

"Part IV: Wood, Fiber and Metals" addresses the craft materials with rich heritages that, except for a few artists, have not yet fully attained art world acceptance but are surely worthy of such recognition. In this sense, we can see the art world as both lagging behind craft practice and simultaneously taking a peek at it. Furniture artists like Brian Gladwell, Tommy Simpson, Albert Paley, Randy Shull and Wendell Castle push functional objects in the direction of sculpture. Since Donald Judd's editioned tables and chairs are now hailed, it is important to note the parallel tradition of these artists. Rather than Bauhaus taboos, ornament and surface decoration play important roles in carrying the expressive intentions of these artists.

Fiber artist Jean Williams Cacicedo, as well as jewelers Ramona Solberg, Don Tompkins, Keith Lewis and Nancy Worden, claims the body as her platform. Activated by the wearer, their constructions comment on everything from Third World politics and the myth of the Far West to AIDS, art history and feminism. These artists are often overlooked because of the smaller scale of their art and, in my discussions of their accomplishments, I attempt to remedy that prejudice.

In some cases, like turned and carved wood sculptures, I have annexed a fine arts history for them, specifically, the sculptural heritage and sculptural implications of early twentieth-century modern sculptors like Arp, Brancusi and Barbara Hepworth.

The final section, "Part V: Two American Masters," reprints my museum retrospective catalogue essay on Rudy Autio, the pioneering Montana artist and unsung colleague of Peter Voulkos. A previously unpublished essay on Dale Chihuly chronicles his evolution as a revolutionary genius and indefatigably imaginative artist updating and enhancing both the decorative power of glass and, in my reading, becoming a suggestive symbolist of great originality.

Finally, besides thanking John Perreault for his preface as well as the benefactors (listed elsewhere) who helped make possible this publication, I want to thank the publisher, Cynthia Navaretta of Midmarch Arts Press, for her unwavering support of the book and her unstinting dedication and critical scrutiny in making the collection as reader-friendly and useful as possible.

Freelance writers are always dependent upon the kindness of editors. I have been unusually fortunate both with the helpful supervision of magazine and catalogue editors and their occasional story ideas. I would like to thank the following for their hard work and continued encouragement: Kate Hensler Fogarty, editor of *American Ceramics* and *GLASS*; Sherman Hall, William C. Hunt and Ruth Butler, editors of *Ceramics Monthly*; Glenn Harper, editor of *Sculpture*; Hyun-Jung Kim, editor of *CRART* (Seoul); Frank Lewis, editor of *Metalsmith*; Lois Moran, Patricia Dandignac and Beverly Sanders, editors of *American Craft*; Patricia Malarcher, editor of *Surface Design Journal*; Koji Matano, editor of Glasswork (Kyoto); Andrew Page, editor of *GLASS;* Michael McTwigan, editor of *American Ceramics*; John Perreault, editor of *GLASS*; Suzanne Ramljak, editor of *American Ceramics, Sculpture, GLASS* and *Metalsmith*; and Satoka Shinoda, editor of *Glass & Art* (Tokyo).

Thanks to their invitations and sensitive follow-through, I have been able to explore an area of American art that is well worth the time and effort. Any contributions these essays make to such a discourse has been reciprocal. They have shaped the kind of art critic I have become.

—M.K.

PART I

ON THE CRAFTS

Edwin and Mary Scheier:
Judgment of Solomon,
1948, earthenware with
matte glazes, 14 ½" dia.
Newark Museum, Purchase
1949, Special Purchase
Fund, 49.370.

Sidney Waugh, designer,
Atlantica, 1938–39, Steuben
Glass Company, maker,
colorless lead glass, cast
and polished, 37 1/8" h.
Corning Museum of glass,
gift of Corning Glass Works,
72.4.22.

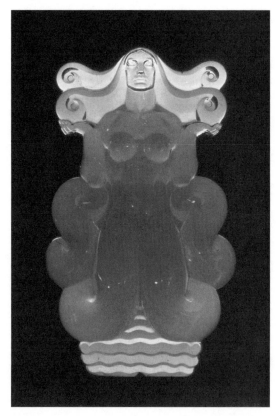

STORYTELLING IN AMERICAN CRAFT 1750–1950

INTRODUCTION: BEFORE THE REPUBLIC

"Once upon a time." That is the way a story begins. However, there are many kinds of stories, many different ways they are told, and many different reasons for telling them. Time or sequence is an important part of written storytelling and it is crucial to point out how time is condensed in the visual arts: all elements of a tale may be present in one image. This difference immediately distinguishes the kind of storytelling or narrative in "Tales and Traditions."

This exhibition, "Tales and Traditions: Storytelling in Twentieth-Century American Craft," seeks to make a case that storytelling in its broadest sense—a person, a myth, a plot, an event, a statement—provides a heretofore unseen and unappreciated dimension of achievement within the development of the living decorative arts—or studio craft—of 20th-century America.

Storytelling in 20th-century American craft is a result of a variety of influences and purposes: social, political, historical, commemorative, personal and psychological. It

reflects the American urge to boast, brag, amuse, and tell a story about one's region, past, family, culture or self with humor and satire, warmth and passion, anger and mystery.

Drawing upon the five basic craft materials—ceramics, glass, metals, textiles and wood—the case for aesthetic content in craft, i.e., *meaning*, can be made by a re-excavation of craft objects already known but never before grouped together or discussed in terms of their potential storytelling properties. As we shall see, craft artists, designers and artisans often delved into pre-existing literary models for the sources of their tales: Judeo-Christian parables; Greco-Roman mythology; Arthurian legend; Shakespeare; American folklore. In addition, they created their own stories growing out of personal experience or responses to political and social events in our turbulent century.

In each case, the force of the story or myth has never led to a sacrifice of craftsmanship. In fact, without the excellence of execution, the story or narrative cannot be successfully carried forth.

An emphasis on analyzing the decoration of surfaces has led to a neglect of other areas of content in 20th-century American craft. The expropriation of the field by decorative arts historians in discussing the art of those no longer living has stressed technical, historical, and contextual aspects of craft rather than its interpretive dimension. This exhibition presumes an active interpretive faculty going so far as to *instill* content where none may have been thought to previously exist. Yet in each case, the clues to interpretation exist in the physical embodiment of the artwork: imagery, juxtaposition of materials, formal properties, and selection. Building on these qualities, it becomes possible to open up the storytelling dimension in American craft and uncover a longer lineage of high artistic purpose than has been thus far been granted.

Surface decoration is one vehicle for artistic content in craft. When it involves the human figure, a potential for narrative is set in motion which will remain intriguing and tantalizing long after the object is made, sold, collected, and measured or assessed by art historians.

Perhaps deliberately, perhaps unwittingly, the furniture maker, the potter or clay sculptor, the glassblower or designer, the jeweler or metalsmith, and the weaver or fiber artist, often present us with a potential story which weds use to meaning and, in so doing, presents his or her art in a different way than a painter or bronze sculptor might. It can be appreciated on many levels. And, just as various periods of history have stressed art as more or less a reflection of society, 20th-century American craft reflects society on a much more pragmatic level.

Since the objects craftmakers create are frequently highly wrought and thus, expensive, their immediate audience might seem narrow or elite. However, many of the finest of these objects are now in public and private collections available to the public or public institutions for viewing. "Tales and Traditions" draws on these newly available resources, upon recent scholarship and criticism addressing the objects, and seeks to place them in a setting—the museum—where they may be visually examined, enjoyed, and seen together. From commemorative plates to ecclesiastical silver, from humorous figurines to stern political satire, from wildly extravagant furniture to a simple Southwest chair, the artworks in "Tales and Traditions" greet and provoke the viewer into reassembling the stories they tell: of their making, of their imagery, of their imaginative potential.

Although "Tales and Traditions" covers the 20th century, our story begins with the origins of the Republic. One could go back even farther, to Greek vase painting, for example, or Egyptian tomb artifacts, for the roots of storytelling in craft but, for our purposes, it is helpful to examine two contrasting works roughly 200 years apart.

Louis XV, a porcelain bust made in France at the Chantilly factory around 1750, tells no story at all; it is the embodiment of absolute power, the king of France who reigned from 1715 to 1774. The seeds of the American Revolution had been sown by French writers like Voltaire and Rousseau but art was still consecrated to those in power. At twelve-and-one-half inches high, *Louis XV* is a diminutive symbol, made for the courtiers at Versailles or for landed aristocracy. The lion at the pedestal's base is the King of Beasts, reinforcing the monarch's primary position among humans but its tiny size renders such puissance a bit absurd.

In contrast, *Factory / Farmworker* (1938), a five-foot-high carved stoneware sculpture by Waylande Gregory, summons up a number of possible stories. Heroic in its own way, it also contains attached symbols of power: the earth below, the factory, the smokestack, the plume of smoke. Made at the height of the Great Depression, it poses the worker with right leg forward, ready to go. Not a symbol of state, like *Louis XV*, but part of a story of American corporate industrial power, the Gregory sculpture's reverse side contains a farmworker. Together, they form the elements for a story about the range of American labor, from farm to factory.

By being surrounded with ample appurtenances on the figures, we make up their stories about grit, determination, sacrifice, and triumph. By 1938, a different effigy of absolute power was rising, however: fascism.

Many stories we love are about humans and animals: "Little Red Riding Hood;" "Daniel in the Lion's Den;" "Beauty and the Beast;" and others. In ancient times, people believed gods could pose as animals to intervene with (or love or harm) humans. "The Rape of Europa," a Greek myth about Zeus becoming a bull to spirit off the lovely maiden Europa, is a mixture of violence and pastoral grace.[1] Around 1750, the Meissen workshop in Germany (where the European discovery of porcelain occurred in 1708–09) made its own completely neutered and docile version. Not threatening but delightful, it suggests how stories repeated frequently can change radically or reflect the period in which they are told. With European world power at an apogee, the toning down or pastoralization of the rape of Europa well suited an indulgent, decadent society eager for pleasure and sensuous distractions. Garlanded with flowers, the symbolic sexual power of the bull—or Zeus—is feminized, diminished, and satirized.

Again, to demonstrate how different the American experience became, *Apocalypse '42* (1942) by Viktor Schreckengost also uses an animal—a horse perched atop the world—but to a totally different end: propaganda. With Europe in flames in 1942, the Cleveland artist depicted three bloody tyrants—Benito Mussolini, Emperor Hirohito, Adolf Hitler—seated on a horse galloping toward the end of the world, the apocalypse. Each figure is associated, like Louis XV was, with signs of his power. The helmeted skeleton among them is Death. Thus we see how similar and yet how different certain building blocks of stories can become across time.

Within the singular art object, an entire story may be told with elaborate or economical means. Sometimes, the story may already be familiar to the viewer. Sometimes, the impetus to create the story out of the elements provided is on the viewer. In emblematic objects, one image might stand for the whole story. In performative objects, the function of the object, its use, might complete the story told about on its surface. Where many images are present, more than one story might be present simultaneously, like reading a short story anthology all at once.

Any traditional story requires a teller and, in our case, the teller is the art object. It is the carrier or mediator of the story between the viewer and the artist. In the same way the bull and the horse are carriers of their characters, so any crafted art work is the vehicle for the story its maker chooses to convey.

Besides the storyteller, that is, the American craft maker, the person hearing the tale or the audience looking at the object also participates in how the story is imparted. We bring our own wealth of experiences as individuals to each story we see or hear; we also participate collectively as an audience, as in the theatre, responding as a group to certain commemorative portraits, for example, of our national leaders. Depending on the audience, then, the story's impact and meaning may change. *Apocalypse '42* had an entirely different meaning—a warning-when it was first made in 1942. The United States of America had a fully established national identity by then but, for the second time in this century, that way of life and those values were threatened by foreign military aggression abroad.

Long before, when the Republic was young, much of the lore that established the American identity was manufactured in England, France, Germany and China and exported to the ex-North American colonies. Often, the subject matter dealt with American themes, military heroes and victors. In an American exception, even a traitor was memorialized. Basic utilitarian wares made of clay, wood, metals, glass and cloth were produced in the young nation but fine decorative objects were not made extensively. To be sure, magnificent examples of silver from New York or Boston were extant as early as the 17th century: the workmen and women were usually of Dutch (New York) or French origin (for example, Paul Revere II, the Boston silversmith and subject of his own Americana myth).

After the Revolutionary War ended, when foreign trade was renewed, Americans set about to furnish their homes by ordering dinnerware, for example, from as far away as Nanjing, China. The household wares ordered from abroad by George Washington, for example, have been the subject of extensive research.[2] It was English and French artisans, however, who shepherded ahead American craft makers by their examples of superlative workmanship, a highly developed way of telling a story—and decorating a useful object at the same time.

BEFORE THE "AMERICAN CENTURY"

> When I peruse the conquer'd fame of heroes/and the victories of mighty generals, I do not envy the generals,/Nor the President in his Presidency, nor the rich in his great house. . . .
>
> —Walt Whitman

It was the founder of Time, Inc., Henry B. Luce, who coined the term "American century" in a February, 1941 issue of *Life*.[3] Regardless of its appeal and widespread adherence, the concept of the "American century" also carried implications of military and moral domination. Many of the objects in "Tales and Traditions" conform to or refute that vision of America as rightly all-powerful. Before examining them, it is worth scanning briefly some of the high points of 19th-century American craft to make the point that, while midcentury American powerbrokers like Luce may have claimed the 20th century as the apogee of U.S. power, the events of the 19th century also accumulated into an overwhelming sense of confidence, pride and even arrogance.

The Civil War, to be sure, wrenched the nation but it also led to extraordinary industrial growth in the North after the war. Add to that the westward expansion both before and after the Civil War, the fulfillment of Manifest Destiny (another shibboleth of inevitable American power), the conquering of Native American peoples, and the atmosphere of God-given rights to prosperity despite human and ecological costs became palpable.

The Industrial Revolution occurred primarily in the East, abetted by the building of the railroad. Like Napoleon crowning himself emperor, American industrial leaders, through related cultural agents and institutions, commemorated their achievements with objects of commanding beauty and richness.

The centennial year of 1876 was a stock-taking year for the Exposition in Philadelphia, the accomplishments of national craft artists were put on view, and many pottery companies, for example, prepared exhibits for the occasion. Chief among these is the *Century Vase* (1876)[4] in the collection of the Metropolitan Museum of Art, designed by Karl L. H. Muller for his employer, Union Porcelain Works at Greenpoint in Brooklyn, New York.

While President Washington presides over the rest of the vase from a portrait medallion, the narrative of power, done in the style of Greek vase scenes, unfolds along the base. Scenes of Native Americans, a Revolutionary War soldier, and the Boston Tea Party are among those abbreviated into instantly recognizable stories which, when taken together, form a grand narrative for the Republic up to that time.

Significant for its execution in porcelain (placing the U.S. on a footing with Europe and Asia), *Century Vase* tells a story whose meaning has changed with the passing of time.

Looking back, the Indians seem glorified as another vanquished and submissive enemy, as the bison head handles remind us of the slaughter of bison and buffaloes which went hand in hand during the opening of the Far West. What was celebrated then might be mourned today. Nevertheless, the vase remains a high point for American craft. An even more elaborate version which includes scenes of telegraph lines being erected is in the collection of the Brooklyn Museum.[5]

If the story of the railroads was celebrated on decorative objects along with the conquering of the Native Americans and the first century of independence, it is safe to say that capitalist entrepreneurship was the underlying driving force in American craft at this time. Patronage determines content in art and the robber barons and new American millionaires of the post-Civil War Gilded Age were well equipped to commission domestic interiors by Tiffany[6], portraits by William Merritt Chase, and a whole panoply of magnificently useless objects, the kinds of things Harvard economist Thorstein Veblen alluded to as "conspicuous consumption" in his 1899 study *The Theory of the Leisure Class*.

BEFORE THE GREAT WAR

The nineteenth century did not really end until 1918, the end of World War I. At that time, the confidence and complacent isolation of the American Republic were shattered, along with conventions and attitudes which had hallmarked the long stretch of peace, monopolistic commodity distribution, and unparalleled growth of wealth.

American craft benefited from a renewed appreciation of the handmade in the face of the factory-made and from the generosity of industrial satraps who, having traveled in Europe, were eager to prove the equal abilities of U.S. artisans. During the 1890–1914 period, the last period of innocent national confidence before the wholesale slaughter abroad, a free-spending atmosphere generated commissions for elaborately fashioned decorative objects which often had stories of their own to reveal.

Made over a two-year period, the so-called "Adams Vase" (1893–95), was sold by Tiffany and Co., but designed by Paulding Farnham. Presented to Edward Dean Adams, chairman of the board of American Cotton Oil Co., it is constructed of solid gold, sterling silver, pearls, enamel and semi-precious stones. Once again, American craft makers were catering to the aggrandizement of patronage, in this case, the giant cotton industry. It was, in a way, the cause of the Civil War through its insistence on slavery.

Within 30 years of the defeat of the South, the *Adams Vase* presented an idealized vision of the product that made a few millionaires and caused suffering and death for thousands. With the vase representing a cotton plant in form, tendrils rising from the "earth" at its base, personifications of Greek mythological figures like Mercury flank either side above seated figures reminiscent of Italian Renaissance goldsmith Benvenuto Cellini.

Cotton bolls are emulated by pearls contained in golden leaves. Four golden eagles surmount the shoulders of the vase. Symbolizing America through an immediately recognizable animal, the eagles also remind us that a gold-eagle coin was issued by the U.S. Treasury during this period. As such, America-as-eagle is represented indistinguishable from wealth or money.

In fact, every aspect of the vase, each of its story elements, conspires to present an overall image of idealized labor. In ironic contrast to King Cotton's origins as slaveholder, the figures exist in a deified, carefree state. With the gilt silver marvelously entangling the vessel and literally overgrowing it, a tale of entangled plantations, divided loyalties, and ruthlessly encroaching brokers (like Adams?) operates on a darker, subterranean level. The *Adams Vase* is an orgy of capitalistic self-congratulation typical of the era before the Great War.

If African-Americans were absented from the story of cotton in the *Adams Vase*, they were sure to be represented—and frequently condescended to—in the coming century. Long before those happy-go-lucky stories appeared in American craft, Native American peoples were subjected to hypocritically romantic treatment of their own. Free-spirited but vanquished (and therefore targets for sentimentalized mythology), various indigenous tribes appeared on decorative arts objects such as the 1898 Rookwood vase made in Cincinnati, Ohio, depicting Chief Joseph of the Nez Percé tribe of Idaho, Montana, and Washington state, painted by William P. McDonald. Contained, if not doomed, by a European form (the porcelain vase), Chief Joseph barely emerges out of a darkened ground as if he and the Nez Percés were already consigned to oblivion. Although McDonald's likeness is not based on a known photograph by Edward S. Curtis, it was Curtis who drew easterners' attention to the great leader. In an October 13, 1904 letter to University of Washington President Edmond S. Meany, he wrote at the time of Chief Joseph's death:

> At last his long, endless fight for his return to the old home is at an end. . . . Perhaps he was not quite what we in our minds had pictured him but I still think that he was one of the greatest men that has ever lived.[7]

If the Indian wars were being consigned to narratives of one-sided nostalgia, the Civil War wounds were still raw as late as 1908. When can a craft work look like a storytelling device but not really be one? A quilt at the Chicago Historical Society, *Daughters of the Grand Army of the Republic* (1907–08), includes all the discrete elements of storytelling—pictures, words, sequential arrangements—without a fully developed tale. Its composition situates each regimental memorial emblem close to one another approximating the logic of a story. However, we re-create the story of the men killed and their diverse backgrounds of national and geographic origins by inference. In this sense, the quilt foretells the major memorial quilt of the late 20th-century, the *AIDS Remembrance Quilt*, also like the Civil War quilt, the work of many hands. Each panel represents an individual dead from AIDS but, taken together, there is no specific story other than their shared tragedies.

Furniture makers on the East and West Coasts actively participated in the creation of stories carved into domestic objects like hope chests and library desks. Influenced by John Ruskin's and William Morris's adulation of medieval English craftsmen's union of art and labor, Providence, Rhode Island painter Sydney Burleigh designed *King Arthur Chest* (c. 1900) and *Shakespeare Chest* (c. 1900) for the cabinet-makers Potter & Co. With the former carved by Julia Lippit Mauran, both works embody fascinating treatments of popular stories.[8]

On the front of *King Arthur Chest* are, appropriately, King Arthur and his Queen Guinevere. Surrounding them on the end and back panels are not the figures of the Knights of the Round Tables but their names, coats-of-arms, and related attributes. For instance, with Sir Lancelot on one end of the chest is his familiar helmet. At the other end, the name Galahad is joined by the Holy Grail which he sought according to legend. The original collection of 1485, *Le Morte d'Arthur*, was given new currency in Tennyson's popular poem "Idylls of the King" which appeared between 1858 and 1872. Readers undoubtedly appreciated Burleigh and Mauran's shorthand way of combining all the characters of the stories in one work, as in a totem pole, constructing a three-dimensional literary entity.

More complicated in that it exposes many characters from different plays, *Shakespeare Chest* also tells us much about which plays were deemed most appropriate to commemorate on the chest: *Taming of the Shrew; Antony and Cleopatra; Merry Wives of Windsor;* and *As You_Like It,* three comedies and one tragedy. Strong female characters dominate each play and, indeed, Cleopatra is depicted alone, resplendent on her throne. Furniture as literary anthology is the underlying narrative principle in this chest, rather than a succession of individual plot elements tied together within one object.

Like Julia Lippit Mauran executing the carving for Sydney Burleigh, Lucia Kleinhans Mathews of San Francisco assisted her husband, Arthur, in choosing colors and in some of the painting and carving.[9] Real collaborators, the Mathewses had their own retail outlet, The Furniture Shop, at 1717 California Street in San Francisco. Inspired instead by Italian Renaissance painting and furniture, Arthur and Lucia Mathews made richly painted and carved wooden objects of all sizes and types, furnishing and supplying the large new mansions of the Bay Area's burgeoning ruling class of merchants, shipping magnates, and financial leaders.

Works in glass perpetuated myths of triumphs and progress which drove forward the nation in an unquestioning pursuit of land, power, wealth, and self-satisfaction. Deep admiration for the art of engraving glass was rewarded with a small masterpiece displayed by the Libbey Glass Co. at the 1904 Louisiana Purchase Exposition in St.

Louis, *Apotheosis of Transportation,* by Hieronimus William Fritchie. Exuberant, rambunctious and absurd, it combines horses, mermaids, a demigod, and even the zodiac, in a stunning composition around a world globe with a map of the U.S. near the plate-form's exact center. More than a tribute to sea travel, railroads or horseback riding, this work foretells America's presence abroad as well and, like some other narrative craft objects, it unwittingly anticipates darker adventures of American empire-building in the dawning century.

In a final irony for the memory of the young Republic, now long gone, Tiffany Furnaces used the Liberty Bell suspended in the talons of an eagle as a symbol for the victory over Germany in 1918. Without the depiction of the hundreds of thousands killed, this souvenir bowl is made of iridescent gold glass, reminding us with an eerie glow of the generous profits made during World War I by the last of the pre-income tax capitalists, the munitions manufacturers, who stayed home.

The Great War was over and, only with it, the 19th century came to an end. Chastened by loss but liberated from Victorian convention, President Woodrow Wilson's America was ready to escape into a frenzy of consumption. Craft artists would cooperate fully in telling the stories Americans wanted to hear, drowning out the other stories of starvation, inflation, and economic collapse coming from Europe.

PLEASURE AND PROSPERITY

We were very tired, we were very merry—
We had gone back and forth all night on the ferry.
We hailed, "Good morrow, mother!" to a shawl-covered head,
And bought a morning paper, which neither of us read;
And she wept, "God bless you!" for the apples and pears,
And we gave her all our money but our subway fares.

—Edna St. Vincent Millay, from "Recuerdo" (1922)

The interwar period, 1919–1939, was an economically divided time, prosperity followed by the Great Depression, yet much American craft remained at the level of fantasy and escape. Painting and sculpture may have more clearly reflected coming hard times but, for the most part, American craft with few exceptions remained on a level of soothing detachment from sobering conditions.

At first, there was a comfortable congruity between life style and imagery. The great illustrator of the age of F. Scott Fitzgerald, John Held, Jr., joined René Clarke and others in designing fabric patterns for Stehli Prints which celebrated jazz and the growing mania for varsity athletics and baseball. Held's *Rhapsody* (1927) was printed in blue dye, punning the title of George Gershwin's descriptive composition for piano and orchestra, "Rhapsody in Blue" (1924). With the musicians playing violins, tubas, banjo, tympani, piano, and other instruments, the repeated orchestra pattern also uses circular forms (cymbals, bass drums, heads, trombone bells) to set up a syncopated visual rhythm similar to jazz and also resembles musical notes. The cumulative effect tells a story of the interface between jazz and classical music which occurred in the 1920s, and in Gershwin's music.

Immigration was a result of growing storms over Europe although isolationist figures like aviator Charles Lindbergh and industrialist-diplomat Joseph P. Kennedy were firmly opposed to any U.S. interventions abroad. The growing presence of Asian peoples on the West Coast was symbolized in a stoneware sculpture of 1921 by Italian immigrant Beniamino B. Bufano who settled in San Francisco earlier in the century. *Chinese Man and Woman* are dressed in traditional clothing replete with embroidered Chinese characters and solemnly staring forward. Their exotic features and attire place them in a category by now common to American craft, the outsider. As dominant a part of the Bay Area's economy as they were, craft treated Asians as "others," fit subject matter for diminutive (31 inches high) execution.

The American Indian had already been subjected to this aesthetic colonization and would continue to be treated so, as in the baptismal font decoration for Christ Church Cranbrook in Bloomfield Hills, Michigan. The Indian brave, drawn by Victor F. von Lossberg for the New York firm of E. F. Caldwell and Co., in 1927, is joined by other figures surrounding the font which include representations of "Africa" (a black man with bird and lion); "Asia" (a robed Asian with birds and blossoms); and "Europe" (a bearded figure with a book and grape leaves).

"America," then, is embodied by the Christianized Indian worshipping the European God, with upturned palms in a degradingly supplicative pose. The characters of the story on the font may be multi-cultural but, like much other art of the period, such representations rest on racial stereotyping and subordination to a dominant, white culture.

If the U.S. received new citizens from abroad who brought their considerable skills with them (indeed, virtually the entire early faculty and administration of Cranbrook Academy of Art are a good example), it also numbered native-born artists who took advantage of superior craftsmanship available in Europe. *At the Gates of Morning* (c. 1925) by painter Arthur B. Davies, for example, was executed at the Gobelins tapestry factory in France: no adequate American institution existed at the time to create a tapestry on this scale.

By 1932, however, Eliel and Loja Saarinen had arrived in Bloomfield Hills, Michigan, to transfer their Finnish-trained skills in architecture, weaving, and art school administration to Cranbrook.[10] In *Sample for the Festival of the May 4 Queen* (1932), the Saarinens imported European pagan festival imagery to America. Here and in other works, deep cultural traditions dealing with seasonal planting cycles, for example, were monumentalized in cloth and made to constitute a neutral, non-ideological educational philosophy for the art school founded in 1925.

Lillian Holm epitomized the European immigration experience in her large weaving, *First Sight of New York* (early 1930s). With skyscrapers looming overhead and the crush of people on either side, Holm's surrounding pattern of window-like rectangles and inverted triangles continues the sense of jazzy rhythm set up in *Rhapsody*. She accentuates the sense of the outsiders looking in with red horizontal lines across the central building image. The lines seem more a barrier to the American dream than access to it.

Two ceramic vignettes, *Ten Nights in a Bar Room* (1932) by Henry Varnum Poor, and *Futility of a Well-Ordered Life* (1935) by Russell Barnett Aitken, comment on the less cheery side of the Depression. The former satirizes Prohibition through a scene from the popular Victorian melodrama, *Ten Nights in a Bar room and What I Saw There* (1854) by Timothy Shay Arthur and William W. Pratt. Poor's tableau approximates a proscenium stage set with its curved front but also splits the scene in two by topping the sculpture with a glimpse of nearby tenements.

It could be the moment captured, a drunk collapsing, alludes to the play's climactic line, "Father, dear father, come home with me now." Made during the height of the "great experiment," *Ten Nights* would have been viewed by Poor's audience with a mixture of sophistication and sarcasm rather than the moral righteousness and approval of Arthur and Pratt's original theatregoers. It is a good example of transplanted narrative, always subject to the shifting allegiances and biases of those listening to the story at a different time in history.

With the New York World's Fair in 1939–40, American craft makers were given a number of opportunities for large-scale commissions using craft materials to tell stories. Despite the coming horrors, brash optimism was the order of the day and allegory—a story that exists on different levels of meaning with each character or plot standing in for something else—was a preferred vehicle for storytelling.

For the Glass Industries Building, Steuben designer Sidney Waugh created *Atlantica* (1938–39). A mermaid, *Atlantica* is the result of several months' work and required many technicians' and workers' involvement.

With the figure's hair echoing the surrounding wave forms, all executed in cast colorless glass, *Atlantica* is not that different in form from heroic, Nazi-period sculptures aggrandizing the Aryan race produced in Germany by, for example, Arno Breker. Grand, imposing, and imperious, *Atlantica* was also a symbol for the achievements of Corning Glass Co. and Steuben (a subsidiary). Corporate power feminized, she may have allegorically represented the ocean connecting North America and Europe but that body of water was soon to be dotted with German U-boats, sunken transport ships, and all manner of peril politely absent from Sidney Waugh's design.

Equally optimistic and chilling in implications, *Fountain of the Atom* (1939–40) by Waylande Gregory played into the fair's theme of "Building the World of Tomorrow with the Tools of Today." Electrons were allegorized into innocent children and joined by monumental figures of fire, earth, air, and water, the basic elements first conceived of by the ancient Greeks. Less than five years later, such benign storytelling would be undercut by the bombs dropped on Hiroshima and Nagasaki, not to mention the subsequent nuclear weapons build-up of the Cold War.

Analogous to *Atlantica*, another sculpture of the same year, *Earth* (1939) personified the planet as a beautiful, dark-skinned woman. Artist Edris Eckhardt created many sculptures dealing with children's storybook figures, for example, and her ability to conflate narrative elements or attributes into a single figure serves her well in this piece. With her blue hair in the form of the ocean's waves, *Earth* answers the sinuous water forms of *Atlantica* and appears equally innocent of any darker meaning. Viewed from our own day of ecological cataclysms, *Earth*, like much art of the late 1930s, seems impossibly naive.

Nevertheless, the considerable beauty and exquisite workmanship redeem these works up to a point and remind us that a literal reflection of society's ills is not always desired by patronage. From *Louis XV* onward during the history of our country, European and American artisans have elevated the pleasing and downplayed the troubling.

With the coming of World War II, the pursuits of pleasure which began in the 1920s and which were perpetuated in craft objects of the 1930s—despite the Depression—gave way to images of power and domination. New stories of military triumph would replace tales of pastoral bliss, scientistic faith, and the subordination of outsiders.

MYTHOLOGIES OF POWER

The dove descending breaks the air
With flame of incandescent terror
Of which the tongues declare
The one discharge from sin and error. . . .

—T. S. Eliot, from "Little Gidding," in *Four Quartets* (1942)

T. S. Eliot's lines were written during the London Blitz and probably refer to the unrelenting bombing of the city by German planes. His cloaking of the horror of World War II in quasi-religious language was one of many responses to the War in which American artists generally avoided the explicit reality of current events.

When not avoiding commenting on the crimes of the Axis powers, some artists were strangely close in spirit to the heroic Fascist style. *Man and the Unicorn* (1940) by Swedish sculptor Carl Milles, for example, parallels male domination fantasies by Nazi-period artists. In this case, the myth of the free, independent unicorn—whom no one could catch—is perverted into a tale of mastery over the creative spirit. It is a celebration of dominance with the ridiculously muscled rider seated on the back of the tense, subdued animal. Milles's extraordinary wood carving sets in motion troubling scenarios about psychological states as well, perhaps the triumph of the ego over the id. Natural forms, such as the vegetation at the unicorn's hooves, are threatening and entangling, too.

Continuing a mythology of power at a time when America was uncertain about involvement in Europe, Steuben designer Sidney Waugh matched his Amazon *Atlantica* with a medley of homegrown stories about dominance in all regions of the country, *The Bowl of American Legends* (1942). Blown and engraved at the Steuben furnaces in Corning, New York, the clear crystal rises in a single curve from a disklike base. Repeating the oldest of all narrative structures for craft, a band around a vessel, Waugh designed a non-sequential series of images which blend together into a long series of "legendary and semilegendary characters"[11] intricately tied to national fantasies about the South, New England, the Midwest, Far West, and Texas.

Rip Van Winkle, Ichabod Crane, and the Headless Horseman remind us that Washington Irving's writings were part polished prose, part fatuous lore. Joel Chandler Harris, another writer associated with condescending racial stereotypes, is represented by Uncle Remus,

Br'er Rabbit and Br'er Fox. Johnny Appleseed, presaging America's agro-business perhaps, grew out of the Ohio territories, and Paul Bunyan, according to Waugh, "brings us to the great days of the opening of the West."[12]

Completing the bowl's circular band, Pecos Bill and Davy Crockett— "in fact, a member of Congress"[13]—blur the line between fantasy and reality and remind us of a cardinal aspect of American craft storytelling: escapist tales must blend with patriotic myths to ensure popularity—and consumption.

To be fair, Viktor Schreckengost's *Apocalypse '42*, a scary blend of humor and reality, remains the paramount craft achievement of the era just before World War II. But then, Schreckengost's vision grew out of his experience as an American tourist in pre-war Germany. Along with other boat passengers arriving in Lübeck harbor from Sweden, he was sequestered briefly before being allowed to proceed southward. Peeking out a window before release, he saw dozens of airplanes "in full war paint"[14] and knew firsthand what the near future would inexorably bring.

Five years later, when *Apocalypse '42* was first shown during the annual "May show" at the Cleveland Museum of Art, Schreckengost was surprised when the work was ostensibly "removed for photography." Upon inquiring further, the artist learned that members of Cleveland's large Italian-American community had objected to the sculpture's depiction of Mussolini sliding off the horse's rump. The dictator had even presented awards to some supporters then resident in the Cleveland area. Eventually, the work was returned to the exhibition area by the museum director.

Three stoneware figures made the same year by Russell Aitken form a beautiful pendant to Schreckengost's unitary sculpture containing symbolic character signifiers. For Aitken, each individual statuette contains explanatory attributes. *Mussolini* is the target of a nose-thumbing African (symbolizing invaded Abyssinia). *Hitler* holds a copy of *Mein Kampf*, wears the cap of the Vikings. A blonde-braided Rhine maiden crouches at his feet. And in a twist away from Schreckengost, *Franklin D. Roosevelt* makes a subtle dig at the President's own possible military yearnings by garbing him as an admiral, alluding to his former post as Secretary of Navy.

After the War, the nation retrenched with a return to deeply conservative values embodied in the Judeo-Christian tradition. These were the values, after all, which the Allies fought to preserve in the face of Nazi barbarism and the extermination of European Jewry.

Three works, two in clay and one in metals, demonstrate the perpetuation of storytelling in American craft up to the midcentury point. The earliest, *Triptych with Virgin and Child* (c. 1940), by Arthur Nevill Kirk, is barely ten inches high yet it attains a monumentality that bears comparison to the great medieval enamels of Limoges. With readily recognizable figures of Magi and Shepherds flanking Mother and Child, this work underscores craftsmanship and high narrative content in 20th-century American craft. A myth of power in its own way, *Triptych* still presents an image of gentle authority and assertion.

In contrast, *Passion of Christ* (1947) by Thomas McClure seems more Christianized than Christian myth with its crude pagan-like carving relief. Through elaborate interlocking sections, the story of Christ's betrayal, crucifixion, and return are told in a blunt, wrap-around sequence. It is almost as if, after the horrors of World War II, a more refined execution would be unseemly. Unglazed, the bowl compresses its story dramatically, like French Romanesque cathedral sculpture but, confined to a clay pot, reverts to the level of symbolic ritual, pre-literate cultures, and a powerfully expressionistic portrayal of sacrifice and renewal.

Finally, concluding the strain of renewed Judeo-Christian subject matter, *The Judgment of Solomon (*1947) by Edwin and Mary Scheier attains a remarkable concision in its balancing of all the Old Testament story elements seen simultaneously on a plate.

Executed in Durham, New Hampshire, *The Judgment of Solomon* firmly illustrates the notion of the craft object as narrator. With palm raised in contemplative pose, King Solomon is telling the story of the two mothers fighting over the possession of an infant son. Literally depicted as embodiments of his memory, the three figures are present on the plate's surface, the King's head.

Both Scheiers were self-taught artists when they began making ceramics in 1937 and much of the freshness of the drawing on the plate rises from its self-invented style, reinforcing, again, a pre-literate sensibility also found in McClure's *Passion of Christ*. We are experiencing Solomon's deliberations prior to his decision, scepter in hand.

Viewed in the context of renewed American power after the War, the Scheier plate also proposes a newfound wisdom for the U.S. about to take its place in the new world forum of diplomacy, decision, and judgments: the United Nations.

Although Edwin Scheier denies a conscious link to such developments at the time of making the plate, he freely admits the possibility in retrospect of such an analogy.[15]

Despite judicious efforts at serious moral subject matter by the Scheiers, McClure, and Kirk, and the explicitly engaged political satires of Poor, Schreckengost, and Aitken, by and large American craft participated in reinforcing helpful illusions about how we would like to see ourselves as a nation.

Rather than reflecting the country's problems, American craft of the first half of the 20th century prepared the way for artists of the second half to react profoundly against such elegant escapism. The stories which would be told next were created by artists who alternately withdrew inward even more or who began to express increasing doubts about the mythologies of confident American values and political power during the Cold War era.

> We shall not cease from exploration
> And the end of all our exploring
> Will be to arrive where we started
> And know the place for the first time.

—T. S. Eliot, from "Little Gidding," in *Four Quartets*

Top: Herter Brothers: Wardrobe, New York, c. 1880, cherry, ebonized and inlaid, 78 ½ x 49 ½ x 26". Metropolitan Museum of Art 69.140. Gift of Kenneth O. Smith. Photo: O. R. Roque

Left: Erik Magnussen: *"Cubic" Coffee Set*, 1927, silver with gilt and oxidized panels, coffee pot, 9" h. Manufactured by Gorham Co., Providence, Rhode Island. Private collection. Photo: Lee Schechter

THE EMBODIMENT OF INGENUITY

The inaugural exhibition at the new American Craft Museum, "Craft Today: Poetry of the Physical," coincided with two other epochal surveys of ornamental and functional objects: "In Pursuit of Beauty: Americans and the Aesthetic Movement" at the Metropolitan Museum of Art and "The Machine Age in America 1918–1941" at the Brooklyn Museum.[1] All three received extensive press coverage, but "Craft Today" in particular garnered some probing and thoughtful critiques.[2] A number of these centered around the unending art-versus-craft debate, as if the two terms were mutually exclusive or somehow in eternal opposition.[3]

While there are those on both sides of the art-versus-craft debate who have reasons for keeping the situation static, I suggest that art and craft are fusing together in the late 20th century. Further, given the achievement on view in "Craft Today," it may be that craft is the alternative influence contemporary art is seeking in its current state of crisis. I believe also that some critics are fearful that the changing paradigm for craft will force them to widen their field, and to alter or abandon convenient preset criteria.[4]

Our world is one of constant change, indeed, of interchange and overlap. The range and volume of aesthetic production in the United States is so vast that no single set of criteria can successfully take stock of this activity. Perhaps case-specific judgments are needed in order to proceed to a general evaluative system. And viewers, collectors and readers would be better served by a new, more inclusive criticism.

Director Paul Smith's selection in "Craft Today" underlined a shared heritage of process and materials that craft-based artists have been implementing for a long time. In this confused and fractious period, when sculpture, for example, is in disarray, much can be learned from the artisan's surer grasp of material. Historians have been repairing modern art's links to the past century despite its long-standing rhetoric of revolutionary severance, but craft never cut the tie at all. As this is realized by the art world, American craft will take on greater stature as a field in which idea and material mastery have always coexisted. In the face of craft's renewed sense of pride and primacy, the art world is scrambling to take a stand toward it and is beginning to recognize the many artists and artisans across the country who never forsook fine technique for trends, and who never heeded the fleeting calls in the 1970s to "decommodify" the art object in favor of "pure" idea or political chic. American craft-based artists always knew they could have it both ways: the satisfaction of fine workmanship and the ability to comment on our culture. At a time when Conceptual art is being "dressed up" again in commodity's "clothing"—and called neo-Conceptual or Simulationist—American craftsmen are able to smile and say, "We never took our clothes off to begin with."

The three exhibitions under discussion play an important role in educating the public about craft's mission to the arts. A hybrid art form that changes from era to era, craft in the late 20th century is accessible to consumers at a range of income levels. By contrast, the beautifully ornate furniture of the Aesthetic Movement (1875–1885) was not. Indeed, it was not until the development of industrial design in the period between the two world wars, highlighted in "The Machine Age," that mass-produced domestic objects were brought into the American home. However, the continuous and parallel development of American craft—what I would like to call the third path— always offered well-constructed, handmade articles for purchase by the middle class. Situated between the extremes of both styles—the high ornamentation of the Victorians and the brutal streamlining of the machine-made—the works in "Craft Today" embody the third path, the application of human ingenuity to the desire for better-looking everyday objects and for attractive, technically complex decorative objects.

Works in all three exhibitions stand outside the strict "good design" promulgated by the Architecture and Design Department of the Museum of Modern Art. Though a few of the artists in the craft museum's inaugural show are also in the Modern's collection (e.g., Peter Voulkos, Toots Zynsky), most would not fit in either because they reject the streamlining mode of the American Bauhaus aesthetic or because they do not conform to the aesthetic of the discreet object subordinate to the totality of the architecturally designed environment. Instead, these artists affirm the independent American spirit, the tendency toward the ingeniously fashioned object that sticks out rather than meshes in, and which calls attention to itself rather than plays down its presence in the overall domestic interior. American craftsmen have chosen to apply the modernist orthodoxy in painting and sculpture—the insistence on the autonomy of the object—to their own work.

Ironically, today's architects have borrowed a leaf from American craft. Rejecting the blending in of modernist chair to carpet or coffee cup to table, postmodern architect-designers like Robert Venturi plan chairs and dishes in mock-Chippendale style that stand out in

the environment—just like a good painting or sculpture. Perhaps the
rivalries between the competing aspects of the visual arts today—fine
art, architecture, design, functional craft, craft-based art—are part
of the same process: the breaking down of art-historical barriers, the
blending together of all kinds of artistic endeavor, the fusion of art
and craft.

Different as the objects produced in the Victorian era and by the machine-age moderns of the 1930's seem to be from each other and from
our own, they often were the result of comparable forces—combinations of individuals, ideas and technological developments—seeking
to ameliorate a living or working environment. Political, social and
economic events intervened to shatter the optimism and confidence of
both periods, but the post-World War II period, with its difficult, post-
nuclear "peace," has nevertheless continued for over 40 years, longer
than either of the earlier eras. Our own time, despite its problems,
has been hospitable to American craft, a sustained experiment in art
and design where artisans pick and choose their sources, conform to,
alter, or reject traditional styles and conventions, and are developing
a collectively pluralistic style which closely resembles the vaunted
individual expressions within the fine arts.

Distressing as it may be to the critic Robert Hughes, who has said
that American craft has "no unifying style of the decorative arts,"[5] it
is important to remember that, even in periods of American history
when one style seemed to dominate, other versions or completely different points of view competed in the free market for attention. The
lack of a unifying decorative style today is a virtue, not a liability. We
can leave it to our counterparts in the coming century to look back on
the American Craft Museum inaugural exhibition and pull together
the threads that seem so disparate to us now.

One can only hope that in the year 2087, the same thoroughness and
scholarship that the Metropolitan's Alice Cooney Frelinghuysen and
her colleagues put into "In Pursuit of Beauty" will be applied to the
accomplishments of our own period. Nearly 10 years in the planning,
this survey of American Aesthetic Movement furniture, painting and
design rescued from oblivion High Victorian taste, the horror vacui
ideal that was anathema to the modern period. Now that they have
been hauled out of storage or borrowed from descendants, the myriad
bedsteads, chests, ceramics and metalwork are testimony to the in-
exhaustibility of the decorative imagination—and to the resourceful-
ness or ingenuity of 19th-century designer-craftsmen. Half-forgotten
figures like Mary Louise McLaughlin and John Bennett have been restored to the growing pantheon of historical American ceramics. The

considerable achievements of the first professional interior designers, like Louis Comfort Tiffany and Herter Brothers, are seen anew,
severed, unfortunately, from the totality of their original settings but
subject to stricter 20th-century judgments conditioned by the modernist autonomy of the object. On their own, some of the highly ornamented, carved and embellished products hold up well. Others do not
pass muster outside the artificed environments for which they were
meant.

Most contemporary craft artists and collectors probably have a nodding familiarity with art pottery of the late 19th century, but thanks
to the Met's exhaustive efforts, the extraordinarily elaborate inlaid
furniture made with precious woods was also on view, as were silken
textile hangings (portières) and exquisitely worked metals such as
silver, copper and brass trays by Tiffany and Company. The decorative motifs, the influences of Asian and English art, the lavish use of
extravagant materials—all were set out before the visitor and can be
savored in the companion book to the exhibition.

The Aesthetic Movement was chiefly for the rich, a conveyance for
what the economist Thorstein Veblen later called "conspicuous consumption." Eventually, it had an influence on the Victorian middle
class through the dissemination of the aesthetic style in wallpaper
sample catalogs and in other areas more accessible to median-in-
come families. A carryover and elaboration of English country house
interior design on a grand scale, the Aesthetic style required huge
projects for its fullest expression. Seeing this elaborate furniture and
accessories in appropriate groupings in the Met's American Wing, one
was struck by the breathtaking levels of craftsmanship, the intricate
forms, ingenious ways of covering a surface and the indulgent use of
fine materials. Even the "better mousetrap" of the Aesthetic period
must have been made of laburnum wood and encrusted with silver
and mother-of-pearl.

William H. Vanderbilt's library table, 1882, built by Herter Brothers,
is more a plinth for finely bound rare books than a platform for the
relay of knowledge. It contrasts starkly with Edward Zucca's *Table of
the Future*, 1986, or Dick Wickman's *Corridor Table*, 1985, in "Craft
Today," though all three are made of fine materials and embody high
standards of workmanship.

Few modern homes lack cupboard space, but that has not stopped
furniture makers like James Krenov, Tommy Simpson and Thomas
Loeser from making freestanding cabinets that bear up to scrutiny
alongside constructions by their anonymous predecessors in the

turn-of-the-century New York. Even though the movement brought new criteria for judging painting and sculpture, refined technique has remained a touchstone for the crafts.

Similarly, Herter Brothers' 1882 silk brocade portière bears comparison to latter-day textiles by Lia Cook, James Bassler and others. The elaborate embroidery in the older hanging has its counterpart, for example, in the intricate weaving technique of Cook. And just as function may have been a pretext for making a pretty cloth to hang in the doorway of the Sloane residence in New York, so contemporary artisans often cite use as a departure point for artistic expression.

The post-Civil War period became the age of the professional decorator—Tiffany, LaFarge, Herter Brothers—but the products were still the achievements of individual artisans. The anonymity and ultimate disappearance of craft was something William Morris and John Ruskin feared, and their efforts in England to prevent this had an effect in the United States. But it is doubtful whether the integrity of American craftsmanship was ever seriously in danger of disappearing. The growth of an affluent middle and upper class kept American artisans working, and the abundance of "subcontractors" uncovered by the Met researchers suggests that the makers, doorknob manufacturers and lamp makers all employed artisans or designer-craftsmen of varying degrees of sophistication.

The adaptation to machine-made objects appears to have happened gradually. After all, even a potter's wheel is a machine. With the advent of industrial spinning wheels, the growth of the economy and the shift of population from rural to urban settings, forces came into play which smooth over the transition from the unique handmade object to the more accessible, multiply produced one. All this coincided with the growing market demands that generated work requiring the supervision of craftsmen who remembered the special qualities of the handmade object.

We pick up the thread after the Great War. In the United States the unrestricted fortunes of the robber barons came to an end with income tax, and the new god, the machine, found ready adherents and critics in literature and the arts. As America was congratulating itself on its incipient modernity after the hollow triumph of World War I, calls for a more widely disseminated, higher "quality of life" were interrupted by the Great Depression.

It was thanks to a new generation of industrial designers, among them Abel Faidy, Raymond Loewy, Gilbert Rohde, Paul Frankl and Joseph Urban, that American ingenuity ignited into the new styles of industrial chic variously known as Art Déco or Art Moderne. The Brooklyn Museum exhibition organizers, Dianne Pilgrim, Richard Guy Wilson and Dickran Tashjian call them "machine aesthetics." Partly influenced by the Bauhaus, and even a bit by the Wiener Werkstätte, the American styles mixed new materials like Bakelite and steel with new technologies such as high-heat casting, plastic forming and pre-stressed concrete. Machine-age America became the laboratory for architectural modernist-utopian thinking, new ideas that Europeans could not afford to implement—until later.

Whether locomotive, skyscraper, expressway or pencil sharpener, the objects in "The Machine Age in America" offer an all-encompassing, delightfully nostalgic look at the 1920s and 30s. They make a strong case that unlike what occurred during the Aesthetic Movement period, more people's lives actually were bettered by the application of machine-age technology to artisan ideals. But was there no place for the craftsman in this futuristic age? In fact, the eye and hand of the maker were still evident either in the overall conception that softened technological possibilities to a more humane scale, or in the finishing process.

If "the business of America (was) business," as Calvin Coolidge put it, then the American office was the new Eden, the test-tube of capitalism, where the businessmen of the day formulated the decisions that would shape the future. The problem is, as one considers the machine-age aesthetic, that everything looks like it was made for the office. Few of us have or want chrome-tubing Naugahyde-covered furniture, though it looks grand in the dentist's waiting room or at the bank. It was not until after 1941 that the harsh angles and slightly authoritarian metal corners were rounded out by Charles Eames and Eero Saarinen, those "craftsmen" of the modern style who innovated the more organic "atomic age" look of the 1950s.

Before then, in the golden glow of the interbellum period, American craft was not lost; it just found its way in through the office door. The elevator interiors of the Chrysler Building, for example, use exotic parquets even a Vanderbilt would have admired. The clothing of the period (such as a mink-trimmed evening wrap of geometrically patterned silk) often matched the smart lines of the cold furniture. And domestic objects like the Erik Magnussen "cubic" coffee set introduced human-scale artisanry into daily life even though the objects might be mass-produced. (Repetition has never bothered American artisan-designers—make a good one, make another—as long as they are able to maintain supervision or control over the outcome.)

It is fascinating to compare examples from "Craft Today." René Chambellan's wrought iron and bronze executive suite gates, 1928, for the Chanin Building, New York, are a symphony of machine-made structural rigor. The broad fencelike form of Gary Griffin's *Cap Gun, Roses and, Middle America*, 1984, echoes Chambellan's gates. Griffin's is more fanciful—casting rose twigs in metal, for example—but it can operate in a similar, ceremonial way as gate or screen.

Looking back (something the machine-age modernists never wanted to do), Russel Wright's 1930 chrome-plated pewter cocktail shaker seems to be from a different planet than that of Tiffany's 1879 chocolate pot or 1878 coffee server. The floral ornament entwining the surfaces of both, the exquisite handling of the silver, copper and brass, and the languid fluted forms distinguish it sharply from Wright's martini can. Yet, all three stress a segmented column shape and offer important solutions as to where the user's hand will grip. Could it be that Wright and Tiffany and Company are more akin than we thought? In fact, aren't the Machine Age and the Aesthetic Movement barely 40 years apart? Seen as parts of the broader stream of American craft, they are close to one another indeed.

Leaping forward, it is also possible to detect links between Wright (who avoided all craft association memberships) and current designer-craftsmen of tableware like Lynn Turner. Her *Expresso* set with its rounded forms has affinities with Wright's *American Modern* dinnerware of 1937. Turner has exaggerated her forms into the realm of personal expression, but another artisan in "Craft Today," James Makins, retains Wright's austerity. He is not designing for the machine age, as Wright did so eloquently, but he shares with Wright the use of monochrome glaze as a sheath for eccentric form.

By 1920, major theoreticians like Le Corbusier deified mass production (and appropriately accepted commissions from both the Soviet Union and the French bourgeoisie!) in the hopes of bringing "good design" to the common man. Fortunately, as "The Machine Age in America" substantiates, American artisans of the period never completely stripped away all the ornament that the great moderns like Le Corbusier thought superfluous. It was the intervention of craft, in its various strains of decoration, ornament and ameliorating pattern that saved machine-age design from becoming the totalitarian style Chaplin parodied in *Modern Times*. Everyday life was improved visually for many and, since the machine would not go away, we owe a debt to the many designers and anonymous artisans who adapted the look of machinery to functional and artistic objects in a humane, attractive way. The nightmare vision of Fritz Lang's *Metropolis* did not come true, however potent and cautionary a metaphor for the future it proved to be.

Returning to the present, how is the interested viewer to cope with the conflicting claims raised by "Craft Today"? Should the question be, "Is it art or is it craft?" or could we more usefully say, "I don't care, but how can I tell it's any good?" Drawing upon the three exhibitions, it should be possible to create three critical categories. First, those objects of an openly functional character may safely be called craft. Next, those made from traditional craft materials such as clay, glass, wood, metal and fiber but in which the nonfunctional content or meaning is uppermost, superseding thee craft or technique, we may place in the fine art category. Finally, the other craft-based objects which do not clearly fit into either category, or about which one cannot yet easily determine the presence of any aesthetic or extrafunctional meaning, may be assigned the term artifact or artifact of the future.[6] Premature categorization? Perhaps, but it seems unlikely that the future will consider everything produced by fine artists or craftsmen during our time as art. We cannot predict which things will be revered and which will be (mercifully) cast aside, but the craft-art-artifact triad could forestall the confusion ahead. It is at least an alternative to the art/craft debate, and it reflects, to the best of my knowledge, the range of objects being produced in the nation today.

As we have excavated the past at the Met and the Brooklyn Museum, sifting through to find the finest achievements of each period, so will our own age be exhumed, along with the rhetoric surrounding it now. As the catalogs of the earlier periods revealed, voluminous commentary already existed. How much of it is helpful in understanding the Victorians and the machine-age moderns is necessarily to be balanced by our own response to the objects themselves based upon the limits of our taste. As I have tried to suggest, it is the interaction of the mind and hand, the embodiment of ingenuity, that speaks across the past to us today. From the achievements of the Aesthetic Movement through the Machine Age to our own time, the very least we can agree upon is the necessity of moving our discussion on to questions of craft-art-artifact, levels of appreciation, revised standards for judgment and criticism, and, finally, a renewed pride in America's longest continuous artistic movement: the third path, American craft.

PACIFIC NORTHWEST CRAFTS IN THE 1950s

INTRODUCTION: COLD WAR CONFORMISTS

Crafts in the Pacific Northwest largely kept pace with the development of other fine arts in the 1945–1960 period. In some respects, activity in the crafts actually set in motion patterns of social and cultural organization that aided artists at the time and during the succeeding period, 1960–80, which is usually considered the heyday of American craft. These were patterns characterized by the formation of artists' cooperative support organizations with both economic and cultural arms, by the specialized sections of art departments at the secondary, junior college, and university levels, and by the close personal relationships between craft artists and middle-class patrons—a connected fostered through annual street fairs, private commissions, and sales through high-quality design-furniture shops. In addition, Northwest artisans gained leadership positions on regional and national cultural-advocate groups such as the American Craft Council, the Northwest Designer Craftsmen, and the World Crafts Council.

At the same time, there was a relative aesthetic timidity underlining a reassuring consensus about the possibilities for craft in America. This was entirely in keeping with the mixture of buoyant relief and traumatized exhaustion after World War II. Whether or not it was indeed the "Age of Anxiety" poet W. H. Auden called it in a poem of that title, the cultural atmosphere in the nation as a whole stressed unanimity, security, and conformity coupled with a sense of numbing optimism, higher living standards for artists, and shared middle-class values. Marriage, family, the home, religion, consumerism, the importance of the domestic interior, and a patriotism veering between American pride and hysterical fear of a third world war dominated public discourse and private life.

Collaboration often involved cooperation with the new planners of American domestic life—architects. Religious, commercial, municipal and residential structures were going up everywhere and Northwest craft artists were called in to ameliorate the stark profile of mid-century modernism, the geometric international style.

Such projects were to become legally institutionalized in One Percent for Art programs twenty-five years later in Seattle, Tacoma, and Portland with a different mixture of success and failure but, for the Cold War craft artists like James FitzGerald (1910–1973), Rudy Autio, Harold Balasz, Irene McGowan (1906–1999) and many others, there

Richard Fairbanks: *Stoneware Drum Bottle,* c. 1959, stoneware, C/9 reduction, thrown body, neck and foot, Fairbanks copper barium matte glaze, 10 x 5 ½ x 3 ¾". Estate of Richard Fairbanks, Issaquah, Washington. Photo: Roger Schreiber

was a remarkable aesthetic consistency of taste with the architects. Perhaps it was because all American craft artists were still closer to a design-arts mentality similar to architectural training. "Problem solving" for society's built environment had been a bulwark of the institutions where many of the Northwest craftsmen and craftswomen had studied: Chicago's Institute of Design (Frances Senska, 1914–1998); Yale (Everett DuPen, 1912–1997); Cranbrook Academy of Art and, most significantly, the University of Washington School of Art.

Individuality was subordinated to the greater, agreed-upon plan in the many residential and liturgical commissions of the period. As a result, many of the art components within these buildings have not withstood the test of time. In retrospect, many appear too cooperative, bland and recessive, and do not stand out as significant artistic achievements.

The nature of the patronage cannot be blamed for, at the time, culture and long traditions held that in working relationships between architects and artists, architects prevailed. Shared philosophies of design allied with the progressive principles of modernism: form follows function; separate elements are subsumed with the totality of the design; the artist and architect may cooperate in creating new realities reflecting Modernity just so long as the greater ideals of the culture were adequately served. These ideals included leisure and comfort promoting American superiority; optimistic Far West "can-do" attitudes; wild confidence in the tremendous new life in the suburbs, and a turning away from negativity or social criticism that would jar the hard-won postwar complacency.

BACKGROUND: BEFORE MID-CENTURY MODERN

On a variety of fronts, the immediate postwar period (1945–50) set in place teachers, schools, colleges and universities which instructed art majors on the G.I. Bill. In Bozeman, new Montana State University art instructor, Frances Senska[1], had pursued postgraduate work with Bauhaus master László Moholy-Nagy (1895–1946) at the Chicago Institute of Design, and with Maija Grotell (1899–1973) at Cranbrook Academy of Art. Both professors emphasized to the new Montana State University instructor that there was no hierarchical distinction between "fine" and "applied arts." In their own work, Rudy Autio and Peter Voulkos, Senska's two most famous students, manifested their beloved teacher's conviction of the fusion of art and craft.

In Seattle, Walter F. Isaacs (1886–1964), director of the University of Washington School of Painting, Sculpture and Design (as it was then

called), devised a curriculum based on his own studies in Paris at the
Académie Colorossi with Charles Guérin, his sophisticated peda-
gogical methods gained at Columbia Teachers College with Arthur
Dow, and his determination to create an art-training institution that
served theory (art education), design (interior design program) and
collaboration (ties to the College of Architecture and Urban Design).
Under Isaacs, ceramics, weaving, printmaking, glass and metal arts
such as jewelry were all eventually established in programs at the
University of Washington.

One outcome of Isaacs's international ties was his hiring at Amê-
dée Ozenfant's suggestion of Paul Ami Bonifas (1893–1967), former
secretary to Ozenfant's and Corbusier's Purist Group, and as a *Seattle
Times* art critic put it quoting a newspaper clipping from Bonifas's
native Switzerland, one of "the world's three most famous ceramists."[2]
Among Bonifas's earliest students at the University of Washington
were John Brendon, Anne Coon, Richard Fairbanks (1929–1989),
Jeanne Hanson, Constance Jarvis, George C. McAnich, Patricia
McCarroll, Sammy Samuelson, Robert Sperry (1927–1998), Beverly
Trautman, and Betty Wolfe.

Lydia Herrick Hodge (1886–1960) of Portland had lived in Oregon
since 1920, when she entered the University of Oregon art program.
By 1937, she became the guiding light behind the Oregon Ceramic
Studio (later Contemporary Crafts Gallery) and was credited by curator Rachael Griffin with a courage and fearlessness "that never quit
trying new ideas and presenting new art that is not readily accessible
to visitors and supporters."[3]

By 1957, Raymond Grimm arrived from studies with F. Carlton Ball
(1911–1991) at Southern Illinois University to set up a ceramics
department at Portland State University. His influence was considerable for the next twenty years, and the strength of functional pottery
in Oregon today is largely a result of his teachings and example as
an artist. Like Autio and Leroy Setziol, Grimm executed liturgical
commissions that remain among the most significant public ceramic
works of the period.

In Montana, Archie Bray (1886–1953), the owner of Western Clay
Co., a brickworks in Helena, hired two young men, Rudy Autio and
Peter Voulkos (1924–2002), who used their spare time to create and
fire their own pots and sculptures. Bray had inherited the company
from his father in 1931. The rise of Montana ceramics at the Western
Clay Co. has been well chronicled by others.[4] Here it is sufficient to
note that in 1951 Bray formed the Archie Bray Foundation as a "non-

profit education corporation handling the business affairs not only of the pottery but eventually an entire art center."[5] (A substantial survey exhibition of forty years of artists' participation through the foundation was shown in Helena and at the Bellevue Art Museum in 1993.)[6]

CERAMICS: FITTING INTO THE FIFTIES

If the 1960s are seen in retrospect as a watershed decade for American ceramics, the preceding decade was the heyday of the Great Depression generation. The gospel of modernism, which had come to the United States toward the end of the 1930s, found full voice at a time when unemployment was low, housing starts were radically up, and mother's heirloom china was simply not "new" enough. A few, like Autio, Sperry and Voulkos, made the transition from craftsmen to artists and then to professors who encouraged experimentation both in the studio and elsewhere. They overcame the chastened conservatism caused by the hardships of the 1930s and faced the uncertainties of the Cold War period with the enthusiasm and fearlessness of youth.

The Puget Sound area was hospitable to ceramists. There were husband-and-wife production potters, among them James McKinnell and Nan Bangs McKinnell[7] and Ralph Spencer and Lorene Spencer, as well as comparatively rebellious potters like Voulkos, who left Montana in 1954 for California, and Sperry who, by 1959, had succeeded Bonifas at the University of Washington.

Sperry's home in Bothell, Washington, with decorations by Norman Warsinske, John Erickson, Alden Mason, and Howard Duell was featured in the lifestyle section of a *Seattle Times* Sunday supplement[8]. This kind of reporting was even then a common feature, and offered frequent coverage of well-designed homes for collectors of crafts. Roland Terry's home for Weyerhaeuser Corporation director John Hauberg and his first wife, Anne Gould Hauberg, was published, as were homes of several artists—the Spencers, jeweler Coralynn Pence, Russell Day, and William Hixson and potter Ngaire Hixson.

The Seattle Clay Club, begun in 1948, flourished in this atmosphere and staged many exhibitions during the 1950s. Along with Lambda Rho, the University of Washington's art alumni association, and the Seattle Weaver's Guild, for example, this group successfully encouraged the Henry Art Gallery at the University of Washington to begin a regular series of exhibitions for Northwest craftsmen and craftswomen. Ivarose Bovingdon emerged from this milieu and later studied in Montana with Voulkos and Shoji Hamada. Jean Griffith later became a pioneer of raku firing techniques and in 1966 founded Pottery Northwest, a cooperative studio on lower Queen Anne Hill in Seattle.

Significantly, by the end of the decade, Sperry's interests had evolved
from abstract expressionism to modern Scandinavian pottery to Japanese folk art and nature. Many of his fellow potters and students,
such as Griffith, also followed this path. Sperry reminisced: "Nature
was a very strong influence. And the sense of the erotic growth of
plant forms. But the Japanese influence of *shibui*—humble, subdued
good taste—was equally important."[9] The presence of both Asian and
Western influences in Northwest ceramics of the period attests to the
breadth of interest among makers and, as usual, to the global context
of the entire American craft tradition.

But where were the clay sculptors? With the coming pop art revolution in West Coast ceramics a full decade off, some artists, like
Sperry, created brooding abstract sculptures that usually ended up
in gardens while others, like Betty Feves (1921–1985) and Ebba
Rapp (1909–1985), created amusing, stylized carved figures and
busts. Feves, along with Hodge, was active internationally at the
time, representing Oregon in exhibitions in Belgium, Japan and
Czechoslovakia. She played a leading role in the Oregon crafts scene
for many years.

An artist who had a limited stay in Montana but who was definitely
ahead of his colleagues at the time, James Leedy antedated Voulkos's
exposure to the New York School through his visits to Manhattan beginning in 1945. Having grown up partly in Montana, Leedy returned
to spend time with Autio and Voulkos between 1959 and 1964. He
brought to them the thick paint surfaces and large bulky surfaces he
had gained from his acquaintances with Willem de Kooning, Franz
Kline, and Jackson Pollock in Greenwich Village.

In Portland, Marie Louise Feldenheimer (1894–1993) created unusual
abstracts in polychrome and unglazed terra cotta. Other sculptors in
clay were Ed Haines, Melba Dennis, Dorothy Travis, and Lela At-
tebery. Northwest ceramics of the period were commented upon in a
Henry Art Gallery exhibition and in LaMar Harrington's substantial
book of 1979.[10]

METALS: TO ADORN OR DECORATE?

In a way, metals were more advanced than ceramics, at least at
the beginning of the 1950s. George Laisner, teaching sculpture and
enamels at Washington State University in Pullman, had a significant impact on his graduate student Rudy Autio. Frederic Littman
(1907–1979) in Portland was creating numerous architectural sculptures in public settings. James FitzGerald (1910–1973), a painter and

sculptor, accepted commissions for liturgical as well as residential and public settings such as Western Washington University. Glen Alps was awarded a large commission for the new city hall in Seattle, a weird combination of bronze, steel, enamels, lighting and water.

For the new downtown Seattle Public Library, George Tsutakawa (1910–1997) made *Fountain of Wisdom* (1957) which ushered in the "City of Fountains" syndrome: it seemed all major outdoor sculpture commissions had to be related to water somehow either as fountains or, in Alps's case, above a reflecting pool. The fountain craze culminated in the 1962 Seattle World's Fair; its many fountains included those by FitzGerald, Jacques Overhoff, François Stahly, and two Japanese architects, Kazuyuki Matsushita and Hideki Shimizu, but the passion for fountains continued for another twenty years.

Russell E. Day was a significant figure throughout the decade. As chairman of the Division of Arts at Everett Junior College, he was professionally active in the Pacific Arts Association, the Council of the National Art Education Association, Washington Arts Association, and the College Art Association. Teacher, artist and author, Day adapted forms of biomorphic surrealism to jewelry constructed of sterling silver and semiprecious stones such as amethyst and pearl. Primary ideologue for a bland modernism in crafts, Day emphasized in various writings the necessity of an inclusive attitude toward the crafts:

> "Art is an expression of beauty in everyman-made thing—whether it be a sculpture, an automobile, a house or a bridge, an industrial building or a photograph, a table-setting or a chair, exquisite jewelry or a drinking fountain."[11]

Day's most important student was Donald Tompkins (1933–1982). Although Tompkins's most influential work, *Commemorative Medals* (1969–72), was made once he moved to New York, his Northwest metalworks of the 1950s featured an engagement ring for his wife, Marilyn Hopkins, which won a special award in the 1954 Northwest Craftsmen's Show at the Henry Art Gallery. Other projects involved a series of mobiles for restaurants owned by Ivar Haglund.

The most senior figure in metals was Ruth Penington (1905–1995). Joining the University of Washington School of Painting, Sculpture, and Design in 1928, she was among the founders of the Northwest Designer Craftsmen as well as being a craftsman trustee of the American Craft Council. Using beach pebbles, agates, jaspers, beads, silver, gold, stones, and wood, Penington created a modern yet regional craft sensibility. She commented upon the relationships between the artist and the patron:

> "I like to work with my hands, designing in the material as I work
> and accepting the challenge of the limitations of the materials,
> suitability to purpose, requirements of the customer, as a way to
> grow and develop as an artist."[12]

Her studies under silversmiths in Sheffield, England and Copenhagen, Denmark grounded her in the grand tradition of workmanship, yet her extensive travels in Europe, South America and Asia opened her eyes to world craft traditions, nudging her work toward more personal expressions that antedated the revival of ethnic jewelry by her most famous student, Ramona Solberg (1921–2005). Solberg's art did not come of age until the 1970s, and, in addition to her debt to Penington, she also was influenced by Tompkins, whose grid format she borrowed from the Commemorative Medals series.

Another Penington student, Coralynn Pence (1909–1994), taught at Edison Vocational School on Seattle's Capitol Hill. She was another artist who influenced Solberg with her use of "bits of abalone shell, rock crystal, mother-of-pearl, Peking glass, tortoise shell, Brazilian topaz."[13] She frequently held fashion shows in her Robert Shields designed home in the Laurelhurst area of Seattle, matching the modern designs of her jewelry to those of her house architecture.

Irene McGowan was perhaps the most successful of the Puget Sound area metalsmiths. She became the sole proprietor in 1952 of Harry C. Lynde Corporation, an electrical lighting fixture concern. Her major art expressions were lamps, sconces, and chandeliers. In 1958, she was part of a unique series of collaborations for architects Robert Shields and Bert Tucker's new restaurant, Canlis. The decor incorporated her dining area chandelier, door handles by Tsutakawa, mosaic planter by Philip McCracken, and a screen divider by Hella Skowronski made of fabric, rattan, and amber beads. McGowan's other commissions in Seattle came from Temple de Hirsch synagogue, the Washington Athletic Club, St. Louise Church of Lake Hills, Frederick & Nelson department store, Broadmoor Golf Club clubhouse, and the Seattle Opera House.

In addition to jewelry techniques, architectural metal welding, casting and electroforming, and freestanding pedestal and public sculpture, enameling caught on in the 1950s and was employed by a number of artists, among them Harold Balasz, Polly Stehman, Lisel Salzer, Katherine Munter, Paul Michaels, and James Peck.

With annual exhibitions beginning in 1952 at the Henry Art Gallery, designer-craftsmen became established in at least one art museum.

This endorsement continued for a decade or more, joining support from the Pacific Northwest Arts and Crafts Fair in Bellevue, Washington which began in 1948. Along with the fair association's official gallery, PANACA, the fair, the oldest and largest in the U.S., provided substantial and lucrative exposure for artists working in all craft media. (Northwest Designer-Craftsmen became a formal members' association in 1954.)

The Henry Art Gallery exhibitions were organized by University of Washington art historian and museum director T. Gervais Reed and assistant LaMar Harrington. Reed and Harrington also held two national craft invitationals, and Reed organized the official American craft exhibition for the 1962 Seattle World's Fair. Both were strong advocates for the crafts. Harrington is also the author of *Washington Craft Forms: A Historical Perspective 1950–1980* (State Capitol Museum, 1982), an invaluable guide to the 1950s period.

WOOD: SEATING OR SCULPTURE?

Leroy Setziol settled in Oregon in 1951. Formerly an Evangelical Reformed cleric, he was already perfectly poised to mesh with the growth of church architecture and liturgical commissions in the Portland and Eugene areas. Allied with architect Pietro Belluschi and others, Setziol eventually completed numerous church commissions along with his pedestal-size carvings in black walnut and native Oregon myrtlewood, all of religious subjects. Setziol referred to himself as an "existential sculptor."[14] Having undertaken postgraduate studies in philosophy at Johns Hopkins University, he was well prepared to articulate the benign humanist dimension of his subjects.

First Grid Relief Carving (1962) brought Setziol into the hospitable realm of Northwest midcentury modern art. Segmented carved-relief blocks of teak set up horizontal and vertical patterns of dynamic movement and prepared an image vocabulary for the formalist triumphs that followed in the 1960s and which continue up to the present day.

Everett DuPen was head of the sculpture program at the University of Washington from 1945 to 1982. Also drawn to liturgical commissions (*Annunciation*, 1954; *Adam*, 1964), he continues to accept and execute them. The tension of DuPen's work in wood (as well as in limestone, terra cotta, and bronze) results from an internal battle between realism and abstraction. Basically a realist, DuPen was subjected to conformist pressures not to be conservative but to toe the line with the School of Art's progressive modernism. Philip McCrack-

en spent a brief period of time in 1954 as a studio assistant to Henry
Moore in Much Haddam, England. His art reflects nature, specifically
birds and animals of the Northwest. A former student of DuPen's,
McCracken became aligned with artists of the Northwest School who
encouraged a "mystical" rhetoric as a profound intentional defense for
his quaint creatures. As Colin Graham observed:

> "To those living sealed off from the natural environment in the great
> North American conurbations, his birds and animals often have little
> to say apart from their formal qualities. . . . His spirit-saturated
> pieces tend to evoke feelings of enchantment tinged with nostalgia."[15]

Only McCracken's *War Bird* (1960) expresses any residual contemporary context or awareness of the "Age of Anxiety".

Among furniture makers of the period, Evert Sodergren, a fourth-
generation Scandinavian American woodworker, is a major figure
both for the innovative laminating techniques and unusual organic
designs. Sodergren's graceful curves and solid physical construction
gained him a wide following among collectors, architects, and interior
designers. A circular coffeetable of 1959 combined bleached rosewood
and brass. A side chair with arms and black leather seat became a
desirable status symbol in architect-designed homes at the time. Sodergren taught at the U.W. School of Art for a short time during the
1950s, but since then has maintained a workshop near the north end
of Lake Washington in Seattle.

Designer-craftsmen Robert Stanton and Harry Lunstead merit mention for their furniture contributions. Lunstead, who worked closely
with interior designers such as Jean Jongeward and others, perfected
a chemical treatment for steel tabletops that made them resemble
patinated bronze. These artisans and sculptors are only some of those
using wood during the 1950s. Seen from the vantage point of the
present, however, with its even more extensive community of artists,
craftsmen and craftswomen using wood, their achievements taken on
increasingly historic stature.

TEXTILES: BEYOND WARP AND WEFT

Ed Rossbach and Katherine Westphal taught at the University of
Washington in the 1940s before moving to Berkeley, where both
became nationally influential figures to generations of students and
artisans. Their open, "try anything" attitude and deep knowledge of
world textile traditions led directly to a renaissance in textile arts
in the San Francisco Bay Area. Lacking such an anchor, Northwest
textiles remained more conservative until the macramé-wall hang-

ing trend of the 1970s, but still managed to break new ground in the decade following World War II.

Jack Lenor Larsen is the other legendary fibers figure to emerge from the Pacific Northwest although he left Seattle in 1950 for New York. Returning in 1954 for a weeklong workshop at Norway Center, Larsen jumpstarted Northwest weaving with his startling and fresh approaches incorporating patterns and weaving techniques from all over the world.

The Seattle Weavers Guild was founded in 1937. Along with the university's Lambda Rho art alumni association and the Seattle Clay Club, the Guild encouraged Henry Art Gallery director T. Gervais Reed to begin the annual competitive Northwest crafts exhibition. Not all artists in clay, metals, textiles, wood and glass belonged to these organizations, but Reed's support and subsequent annual exhibitions set in motion an endorsement by the establishment that came to the artists and community as a whole for decades. (To mount such exhibitions on a regular basis at the Seattle Art Museum, Portland Art Museum, Tacoma Art Museum, or Vancouver Art Gallery apparently is unthinkable; the Bellevue Arts Museum today is a notable exception.)

Harrington's discussion of 1950s textiles in *Washington Craft Forms* lists thirty-one women and six men. Even a cursory survey reveals, as for other materials under review, artists seemed split between those who embraced modernism and the "age of progress," and those who clung to traditional techniques which went as far, in Jean Wilson's case, as raising her own sheep.

Hella Skowronski took a cue from Dorothy Liebes, who gave workshops in Seattle during the 1950s and also combined materials such as wood and metals in loose casement weavings. Skowronski, like Liebes, went on to great acclaim, had her work exhibited and purchased at the Museum of Modern Art, New York, and set up her own business for corporate and residential clients.

Skowronski mixed raw silk threads with mohair, added redwood strips, leather and jute, and ended up creating work of refreshing informality which gently ameliorated the stark international style forms of 1950s architecture.

Harrington calls her work "romantic" but the strong forms—linear, alternately transparent and bulky—seem progressive, clear-eyed and pragmatic. Indeed, her switch to industrial powerlooming followed Larsen's and Liebes's lead and indicated complete endorsement of the free market system. Many of Skowronski's subsequent clients were corporate, industrial and international. The young woman who had come from Germany in 1929 easily transcended the condescending newspaper headline of a profile on her in the *Seattle Post-Intelligencer*: "Hobby Now Big Business." Weaving had never been a hobby for Hella Skowronski.[16]

GLASS: BEFORE TOLEDO

Although a fateful workshop given at the Toledo Art Museum in 1962 by Harvey Littleton and Dominick Labino introduced a way of making art glass in a home studio, it is not widely known that Russell Day was exploring the same problems—hot to melt glass at a low enough temperature to avoid having to work in a factory. In his master's thesis for the University of Washington, "Experiments in Glass and Colored Light," Day

> "first began with the idea that glass could be used sculpturally with other materials...Planning a construction of overlapping planes of various colored glass, I attempted to fuse metal rods at right angles to the plane...[17]

He ran his small kiln at approximately 1350° F., considerably cooler than factory kilns. His experiments were spotty and plagued with failures as he amusingly relates:

> Later, using a sheet of fractured glass as large as the kiln shelf would support, I laboriously laid out a fantasy of colored glass, and glass rocks, and fired it. . . . The room was filled with a heavy, sooty black smoke, very acrid and penetrating. Hardly able to wait for the kiln to cool so that I could look at my masterpiece, I was somewhat shocked to find that numerous small explosions had taken place and that instead of one piece of fused glass, I had thousands of fragments of glass scattered all over the kiln.[18]

This may have been the real birth of Northwest glass rather than Dale Chihuly's vaunted experiments at a friend's house in 1964.

It was left to Chihuly to revolutionize not only Northwest glass but American and Venetian glass as well. By the dawn of the 1960s, the young Tacoma native had entered the U.W. interior design program, executed his "secret" Saturday night experiments, and been inspired by the only other significant glass artist of the day besides Day, Steven Fuller (1911–1999).

Fuller dealt with color by layering colored glass over clear glass and later fused green-tinted strips of glass into intersected conformations, which he then heated in a kiln and formed into abstract configurations. A combination of clear lines and lumpy shapes, Fuller's art has more instructional than aesthetic value although, again from the vantage point of today, he takes on added stature simply because he was Chihuly's first glass teacher.

As a major beneficiary of Fuller's guidance and of his strong design training under Hope Foote and Warren Hill in the interiors program, Chihuly was singularly well equipped to forge ahead in his own daredevil experiments after leaving the university. Interestingly, in contemplating Chihuly's work of the 1990s—private residential and corporate and public installations—one can make the case that he has embodied many of the principles set forth by his elders in the 1950s: Try anything, combine materials, relate the handmade object to the containing built environment, have an open attitude to color, and emphasize the decorative.

By avoiding any troubling subject matter and exuding the cheerful optimism of the "age of progress" in the Pacific Northwest, the area's greatest craft artist owes a huge debt to the 1950s. While he did not face the same pressures as the Cold War conformists (except as an unruly adolescent), Chihuly benefited from their undertakings and exuberant pride in the crafts as a high calling. In that sense, the many artists mentioned above deserve praise, recognition, and continued critical scrutiny.

BREAKING BARRIERS:
RECENT AMERICAN CRAFT

The artists of *Breaking Barriers: Recent American Craft*, through technical mastery combined with intellectual, social, formal, or psychological content, illustrate the maturity of American craft in the late twentieth century. They break with tradition in basic ways: content, scale, technique, material, and function. Representing every region of the country, the nine women and eight men have African American, Asian American, European American, and Hispanic American heritages. They have frequently crossed cultural boundaries in their search for individual expression, thus creating an American sensibility that reflects trends in world craft.

Among many new developments reflected in this exhibition, one discernible change, according to American Craft Museum director Janet Kardon, "has been an intense scrutiny and active dialogue with the history of craft, making the historical continuum a fertile ground that has been deconstructed and energetically reassembled."[1] Viewed in this light, it makes sense that *Breaking Barriers* artist Wendell Castle reinterpreted nineteenth-century and early twentieth-century high-style French furniture, that Albert Paley filters much of early 20th-century northern European decorative arts, such as Art Nouveau, that Michael Lucero appropriates the forms of pre-Columbian terra cotta figures and that Dale Chihuly in his recent work reassesses art glass made in Venice between World War I and World War II. Craft artists have assimilated and reconfigured historical traditions while pushing forward into an avant-garde of their own making.[2]

The artists in *Breaking Barriers* go beyond the functional without necessarily giving up functional references. Just as the production potter or quilt maker honors the fundamental requirements of design, so the artists included here respect those requirements, even though they are equally driven to violate, explode, and reassemble them. This is what separates these seventeen artists from more conservative traditions as well as from contemporary art trends which privilege ideas over materials.

The most adventurous American craft makers today want both aspects—ideas and materials—just so long as the artwork is able to retain a physical autonomy while conveying the possibility of complex meaning to the viewer. That interplay between artist and viewer, craftmaker and consumer, art object and connoisseur, is an essential part of the contemporary art contract. Fortunately, the rich material

involvement in these works tempts us into the experience of appreciation. Seductive and sensual indeed, craft art begins with the vibrant,
life-affirming perception of making and then, if we are willing to carry
on, other levels of experience may be revealed. As with all contemporary art, it is a two-way street. The broad avenue of enjoyment may
only be reached when the viewer actively engaging his or her imagination by first unraveling process and then perceiving nuances of
meaning.

LANDSCAPE AND THE OBJECT

Wendell Castle, Jane Sauer, Albert Paley, and Dale Chihuly make
art that is tied to the American landscape. All emerge out of the
dominant art style of the century— modernist abstraction—yet each
ameliorates the severity of abstraction with natural growth forms
and symbolic landscape environments. In their work, the meaning is
subtle, submerged, and awaiting interpretation.

Wendell Castle makes furniture that echoes his childhood on the
farms and plains of the Midwest. Defying the traditional upright and
rigid nature of wood, he laminates planks of mahogany, which he
then sands and attacks with a chain saw, producing functional objects
that attain strong sculptural presence. Whether making a chest of
drawers, a wedding chest, or a drop-front desk, Castle completely
reconceives historical furniture genres through the force of memory
and powerful imagination. Having grown up surrounded by images of
plowed fields, cleared landscapes, and encroaching nature, Castle has
conquered and civilized wood's rigidity while retaining the memory
of its plasticity. Each piece bends materials to a softer end: organic
growth.

The feeling of land is always present in Castle's art. Castle's memories of his father's agricultural experiments with seedpod formation
have spurred his own recent explorations: chairs, desks, and tables
with ungainly legs resembling irregular plant growth, or even animal
anatomy. Supports often mirror natural leaf forms, and upper surfaces convey the impersonality of man's impingement on the landscape.
Contrasting materials symbolic Castle's contrasting emotive states,
while asymmetry and teetering imbalance give his work a tour-de-
force quality often at odds with our belief in gravity.

An Anxious Object #2 (1992) stirs a greater sense of anxiety with its
heavily massed double-drawer section balanced by a graceful black
support at the opposite end. The large, irregular leaf form of the desk-
top hovers above the legs. Castle's objects force us to reconsider our

belief in gravity, as their legs seem to come directly from the American soil. They may have their roots of midcentury modernism but today they take their place in an idealization of the land.

Jane Sauer's sculptures are also implanted in the environment, specifically the American Southwest. Sauer makes art that embraces nature or faces urban reality. The pieces for which she has become best known are fiber works wrapped against an inner Styrofoam core, sometimes rising in paired vertical forms to suggest buttes, eroded landforms, and perhaps anonymous abstracted figures. They derive from pre-European North American craft traditions, particularly Neolithic basketry. Weaving off the loom, Sauer adapts an ancient technique to a contemporary end. Painting the threads with contrasting oranges, reds and blues and blacks, she echoes the colors of the malleable earth and the glare of the setting sun in the Southwest. Recently, she has shifted from purely abstract-organic forms to the realm of women's issues and social commentary.

Although originally a jeweler, Albert Paley switched to bent-steel furniture in 1989. Like Chihuly and Castle, he employs up to ten team members to work on a single piece. He has broken geopolitical barriers, frequently exhibiting, lecturing and accepting commissions abroad. Especially respected in Central and Eastern Europe, his art is a battleground for natural forms and the power of steel. This conflict is appropriate for an artist living in the rust belt city of Rochester, New York, with its legacy of cast-iron turn-of-the-century architecture, its heritage of once-pristine natural beauty, and its tug-of-war between the vanishing natural environment and the fading industrial infrastructure.

Inspired by Gothic and Art Nouveau styles, Paley has pushed the limits of steel, twisting it into tortuous lines, sinuous curves, and implausibly turned shapes, all underlying ceremonial entablatures made of marble or slate. The sense of occasion is heightened in a Paley furniture-sculpture, which evokes the lost world of ornate consumption by turn-of-the-century industrial magnates. His overscaled objects—plant stands, hall tables—turn simple functions into aggressive, histrionic events.

Paley is a poet in steel, not elevating its process à la Carl Sandburg, but symbolically chronicling man's shaky relationship to metal structures and nature's matching need to reclaim any built structures in decay. The dark side of nature is operative here, as it was for Art Nouveau artists such as Hector Guimard and Antoní Gaudí. Far from reassuring or life-enhancing, nature in Paley is overpowering and threatening. His objects dominate any setting, proclaiming themselves as marvels of fabrication and announcing their art status. Genetically mutated, yet visually mesmerizing in their tour-de-force construction, they strongly suggest late-twentieth-century visions of nature gone wrong.

Dale Chihuly embodies a European designer-craftsman attitude, using traditions of Italian teamwork to unparalleled extents. In his works, the extraordinary translucence and reflective qualities of glass reinforce an illusion of natural sunlight. Romantic versions of sublime nature and the delicacy of the vine, the bud, and the flower are summoned up and wildly idealized. Nature, however, is not treated as a purely pastoral theme but is depicted as assaulted by toxic pollution. Chihuly's recent pieces involve wildly curved floral elements that seem to envelop the vessel. Throughout, the urge toward "beauty" and the right to decorate are held at a hysterical and provocative pitch.

Among the largest of the "Venetians" series, *Cadmium Orange Putti Venetian with Gilded Putti Stopper* builds up sequential blown shapes that are combined with wraparound gilded leaves. With its brittle gold-leaf fragments, the work moves beyond any rootedness in the landscape, toward ritual vessels or palace presentation objects. *Confetti Float* grows out of a series based on the Japanese fishing-net floats the artist saw wash up on the beach near his childhood home in Washington State. Perhaps the largest single glass ball ever blown (nearly three feet in diameter), *Confetti Float* epitomizes the artist's literally expansive attitude to nature. The sphere, an ancient metaphor for the planet, seems to have come out of the water but, in reality, emerged from an oven of the most intense heat. Its pale yellow ground speckled with colored spots, the large ball suggests a heavily populated environment. Humanity is dependent on nature, and Chihuly, along with Castle, Sauer, and Paley, reminds us of this fragile, enhancing, yet fabricated relationship.

NARRATIVE FIGURATION

Storytelling is perhaps the oldest of all strategies for content in American craft. Throughout this century, while modernist abstraction reigned, potters, weavers, and others kept both the figure and the narrative convention alive in order to tell a nation's stories: folk tales, legends, secrets. Recent exhibitions and scholarship have chronicled this development. Jean Williams Cacicedo, Ke Francis, Viola Frey, Michael Lucero, Sherry Markovitz, and James Tanner all tell us stories about neighborhoods, families, our cultural and racial roots, and our shared, multicultural heritages as Americans.

Ke Francis combines wood, ceramics, glass, and paper in mixed media sculptures that hark back to Mississippi folk art traditions. He mythologizes fishing, hunting, and fly tying as nostalgic male activities gone the way of the Model-T and the Old South. We enter a world of floods, tornadoes, and the power of the Big River through prints, artist's books, woodcuts and multi-media sculptures. Francis insists on the power of the subjective personal vision, fighting the culturally predetermined expectations of why we make art, as well as the attitude that cultural practice is a social construction of conditioning and education.

Francis has not only created pictorial narratives in his extensive woodcuts and sculptural installations but has also gathered stories about the people of Mississippi and turned them into limited-edition artist's books. Some, like *Dixie Compass* and *Boot Knife*, come in the shape of the story's subject. In this sense, they are reflexive objects that comment on their own process and content. Others, like *Jug Line* and *Babylon / Babble-on*, are parts of larger temporary installations but nonetheless stand on their own as examples of the art of the book. With careful attention given to handset letterpress typeface, binding and illustrations, these constructions literalize narrative. In *Penumbra*, the analogy goes even farther with the title character making boxes that are heralded for the memories or evanescent qualities they "contain." Francis stresses the careful handmade character of the book, thus expanding the power of the narrative—first unraveling the process of making in a sequential manner, then including a story, and finally, when the story becomes an allegory of its own making, turning the experience on itself in a twist of gentle humor.

Jean Williams Cacicedo's huge felted and sewn coats, almost too heavy to wear, contain patterns, symbols and ornaments which address American myths of the Far West such as cowboys and native Americans. Stitchery, weaving, felting, and placing of fabric parts comprise the material construction of her work but are, more importantly, the basis for a continuing narrative of subjective simplicity. Black-and-white borders line each coat, surrounding images of wigwams and campfires. The wearer becomes a spokesperson for the artist in this sense, open to discussions about the coat more than a collector might have to defend or explain a painting. Much women's art of the past decade re-evaluated clothing or "wearable art" as a valid expression; Cacicedo is among the most provocative.

Cacicedo's recent works, like *My Father's House* and *Coat of Arms*, focus on her grief over the death of her father. *Coat of Arms* stacks three separate planes of cloth, compressing time into stylized outlines of an old man fishing. Protective, paternal hands touch the cornered hems and metaphorically embrace the wearer. *My Father's House* emulates an Old Testament cape which has, as its lining, the text from Psalm 23, a comforting allusion to prayer for the soul of the departed. Thus, Cacicedo makes a narrative journey of clothing by using the functional convention of the robe both to sculpturally stand in for a figure and to act as the container for a text of grief.

Viola Frey, like Cacicedo, draws on family relationships as a strong source for storytelling. Frey is the most important figurative ceramic sculptor in the United States today. The startling primary colors, construction, and scale of her single and multiple human figures convey a sense of physical and psychological disorientation. Recognizable authority figures such as parents, grandparents, and businessmen challenge our relation to power, family, and childlike scale, intimidated by the larger object. When it is small and toylike, we become children again. Frey has challenged the diminutive heritage of clay figurines and answered the legacy of monumental public art statuary with vivid confrontational beings.

Michael Lucero also deals with scale. With elaborate illusionistic surface decoration, he explodes preconceptions about sculptural mass, leading the viewer to gaze through the object. Images of natural history, landscape, and animals cover clay objects resembling pre-Columbian votive sculptures. Lucero produces fantastic combinations of figures and animals, often incorporating found objects such as baby buggies, chairs, and tables. Tall totemlike sculptures in clay and bronze create vertical narratives about ecology, memory, and the history of everyday functional objects. Drawing on his Hispanic American background, Lucero was engaging multicultural issues long before they became popular.

Lucero's earlier work appropriated pre-Columbian pottery figures to create cross-cultural and cross-historical displacement. Today, with abstracted baby forms alternately hanging from swings or seated in strollers, the California native joins Frey and Cacicedo in creating surrogate family members. Lucero skews the narrative with Surrealist interventions on the clay's surface decoration. Dripping color obscures illusionistic landscapes and other images, which the viewer pieces together to form a story. Unlike pictorial Surrealism, Lucero's sculpture reveals itself in three dimensions, both through the presence of the figure and via the all-enveloping glazed surface.

James Tanner makes spattered clay and bronze wall relief that, on one level, are figurative sculptures—with their abrupt, glaring faces—and, on an another, are statements about the struggle of African Americans to attain a separate identity in the midst of strong social, economic, and peer pressures to conform. Some pieces recall West African bronzes of the ancient kingdom of Benin; others echo a major African American art form of the slave period: carved face jugs. Sculptor, painter, and printmaker, Tanner uses brightly colored, celebratory glazes to overlay the stylized faces pushing toward visibility. The improvisatory manner of the painting echoes the spontaneous nature of African American jazz.

Sherry Markovitz also uses the object's surface as a departure point for narration. Her works comment on the sanctity of life, interspecies relationships, the savagery of hunting, and the vanished traditions of Native Americans. For over a decade, she has used papier-mâché on taxidermy molds of moose, deer, and other wildlife, dressing up, spangling, and beading them. She cross-dresses the animals, from male to female. By decorating them, Markovitz cancels out the life extinction of blood sports, feminizing a male province, and subverting gender stereotypes. Like Frey, she deals with parent-child relationships, but with the difference that family members are all animals. Warnings against the barbarism of sport hunting, the beaded animal heads were at once alive and dead, their vitality ignited by the extraordinary process of glass beading, their morbidity underscored by a resemblance to taxidermy trophies.

Markovitz's recent work explores themes of organic growth in a more abstract fashion. Dried gourds from New Mexico and the Southeast are covered with glass beads—all hand-strung by Markovitz. The new work delves deeper into primal forms with pink beads, closer color-values, and the limb-like appurtenances of gourds standing in for the human figure. *Yellow Bear* makes allusions to Plains Indians beading traditions and to ceremonial Native American face painting but its riotously incongruous appearance, staring out directly at the viewer, separates it from authentic indigenous art, thrusting into the contemporary moment. *Twins* and *Pink Belly* continue the elaborate surface-covering conventions but shift away from animal imagery toward an earlier stage of life, cell division after conception. At this point, Markovitz slides into organic abstraction without sacrificing figurative or narrative implications. An icon of pregnancy, *Pink Belly* juts out from the wall without explanation, throbbing with life in all its irregular bumps and depressions. Formalist and figurativist at once, Markovitz confounds observers who insist on such arbitrary classifications.

COMIC RELEASE

Viola Frey and Michael Lucero provide a transition from narrative figuration in clay to related expressions using humor in the art of Ginny Ruffner, Wendy Maruyama, Tommy Simpson, and Joyce Scott. These artists use humor to differing ends: satire, surprise, nostalgia, and social critique. In Frey's work, the improbability of scale (giant authority/parent figures) shocks or intimidates us into an uneasy laugh of fear. Rooted in cartoon imagery rather than realism, her Pop associations also evoke smiles. Frey's narrow primary color glaze palette in turn recalls the colors of comic strips.

As for Lucero, the Surrealist strategy of disjunctive juxtaposition stretches potential humor to its limit. His sun-filled colors alternate with scenes of nature by night. The artist's broad range of imagery—babies, dogs, animals, insects, amphibians, etc.—suggests a profoundly American embrace of the universe. He accepts the raucous complexity of American life and filters all of it through his unceasingly inventive imagination. The "New World" of Lucero's series title is actually the new world of his own imagination: witty, exaggerated, starling, and teeming with life.

Like Lucero, Ginny Ruffner indulges in an aesthetic of excess. For her, however, sculpture is a disembodied volume. Using glass lampwork tubing, she assembles linear phantasms of clustered forms around a central empty space—complicated structures resembling DNA helixes, string networks, and three-dimensional drawings. She derives humor from upsetting expectations, scattering a playful vocabulary of objects on the same piece. Ruffner also satirizes art history by shrinking the scale of objects and by appropriating fine art images.

Garden Party and *Circuitous Path* both celebrate life's abundance of event and anecdote, tempting us into narrative only to defy any logical plot. The outward-stretching squiggles of *Garden Party* suggest expanding growth forms. The cube, typical of Ruffner's internal symmetry, might also be seen as a metaphor for highly planned formal gardens. Such logic is denied in the dizzying line of *Circuitous Path*, which unveils a light-hearted walkway similar to a game board. Dice, striped tubing, cherries and strawberries—recalling a slot machine— jolt the viewer into a complex mood of gentle humor and spatial disorientation.

Wendy Maruyama has broken the barriers between functional objects and aesthetic objects made for contemplation first—and use second. Playing up the wit of improbable structures, Maruyama calls on the

colors of wood and paint
to dominate the form.
Violating the wood's
surface by gouging and
sawing, she emphasizes
how the object can depict
its own making. Her
work in the last decade
reflects a greater appearance of hands-on action
and painterly surfaces,
taking construction
beyond function into an
expressionistic realm of
color and touch.

Disrupted expectation is
a key to Maruyama's hu-
mor. *Candelabrum with
Cone* looks more like
a carnivorous tropical
plant than a torchère. In
contrast, *Peking* seems
a parody of classical
Chinese lacquered court
furniture. With its gold-
leafed "collar" and bur-

Tommy Simpson: *Children of Love*, 1992, maple,
satinwood, cherry, oak, rosewood and photos,
24 x 14 x 2". Courtesy of Leo Kaplan Modern,
New York. Photo: William Seitz

nished red "shawl" or "lapels," and drawer pulls that act as "buttons,"
the cabinet's facade takes on strongly figurative overtones. Inside, the
humor is reversed by the sober symmetry of the shelves and cubby-
holes. Facades are always light-hearted in Maruyama while interiors
are secretive and sober.

For Tommy Simpson, painted wooden furniture is part of a wider
range of sculptural explorations, all united by his subjective sensibility.
Clocks resemble kangaroos, and armoires are shaped like telephone
booths. Everything is a departure-point for the viewer's interactive
role, a journey to an innocent, lovingly constructed world of stars,
roads, paths, ponds, and glens. Simpson's art involves a willful regression to childhood. Chipping at the wooden surfaces, Simpson takes
the time a child takes with a homemade toy, eschewing deadlines or
external realities. His sense of humor is double-edged, gently clever,
redolent of a resistance to technological culture as well as to issues of
adult responsibility. His is an art of escape, but an escape into a height-

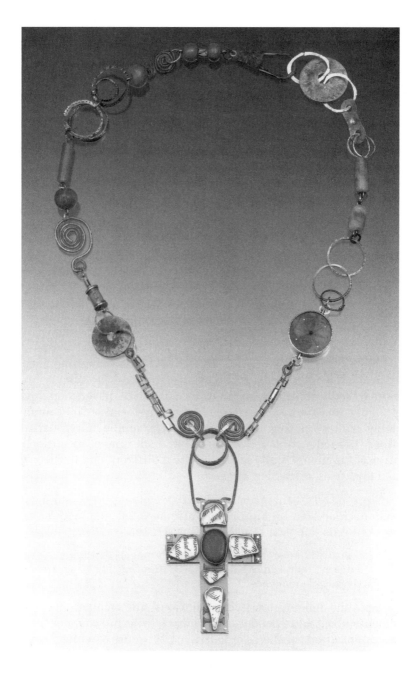

Robert Ebendorf: *Necklace/Cross*, 1993, sterling silver, iron wire, amber, carnelian, nickel silver, and found objects, ¼ x 25". Charles W. Wustum Museum of Fine Arts, Racine, Wisconsin. Photo: John Lenz

ened sense of the distance between whimsy and seriousness. Integrity of workmanship enables Simpson to balance both extremes.

H. C. Westermann had a major impact on Simpson. Throughout the 1980s, Simpson doubled Westermann's love for and mockery of American folk art, adapting it to his own image vocabulary. Since then, he has extended the development of curves, triangles, ovals, and circles into a more fully individual expression. Adopting other materials, like brush bristles, upholstery fabric, and metal, Simpson stresses the labor-intensive aspects of American folk furniture while adding sophistication.

Joyce Scott uses humor to shock us into a recognition of deeper concerns such as racial injustice, relations between blacks and whites, and sexual stereotyping of minorities. The doll-size scale of her sculptures tricks us into thinking they are sparkling toys. The glittering reflections of the colored beads generates a deceptively upbeat atmosphere only to be undercut. Scott is a transitional artist who links the comic release of Ruffner, Simpson and Maruyama to the topical references of another group of artists in the exhibition.

SOCIAL SUBJECTS: TRANSCENDING ADORNMENT

Joyce Scott, Robert Ebendorf, Thomasin Grim, and Jane Sauer break barriers by addressing sex, religion, race, violence, poverty, and pollution. They also broke barriers of enforced material purity common to earlier craft when they use found objects, combine materials, and downplay refined technique. Ornament and adornment, traditional features of functional craft, are turned to a different end in their work or, in a few cases, discarded altogether.

Joyce Scott, a third-generation craft artist, conveys universal messages in necklaces and sculptures of intimate scale and monumental power. As Linda Johnson Dougherty has written,

> Integrating humor, social issues, and formal aesthetics. . . . Scott creates art that achieves its goal of confronting, agitating, and activating an audience.[3]

She adapts the doll as a terrifying, hilarious, and stringent focus for statements about race, gender, and politics. Whether commenting on the exploitations of slaves or satirizing the fears of white South Africans, however, Scott never becomes tendentious or dogmatic. Also a performance artist, she employs humor in making her stinging but valid claims about life in American society as a member of a minority culture.

Three Graces Oblivious as Los Angeles Burns, built around a blown-glass column, is one of Scott's most important works. It combines great beauty with terrifying subject matter. An image of bitter violence, the sculpture's inner core is a frieze of flames, rioters, and burning buildings. Noticeably white, the Graces stand with their backs to the carnage, arms upturned or akimbo, gazing away impassively. Above, the head of police brutality victim Rodney King supports a looter holding a flame. The mermaid-like Graces also act as Sirens, either warning us of such horror or perilously seducing our attention away from reality.

Robert Ebendorf has redefined the province of American art jewelry by fashioning found objects and fine materials into intricate pieces of body ornament or independent sculpture. Not so much ready-mades as recycled junk, the components of Ebendorf's art emerge from the seashore, parking lots, back alleys, architectural blueprints, and even a simple stroll in the neighborhood. Behind it all is the artist's sensitivity to the plight of the homeless, the hidden key to understanding the origins of his recent work. Ebendorf combines fine and mundane materials such as sterling silver and stone, Scrabble letters, pencils, wires, metal tape measures, and Color-Core Formica, arranging them into fragments of memory that echo chapters in American history or stand in as mementos of the wearer's experience. The human body affects the content of his work: the wearer lends sculptural support to a necklace or brooch and creates a backdrop for elaborate symbolic combinations. At other times, Ebendorf subverts jewelry's primary mission of body adornment by creating unwieldy, possibly unwearable forms, and by using detritus of our throwaway society: crab shells, plastic forks, and paper clips.

Architectural Brooches literally cuts down to size the grandiosity of buildings designed during the boom years of the 1980s. Worn separately or displayed as a group, the pins are a wry commentary on the building arts and draw attention to how humble materials like cardboard and paper may stand in symbolically for stone and metal. Ebendorf responds to the two extremes of our environment, slipshod shanties and sleek, upscale buildings.

Thomasin Grim addresses issues such as the perception of information and the world's inundation by visual messages. Making up signs that double as metaphors for language and syntax, she reinforces a West Coast preference for internalized, meditative artwork. Although mystical in its indeterminate symbolism, Grim's art seems to refer to computer circuit boards or computer printouts—ironically executed in time-consuming weavings. She stresses the necessity of the handmade, the primacy of craft as a humanizing element in a society increasingly controlled by electronic and digital means.

By using a traditional eight-harness floor loom, Grim deliberately invokes historical weaving traditions at the same time she presents subjects of global concern. The contemporaneity of her subjects wrenches them out of a West Coast fantasy world and into the adversarial postmodern condition. The rayon and cotton thread weavings are bluntly frontal, with firmly centered compositions that are read as signs rather than dream imagery. *Cards* refers to semiotics and the pervasiveness of mass communications and advertising. Grim wittily adapts the grid structure of quilts in *Cards*, which depicts homes on fire, scales of justice in flames, and couples in domestic settings. The overall sensation is one of warning and impending disaster. *Bloodlines* and *Tic Toc* deal with ecology. The former connects Grim's generic figures to a stylized root system below a leafy tree. The interdependency of people and the land is reinforced by the ghostlike tree. Vivid in color and pictorially more complex, *Whence* deals with the new image of Africa as the site where the human species originated. With a cut-away view of the ocean at the picture's base, Grim sets up a primordial soup "whence" the earliest protoplasm led to all life, not just our species.

Since 1990, Jane Sauer has incorporated writings by and about women into gall oblong container shapes resembling thread spools, vases, or baskets. Expressing her feelings about such issues as abortion, violence against women, and the position of women in the labor force, she represents the shift of some American craft artists toward art with more direct social involvement, if not reformative impact. The laborious process of weaving the lettering draws attention to the history of women as a part of America's textile industry, often unappreciated, or worse, exploited and endangered. Now no longer formalist vessels, Sauer's works take their place alongside some of the most politically committed art using craft materials.

In her series, "Running On Empty," Sauer addresses problems that plague her home in St. Louis: teens and guns, lack of daycare for working mothers, and the disparity in the U.S. between military spending and housing, social security, and welfare. The tombstone shapes signify the many deaths of young people caused by inadequate social programs and the lack of gun control. Several critics hold that human relationships, specifically family relationships, are the themes that link Sauer's earlier "organic obelisks" with the current text pieces. Others proffer a gender-based reading of her forms, claiming she "explore[s] the male-female dichotomy."[4] Like Grim, however, she relies on fiber and textiles as vehicles for meaning, and both artists transcend traditional adornment in order to make social comments.

ADORNING TRANSCENDENCE: REBECCA MEDEL

Rejecting topicality altogether, Rebecca Medel embraces adornment as a means for discussing religious or spiritual transcendence. Using knotted predyed linen threads which are immersed in liquid adhesive to render them rigid enough to be suspended behind one another, Medel creates frontal, illusionistic, subtly kinetic, three-dimensional mandalas that push the viewer toward a hypnotic state.

Pattern is an organizing principle in Medel's compositions: she turns repetition, an essential compositional element in weaving, to a symbolic end in her geometric three-dimensional wall reliefs. Her knotted net patterns are deceptively modular and abstract; in reality, they refer to structures within certain Buddhist temples, the passage of time, and issues of concealment and revelation. The works thrust outward and, at the same time, draw us into an unattainable center. Medel's giant weavings are another answer to traditional sculptural weight or mass: they take up space but seem on the verge of disappearance. The net structure also implies containment or imprisonment, but the off-centered coloring and glowing presence suggest spiritual, if not physical, escape. Medel's art represents the interface or conflict between the material and immaterial worlds, between the public space where the body stands and the invisible inner world where the personality resides.

Semiotics encases the knotted nets in two Plexiglas cases, thereby literalizing the feeling of a closed system. Each module is a reverse of the other, suggesting the binary structure of a computer more than a heightened state of spiritual awareness. More open-ended, *Two Views* and *Star Map: Crater* present, respectively, highly planned and comparatively random compositions. *Two Views* uses multiple suspended transparent planes which contain two centered "windowpane" images.

With her suspended compositions, Medel breaks the barrier of gravity, leaving the cares of the world behind. Discarding social issues, she returns us to the spiritual precepts of modernist abstraction and points upward to the cosmos. As we approach the end of the millennium, art may take that direction. But one critical aspect of Medel's art will always tie it to the human condition and, hence, give it a social context: it must be made by hand. No matter how transcendent the ultimate image may be, no matter how devoid of partisan content or topical references, her art shares with that of all the other artists in this exhibition a reverent devotion to the act of making.

Martin Puryear: *Thicket*, 1990, basswood and cypress, 67 x 62 x 17".
Seattle Art Museum, gift of Agnes Gund. 90.32. Photo: Paul Macapia

THE REMATERIALIZATION OF THE ART OBJECT

> The idea has to be awfully good to compete with the object and few of
> the contemporary ideas . . . are finally that good.

—Lucy R. Lippard and John Chandler, 1968[1]

During the 1990s, antimaterialist, intellectual processes of artmaking characteristic of the last two decades have begun to give way to an ultramaterialist art that emphasizes the fabrication process. Such a trend appears to be provoking a profound rematerialization of art as object. We have come a long way since Lucy R. Lippard and John Chandler's 1968 essay, "The De-Materialization of Art,"[2] and her 1973 anthology, Six Years: The Dematerialization of the Art Object from 1966 to 1972.[3] in which Lippard posited a coming brave new world wherein art would experience a "gradual de-emphasis of sculptural concerns" and a "heightened alertness to sensorial or visual phenomena."[4]

In retrospect, there was a strange union between object-oriented art like Minimalism and the de-materializing art of Conceptualism. The former still depended on the presence of objects, as critics like Michael Fried and the British group Art & Language pointed out at the time. Responding to Lippard and Chandler's essay in Art International which held among other things that "Idea art has been seen as art about criticism rather than art-as-art or even art about art,"[5] Art & Language wrote in a letter reprinted in Six Years, "All of the examples of art works (ideas) you refer to in your article are with few exceptions art-objects."[6]

Other critics of Conceptual art damned it along with Minimalism and Arte Povera as "novelty art," (Clement Greenberg), "the emperor's new bikini," (Hilton Kramer), and "de-aestheticized art" (Harold Rosenberg). Rosenberg concluded in his 1970 tirade: "Art in our era oscillates between the conviction that meeting the resistance of a craft tradition is indispensable to acts of creation and the counter-conviction that secrets can be fished alive out of the sea of phenomena."[7]

Why did Conceptualism eventually become so mainstream, so institutionalized, so academified when it was revived in the 1980s as the establishment taste of curators and critics like Laura Trippi, Dan Cameron, Craig Owens, and Hal Foster, to name but a few? The answer must be in its greater discussability and teachability. Lippard gave a hint of what was to come when she commented in the same essay "Sometime in the near future, it may be necessary for the writer to be an artist as well as for the artist to be a writer. There will still be scholars and art historians of art but the contemporary critic may have to choose between a creative originality and explanatory historicism."[8]

Precisely. Art became a succession of texts sidestepping the need for interpretation by critics and elevating the curator to the powerful (and appealing) position of village explainer. However, to paraphrase Gertrude Stein's comment about Ezra Pound, that is fine if you are a village, if not not.

Indeed, Lippard was soon accused of this herself by critics of her 1969 Seattle Art Museum Modern Art Pavilion exhibition, "557,087" (the population of Seattle at the time). As Peter Plagens pointed out in Artforum, "There is a total style so pervasive as to suggest that [L.L.] is in fact the artist and that her medium is other artists. . . . "[9]

Nearly three decades later, it is necessary to now forecast Conceptualism's own demise and to recast recent art history, including Minimalism, in terms of its material involvement, review it in relation to the object's new status, and to examine material-fashioning as a chief criterion over discussability. We can even borrow from the Minimalists' tactic of unapologetically admitting that much of their art could be about "nothing." The rematerialized art object might be about "nothing" other than its own construction. Art made now that elevates decoration, function, and construction can also carry other contents but all such ideas are transfused through the apprehension of fabrication.

Seen this way, Postmodernism was a period style (1975–1995) that favored discussability over physical presence, intention over interpretation, text over image, and ideological content over the visible residue of making. Cleverly twisting Frank Stella's "What you see is what you get," Postmodernism's rejoinder was "What you say is what you get." Postmodernism kept alive the myth of an artistic avant-garde long since vanished. Oddly enough, such anti-establishment art required explicit state approval and government funding for its many alternative non-profit exhibition sites from Seattle's and/or to New York's Franklin Furnace Archive, Inc.

Two artists who were ahead of the curve leading to the awareness of the renewability of the art object are Ulrich Ruckriem and Martin Puryear. As early as 1981, in his first U.S. museum show at Fort Worth, Ruckriem spent weeks with German-American stonemasons in Fredericksburg, Texas working with large quarried pieces of granite. The artist has a background as a stonemason, having worked on the Cologne Cathedral. Similarly, Puryear's studies of maritime carpentry in Sweden provided crucial training in the stacking and laminating of hardwoods so central to his highly praised sculptures like Thicket (1990) of cut and pegged basswood and cypress.

Taking the implications of these and other artists one step farther, critics like Donald Kuspit have concluded "the days of 'anything goes' are over." He adds a provocative defense of crafted art in, of all things, moral terms. Kuspit echoes Victorian art critic and theorist John Ruskin in claiming that one salutary value of such a paradigm shift from idea to making is "to save the dignity of work [involving] a re-emphasis in art as hard work."[10] Such comments reveal a realization that the nature of art is inextricably tied up with technical mastery of materials, done alone or, more frequently, in tandem with other skilled assistants executing complicated commands: cutting, polishing, sanding, sewing, throwing, carving, and other studio procedures.

This shift has revolutionary implications for contemporary art and criticism if taken to logical conclusions. Art school students will have to master art materials once again. And what will critics say about the rematerialization of the art object? After the endless, reassuring discussability of Postmodernism, critics will have to deal with issues of fabrication, ornament and decoration as potential conveyors of meaning (though social content will surely remain, as in the work of Thomasin Grim or Lou Cabeen, as part and parcel of the object's total presence.). New critics will appear who enjoy and appreciate the challenge handmade art makes to a world increasingly involved in virtual reality and disembodied computer operations. We are far from such a stage yet but there are encouraging signs that not only are we indeed beyond the "anything goes" phase of Conceptualism, we are also past the claims of Andy Warhol and Joseph Beuys that "everyone is creative."

Today, under Kuspit's neo-Ruskinian paradigm for art, a reassertion of the made properties of art constitute a revised aesthetic status and legitimacy for art. Transitional figures like Michael Lucero and Therman Statom mix found objects with highly manipulated clay and glass. Lucero's "Reclamation" series (1995–96), for example, retrieves broken cement garden statuary or damaged ethnic art and "mends" them with elaborate ceramic add-ons. Statom's many glass installations reposition everything from thrift shop detritus to children's toys within plate-glass walls and broken hand-blown glass fragments. The power of their work has to do with the retrieval and rescuing of the handmade. After all, during the Postmodern period, artists with craft talents have kept sculpture alive on a life-support system.

Elaborate techniques like jewelry making (as exemplified in the work of Joyce Scott and Nancy Worden), glass tube lampworking (Ginny Ruffner), glasscasting (Hank Murta Adams), glassblowing (Dale Chihuly) and many other processes, are being turned to on the part of younger artists who seek satisfaction in hard work that matches a quest for profound personal expression.

Postmodernism has been unable to kill the individual artist, to kill off painting and sculpture for good; unable to eradicate the subjective and the personal, to demolish the autonomous object in favor of the relentlessly contingent and didactic.

In view of Conceptualism's brief lineage (less than 30 years), the new sculpture sensitive to craft traditions may tap into global heritages at least two millenia long. More than just "appropriating," or ransacking art history, these artists meet, master, and reinvent processes widespread throughout the world: weaving, ceramics, metalsmithing, wood carving, woodturning, to name but a few.

These are transferred to contemporary expressions that unite diverse cultures (like Lucero's "New World" series) and reorient the viewer's relation to the passage of time through the apprehension of process.

Lucero and Mark Lindquist, two artists with nationally touring retrospectives at this time, achieve dialogues with international traditions of fabrication. With Lindquist, the age of the wood as well as the intervention of the tool is signified in a way that is not true with Puryear. For Lucero, the blending of the found and handmade object can be a tactic that unites humanity rather than ghettoizes it through cultural separatism.

In writing about Lucero so sensitively, Lippard's retrospective catalog essay[11] shows how far her own thought has traveled since 1969 when she wrote that "it has become feasible for artists to deal with technical concepts in their own imaginations rather than having to struggle with constructive techniques beyond their capacities and financial means."[12] Indeed, with the rematerialization of the art object, critics and artists alike recognize that what matters is the "struggle with constructive techniques."

THE MYTH OF THE NEGLECTED CERAMICS ARTIST: A BRIEF HISTORY OF CLAY CRITICISM

Sometimes, as scholars, historians and researchers well know, a light bulb can go off or a *eureka* moment can occur months or years after exposure to certain sets of figures or data. In my case, the year of my James Renwick fellowship in American craft research at the Smithsonian American Art Museum in 1989–90 eventually led to a comparable experience.

In the process of writing the introduction for a proposed anthology of clay criticism and re-reading all the entries which came from a variety of sources—magazines, monographs, gallery and museum catalogs and art and craft journals—I received the blinding insight that my initial thesis had been disproven by my own activities and that, like a good philosopher in the tradition of Sir Karl Popper, I would have to prove or refute my own hypothesis, that American ceramics had been the ugly bastard stepchild of American art. What I realized, instead, was that no such thing appeared to be true according to the materials I was re-reading. Lo and behold, in one newspaper and art magazine after another, clay has been taken seriously, commented upon thoughtfully and that the entire party line of the put-upon "neglected ceramic artist" that I had inherited as a budding art critic more than 25 years ago had been a big pile of—misinformation.

What I would like to share with you are some of the high points in the brief history of clay criticism since 1945. After World War II, as the whole university-based ceramic training system got going, there was the Syracuse National. Reviewing the 1949 touring exhibition organized by the Syracuse Museum of Fine Arts (now the Everson Museum), the art critic Mary L. Alexander reviewed the exhibit very favorably in the *Cincinnati Enquirer*:

> Ceramic sculpture, which is of excellent quality, has qualities peculiar to its medium—clay. Its very plastic quality determines its treatment. It must not be carved like wood or chipped like stone, but it should be handled so as to preserve the character and feeling of the basic material.[1]

But it was at the Great Gray Lady, the *New York Times*, in 1960, the year before Rose Slivka's better-known "New Ceramic Presence" piece in *Craft Horizons* appeared, that the estimable John Canaday first brought up the link between Abstract Expressionism and American ceramics.

Robert Arneson: *Doggie Bob*, 1982. Glazed ceramic and bronze, 36 x 33 x 21".
Stephen and Pamela Hootkin Collection, New York. Photo: Courtesy of George
Adams Gallery, New York

Canaday touched on the clubby aspect of American ceramics at the time, how "They are specialists in a field of aesthetics in which responses are so acutely refined that, to an outsider looking in, the initiated seem to be communicating by extrasensory perception." But Canaday, not Slivka, was the first to ask what potters shared with New York painters of the day. He answered:

> Only this: that in their relationship to their material, painters seem to be nudging hopefully around the boundaries of the idea that has sustained the earthy life in the art of the potter in spite of the esoteric extremities of his aesthetics. The painters—we are speaking of abstract painters—investigation of new methods and new media is generally explained as an effort to extend the boundaries of expression, but the effort may really be to try to touch ground by working with material more tangible than the thin skin of pigment that used to satisfy the painter of pictorial images. As evidence, look at the kind of new materials the painter chooses. He loads his pigments with sand, ashes or other coarse matter; he composes with wire, screen, cardboard, gravel, until his work is painting only by the loosest use of the word. He seems to be gravitating toward the direct manual manipulation typical of the art crafts.[2]

I wish to mention briefly the purported breakthrough essay of Voulkos's greatest champion, Rose Slivka, her "New Ceramic Presence" essay in the April, 1961 *Craft Horizons* (of which she was editor-in-chief) to note that, not only was she superseded by Canaday, but that, although her article was heavily illustrated, not one artist other than Picasso and Miró, was mentioned by name. One passage, however, seems inspired by Canaday's of a few months earlier, when she says:

> The painter, moreover, having expanded the vistas of his material, physically treats paint as if it were clay—a soft, wet, viscous substance responsive to the direction and force of the hand and to the touch, directly or with tool; it can be dripped, poured, brushed, squeezed, thrown, pinched, scratched, scraped, modeled—treated as both fluid and solid. Like the potter, he even incorporates foreign materials—such as sand, glass, coffee grounds, crushed stone, etc.— with paint as the binder, to emphasize texture and surface quality beyond color.[3]

Art in America got into the act early on. In 1956, they published William J. Homer's 2,000-word memorial essay on Carl Walters, a ceramic sculptor of animals who had exhibited at the Metropolitan Museum of Art. Homer used a tone of great respect and admiration: He concluded:

> Had Carl Walters continued his youthful efforts as a painter, he might have become a nationally known American realist. But by the

peculiar turns of circumstance which seem to draw artists to one medium or another, Walters steered in the direction of ceramics. In this field he was unexcelled. Perhaps he was born a few thousand years too late, but, by fulfilling his talent completely in this medium, he commanded the respect of connoisseur and layman alike.[4]

Another revelation that occurred to me was when I found the only review of Peter Voulkos's first show in New York at The Museum of Modern Art. The convention wisdom is that either the show was ignored or panned. I could not find material to support either claim but I did find Dore Ashton's 1960 *New York Times* review. Although less than 300 words, I'd call it a rave. Ashton noted:

> Peter Voulkos, whose sculpture and paintings are on view in the Museum of Modern Art's thirteenth "New Talent" exhibition, is an artist of exceptionally vitality. Not only is he considered by many to be America's most original potter, but also he now proves himself to be a naturally gifted sculptor as well.[5]

Six years later, another important figure, the late John Coplans, co-founder of *Artforum*, published the catalog that was later printed as an essay in *Artforum*, "Abstract Expressionist Ceramics." Coplans's exhibit at University of California—Irvine presented the first real canon of AbEx clay. Besides Voulkos, it included John Mason, Billy Al Bengston, Kenneth Price, Malcolm McClain, Michael Frimkess and Henry Takemoto, adding later in the article, James Melchert, Manuel Neri and Ron Nagle.[6]

We cannot fully analyze here another cardinal clay essay of the 1960s, Peter Selz's "Notes on Funk," recently canonized and codified at a symposium at the Arizona State University in Tempe. Selz's survey of the new Bay Area ceramics at the University Art Museum of Berkeley at least took seriously artists after Voulkos who had a radically different sensibility, like Robert Arneson, Robert Hudson and Ken Price. People forget that the end of "Notes on Funk" pushes Funk away from ceramics toward plastics, metals, fiberglass, and even redwood. The movement so loudly claimed as private property for California clay artists ever since was never really wholly theirs to own.[7]

Numerous museum curators, art critics and art historians have taken the time to seriously and sensitively learn and write about American ceramics. They include Barbara Haskell's definitive 1974 Pasadena Museum of Art monograph on John Mason and Alfred Frankenstein's 1976 *ARTnews* piece on Arneson, the first art magazine article ever written about Arneson. Frankenstein noted midway through his essay: "Arneson is almost singlehandedly responsible for the fact that ceramic is now a major sculptor's medium."[8]

Thus, with the interest of a few art critics among the many who, let's face it, largely ignore the ceramics and craft magazines, the whole movement could be re-invented where it really mattered: in the art magazines. The 1970s and 1980s were a heyday for clay in the art world. There were Alexandra Anderson's discovery of "George Ohr's 'Mud Babies'" in the January 1979 *Art in America* (four pages in color!) and Prudence Carlson's 1980 *Art in America* review of Daisy Youngblood, one of the most moving and beautiful pieces of writing on any American artist. While she gives due space to Youngblood's choice of clay and her miraculous powers over it, she concludes on a deeper note: Rather,

> With the craft and black mischief of a Trickster, she has inspirited her clay material with an unorthodox life, realizing an aesthetic and describing a zoology the likes of which are to be found nowhere else. What her violated heads hold in common is an intriguing multiplicity of allusion together with an intrinsic eloquence of proportion, contour and line—a formal self-sufficiency—that share equally in the work's oddity and impact.[9]

The 1980s also brought to the fore the return of art pottery thanks to the influence and power of two dealers, Alice Westphal and Garth Clark, the latter of whom had failed as an art critic and had to fall back on becoming an art dealer. Westphal's 1985 address to the members of the High Museum of Art in Atlanta, "Disruptions and Eruptions in 20th-Century Ceramics," was a deeply philosophical treatise justifying what Rob Barnard so shrewdly called the "gallery vessel," but at least Westphal brought more than Clark's dry decorative arts background and teacup fancier's point of view to her enterprise. Whether or not the ideas of Martin Heidegger clarify Westphal's efforts, at least she had read the German philosopher and could draw on his theories of "The origin of a Work of Art."

Gerald Nordland made a valiant stab at one of Westphal's pets, Richard DeVore, but was not interpretive enough in his 1981 catalog for Westphal's Chicago gallery, Exhibit A. He resorted to a familiar approach: when you don't have any ideas about the art under discussion, just interview the artist and quote him or her! Nor is it clear whether a discussion of DeVore's sessions with his psychiatrist, Dr. Hilbert DeLawter, strengthened Nordland's overall analysis.

Speaking of psychoanalysis, probably the single most brilliant mind to address American ceramics in this period is the art critic and now credentialed lay analyst, Donald Kuspit. Dr. Kuspit, who holds Ph.D. degrees in philosophy and art history, and who studied at the Frankfurt School of Advanced Studies under Theodor Adorno, has done an amazing job of combining social and psychological sciences with the disciplines of art criticism and art history.

Although his writings on Arneson are unparalleled in their psychological insights, it's worth sharing a few gems from his "Elemental Realities," a feature-length review in *Art in America* of Garth Clark's mega-survey, "A Century of American Ceramics 1878–1978." Kuspit begins significantly by quoting a 1930s *Fortune* magazine article's description of American ceramics as the "art with an inferiority complex" and continues by praising Clark's efforts to "overturn the deeply rooted negative attitude that ceramics is inherently trivial." Kuspit openly discusses "the contempt in which ceramics is held" and claims this is so because "a fixed hierarchy of the arts [still] lingers."

Kuspit's wide-ranging analysis of the show concludes:

> Until recently, however, ceramics has lived in the shadow of painting and sculpture. But now it has been realized that there are no privileged modes of art, and that the ceramic material, while frequently considered the sculptural medium of last resort. . .[is] also the medium which makes self-evident the fundamental tensions that inform art. Clay's great flexibility implies freedom from preconceived forms; its elemental character suggests the possibility of an art at once profound and intimate. . . . Ceramics may thus be the most truly universal art: its material is highly responsive to human aspirations, while the final product is as risky and difficult to achieve as any human individuality.[10]

Less than a decade earlier, clay really came of age in the art world: it was the subject of a tremendous cat fight between two leading art critics of the day, the redoubtable Hilton Kramer of *The New York Times* and John Perreault at *SoHo News* and *Artforum*. Richard Marshall and Suzanne Foley's "Ceramic Sculpture: Six Artists" at the Whitney Museum of American Art brought to New York the whole crowd, that is, Voulkos, Mason, Price, Arneson, and Richard Shaw and David Gilhooly.

Kramer's Sunday *Times* piece in December, 1981 was ruthless in exposing his own taste and unguarded prejudices. He opens by mentioning the "fact that ceramic art—in this country, at least—has traditionally been associated with regional styles and a provincial ethos," and then goes on, quite humorously, to get out of the way once and for all the link between Abstract Expressionism and ceramics: "My own view is that it never really worked, and resulted more often than not in making ceramic sculpture a displaced satellite of a style conceived for another medium. Kramer dismissed Mason first by calling his work "a glazed stoneware response to Donald Judd," even though, of course, Mason used neither glaze nor stoneware in his leg-

endary firebrick installations. Price is favorably compared to Frank
Stella. Arneson, Gilhooly and Shaw are the worst, saved for the last:
"Kitsch, low taste, visual gags, facetious narratives and a certain vein
of sophomoric humor, more or less akin to the Pop Art ethos of the
1960s, takes over with a vengeance." While conceding Arneson to be
the best technician in the group, Kramer still accuses him of "egre-
gious banality" and "moral smugness."[11]

Two important things happened as a result of Kramer's diatribe:
Arneson responded with his greatest self-portrait, *California Artist*, of
1982, and Perreault's hysterically funny riposte appeared in the *SoHo
News*, later amplified to "Fear of Clay" in the April, 1982 *Artforum*.
Perreault's initial response codified the source of Kramer's hatred:
"Pots! That's what it is. The prejudice against clay is the prejudice
against pots and—dreaded term—the crafts." He went on with a more
spirited attack on Kramer, adding ridicule to the notion of defining
or respecting any artwork solely because of what material it is made
of. He suggests that, after the 1970s, when even paint or bronze or
marble were rendered suspicious choices, now art could be made of
anything—even clay. He defends "Ceramic Sculpture: Six Artists" but
also points out its faults. Nagle and Stephen DeStaebler should have
been included. Why was it all men? Why was it limited to California?
Amusingly, Perreault gets down and dirty when he boldly proclaims
the real reason people hate clay: it's too much like excrement. He also
turns the art/craft conundrum on its head by saying the problem with
the show is that "it's really all about art," calling this its "superficial
message."

Perreault concludes with his own psycho-phobia lesson à la Kuspit:
fear of clay.

> Fear of clay is mainly the fear that the utilitarian and the aesthetic
> could be once again truly united. It is a fear of pots, a fear of objects
> that don't fit neatly into given categories, of objects that can be more
> than one thing at once. A pot can be utilitarian and esthetic; there is
> a long history of this that we are supposed to know but for the most
> part we remain ethnocentric, sexist, and full of class bias. A pot can
> be art and craft; sculpture and painting; masculine and feminine.[12]

If Perreault's analysis is the queer eye for the straight pot, could we
call Peter Schjeldahl's essay on Adrian Saxe, the straight eye for the
queer pot? Just one passage is worth savoring especially although the
whole essay, called "The Smart Pot," is a masterful interpretation of
why Saxe's pots are so amazing to look at:

> I don't imagine that many people in the ceramic world take Saxe's
> work in the heady way I do. Undertaking to write about it, I'm aware

of encroaching on a field where suspicious of intellect is a given, anti-intellectualism being the shadow of certain positive values embodied in most modern craft movements.[13]

There you have it in a nutshell, the whole reason that not even more art critics have written about clay: the not-so-subtle suspicion by ceramists of intellectuals in a field that is so earthy and physical. Schjeldahl is courageous for writing about Adrian Saxe at a time when "amateurs in the field," among whom this distinguished art critic for *The New Yorker* counted himself later in the essay, continued to be attacked by insiders.

Along with Janet Koplos on Rudolf Staffel, Carter Ratcliff on Michael Lucero, and Robert C. Hughes on Ken Price, there have been many other art critics who risked attack by the inbred clay establishment, the very field they were curious about. Schjeldahl has articulated with great modesty and humility a hidden gap between the professional ceramics field and curious art critics.

I conclude with a plea to *Ceramics Monthly* readers, and all teachers, students and artists. One day, some of you may be in a position to open the door to an art critic, as Patti Warashina did for me many years ago. Risk your own ego, give up control of the meaning of your work, and let them write about you without interference.

I beg of you, don't settle for writing about yourself or reviewing your best friend's or colleague's work in chummy publications. You are doing no one a favor. Please build on the substantial critical heritage I have introduced to you here, but don't do it by writing. Don't let the gap between clay artists and writers grow big again.

Finally, there is something even bigger at stake. The need for the American ceramics movement to attain the same intellectual maturity demanded by painters and sculptors. It will never be arrived at by artists writing about themselves and one another. It can only occur if you hold the door open and lend a hand—to us.

PART II

CERAMICS

Patti Warashina: *Ketchup Kiss*, c. 1969, earthenware and glazes, 36" h.
Photo: Courtesy of the artist

Beatrice Wood: *Goblet*, 1987, glazed earthenware with lusters, 13 ¼ x 6 ¼ x 5". Stephen and Pamela Hootkin Collection, New York. Photo: Noel Allum

TOWARD A BICAMERAL ESTHETIC OF CLAY

Criticism surrounding clay is in disarray. The gaping inadequacies of the few critical methodologies extant have forced the issue to be raised: Can a single encompassing critical approach to clay be formulated at all? Conversely, should a special case necessarily be made for clay, or should the character of such discourse be subsumed within a general aesthetic—say, one which we already work from, each of us in our own way, while inspecting and responding to any work of art?

These questions are not easily answered. To disregard the role of the medium—the clay itself—in shaping forms and in creating an appropriate criticism would unnecessarily diminish its historical achievements in applied-arts tradition. Yet a special class of clay criticism must be combined with current and evolving critical modes in order to better address the range of issues clay may now embrace: image, social placement, iconography, function, social criticism, and ideology.

Part of the reason a sufficiently compelling philosophy of clay—I mean a way of looking at it and even judging it—has not arisen rests in the different way clay has emerged as a thread of our cultural fabric. I need not reiterate here the long historical legacy of pottery or clay figurines or how all that has unalterably molded the nature of our own responses to comparable objects today. That academic, art-historical backfilling—very necessary, no doubt about it—has ironically dictated the form clay criticism has taken in recent years. That is, predominating clay commentary, analysis, or criticism have been shaped by a hyperconsciousness of one particular aspect of the medium, vesselmaking.

I care to argue here for a bicameral approach. The morass of language smothering clay must be channeled into at least two "rooms"—sculptural and vessel—and taken out of a single, stifling closet. Picture a cutaway view of a house with two rooms side-by-side, connected by a free-swinging door. In one room, purely functional objects are stored, some of which resemble functional things—jugs, pots, cups, archaeological and architectural relics, and all types of holders—but because of their size or exaggerated appurtenances are only superficially functional. The other room is full of sculptural objects made of clay: dolls, figurines, statuary, entire walls, and decorative tablets, as well as more archaeological treasures that serve no functional purpose to speak of. These odds and ends, however, by virtue of their sole decorative function, point toward meanings and interpretations usually only associated with paintings and sculptures of stone or metal. Together these rooms form the bicameral, that is, two-chambered, house of clay. This dual construction will consist of functional and nonfunctional considerations side by side, it will undertake to elucidate and evaluate vessel and non-vessel art made with clay, and it may conceivably elicit a more comprehensive revelation of the medium.

The waning primacy of vessel criticism is partly due to a rising awareness of the full plurality of the medium's history. The purely sculptural accomplishments in clay, for example, are every bit as towering throughout history as the achievements of functional forms. This broader picture of clay takes into consideration the role of vessels in a non-ritual, non-spiritual context, and seeks a rationale for the economic, social, and political dimensions of clay. The significance of Portuguese majolica nativities or Hispano-Moresque luster plates lies not only in the evolution of glazes—the teacup fancier's view—but in the role those objects played in their respective societies. It also lies in their meaning for us today. For clay has an inextricable relationship to political and social institutions, both past and present. It is a gripping, fascinating tale too important to leave to connoisseurs or anthropologists. It is a task that serious art criticism is only beginning to attack.

The sculptural, nonfunctional continuum, a parallel and equally surging stream in ceramics, must also be immersed in this new ideological context. The development of the formula for porcelain at Meissen is important only to the degree it reflects the level of German scientific and economic development in the early eighteenth century. The vast production of northern European tableware is meaningful to the extent that we can compose a picture of that society by creating an iconography of its tableware decoration. Likewise, the extraordinary production of German religious statuary not only displays a comparable assembly of fertile images to be interpreted, it represents the central place of ceramic art in European institutions of the period: economic, social, and religious.

All the same, the impossibility of accurately recreating the atmosphere of history's ritual vessels or porcelain Madonnas is one reason a bicameral aesthetic of clay must be given a try. The dual nature of such an approach could—like a cell dividing—lead to a newer, more comprehensive understanding of clay's presence in humanity's home. For instance, it might elaborate upon both functional and nonfunctional aspects of a particular object. A teacup's rim decoration and that particular meaning within the history of ornamental iconography are equally if not more important than the presence or absence of the teacup's handle. Similarly, the origins and meaning of pastoral or maritime scenes on a Genoese fish platter ought to be considered within an iconographic, excavative history of European art. The platter's curved or braided handles and the level of preindustrial technology they embody are another part of their total, bicameral meaning. So is their relation to the development of labor and management in Italian potteries of the period.

Unlike fire, its helpmate, clay has been ripped from its original, primordial context aeons ago. Its overriding meaning to us—as art, as icon, as demographic statistic, as mug—must begin with its complex social functions and relationships.

Given this, a bicameral aesthetic of clay does not toss out function. Function is the handmaiden of work. The narrowly focused lens of china connoisseurship has ended to neglect work's relation to clay and in pursuit of the objet d'art has overlooked clay's functional heritage. Given a new critical framework, restaurant cups are as important as raku teacups used in Zen ceremony. Given a new social unification, tile-maker and tile-setter are as important as the master crafts-maker worrying about tenure; the Gentleman Potter of eighteenth-century England is as important as the contemporary production-ware potter. "Work" is not a dirty word when it comes to clay; neither is "production"; neither is "function." By reincorporating these terms into a new aesthetic of clay, one can reinvigorate its criticism.

I cannot deny the seeming loggerheads to which a bicameral aesthetic of clay may lead. Some will insist clay be confined to a narrow history, that the Flame of the Vessel must be held forever aloft and protected as fiercely as the Greeks guarded the Fire at Olympia. Metaphysically oriented criticisms of art have always placed metaphorical conceptions high above the objects themselves. In the long run, they diminish clay's significance as art by whittling down the object's importance in favor of Spirit, Soul, or some other abstract virtue or moral imperative.

The delicately important thing to admit is the likelihood that critical judgments against the accomplishments of contemporary clay artists will get worse—even harsher—before they get better. This has nothing to do with clay's having been treated like the forgotten stepsister to Cor-Ten steel or anything like that. As with photography, the real reason probably has more to do with the great numbers of people doing things with it at this time. Achievement may indeed be the most important thing to bear in mind, as critic Clement Greenberg pointed out in an address at Syracuse University.[1] Nevertheless, clay's achievements can never be understood in quite the same way

Greenberg understands the paintings of Kenneth Noland or Helen Frankenthaler. That is to say, Greenberg's praise of "achievement" vaguely sidesteps clay's many manifestations beyond the purely medium-related aesthetic that is at the base of Greenberg's view of modern art. His championing of the Abstract Expressionists and the Post-Painterly Abstractionists revolved around their emphasis on the nature and presence of paint itself, referring to what paint can physically do to a flat canvas, not on what the paint was used to depict or transmit. His elevation of such questionable masters as Noland and Jules Olitski was connected to a conviction that their triumphant concentration on the flat, inviolable nature of the canvas was part of what comprised their significance as artists. Thus, despite the flattery of having so distinguished (and controversial) an art-world figure give his belated imprimatur to clay, the validity of that compliment must be seen in the light of Greenberg's overall writings. Such an examination can only lead to the conclusion that it was an implicit endorsement of an art that sticks to medium-based, clay-for-clay's-sake traditions, rather than one that seeks to break away from or expand the medium's boundaries. Today's art critics, who cast a wider net, seek to encompass contexts beyond Greenberg's "truth to medium" and aim to grapple with issues broader than formalism or materialism.

Clay's importance in this cultural drama must be wrenched from false hierarchies of medium or material, even if this may at first seem to lessen clay's significance rather than enhance it. Uncle Tom-style integration or safe assimilation into the art world are not desiderata. An independent, parallel availability for viewers, makers, critics, and users is one ideal. What seems sure is not that clay is on the verge of some great new era, but that criticism (the *New York Times* notwithstanding[2]) finally appears to be catching up with clay.

Metaphor, a much-touted critical tool, ostensibly lends literary connotations to art, thereby giving it the quick illusion of deep meaning. Profoundly understood, metaphor is a time bomb waiting to explode: it can go off in any direction. Improperly understood, it places meaning where none exists.

Taken to one geophysical extreme, Mount St. Helens's crater now best demonstrates the Vessel's ultimate possibility as a container of space. Beside such an overwhelming example of majesty and mud, contemporary clay vessels' metaphorical level shrivels to souvenir status. Anything, in short, can carry a metaphor. The comical implications in the "vessel as metaphor" slogan have crept directly out of its insufficiently encompassing matrix for discussing the entire range of contemporary clay. The proposals made here seek to circumvent its weaknesses and, if such a thing is possible, amplify its strengths.

The ideology of a medium is the ideology of its maker; clay's future, finally, lies in the hands of the artist. Clay can, however, also express the ideology of the viewer, the user, and the critic. Here there need be no pat equivalencies such as "vessel as metaphor" or "medium equals meaning." Only by admitting the bicamerality of the medium—and then getting on with the business of interpreting and appreciating— can an illuminating aesthetic of this or any other function-based art be achieved. Let that process of introspection and subsequent action truly begin.

Robert Sperry: *Untitled*, 1981, clay slip on stoneware, 16 x 16 x 2". Courtesy of the
Estate of Robert Sperry. Photo: Ed Marquand

ROBERT SPERRY: PLANETARY CLAY

Sperry: I always said I should have just become a 2-D artist and
forget this other stuff.
Kangas: You have, Bob, you have.

—From a conversation in Seattle, September 22, 1981

Let me begin by dispensing with any discussion of form or function in
the art of Robert Sperry (1927–1998). What I offer is a radical reap-
praisal of an American artist's work; it flies in the face of previous
views categorizing him as production potter, vesselmaker and sculptor. Sperry is, in fact, a painter in clay.

It was LaMar Harrington, author of *Ceramics in the Pacific Northwest* (University of Washington Press, Seattle, 1979), who rightly
pointed out in her analysis of Sperry's carved sculptures of 1959–62
that he was "not as involved in destroying past references to function-
alism as were (Peter) Voulkos and his colleagues." During the ensuing
20 years, however, the chief stylistic development of Sperry's mature
period has been an undermining of the vessel, which had preoccupied
him for a decade, and a replacement of those concerns with a decorated flat surface attaining to complex levels of meaning.

Sperry's "arena" for this activity, to borrow the art critic Harold
Rosenberg's term, has been the floor and table of his studio in the
Montlake area of Seattle, Washington. The perfection of a spontaneous touch and drag of liquid slip over a glazed surface has been the
recent technical problem which the Canadian-reared artist set for
himself. In order to achieve this pictorial goal, he separated himself
from most mainstream American clay activity (e.g., William Daley,
Wayne Higby) as well as from what became the mainstream West
Coast Surrealistillustrational style (e.g., Patti Warashina, Richard
Shaw), and subsequently concocted a chain of images which operates
on may levels: personal, abstract, materialist, natural.

Like Franz Kline and Jackson Pollock, the Abstract Expressionists whose work his most resembles (and whom he most admires),
Sperry, a professor of art at the University of Washington, turned to
his chosen medium as a vehicle for direct but private expression, and
for a dialogue with an essential aspect of that medium—firing. It is a
focus for creating his own worldview, which is rooted in the depiction
of the earth's crust as an "all-over" surface. It does not rest on historical or primordial associations of the vessel form. Rather, it glances
downward and upward simultaneously: to the muddy earth which is

subject to the kiln's fury; to the stars and planets which have surfaces of their own akin to earth's in a literally infinite variety.

This resemblance is the key theme in Sperry's newest art. It is a subject I call planetary clay.

Harrington also pointed out how Sperry's work of the early 1960's contained two seemingly contradictory streams, one a spontaneous, sparing application of glaze, and the other, "drawing designs on every conceivable inch of space in the manner of the horror vacui of Barbarian or Islamic art." Ultimately, these opposing strains were fused into one style as Sperry achieved a surer control over surface decoration.

This balancing of a restrained freedom and an obsessive decorative impulse has as much to do with Sperry's ceaseless experimentation upon a flat surface as with any devotion to some ideal of appropriate form such as the vessel. The results of those investigations into a personal symbology may be seen on the hundreds of plates, platters, slabs and bowls which he has made during the past decade.

They involve, more specifically, another twin stream of decorative devices—black and white, dark and light in the form of dark glazes and creamy liquid slip—which Sperry has alternately worked at throughout his prolific production periods. This development has its historical roots in the Abstract Expressionists, too. From de Kooning and Pollock to Kline and Robert Motherwell, the use of black and white took on an especially American and urban urgency.

The attempt here to create an iconography based on the decoration of tableware and clay slabs may seem odd to some, but to do less would be to miss the crux of Sperry's art. All of his images—the x-marks, crosses, circles, infinity symbols, spatters—have been tied up with the appearance of clay itself as a tabula rasa for personal expression. That the creation of such images is slowly becoming an indelible chapter within American art is due partly to his adaptation of Abstract Expressionist painting methods to clay. It also has much to do with Japanese ceramics, but that influence is another subject entirely.

Sperry left sculpture behind long ago and determined, for better or worse, to let liquid clay dictate the manner of surface decoration. This medium-based link—between clay and the images it creates—is the essence of his modernism. Even while tracing the origins of spontaneity in Sperry's marks back to New York School paintings of the 1950's, it is important to note that his search for "universal symbols' corresponds to Mark Rothko's and Barnett Newman's own interests at the time. Pacific Northwest artists of that era besides Sperry (e.g., Mark Tobey, Kenneth Callahan) also were seeking global pictorial images, and Sperry's work might be seen as an intermediary spin-off or manifestation of those shared East and West Coast art-historical preoccupations. The reason Sperry's linear shapes look somewhat different is that he was not painting on canvas. He was applying slip over glaze, two elements which become successively transformed during the firing process.

Before his abandonment of the slip decoration to the explosive vagaries of the kiln, Sperry's luster-decorated plates of the 1970's grew out of a completely opposite approach, one that he calls a "creative control over disorder." It involved the piling on of glazed blister-dots and the meticulous application of gold and silver luster lines. Some of these pieces were even modified container forms. Beginning with his use of lusters in 1965, Sperry went against "tasteful" clay traditions of the time and turned them to his own ends. The results were a satiated metallic decoration with green, red, brown, gray and blue accents. Together, the colors and lusters created a sense of ecstatic flux and anticipated by several years the use of gold as a personal emblem by other artists (e.g., Lynda Benglis).

What art critic Donald Kuspit described as "cosmetic transcendentalism" in Benglis's gilt papier-mâché pieces was already a highly developed and compressed convention in Sperry's work of the early 1970's. It afforded this impulsive intellectual a measure of control over imagery which at the time was tending more and more toward circular forms and cancellation signs. As Sperry put it, the application of lusters was a "totally rational act" as opposed to the unpredictable "dynamism of glaze and the 'unknown' of the fire."

Though the luster and color glazed plates rank among Sperry's finest works, they led eventually to a diminution and temporary suspension of color. *Untitled* (1980) subordinates a rose "underpainting" to a roughly cracked surface.

When Sperry's "cosmetic transcendentalism" extinguished itself in the kiln, it became cosmic instead. That is to say, the current black-and-white period, as evinced in the series of wall tiles of almost unprecedented size for Sperry, takes as its unifying image a portrait of the cosmos. The literal pocking, pitting and blistering away of clay on the new pieces summon up moments of fiery planetary birth. Whether one sees individual tile as images of planetary covering or as horizon-sky cross sections, the suggestions of volcanic and geological activity of some sort are inescapable.

A subliminal theme of Sperry's newer work was foreshadowed in his 1966 award-winning film, *Village Potters of Onda*. This deeply humane document contains the threads of the current work: a return to the humble origins of clay and an insistence upon black and white as the only color scheme capable of carrying symbolic meanings. To understand Sperry's achievement as the director, cinematographer and narrator of *Village Potters of Onda* is to perceive the delayed but determined effect of that film on Sperry the artist. The blunt presentation of the townspeople and Sperry's monotonous halting delivery of Edythe Sperry's poetic script austerely document the place of man in a changing technological society.

In addition to borrowing glazes or forms from the Japanese antecedents he admires, such as Bizen or Shino ware, Sperry took from the year-long stay in Onda techniques which would emerge in his art 20 years later: liquid slip "painting," the use of casually applied decoration and an abstract imagery rooted in natural phenomena. In the film, Sperry speaks of the villagers' finding a "form of serenity that stems from a way of life that is productive and satisfying." This might well serve as Sperry's credo since he has always described himself simply as a potter.

Around the hardworking men and women of Onda, Sperry placed images of flowing water, forests, rocks and rows and rows of production ware. The 25-minute film's interplay of natural abstracted forms sets up a theme which would propel Sperry's art for years to come.

The culmination of the Japanese experience was a later body of work which affirms both the strength of the modernist aesthetic and its relationship to Asian art in an unexpected way. Sperry's gestural calligraphy bears comparison to that of Tobey, who worked in tempera and sumi. Sperry has adapted the calligraphic stroke to the clay surface. Whereas Tobey's "white writing" became transparent, ethereal and "mystical," Sperry's own "white writing" has been fired and cracked, accentuating its own materiality and binding it eternally to the "objectness" of the clay slab. Thus two artists, both responding to Asian brushwork, arrive at completely contrary ends.

Unlike Tobey, the only thing remotely "mystical" about Sperry has been his Zen-like belief that creativity can only be a casual byproduct of the day-in, day-out monotony of the potter's life. And yet, this has in no way prevented him from creating an art which submits to varied critical interpretations and retains aesthetic autonomy.

The durability of clay—one thinks of all the archaeological pottery shards ever discovered—may one day be seen as the ultimate meaning for this 30-year collection of plates, bowls, bottles, paintings, drawings, slabs and films. The Seattle artist's quiet evolution from painter to pot-thrower and back again symbolizes how certain American artists were caught mid-century between paint and clay. Robert Sperry's decision to combine both, so to speak, was an historic compromise for American ceramics. It was a compromise from which has stemmed an art of timeless signs and energy.

Robert Arneson: *A Hollow Jesture*, 1971, fired ceramic clay and glazes, 20 1/4" h. Collection of Drs. R. Joseph and Elaine Monsen, Seattle. Photo: Dudley, Hardin and Yang

Jack Earl: *Grandmother*, 1987. Painted earthenware, 27 x 8 ½ x 10 ½". Stephen and Pamela Hootkin Collection, New York. Photo: Noel Allum

AMERICAN FIGURATIVE CERAMICS
In Memoriam Howard Kottler 1930–1989

INTRODUCTION

> What is man but a mass of thawing clay? The ball of the human
> finger is but a drop congealed. The fingers and toes flow to their
> extent from the thawing mass of the body. Who knows what the
> human body would expand and flow out to under a more genial
> heaven?

—Henry David Thoreau

American ceramics may be seen as developing in three essential categories: functional ware, art pottery, and figurative sculpture. At the
current moment, slouching toward the end of our century, figurative
ceramic sculpture seems to be the area of the highest achievement.
This is not to deny the strengths of fine handmade dinnerware or the
beauties of the revived "vessel" or art pottery movement-that curious
hybrid between vases and abstract sculpture—but only to point out
that critical consensus seems to have favored the accomplishments of
those artists whose use of the figure has contributed to the broader
category of commentary on the human condition in contemporary art
if the 1980s were a period, in general, of expressionistic figurative
art, then this branch of the ceramics field may be said to have had the
most impact and attracted the most attention.

Unusually, it has begun and flourished almost completely outside of
New York City, America's conceded art center. And that may have
been as it should be, for the market pressures of New York rarely allow artists to continuously pursue individual visions over long periods
of time without interference from the swiftly changing trends. American figurative ceramics, then, are also a triumph of de-centralization
or the new regionalism in American art. Though many of the artists
in this exhibition are seen regularly in New York shows, they choose
to live elsewhere, often in geographically remote areas. In an age of
rapid air travel and increased telecommunications, they are also free
to pick and choose their influences free of economic and peer pressures, as well as critical scrutiny.

Seen as a series of separately evolving artists, they have formed no
school but, rather, drawn upon ceramic sculpture's long heritage
in Europe, Asia, and Africa, in order to add to that collective world
heritage the force of their own individual and often private visions.
Nevertheless, it is possible to draw certain conclusions: American

ceramic sculpture has developed in tandem with other contemporary art movements, not behind them, and it is possible to trace certain affinities among the artists of this exhibition so that the rich diversity of styles may also be seen as various clusters which relate to styles also prevalent in painting and non-ceramic sculpture over the past twenty-five years. For American figurative ceramics have become the single most important and successful "cross-over" medium for the entire American craft movement. Taking their rightful place in art galleries beside painters or bronze sculptors, for example, they have benefited from the eventual breakdown of prejudices associated with the hierarchy of art materials. It has been the content and execution of their art that has mattered, not the dominant culture's approval or disapproval of the given medium, clay. No matter what context they have exhibited their work in, they have been the joint beneficiaries of a twin heritage: crafts and fine arts.

Developing as they have since the end of World War II, most have been associated with one or more university-based settings. Without going into great detail about the sociology of American higher education, it is worth noting that the exhibition spans two or possibly three generations of students, some of whom also became teachers. It has been the sanctuary and economic security of the ivory tower that has allowed many of these artists to forge ahead regardless of early market neglect, and allowed them to come into contact with one another's ideas for transforming the medium into the strong forum for expression it is today.

Briefly, the University of Montana (Missoula), the University of Washington (Seattle), and the University of California (Davis) were the chief training centers.

For Rudy Autio at Missoula, after the formative experiences with Bernard Leach and Shoji Hamada at the Archie Bray Foundation in Helena, university teaching freed him to concentrate on creating his long succession of slab-built cylindrical forms covered with men, women, and animals. He became Professor Emeritus in 1984.

Farther to the west, after having met Peter Voulkos and Autio in Helena in the summer of 1954, Robert Sperry took over the reins of the University of Washington's nascent ceramics department from Swiss potter Paul Bonifas, original secretary to Le Corbusier and the Purist movement in France. By 1982, Sperry handed things over to his wife and former student, Patti Warashina, who had joined the department in 1968.

To the south, Robert Arneson's presence in Davis, California, attracted students from all over the country, including Montana and Washington State. The result of all these activities, the fertile cross-continent exchange, and the popular custom of visiting artists giving demonstration workshops, all contributed to a support network unusual among American artists in any medium. The atmosphere of healthy competition among teachers, and then between teachers and students, only fueled their efforts to excel and break new ground.

Just as Chicago painters like Leon Golub and San Francisco painters like David Park were keeping the figure alive during the 1950s heyday of Abstract Expressionism, so these ceramic sculptors committed to figurative content in the ensuing decades, regardless of the more and more reductive elements of abstraction dominating the rest of the art world. In retrospect, they all may be viewed as upholders of liberal humanist content in art using the figure as heroic emblem in the bewildering climate of minimal and post-painterly abstraction.

By the 1970s, several of the artists, Arneson, Frey, Autio, and Warashina, for example, were beginning to produce some of their best work and, again, it is a tribute to a peculiarly American—and Australian—quality, rugged individualism, that they avoided resembling one another or forming a common school. In each case, scale, technique, and particular medium (stoneware, porcelain, etc.), they found their own path to a personal expression.

The rest of the art world, i.e., New York City, was beginning to pay more attention, too, but it was always at one remove. The issue of regionalism always matters more for those in the "capital" than for the artists hard at work in distant places. It is a false power issue employed to reassure those in the center of their power. Nevertheless, media attention grew through the art magazines centered in New York, and percipient museum curators and dealers began to pay attention to all of these artists.

The achievement of their former students also became hard to ignore. Sometimes building on their teacher's lessons, sometimes vigorously opposing them by example, younger artists like Nancy Carman, Mark Burns, and Anne Perrigo pursued wildly diverse routes employing, respectively, Surrealism, kitsch, and French academic sculpture as inspirations and newly invented taproots.

Looking back before we look ahead to the present and future, one cannot argue strongly enough for the Janus-like character of these artists' efforts. On the one hand, they drew from the entire history and pre-history of the clay figure, equally as old if not older than the tradition of the pot or vessel. Figurative ceramics must be seen as a simultaneous development within art history, hence the frequent references to archaic or pre-historic forms. Conversely, there was a pulling away or quasi-disassociation from decorative arts or crafts traditions in order to respond afresh to the contemporary world's cry of "Make it new!" in Ezra Pound's memorable words. Though a will to the avant-garde and attempts at originality have been reduced in the U.S. to cheap marketing devices at this late point in the twentieth century, it is crucial to recall the sparkling atmosphere affecting all artists and inspiring them to outdo one another. Breakthroughs in subject matter, the violation of taboos, and the use of extravagant or unexpected materials unite American figurative ceramics with the modern movement of the twentieth century. The abstraction, reduction, or distortion of the human figure has strong precedents in such unquestionably modern artists as Amedeo Modigliani, Alberto Giacometti, and Pablo Picasso. In fact, American figurative ceramics could be seen as part of an historical mopping-up operation, building on the breakthroughs of the early Moderns, and contributing revisions, refinements, and summations of their own. Just as Giacometti's plasters got smaller and smaller, reflecting an existential malaise toward the fate of France after World War II, so Viola Frey's tall, looming figures are an oblique commentary on exaggerated American power in the world thirty years later. The man in the blue business suit can seem every bit as evocative of our period as Giacometti's shrinking men do of theirs.

THE RIVER AND ITS TRIBUTARIES

Realism, Surrealism, and Expressionism are the three main strains or "tributaries" of American figurative ceramics. Together, they comprise the "river" of American clay sculpture, waywardly flowing beside and occasionally touching the rest of contemporary American art. However much craft-based artists may yearn for acceptance by the dominant artistic culture, it is important that they keep track of the sources and origins in the ancient mud-bed where clay was first found. Mainstream endorsement is fickle at best, often driven by wildly fluctuating economic factors rather than cautious, assured assimilation. In time, in exhibitions such as "American Figurative Ceramics," validation will come from outside or abroad, or from the occasional curator who treats groups of artists according to shared ideas or concepts rather than simply a shared medium. The artists themselves are ambivalent about these issues, making it impossible to generalize about any collective attitude they may have about their status.

As Clement Greenberg once told a gathering of clay artists in Syracuse, New York, "opinion changes, achievement stays. . . results. . . are all that count when it comes to art as art."

REALISM

Jack Earl is in a class by himself. The leading Realist or strictly representational clay artist in the U.S. today, he blurs the distinctions between reality and memory, blending them together in pictorial vignettes on his double-sided tableaux of white, mid-western Americans. Whether religion, family, or childhood is invoked, the viewer marvels at the intricate small world Earl has created. The detail of workmanship is admirable and allows us to enter visually into the small world on view. The similarity to photography, family snapshots, keeps us at a certain distance at the same time. If there is a weak link in Earl's chain of memory, it is the elaborate text-titles accompanying each piece. Superfluous appendages, they are not really necessary for appreciation and act like a literary ornament, as in the British painter Turner's poems accompanying each painting. Earl's images are strong enough without their anecdotal reminiscences. Seen on their own, as in "On the Path", they both evoke the American scene and stimulate the viewer's own memories about shared and private moments.

SURREALISM

The eye exists in its primitive state. The marvels of the earth a hundred feet high, the marvels of the sea a hundred feet deep, have for their witness only the wild eye that when in need of colors refers simply to the rainbow.

—André Breton, 1928

Closely tied to Realism in its sources, American ceramic Surrealism is also aligned with the original French development which sought a reality based in escape into the "marvelous." As it moved from conventional representation to an arbitrary juxtaposition of disassociated elements, Surrealism shocked the viewer into accepting an altogether different, if not higher, plane of reality. This has taken many forms for the American clay Surrealists. For example, for the senior generation, Richard Shaw and Patti Warashina have taken two distinct journeys down the river of American figurative ceramics.

For Shaw (*Singing in the Bathtub*, 1986), figures constructed out of everyday objects, made of cast molds, make no pretence at conventional representation but, rather, propose a metaphor for the individual constructed of personal belongings and consumer objects. We are what we own or buy. He harks back to the Italian painter at the court of Rudolf II in Prague, Giuseppe Arcimboldo, who painted faces made of fruits and vegetables. Also, closer to home, Shaw recalls the nineteenth century American trompe l'oeil still life painter William Harnett who reveled in tickling the senses and literally fooling the eye. Curiously, there is a vital quality to Shaw's assemblages that defies the viewer's knowledge of their artificiality.

Patti Warashina, by contrast, constructs completely enclosed worlds comparable to dream states that depend upon the viewer's willingness to trigger unconscious associations between her multiple figures. As in classic Surrealism such as Salvador Dalí's, we are forced to piece together a narrative from the elements the artist provides. The small scale of the figure (doll-size), the surprising and unusual settings they find themselves in, and the sparing use of color, all conspire to remind us that, however, we release our imagination into full play, we are still inspecting an artwork, an imaginatively built object. *Kiss Off* (1989) recalls an earlier work, *Carrier* (1986), by another artist in the exhibition, Arthur González.

González's work is a fascinating foretelling of Warashina's. She has expanded and multiplied his lonely figures into a drama of elaborate action and symbolic implication.

Borrowing from Richard Shaw, Tom Rippon fashions his own version of the human figure made of separate objects (*Oskar's Gift*, 1989) but shies away from Shaw's dependence on recognizable things; instead, Rippon accentuates his quality of a private world by incorporating a composition of shifting imbalance. Vases teeter on tiny pedestals. Tables seem to verge on collapse, and the figure nearly residual, operates as an effigy or stand-in for humanity. The fantasy world common to much Chicago art is fully expressed in Rippon's work and offers a unique logic of its own. Surrealism challenges our preconceptions of anatomy, gravity, and balance. Rippon emphasizes Surrealism's dislocating aesthetic.

Unlike their teacher at the University of Washington, Patti Warashina, Mark Burns and Nancy Carman have concentrated on individual figures. They join Yoshio Taylor within the Surrealist wing of American figurative ceramics as artists who present the figure in situations of fear, revelation, and a state of evolution or becoming.

Carman and Taylor often use the female figure but present differing views of the individual's relation to the larger world. For example, Carman's *Grounding* (1989) places the figure at the top of the sculptural form, seated "on top of the world", if you will. Conversely, Yoshio Taylor's *Kitakaze* (1988) emerges from the sphere or ball of clay at her feet. These artists present contrasting images of power and also comment obliquely on the supporting base as a metaphor for ceramics itself, carved and refined in Carman's instance, irregular and malleable in Taylor's case.

Mark Burns's work has long embraced the vulgarity of kitsch figurines, as did his teacher in Seattle, the late Howard Kottler. Burns has gone beyond found objects or a thrift-store aesthetic in favor of combining fabricated elements together in tableaux of horror, humor, and questionable taste. Like Kottler, he reminds us of ceramic sculpture's darker heritage, the cast-mould, cheap, garbagey knickknacks arising out of the late nineteenth century and reaching an apotheosis in mid-twentieth century souvenir America. Not content to rest on that level, however, Burns has shifted toward stylized figures caught in frightening and emotional moments (*Despair*, 1989). He has built on Kottler's legacy of appreciation for the lower forms of American ceramic history, restaurant china, tourist clutter, commemorative liquor decanters, yet steered toward a more expressive, less Surrealistic content.

EXPRESSIONISM

The state of awareness of visions is not one in which we are either remembering or perceiving. It is rather a level of consciousness at which we experience visions within ourselves.

—Oskar Kokoschka, 1912

If Burns is the transitional artist between Surrealism and Expressionism, then other young artists like Robert Brady, Arthur González and Peter VandenBerge appear to have side-stepped Surrealism completely, landing four-square in the land of ragged and grotesque, neo-expressionist ceramics. Whether incubus, demon or monster, their sculptures opt for the darker, mythic dimension of life, pushing us toward recognition of subconscious drives which we prefer to ignore or repress. A welcome sense of discomfort emerges from their work, questioning the status quo and the everyday complacencies of American life.

Robert Brady, Christine Federighi and Peter VandenBerge posit the human figure as a static monolith, a cultural artifact dredged up from the present. Arthur González, Judy Moonelis, and Anne Perrigo present the figure in an emotionally and physically dynamic condition. Both approaches elicit a strong expressionistic undercurrent.

Brady's *Virtu* (1987) and Federighi's *Two Rivers* (1989) are a fascinating pair of statues commenting on humanity's relationship to
nature. For Brady, the full-length figure spouts sphere-like organic
forms where the head would be, as if the figure were a genetic mishap
due to our poisoning the environment. In Federighi's case, the head
is present but appears to be literally the "headwaters" for two flowing
rivers down each side of the body. Grooved into the clay, the illusion
of water ends at the base where the figure's feet would be.

In an extension of the human/nature juxtaposition, Dutch-born Peter
VandenBerge places a cow atop the hat of a solemn-faced boy. *Animalman* (1989) may be a commentary on the memory of nature or,
more appropriately perhaps, a symbolic reference to the minute importance we Americans have given to nature at a time when impending ecological disaster is a very real concern for our society. With his
pockmarked features and squinty eyes, *Animalman* appears to have
undergone some sort of vitamin deficiency at the very least.

Both Anne Perrigo and Arthur González attended the University of
California-Davis yet both have strikingly different approaches to the
figure. González revels in the dry, dusty look of clay with sparingly
applied glaze that operates as make-up on his female figures. They
are caught mid-pose, turning, nodding, scowling, or just mugging for
the camera. Affixed to the wall, they appear to come toward the viewer aggressively and often melodramatically. With ludicrous haircuts
and truncated torsos, they seem survivors of some odd sub-culture.

Perrigo pushes the references to popular culture such as old mov-
ies even further. Piling on found objects, as in *Magnetic Attraction*
(1985), she links the tacky objects to the figures like emblems or
badges associated with their "roles". While González indulges in
melodrama or the campy pose, Perrigo's work seems closer to pulp
magazines or even opera in those worlds, emotions run at high pitch
and a slap is just as close, and likely, as a kiss. Perrigo's recent work
explores the evocative gestures more closely and she pays strong allegiance to the French sculptor Jean-Baptiste Carpeaux who worked
in terracotta, plaster and stone.

Judy Moonelis's *Refuge* (1989) does not deal with nature or popular
culture but with the plight of the homeless. Like González, she lives
in New York and, whereas many of the other artists seem to be dealing with ecology or psychology, Moonelis addresses directly the effects
of a gigantic urban culture on the unfortunate and the dispossessed.
Never resorting to headlines, she manages to render the topical into
the timeless, something very few socially conscious artists are able

to do today. Huddling on a pile of rags beside two crumbling tenements, her figure simply and bluntly states a human dilemma all too
common in advanced western societies: those who have nothing in a
culture of abundance.

FOUR AMERICAN MASTERS

Rudy Autio, Robert Arneson, Stephen de Staebler, and Viola Frey are
the leading figurative ceramic sculptors in the U.S. Over a long period
of time, each has attained not only a degree of recognition outside the
craft field but, far more importantly, created art of incomparable and
haunting beauty, urgency, and skill.

De Staebler is the only artist of the four whose art does not comment
on American history or culture. Part of a growing trend in contemporary art, the neo-antique or neo-archaic, his slab-built ruins of figures
evoke ancient Egyptian art. His decapitated figures arise from the
past as ruins silently accusing the present. They are reminders that
the profligacy and waste of American society could easily become a
comparable wreck or salvaged series of artifacts.

Considering, then, that De Staebler's figures make no pretence about
reflecting the present condition in the world, it is still worth examining briefly two aspects of their appearance: their lack of individual
features and their absence of distinguishing gender. Although each
"stele" is carefully fashioned and differs from the rest in size, color, or
scale, there is a potential danger that, in the absence of distinguishing features or gender, they run the risk of becoming repetitive and
generic.

Remarkably, De Staebler defended this gender-neutrality in an interview with critic Donald Kuspit by claiming that "for years", he has
been involved with the "male-female polarity. . . . All of my figures
are either androgynous or nonsexual." Switching to the offensive, he
added that "people who are insecure about their own sexual orienta-
tion, or who like things clear-cut, do not like this kind of ambiguity." This is a regrettable and inaccurate conclusion. Whatever De
Staebler's reasons might be for fence-sitting on the gender question,
it is not at all the case that criticizing his indecisiveness on one of the
most important social issues of the day, "male-female polarity," is the
result of the viewer or critic's "insecurity".

Nevertheless, the statues in their condition as damaged goods, crumbling and appearing to rot, operate on a metaphorical level as representatives of twentieth century humanity in that most violent of all
centuries. Such an impact would be increased, not lessened, were they

to have clearer features. As they sit, they seem more interchangeable ciphers than resolute stand-ins for the people they memorialize.

Rudy Autio's art deals with history, too, the rough-and-tumble American West. Ponies, livestock, wolves, and nude male and female figures cavort together on exuberantly slab-built constructions hailed in Finland and Japan as well as in the U.S. and Australia. Most European of the Americans included, his art may grow out of his early friendship with Peter Voulkos but it has an aesthetic and vision all its own. With the forms a fusion of painting and sculpture, the drawing alludes to Matisse and the figures covering the forms date back to Picasso's ceramics at Vallauris, France.

Robust and vigorous, there is nonetheless a tenderness in Autio's sculptures, too, which extends to animals. Caught in an ecological paradise, the Old West, his cowboy and cowgirl, cattle and coyote, horse and rider, should find a ready audience in Australia with its own heritage of ranching and mining, just like Autio's home state of Montana.

Robert Arneson and Viola Frey have become the social consciences of American ceramic sculpture. With the former explicitly criticizing the military establishment and the latter indirectly commenting on the ghouls of American business, both artists have shifted away in recent years from the obsessions with self, memory, and the childhood and toward a more open critique of America.

Humor also plays a less important role than before. The California clay artists like Arneson, Frey, and Shaw have used wit as an integral component of their work but, with the advent of Arneson's recent sculptures, wit has turned into angry satire.

Sarcophagus (1985) draws from an earlier painting on paper, *Joint* (1984), which refers to the Joint Chiefs of Staff, the heads of the American military forces. As Neal Benezra observed, "Based on a news magazine photograph of three smiling generals seated at a press briefing, Arneson's image transforms the faces into mask-like caricatures, the medals on their chests drip blood, and before them is a sarcophagus occupied by a prone corpse."

The art of Viola Frey may be based in a reverie of childhood but it is very adult in its confrontational character. By making the figures over-size, the artist creates a scale relationship in which the viewer and artist appear like children beside the tall authority figures. *Leaning Man II* (1985) seems like Boris Karloff on Wall Street. Frey reminds us that the white male is still the dominant power figure in American life yet, by daubing him all over with bright blue and orange glaze, she exerts the artist's control over even the most intimidating of stereotypes. Like the other artists in the exhibition, she has used her towering powers as a craftsman to create her own population of individuals.

Collectively, these artists shove all combined private, social, political and psychological concerns into sculptures which simultaneously perform on subjective and objective levels. It is the coincidence of idea and craft that has given their work its highest artistic attributes and ferried them along the river of American ceramic sculpture to the headwaters of art.

SHATTERED SELF:
NORTHWEST FIGURATIVE CERAMICS

> I think I am going up,
> I think I may rise—
> The beads of hot metal fly, and I,
> > love, I
> Am a pure acetylene Virgin
> Attended by roses,
> By kisses, by cherubim,
> By whatever these pink things mean.
> . . . .
> (My selves dissolving,
> > old whore petticoats)—
> To Paradise.

> —Sylvia Plath, from "Fever 103°"

Just as Sylvia Plath's persona or heroine witnesses her disintegration under psychic duress, so Seattle ceramic sculptors of the past decade have taken as their subject matter their own dissolving selves. Instead of the poet's "kisses . . . cherubim . . . and pink things," they have surrounded their figures—often self-portraits—with fragments of anatomy or ceramic shards, shattered hobby-shop knickknacks. These elements make up a body of work that has shifted away distinctly from the influential wit and humor of Bay Area clay toward what might be called the fragmented or shattered self of the evolving Seattle sensibility. Where once artists used puns, they now use double images; where once the one-liner was king (or queen), they now probe into the dangerous territory of the unconscious mind. Indeed, the transformation of formerly suppressed personal quirks or vagaries into art has become the content of the work of Ann Gardner, Howard Kottler, Anne Perrigo, Debra Sherwood and Patti Warashina.

Shattered self. The term may be divided into two parts: the shard and the self-portrait, or autobiographical persona. The artmaking process for these ceramic artists is one of continual deconstruction and restoration, both literally and figuratively. As the self is repaired and reconstituted by piling shard upon shard, or face next to face, so the violent expressionistic process of breaking clay is mitigated by the healing, holistic act of putting an artwork—and perhaps a life—back together again.

Viewed another way, the fragmented anatomy of their sculptures is a metaphor for both the "un-whole" state of Becoming and the "whole" of the completed artistic act. In fact, much of this art is about re-integrating the self into a psychic and an artistic totality. It is this somewhat hidden agenda—individually arrived at in each case—that unites much of Seattle ceramic sculpture today and distinguishes it from other American clay dealing with the figure or the shard. Auto-biography is the key to understanding some of this work on one level, yet the residue of anger, range and self-obsession is ameliorated and made universal by the beauty of the objects themselves.

As Patti Warashina put it, "representational imagery and beautiful surfaces" are in a dialectical relationship to the "anger underneath." Though Warashina executed a two- to three-year commission for the Seattle Opera House, an installation using myriad small porcelain figures *("A" Procession)*, the bulk of her work since 1980 has dealt with specifically autobiographical issues transformed into generalized feminist tableaux. Though her altars and triangular shrines are well known—*Wash and Wear, Happy Anniversary*, etc.—it is important to note that she was the first of these artists to deconstruct the figure.

Untitled, 1972, in which a woman is depicted as a helpless prisoner of ritual hospitality, set the stage for much of Warashina's later work. The debased suppliant gestures of the upturned palms, the severed head encased in a breast-like form, and the "golden egg" at the center are succinct symbols of a woman's traditional confining roles: sub-servience, entertaining and childbearing. By the mid-70s, the paisley patterns and bishop's-crook imagery of her early works had given way to outrageous domination fantasies scarcely concealed by "beautiful surfaces."

As Warashina recalled, "I didn't realize the hostility in those pieces, but I've always loved attractive surfaces covering up unsettling de-tails—like those crowns of thorns going into that beautiful pink flesh in Northern Renaissance paintings."

Barking Up the Wrong Tree, 1977, turns the tables on the disembodied submissive qualities of *Untitled,* 1972. The low-relief (and low-life?) "nudie-cutie" alter ego emerges from the "altar" back wearing claw-like gloves and petting a bulldog's snarling head replete with studded collar. Salomé and the head of John the Baptist may be one icono-graphical precedent, but the artist's appropriation of pop culture and sadomasochistic imagery is another sign of her hidden agenda. Seen in a feminist context, the bulldog's head is maledom in general, and the tableau finally operates as a spoof on sexual power—and politics.

Debra Sherwood is an artist whose concerns owe a debt to Warashina, her former teacher at the University of Washington Graduate School of Art. However, unlike Warashina, she is addressing on a monumental scale the twin themes of recent Seattle ceramic sculpture: autobiography and the shard or severed figure. Though a wedding bust of bride and groom (Sherwood and her husband, Rowan Snyder) marked a return to a realistic rather than expressionistic style, an installation at Traver Sutton Gallery, *The Petrification of Garnet*, 1985, was a startling revelation of the helplessly narcissistic roots of Sherwood's art. Subject of a Seattle Art Museum exhibition in 1986, she previously concentrated on large-scale female idol or goddess figures, some more than eight feet high. *The Petrification of Garnet* expands any feminist content by combining a male and female figure in one vignette. Sherwood's own head (her Garnet persona) is severed and placed on a pedestal (another allusion to Salomé and Saint John), gazing at a vanity table full of mirrors. Nearby, the bottom half of a male figure dressed in trousers and shoes is frozen into powerlessness and immobility by the reflected gaze of Garnet-Medusa in the mirror. Sherwood has extended Warashina's domination-and-control fantasies into the seemingly submissive metaphor of a woman looking into a mirror. The cosmetics of lethal, as is Sherwood's devastatingly honest use of her own image—and life—combining bits and pieces of bodies and psyches.

Her other teacher, Howard Kottler, deserves credit along with Warashina for innovating both the potentially searing subject of self and the literal explosion of the art object. In his case, he has reconstructed the ruins into a series of archaic or Greco-Roman self-portrait profiles. Robert Arneson long ago used himself as a subject though never in order to peel away the outer layer for a look at Arneson, the man with private terrors. Kottler, au contraire, has reveled in the vagaries of his own psychosexual dynamic. He began his odyssey toward self-recognition and sanity with his silhouette self-portraits partly composed of shards. In his hands, the shard took on a powerful symbolic meaning as section-of-the-self arising directly and naturally out of its original material, clay. This was picked up by some other artists, to be sure (and lately discovered by Ann Gardner and Anne Perrigo), but by 1975 Kottler fashioned a material and iconic vocabulary that led by a process of exhaustion and elimination to his highly simplified and fiendishly stylized *Face Vase,* 1986.

Again, echoing Warashina's severed heads at the mercy of snarling nudes, Kottler took a gamble by using his own image to perpetrate a series of outrageous conceits: male narcissism and the love of kitsch memorabilia. *Kottler by Kottler*, 1977, turns the artist into a still life surrounded by his own exotic mementoes: the commercial coffee cup, mirror fragments. It recalls Roman funerary reliefs and the somber but sincere bad taste of contemporary Italian cemeteries. Freestanding and worked on both sides, this sculpture, along with *One for the Road*, 1977, *Smoke Dreams*, 1978, and *Nuts and Bolts*, 1978, marked Kottler's decisive turning away from the one-liners and visual puns of his previous work. To be fair, it was Michael Lucero, another Kottler student at the University of Washington Graduate School of Art, who began stringing together ceramic shards as early as 1976 (*Golden Fleece*). But the shard convention only preoccupied Kottler for a few years. As such, his silhouette-shard pieces represented the most perfect union—up to that point—of the shattered-self theme.

Ann Gardner moved to Seattle from Eugene, Oregon, in 1979. Her immediate response to her new circumstances was to begin breaking things into pieces. These studio tantrums took on far greater import in the light of her subsequent ceramic-and-glass masks and statues. On the one hand were her pillar goddesses fallen on hard times (*Two Ladies*, 1980), shoved back together, bewildered and modest with flying hair. On the other were her genderless impassive masks that drew upon primitive art and hid the artist's rage; their bright colors ameliorated and healed the sense of fury suggested by the jagged shards.

Kottler's work had sharp edges, figuratively speaking, but Gardner's masks and full figures (*Two Figures*, 1983, destroyed) had dangerous-looking splinters that made explicit the volatile subject matter of a shattered self. Interestingly, by the mid-80s Gardner, like Warashina, had shifted to the full figure. *Two Figures* filled clear glass "bodies" with unglazed shards. The colors—red, green and yellow—had a semiotic, or "stop/go" effect, avoiding issues of autobiography in favor of the look of children's toys or of straw dolls from Third World markets. Gardner left these behind, too, with her *Bandits*. In these tall totems Gardner fused the shard with the segmented anatomy. Working in an entirely more minimal and impersonal vein than the others, Gardner concentrated on transmuting the splinters and cast-off extrusions of clay into smoother painted surfaces. The effect is hierarchical and celebratory but may be traced directly back to the shamanistic masks (*Popsicle Man* or *Mask #2*, both 1981) in their efforts to ward off "evil spirits" or to create an aura of manic, forced cheerfulness. What began as a feminist strategy—making masks of men wearing makeup or war paint—developed into large-scale figurative sculpture of startling freshness and chromatic appeal. She had a major exhibition at the Bellevue Art Museum in 1986.

Anne Perrigo:
Magnetic Attraction,
1985, clay, glaze,
magnets and nails, 30 x
27 x 18", The Estate of
Howard Kottler. Photo:
Roger Schreiber

Anne Perrigo has synthesized the dichotomy of self and shard so successfully that she is one of the most innovative and psychologically courageous of American clay artists of recent years. Reclusive by nature, she grew up in national parks with her mother and forest-ranger father and tamed wild animals for her pets—and sole companions. She was an only child, and her art is a lonely sequence of remembered and imagined vignettes from childhood, adolescence and adulthood. This expression takes extreme but dazzlingly beautiful forms. Built like hollowed-out bookends, Perrigo's sculptures seem bemusedly resigned to their dilemmas. Like dogs dressed up in human attire, they stare out at us in pained humility, blatantly obvious by their absurd clothing and wardrobe appurtenances yet strangely affecting in touchingly human situations. These sculptures always border on the repellent or tasteless—a child kissing a pet dog (*Do Dogs Dream?*, 1983), a redheaded girl kissing a man with a crewcut of nails (*Magnetic*

Attraction, 1985) or two comedy/tragedy-masked women illustrating menstrual cramp relief tablets (*Betty's Sad / Betty's Glad*,

1982)—but by virtue of their exquisite china-painted surfaces, their vigorous handbuilt spontaneity and their brutally truncated anatomy, they become survivors of an embattled private world.

If we are looking for origins, we must turn to Kottler and Arneson, both Perrigo's teachers. However, in some respects, Perrigo points the way beyond the complacent variations of Arneson's self-portraits and Kottler's gold-and-glitter monuments to Kottler. She creates emotionally frantic art which retains its expressionistic urgency without sacrificing its potentially great beauty as ceramic sculpture. Taking Kottler's thrift shop ready-mades to the nth degree, she uses the gaudiest and goriest souvenir trash to supplement her figures' character "flaws": cheap tin Mexican masks for a sleazy suitor, a Lassie jigsaw puzzle for a "dreaming" doggy and square Color Tile discount-store tile for a square "embarrassed" housewife.

Perrigo has also learned from the dual virtues of Warashina's "attractive surfaces covering unsettling details," and the more one contemplates Perrigo's assaulted busts and bookends, the more sinister, troubling and beautiful they appear.

Along with Gardner, Kottler, Sherwood and Warashina, Perrigo has turned the corner for Northwest ceramics, bringing it out of the period LaMar Harrington so eloquently chronicled in her 1979 book *Ceramics in the Pacific Northwest: A History* and into the postmodern world of destabilizing urban art centers, pluralistic attitudes about the crafts, and uncertain, shifting value judgments. All the same, the Seattle figurative ceramic sculptors have intensified what they were already doing quite well and edged into the darker realms of the shattered self.

Howard Kottler:
Silent White Majority,
1971, porcelain dinner
plate and decals, 10" dia.
Photo: Paul Macapia

Howard Kottler:
Radio City Pot, 1967,
clay with glazes and
metallic lusters,
17" x 20 x 6".
Collection of Drs. R.
Joseph and Elaine
Monsen, Seattle.
Photo: Dudley, Hardin
and Yang

HOWARD KOTTLER

Although grouped with West Coast clay humorists, Howard Kottler's art is far from funny. Instead, humor has been a ruse, a ploy to a more subversive end: challenging our conditioned notions of reality by using clay to an illusionistic end, and upsetting the prevailing notion of "good taste" surrounding the vessel by appropriating offbeat examples from the long history of clay, such as mass-produced exportware and decal souvenir plates. To laugh or not to laugh, that is the question. The resistance to Bay Area ceramists' sense of humor on the part of New York critics is long-standing, and Kottler has often been seen as an adjunct or ancillary figure to Arneson and company. While it is true his obsessive use of the self-portrait and his evolution of low-fire glazes owe much to Arneson's pioneering efforts, it is also true his range of subjects and persistent devotion to the vessel have set him apart from the Clown of Benicia.

As Arneson himself turned away from humor toward public and social subjects such as nuclear war or the military establishment, Kottler's shift away from humor involved opposite issues: instead of politics, the development of private, autobiographical issues and the parallel connoisseur's fascination with the lowliest of ceramic objects, mass-produced Japanese exportware of the pre-World War II period. But by doing so, by honing in on a kind of fragmentation and reconstruction of the self in his portraits, he has developed a psychological level of content for American ceramics rarely attained and barely acknowledged despite his inclusion in many group shows.

His concomitant immersion in Noritake ware and other examples of New York-designed, Japanese-made knickknacks has led to the current body of work, which seems equally divided between large-scale, full-figure self-portraits (built in sections) and a series of vases and pots, which allude to and in some cases directly appropriate historical examples of ceramics' forgotten dime store heritage.

Literally and figuratively, Kottler has been the underdog of American ceramics. Occasionally using dogs as metaphors for the self—guardians of secrets (*Waiting for Master*), alternately loyal and vicious (*Devil Walk*, 1986)—he has also drawn from Chinese iconography of tomb guardians and from kitsch statuettes of dogs to press home the point that any image, no matter how humble or vulgar, can be instilled with meaning and subjected to elaborate material indulgences.

Growing up in Cleveland, attending Ohio State University, Kottler dropped out of optometry school because his teachers found him spending more time in a basement ceramics studio on campus. Little did he know he was attaching himself to one of the nation's oldest university ceramics training programs. Arthur Baggs had founded it in 1929 and Carlton Atherton, Paul Bogatay, Gene Friley, and Edgar Littlefield were among his teachers. Receiving his M.A., he proceeded to an equally conservative institution, Cranbrook Academy of Art, and spent a year with Finnish-Swedish potter Maija Grotell, getting an M.F.A. degree. Grotell's influence and assistance was negligible, according to Kottler. After a year's work, "she lined up ten pieces, said this one was the best, and walked away."

Not surprisingly, it was exposure to a roomful of Peter Voulkos's work at the Art Institute of Chicago in 1957 that provided one turning point. He later met Voulkos in 1962 at a workshop at O.S.U. By that time, Kottler had already spent a year "starting to break loose" as a 1957 Fulbright student in Finland, where he was told by the director of the Arabia Company that he was the first visiting American to create work that looked nothing like Arabia ware.

Returning to Columbus, Ohio, he embarked in earnest on what became his Ph.D. degree in ceramic arts. The handbuilt pots were done while working as a teaching assistant and later instructor in art history and led to his dissertation exhibition of 1964 that featured both thrown and handbuilt pots, recalling Japanese Bizen ware and a strong influence of Abstract Expressionism.

Kottler had also developed a strong interest in Tiffany glass while working on his doctorate, collecting it heavily and admiring its shiny, iridescent surfaces. Coming to Seattle to teach at the invitation of University of Washington ceramics chair Robert Sperry in 1964, Kottler joined Harry Myers, Mutsuo Yanigahara, and Marie Woo. Patti Warashina had just graduated with Fred Bauer and both went off to Wisconsin State University to teach.

The crucible of Northwest ceramics had begun to boil. Leaving behind the "controlled Abstract Expressionism" of his Ohio period, Kottler finally found a way to combine his interest in the heritage of mass-production ceramics with his highly refined aesthetic sensibility. One could say, settled in the Lake City area north of the university, Kottler found his own place and created his first distinctively individual work.

To be sure, Ken Price had already begun using low-fire, "hobby-shop" glazes in order to attain a wider palette and had also begun using the cup form, but Kottler's 1965 *Chalice* was a transitional piece. Thrown and altered, handbuilt, raku-fired, it had a yellow and green irides-cent color vaguely akin to Tiffany glass. Neither was it influenced by

George E. Ohr, the eccentric Mississippian he was later often compared to, whose work Kottler did not know until 1970.

The Chiquita Banana series (1967) was pure Kottler of the first order. Along with *Hustler's Delight* (1967) and *Orange Angel Pot* (1969), *Lemon Punch Pot* (1967) played off the sexual innuendo of Carmen Miranda's Fox musical persona—"the lady in the tutti-frutti hat"— and introduced the glaring gold and silver luster glazes (only $37 an ounce in 1966). They presented what would become the artist's hallmark erotic form, the vessel displaying both male and female symbolic sexual parts. Brightly colored in oranges, chartreuses, lemon yellows, the Chiquita pots were simultaneously attractive and outrageous. They carried the vessel tradition to a dizzying, hallucinatory height and long antedated Judy Chicago's ceramic vagina-plates of *The Dinner Party*. Rather than pretexts for sexuo-political ideologies, all of Kottler's work of this period and much that would follow dealt with the male and female natures within each of us. The subliminal content was ambisexual in form rather than phallocentric or gender-segregationist.

Peter Selz's pathbreaking "Funk" show was in the air, too. Collecting various California clay artists such as Arneson, Voulkos, Gilhooly, Price, and Melchert under the common rubric of "funk" for a show at the University Art Museum in Berkeley in 1967, Selz summoned up the mysterious West Coast sensibility of the day. Kottler was already working in a similar vein and had created his own variations, the fur pots and the decal plates. Political, religious, and sexual in inspiration, the mass-produced blank porcelain plates with altered decals drew upon the artist's Ohio heritage where the major manufacturers of souvenir plates were headquartered in East Liverpool (Homer Laughlin), Zanesville (Weller, Roseville), and Cincinnati (Rookwood). *Peace March* (1968) with its marching dueling pistols and *(sticks)(stones) = bones* (1968) referred to anti-Vietnam demonstrations and to Robert Kennedy's assassination that year. *American Gothicware Look Alikes* (1972) made Grant Wood's popular painting an early victim of Kottler's appropriation strategy and an oblique commentary on hippie commune lifestyles. *Leonardo's Supperware*, consisting of thirteen plates, continued the shameless art-historical lifting. *Da Vinci's Revenge* (1967–71), drove the device into the ground, drawing on the mealtime subject of the Renaissance masterpiece *The Last Supper*, its vulgar adaptation into Italian souvenir plates, and the deconstruction of a cultural icon, by cutting away all the Apostles to leave only ghostlike figures about to dine. Together, the decal plates sum up many of the social concerns of the sixties and paved the way from Kottler's amorphous funk vessels to his own version of a Pop Art pointing toward more conceptual concerns. In addition, as Warhol anticipated the postmodern return to representation with his use of photography and the elevation of consumerism as subject, so Kottler accomplished exactly the same thing for American ceramics.

Exhausting the decal convention by 1973, he turned to molds. In a set based on the industrial evolution of the cup form, Kottler turned the mold for the average coffee cup inside-out and upside-down. Like conceptual art of the period, he was examining process and elevating it to the status of subject.

Precious Cup (1973) exaggerated the process by having an inordinately long, thin pouring shaft for a tiny cup that was covered in gold luster. *Schmaltzy-Paisley* (1973) encased a plain cup in a mold and a Plexiglas box, both covered with blue paisley decals. It literalized and codified the process of decoration by separating it from the cup's surface and surrounding the cup in a mold and a formal box, which acted as an all-over environment maintaining the "purity" and blankness of the cup form. *Cup of Light* (1973) is a two-part mold deconstructing the process step by step, showing the cross-section of the cup form. By uniting it side by side with the other half of the mold, Kottler created an aesthetic unity for the piece while exposing its latent, rather than overt, function as a container.

Homage to Oppenheim (1973) continued the artist's blatant appropriation of art-historical models and reinforced his link to Dada strategies, including what he called "the twentieth century's first important work of ceramic sculpture," Duchamp's urinal readymade, *Fountain* (1917). Using the mold, he subverted Méret Oppenheim's *Object* (1936) by placing the fur on the outside of the cup mold on one side and on the inside of the cup on the other. By the late seventies, Kottler had set aside both Pop and Conceptual themes to concentrate on a series of self-portrait works that continue to occupy him at the present time. Spending a semester at the fountainhead of Funk, the University of California-Davis, in 1977, Kottler pressed his interest in the nature of reality into the realm of fake materials, asking the question we all ask of ourselves, "Am I a fake?"

Actually, a wooden piece satirizing the King Tut phenomenon with Kottler as the Egyptian scion was the first figurative, self-portrait work in the series. It used cut-up wood-grain Contac paper. More importantly, *Rock Vase* (1978) and *Nut Art is Nutty* (1978) were more successful, both because they returned to the clay medium and because they used double silhouettes to stress the dual nature of the psyche. *Rock Vase* played upon clay's origins in geological time and incorporated the so-called Rubens vase as an illusionistic platform for two facing profiles of the artist. Monochromatic in black with one white "rock" at the base of each silhouette, *Rock Vase* also acted as a metaphor for the artist's devotion to the vessel form. Just as the faces create the outline of the footed vase, so Kottler, the artist, plays off the vessel notion by using it as a conceptual playpen for his own narcissistic pursuits. Add to that the determinedly two-dimensional nature of the piece and one begins to get the idea that Kottler's interests all along have been to explode our preconceptions of the limits of ceramics while at the same time using it as a forum for self-exploration and artistic expression.

Nut Art is Nutty, a wall-relief of the artist in double profile, made a point about the distinctive singularity of West Coast ceramics that Arneson would later comment on in his own *California Artist* of 1982. Using the silhouette of his face as a meandering river over a map of the Far West, Kottler symbolically severed the more conservative East Coast clay community and capped himself with a clay walnut shell.

In the following decade, Kottler concentrated on mixed-≠media tables and chairs using figurative references. He continued working in clay the whole time, made more self-portraits, and began another set of vases and pots in 1982, working in a borrowed New York studio on Washington Street. *Blue Balls* (1982–86), *Pot Twister* (1986), and *Skyscraper Vase* (1986) were completed in Seattle and are an attempted fusion of vessel form and abstracted human figuration. Drawing upon architectural forms, specific Japanese Déco exportware examples, and stylized male and female sexual anatomy, Kottler has attained a new level of craftsmanship and content. Harking back to the fur-and-clay pieces like *Hole Grabber* and *Gilt Feeler* (1966), Kottler's new work combines phallic forms (the vase's column, the protuberant floral bud) with concealed and recessed female openings, surrounded by overlapping angular or wavy areas. The colors are bright to brilliant, invoking the garish, mass-produced predecessors Kottler has so successfully assimilated over the years and lending the works an assertive, symbolic character of their own. Ambisexual in appearance, they function as votive objects for some mysterious, luxuriant, and libertine cult of the postmodern era. They also operate as more detached foils to the ongoing self -portraits.

After the ego-indulgent work of the Davis period (1977–78), Kottler sublimated the artist's profile form in his new work. One side of *Northwest Dreamer* (1986) is a 3-D Braque cubist landscape covered with light and dark brown, cut-up woodgrain Contac paper. The other side more clearly suggests the head lying on its side with eyes and neck punctured by fake wooden points. Instead of the double silhouette, Kottler has manifested his double nature through waking and sleeping sides, conscious and subconscious states, perfectly reflected in the active and passive material treatments.

Finally, working in sections that when disassembled reveal further niches with hidden written messages, Kottler's latest sculptures are a large-scale apotheosis of his exorbitant preoccupation with his own image. Unlike earlier works, they also operate as more generalized figures.

Tongue Twister (1986) piles on simulated gold leaf over a six-foot-high self-portrait head with the telltale double profile in red aluminum spewing out of the mouth. The effect is strangely attractive and threatening.

Howeird (1986) cloaks a recessed head in a black leather box. Gold luster glaze covers the interior landscape of the artist's head. The ultimate step from the sexual to the sacred has occurred and Kottler has finally made a god of himself in these two works. Though they still deal with the pervasive themes of illusion, self-examination, and marginal "bad taste," they have slid over the line to the mock-sacred object wherein that most previous of materials, gold, is turned to an auto-deifying end.

The fate of the vessel has ended up where it began, inside the artist's head, and as we examine *Howeird* with its cross-section of the skull's interior, it becomes clear that here as elsewhere Kottler has seized upon ways to combine figuration and the vessel tradition. In this case, the artist's head is his ultimate container-form, with the traditional surface covering of glaze peeled away to expose the stylized workings of the mind. Shedding the one-liners, the puns, and the fussy material conceits of the earlier work, Howard Kottler intensified his psychological and aesthetic researches culminating in a body of work that pits monumentality of form against the illusionism of clay, the "sacred" quality of gleaming colors and gold against the "profane" nature of the self.

PATTERN RE-EXAMINED
IN AMERICAN CERAMICS

The extraordinary evolution of American ceramics from the work of
the earliest native potters and Moravian immigrants to the sleek forms
of contemporary university professors may be interpreted as a series
of shifting attitudes toward pattern. By pattern, I mean a repeated
abstract motif. Separating out relevant examples and determining how
they reflect changing aesthetic attitudes is the purpose of this essay.
In touching upon one thread within American clay art, pattern, it may
be possible to perceive how deeply ingrained is the need for reassuring
order in an often chaotic and uncontrollable medium. In tracing the
differing forms that pattern takes, we may reveal not only the vaunted
diversity of American ceramics but also a unifying strain which marks
much of the strongest and best work created.

Pattern, whether non-representational or highly abstracted, is a
repeated line, form, or shape. Thus, figurative imagery or decoration
is not the subject of this essay. Instead, let us delve briefly into the
growth of the decorative impulse which brings order to the disorderly medium of clay. By glancing back to our origins, we may better
understand why pattern is an important but misunderstood aspect of
clay surface decoration today.

Pattern is conveyed in many different ways, as we shall see: the use
of slip and glaze; the piercing or incising of marks; the breaking up
of parts and re-assembly into a whole. All these methods carry forth
pattern in a way that leads the eye in and around the object. It can be
delightful or subversive but it must relate to the container's shape or
the extent of the given surface.

Long before the European settlement of North America, the Salado Indian culture (850–1150 A.D.) and the Anasazi people (950–1100 A.D.)
of the Southwest, respectively, used corrugated exterior patterns and
parallel straight-line patterns on their earthenware. With the advent
of the European-style kilns such as those built by the German Moravian settlers near what is now Winston-Salem, North Carolina, pottery
became slip-decorated, involving the use of liquid clay in colors which
were dripped in linear and circular patterns around "sugar bowls" and
other functional shapes. The work of these 18th-century settlers was
echoed around 1800 by that of another group of Germans, the so-called
"Pennsylvania Dutch", who were much more restrained in their use of
patterning. One redware plate, for example, has eight simple zigzags
with a wavy line above and below the pattern.

During the first half of the 19th century, stoneware utility jugs were prevalent in upstate New York and an unusual example in the Everson Museum collection in Syracuse has a single area of grid decoration. Within each square is a single dot that could be either a comment on quilt design or a game board.[1]

Most Victorian art potters eschewed the use of regular pattern in favor of Japanese-style asymmetrical design or crowded scenes. Abstract pattern appeared to go underground. By the turn of the century, however, Frederick H. Rhead of Roseville Pottery (Zanesville, Ohio) and Adelaide Alsop Robineau of Syracuse, New York, intensified the repetitive nature of pattern into impressively extravagant expressions. Rhead's stylized flowers on earthenware vases were more abstract than representational. Robineau's *Lantern* (1908) and *Scarab Vase (The Apotheosis of the Toiler)* (1910) represent highwater marks within the history of American ceramics. Both artists shifted the trend away from Victorian pictorialism and asymmetry toward the abstract and modern revolution about to arrive.

The advent of Art Nouveau to the United States gradually favored a more unified form of decoration in pottery evidenced in the striated water-lily leaves on Grueby ware from Boston, as well as in the intricate sunflower patterns on later Roseville jardinières during the 1920s.

It was not until the arrival of European émigrés during the interwar period (1919–39) that the gospel of Modernism, specifically that of the Bauhaus, reinvigorated abstract pattern in American ceramics. Maija Grotell, the great Finnish-Swedish ceramic artist, joined the Cranbrook Academy of Art and offered in her own work a more sophisticated version of pattern—-one which was complex enough to appear irregular but which, at the same time, set up a system of orderly covering.

One of her students, Howard Kottler, deserves credit for further reviving pattern after the exciting but formally chaotic excesses of the Abstract Expressionist ceramics of the 1950s. His cut-up decals of paisley patterns, for example, employed a Cubist technique—collage—to disorient the viewer and lure the eye into a hallucinatory realm completely under the control of the artist. Here and throughout his career, Kottler kept an eye on both the past and present. Whether psychedelic, Art Nouveau, Noritake, or hard-edge, Kottler's unending variations on the use of pattern marks another epic achievement within the field. Even though his life was tragically cut short in 1989, his work ranks with that of other great Ohio ceramic artists like Maria Longworth Nichols, Mary Louise McLaughlin, and his teacher at Ohio State University, Paul Bogatay.

As the modern movement wound down in the early 1970s, older artists like John Mason and Robert Sperry, who had benefited from the Ab-Ex breakthroughs, found themselves reassessing pattern as an escape route out of the material excesses Rose Slivka praised in her 1961 essay, "The New Ceramic Presence."[2] By the 1980s, it was no longer a "new" presence but one generally evacuated by overkill. It was also under critical scrutiny in an age when figuration and representation offered serious alternatives to pattern. Mason's conversion to a Minimalist aesthetic perfectly adapted pattern's repetitive component to Minimalism's dull, additive structures. After the firebrick pieces (*Hudson River Series*, 1978), he returned to the vessel in the 1980s. By employing mathematically calculated pattern systems as an austere surface covering, he further extended pattern's evolution in ceramics to a cold, technological phase tempered only by sections of warm, unglazed clay.

In Sperry's case, the Cubist grid organized otherwise chaotic slip decorations on large wall murals. Always at home with the two-dimensional surface, Sperry gradually reduced his explosive pictorial imagery suggestive of planetary bodies or galaxies (white slip over black) and, in the past decade, his work resumed an intellectual clarity common to his earliest pottery of the 1950s. *Untitled #951* (1989) may be a tribute to Mason's *Red X* (1966) but, suspended on a wall rather than free-standing, it creates a powerful effect involving the use of a pattern component—the "X"—with the gridded surface underneath.

While Sperry and Mason were making the shift from the formless spontaneity of Ab-Ex to the intellectually liberating world of pattern, three other artists were reexamining pattern through distortion, imbalance, and glitter. Ralph Bacerra, Bennett Bean, and Rick Dillingham retained conventional pottery forms—patterns, vases, and spheres—but became leading figures in the gallery vessel movement. Pattern and decoration were eagerly embraced, as boldly defensive critics like Jeff Perrone ceaselessly pointed out.[3]

Surprisingly, the very fine arts movement that one would have thought most applicable or sympathetic to ceramics, Pattern & Decoration (P&D), produced much of the worst work imaginable in painting. Painters Miriam Schapiro, Joyce Kozloff, Valerie Jaudon, and Robert Zakanitch drew heavily from Matisse and Islamic ornament theory and, with the help of critics like Perrone and John Perreault, attained a moment of recognition and respectability during the mid-1970s. Adapting patterning from tile and the decorative arts to another medium, painting, and then emerging from the puritanical austerity of Minimalism, P&D was bound to fail. Add to this the nascent psychological expressionism of the early 1980s, and a reaction to P&D set in. It came in Donald Kuspit's 1974 essay "Betraying the Feminist Intention: The Case Against Feminist Decorative Art."[4]

Kuspit argued that the use of pattern gave painting a "superficial vitality" and that P&D was caught between feminist wishes to be a part of a male-dominated world and Modernism and "transcendent abstraction's" rejection of the "life-world". He hit close to craft when he accused the feminist P&D of being "more easily read as a technical exercise than as a symbolic form."

For our purposes, Kuspit's critique of pattern in painting actually appears, in retrospect, to have raised clay's application of pattern to a comparatively higher status. Already at home with "technical exercises" or craft, artists using pattern in ceramics fit into the existing feminist heritage of china painting, and neatly sidestep the Modernist category of "transcendent abstraction" of which Kuspit was so protective. Perhaps better suited than painting to pattern as decoration, ceramics has a forthright functional honesty that saves it from political, ideological, or spiritual confusion of content.

Ralph Bacerra draws on Japanese Imari ware as a paradigm for complex patterning that is both modular and erratic. Along with Bean and Dillingham, he uses fragments that fit together to form a new whole, aided by the addition of gold lusters. All three were part of the gallery vessel movement arising during the 1980s, and individually invoke that sense of material indulgence that is key to an appreciation of their work.

Far less successful, though equally astute concerning the subtleties of fragmentary pattern, Jeff Perrone's multipart glazed earthenware gallery vessels do not share Bean's, Dillingham's or Bacerra's consummate technical control. How a critic of such towering erudition could create objects of a barely high-school level of craft is astounding. New to exhibiting after nearly twenty years of reviewing, Perrone expresses ideas that are far from fresh. They still appear steeped in a P&D mentality that other clay artists have already mastered or rejected and left behind in favor of to the pattern problem.

Pattern in American ceramics is again under scrutiny and examination. A few artists like Eileen Horner, Kathryn Sharbaugh, and Silvie Granatelli are exploring the strict divisions of black and white in functional ware of great beauty. And two Japanese artists living in the United States, Jun Kaneko and Yumi Kiyosi, may be showing the way for future revelations of pattern. Kiyosi creates large concentric spiral in clay that are wall-mounted. Possibly floral or sharp alternatives to the linear or geometric legacy.

Finally, Kaneko manages to defy pattern's often diminutive character by making entire paved plazas of patterned tiles and tall dango forms which, covered in idiosyncratic pattern, retain completely individual qualities. It could be that a combination of deep subjectivity and knowledge of the world around us is needed to refresh pattern in an increasingly technological world. Along with the other artists mentioned above, Kaneko joins the long thread of pattern in American ceramics.

From the simple zigzag through the abstracted leaf; from the streamlined V-shape to the Minimal module; from the reconstituted decorative fragment to the simplicity of black and white, American ceramists have used pattern to enhance surface decoration, convey personal expression, and reflect the age in which they live.

Richard Fairbanks: *Stoneware Jar*, 1980, stoneware with pale blue glaze, 9" h.
Mrs. Richard Fairbanks collection, Issaquah, Washington. Photo: Roger Schreiber

RICHARD FAIRBANKS:
TURNING POINT

DOOR TO THE WORLD

You are very fortunate here in Finland to
have a fine appreciation and understanding
of handmade things.

—R. F., *final line from unpublished lecture to*
undetermined group in Helsinki, 1960

The academic year Richard Fairbanks spent in Finland as special
student at the Institute of Applied Arts (later University of Industrial
Arts) and as guest of the Arabia Wärtsilä OY ceramic manufacturing firm (later Hackman Arabia OY) was the single most important
professional experience of his life. A recipient of a United States government grant, the Fulbright Fellowship (Act of 79th U.S. Congress,
Public Law 584), Fairbanks found himself overwhelmed by experiences in a country that, like Japan, elevated the design and making of
functional pottery over that of painting and sculpture.

The ramifications of his year in Finland would touch his life for many
years. Besides providing a virtual electric charge to his creative life,
it triggered thoughts about the nature of pottery delivered in two important lectures while in Helsinki, made him a committed Europhile,
and gave him a peer group of like-minded artists, some of whom
would become lifelong friends and colleagues.

When 30-year-old Richard Fairbanks embarked from New York
aboard the *S.S. Kungsholm* on August 12, 1959, he had no idea
that the experiences he was about to have, the people he was about
to meet, and the things he was about to see would change his life
forever. Early journal entries comment on the cross-country train
ride to New York City, his first impressions of Manhattan, and his
enthusiastic participation in shipboard life. Studying Finnish daily
aboard the Swedish liner, he reveled at the Gammeldans group who
performed traditional Scandinavian folk dances each evening after a
sumptuous dinner. Slowly, he tried out his newly learned language,
first in the diary entries ("Maanantai, Tuesday, Keskiviiko,
Torstai. . . . "), next at the dinner table with newly found traveling
companions.

Landing in Göteberg, Sweden, the Fulbright group continued on to
Stockholm and, after a day's sightseeing, Fairbanks boarded the *S.S.*

Bore II where he was offered a white porcelain chamber pot (no doubt made at Arabia, Europe's largest toilet manufacturer) in addition to other steamer conveniences.

On August 23, he arrived in Helsinki harbor and immediately remarked how much the city reminded him of Seattle, Washington. His living quarters assigned in suburban Otaniemi, and "very glad to be settled for a while," Fairbanks was pleased to be given "a private room with a huge picture window overlooking the inlet and across to the woods on the other side."

It was the driest summer since 1914, he recorded, and, sitting on the beach, he read mail on August 26 from "Papa" Bonifas. After recovering from the Atlantic crossing and the less comfortable steamer trip across the Gulf of Bothnia, Fairbanks spent a week traveling to various sites including the ancient port of Turku, the glassworks at Nuutajärvi, where he met the greatest Finnish designer of all, Kaj Franck (1911–1990).

Back in Helsinki on September 4, he was given a tour of the Arabia facilities by Art Department head Vaino Kankunnen and introduced to Kyllikki Salmenhaara (1915–1981), Aune Siimes (1909–1964), and Karl-Heinz Schultz-Köln, all top clay artists and designers at the time. The following day he met other leading figures of the golden age of Finnish design: Birger Kaipiainen (1915–1988), Oiva Toikka, and Sakari Vapaavuori (1920–1988).

Within a few days, he had cleaned up the studio he was assigned and was happily throwing pots. Gradually, he was attracted to the rougher clay body used by Salmenhaara and another artist, Raija Tuumi. As he wrote to Carolyn Price Dyer:

> My work at Arabia goes on. I have my own studio on the 8th floor overlooking a fine bay to the east, from whence the winds and snows savagely rage. Have met the artists there. Am on very friendly terms especially with Kyllikki Salmenhaara. Her pieces are rugged & simple. She works like a whiz, and glazes her pieces in the green [i.e., unbisqued] state. Some others, too, are potters, but several are "artists" designing for anonymous throwers to execute...[1]

His annus mirabilis was underway.

IN THE COURT OF CLAY

> Do not cherish and shelter an object if you do not
> like it. Break it; you have again learned something. You have been
> humbled. It is even better if you grow angry and make a new one.
>
> —Kyllikki Salmenhara, in Marianne Aav,
> *Kyllikki Salmenhaara 1915–1981*, 1986

The story of the relationship between Fairbanks and Salmenhaara could probably fill a book all its own and occupy several exhibitions. Readers are referred to *Kyllikki Salmenhaara 1915–1981* by Marianne Aav[2] for a sketch of her life and work. It is worth noting here that by the time she met Fairbanks, Salmenhaara had already exhibited abroad widely in postwar design exhibitions and was considered a highly significant cultural figure in Scandinavia.

Aav points out in her introduction to Fairbanks's Helsinki Journal that the three Arabia artists besides Salmenhaara who were closest to Fairbanks in spirit were Francesca Mascitti-Lindh, Raija Tuumi, and Liisa Hallamaa. Calling them the "down-to-earth" school, she touched on a theme that should be seen in the context of the times, the Cold War period (1946–1990). Meeting them at the height of the Cold War, the young American was immediately attracted to the rough or rustic character of their wares. These four high priestesses of Finnish ceramics leaned on a coarse look in their wares, closely dependent on a clay body called chamotte. Their approach was in tune with Fairbanks's own agrarian background.

The reason for their "down-to-earth" approach is complex, but one possible explanation may lie in Finland's geo-political history as an occupied nation. Russia to the east had occupied Finland between 1809 and 1917; Sweden to the west had occupied Finland between 1100 until the early 19th century. These women may have been proffering a uniquely Finnish national craft style by reviving such a rustic farm appearance in so highly official a setting.

Expressive of the land, rarely glazed to conceal the clay body, and inspired by farmhouse forms (just as Fairbanks had been), their pottery gained great international recognition for Finland precisely at a time when the Soviet Union was nearing its most adventurous and reckless expansionist phase under Premier Khrushchev. Acutely aware of the size and threatening power of their neighbor, the Finnish government had steered a neutral course in foreign policy so as not to offend the Russians in return for a hands-off approach to Finnish free-market economies and national autonomy. What was often disdainfully referred to as an accommodation, "Finlandization" became a positive

model for independence and national aspirations 25 years later in
Eastern Europe.

Long before the wisdom of the official Finnish response to the Cold
War was recognized, the Finns were rebuilding their economy
through hard work and various examples of cooperation between
private industry and government guidance. So it was that artists
were hired full time at Arabia, Europe's largest industrial porcelain
factory, named after the suburban "villa" neighborhood where it had
been built in 1874.

By 1959, having endured the vicissitudes (and fluctuating markets)
of large and great wars, the company was relatively prosperous and
owned by a huge shipbuilding conglomerate, Wärtsilä OY. Under
design director Kaj Franck (who left in 1960) and general director
Holger Caring, a number of artists were subsidized to do their own
work, which was subsequently sold as individual art pots in the Arabia shops, or exported around the world.

One of the earliest U.S. importers of Arabia goods, Seattle business-
man James Egbert (who became a close friend of Fairbanks), recalls
the prima-donna rivalries among the four high priestesses. Partner in
a Seattle fine-design furniture store, Keeg's, Egbert insisted on buy-
ing trips, going directly to the European factories rather than depending on their New York City showrooms. Describing them as

> both exotic and provincial, the women were outwardly polite but,
> between them, I sensed a tremendous tension, rivalry,
> and egocentric jealousy.[4]

In an observation that suggests an embarrassing Cold War atmosphere, Egbert called them

> court artists in a socialist state. They were almost imprisoned
> workers, rarely allowed to leave the country. It was as if the
> directors of the company felt they would be tainted by other
> influences, that their Finnishness would be impaired.[5]

Based on conversations with Fairbanks a few years later, Egbert also
remembered that the young American was "probably in awe somewhat and disturbed by their carping and bitching all the time."[6]

If so, he concealed it well in his journal and letters to Carolyn Price
Dyer. On February 13, 1960, he wrote of a new bond with Salmenhaara:

> I've made several of what others . . . feel are strong, live, sizable
> pots. Am really interested at present in how fingers and tools
> yield characteristic surface texture and have [been] combining
> (juxtaposing?!) 2 or 3 on one pot. Have gotten this awareness

> somehow from seeing Salmenhaara's pots. I find in her pieces the
> strength of rugged Early American folk pottery— she was in USA 6
> months in 1956. Also I've had a chance in Iowa and Mo. to see plenty
> of such jugs, jars, etc.—fine sturdy, no-nonsense forms.[7]

Their bond cemented by a love of American folk pottery and a shared
dedication to pottery, Salmenhaara (14 years older) and Fairbanks
saw one another on a daily basis, and according to the journal,
frequently lunched or dined together. In the same way that Bonifas
had become a surrogate father figure, Fairbanks may have turned
Salmenhaara into a maternal substitute, or at the very least, a sister.

By late November, he was seeing Salmenhaara frequently (November
24), giving her a box of Fazer chocolates (November 28) and, two days
after witnessing a moving Independence Day parade (December 6),
celebrating Salmenhaara's "name day" (December 8) with her before
the Fulbright fellows' Christmas party at the Angleterre Restaurant.

On Christmas Eve, he was "surprised and flabbergasted" that
Salmenhaara "came with a big box" of presents for him.

> So many things: a wonderful black pot for apples and a big white
> teacup with 2 dwarf red tulips sprouted from the bare bulbs, a
> molded fruitcake, bonbons, 3 wooden spoons and a promise of a
> sweater handknit of handspun...wool... Earlier, I had given her 2
> pots, one a candlestick; one a teapot that she was fond of.
> (December 24)[8]

The significance of the exchange of pots should not be understated.
The world over, when potters exchange pots, the assumption is of a
gift between equals. Quite apart from the typical Finnish generosity, to a visiting foreigner, Salmenhaara's ceramic presents should be
seen as an acceptance of Fairbanks as a peer.

The day after Christmas, he and Salmenhaara walked in the snow to
a church in Seurasaari where they happened upon Uhro Kekkonen,
President of the Republic, "walking very briskly. . . . Followed at a
distance by detective in black fur hat. (December 26)"

Well into the northern winter, Fairbanks plunged into his own work
making more candlesticks on Twelfth Night (January 5) and discovered that the date on an antique wooden bucket he had purchased
had been altered from 1936 to 1836. With new confidence, he undertook a series of larger pots along with pitchers, lidded jars, coffee
servers, and a tall cylindrical milk pail, *Stoneware Jar* (1960).

On a technical level, it could be said that Salmenhaara provided four
main influences on Fairbanks's work at this time. As stated before,
the coarse chamotte clay body added a needed tactile dimension of

Fairbanks's pots after the Mediterranean refinements of Bonifas and Prieto. Next, besides encouraging him to make larger pots, she also was highly adept at making spouts and handles which seemed to emerge effortlessly out of the vessel without appearing added on. In fact, so skilled did Fairbanks become at handles that, after a serious studio injury that basically ended Salmenhaara's throwing career,[9] she allowed Fairbanks to make all the handles for the work she sent to the 1954 *Milan Triennale*[10]. Finally, an extraordinary blue-green glaze (copper, barium) was common to her work and was adapted by Fairbanks during his sojourn. In fact, Salmenhaara made a gift of blue plate to Fairbanks on March 13, 1960. For many years the plate hung on the wall in the Fairbanks home in Ellensburg, Washington.

According to William Tyner, Fairbanks's foremost student during the Ellensburg years, the blue glazes in Fairbanks's wares were always "slightly underfired to retain glaze color," rather than letting it burn out in a highfire kiln.[11] Salmenhaara's blue glaze application, by contrast, was always sparser, allowing the natural clay body to show through in areas but richly pooling and accumulating in other areas.

Two of Fairbanks's works from this period, *Stoneware Drum Bottle* (1960) and *Stoneware Plate* (1967), display an extraordinary range of color. *Bottle* employs the drum-shape Fairbanks devised by combining separate thrown forms and alluded to in his letter to Dyer. Made two years after his "spinach-and-egg" bottle, it demonstrates a fuller, bulging form and a new direction in glazes. Spattered with copper to create the green highlights, it shares the pedestal-type foot and a decisive neck. The lip is far more decisive, however, and extends downward into a band that finishes the piece confidently.

With their shared love of the American vernacular pottery of Tennessee, North Carolina, and Missouri, their affinity for multiple use-specific shapes, and their shared inversion of thrown forms on a simple pot, Salmenhaara and Fairbanks's relationship developed over the course of the year from teacher-student into colleagues. Their gift exchanges, long walks, and frequent lunches and dinners alone together provided a model of intellectual and domestic life for the young loner. Their friendship would continue for many years and involve a number of visits between Finland and Ellensburg. It was shared after 1966 by Fairbanks's young wife, painter Dixie Parker.

Before he sailed from Turku on May 20, 1960, to return to the U.S., Fairbanks said good-bye to Salmenhaara. This time, it was she who brought a gift of "2 small boxes of Fazer chocolate," along with "some sandwiches and a tiny pot with flowers." (May 19, 1960).

JIM LEEDY: PREHISTORIC MODERN

The history of American ceramics is riddled with gaps. The literature grows, and the list of critics and historians becomes longer, yet there are still many neglected figures worthy of serious scrutiny. Jim Leedy is one of them. Though he was in Missoula, Montana, during the early 1960s, his contributions were barely touched on by LaMar Harrington in her pathbreaking study, *Ceramics in the Pacific Northwest: A History* (1979). Though he was probably the first U.S. clay artist to revel in the Abstract Expressionist milieu in New York City, Rose Slivka made no mention of him in her article "The New Ceramic Presence" (*Craft Horizons*, July/August 1961). And lately, Leedy has been passed over by both Garth Clark and Elaine Levin, to name two authors plotting the genesis of postwar American ceramics.

The oversight may be partly Leedy's own fault. He has always bent over backwards to help others expecting little and rarely receiving reciprocal favors. Moreover, his full-time job as professor of sculpture at the Kansas City Art Institute in Missouri has paralleled an ongoing studio life, and both have competed for attention with art-historical studies and supplementary activities as author, folk singer, art dealer and curator.

In assessing Leedy's art, I intend to focus on one aspect—his vessels and sculptures of clay—and leave for other critics his hot-air balloons, realistic figurative assemblages, prints and photographs, and his collaborations with Rudy Autio and Peter Voulkos.

If Voulkos and Autio have been perceived as the demigods of American ceramics, Leedy might be seen as a Vulcan figure, invoking the Roman god of the forge or kiln. All his work is inextricably tied to the blazing, charring flame which bakes and transforms the clay. Its appearance illustrates the process of firing, rather than the "power throwing" of Voulkos or the hand-building of Autio. And the origins of this burnt, ancient-artifact look in Leedy's art is a fascinating story. When Leedy was made an honorary fellow of the National Council on Education for the Ceramic Arts in 1989, it was partly in recognition of his contribution to American raku. Though the widespread discovery by American ceramists of this Japanese method of firing occurred around 1961, Leedy, in fact, had been experimenting with it as early as 1950.[1]

Born in McRoberts, Kentucky, in 1929, Leedy, the surviving son of a twin birth, grew up in the remote hills where he periodically returns

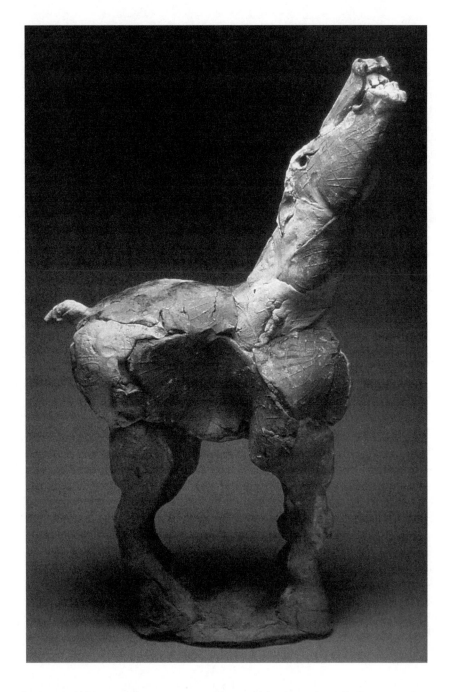

Jim Leedy: *Whinny*, 1981, terra cotta with porcelain, 43 x 42 x 10". Courtesy of Leedy-Voulkos Art Center, Kansas City. Photo: Jim Walker

to visit family. Had he remained behind, he might have become an heir to the Appalachian folk pottery tradition. Instead, he became a major, if unrecognized, proponent of the most significant 20th-century art movement to influence ceramics: Abstract Expressionism.

Before Leedy's initial visit to New York in 1945, his family lived in Montana, Ohio and Virginia. His service in the U.S. Army during the Korean War was the occasion for the first of four crucial trips to Asia (the others were in 1963, 1987, and 1990). The full force of Asian art and culture hit Leedy each time and affected his work profoundly. Studying on the G.I. Bill, Leedy completed a B.F.A. degree with honors in 1957 at what is now Virginia Commonwealth University in Richmond. But long before his studies there, which centered on Asian art history, he had turned to clay as an extension of his interest in painting and sculpture. As early as 1950, inspired by a picture of an African stack kiln, Leedy set up an outdoor pyre in his backyard, and, making the most of the lower temperature, added dabs of colored polyester resins to his crude-looking "stilted vessels." The results may be seen as the first Abstract Expressionist ceramics.

Living in New York the summer after graduation, and spending the subsequent two summers there, he continued to paint and to frequent the Dillon Bar in Greenwich Village, where, some years earlier, he had met and "wrestled to the ground" the painter Willem de Kooning in a friendly brawl over an ex-girlfriend of the Dutchman's whom Leedy befriended at the counter. He also took graduate courses in art history at Columbia University with Meyer Schapiro and architectural history classes with James Marston Fitch.

Looking back on the heyday of the New York School, Leedy recalls: "I got to know de Kooning and I met [Franz] Kline, [Jackson] Pollock, Phil Guston, Grace Hartigan and Joan Mitchell. But there was another gentleman who meant much more: Benjamin Benno, the painter. We were philosophical friends. He had been in Paris and had autographed letters to him from Picasso and Matisse. Benno was the greatest teacher I ever had who never taught formally. He created his own group of friends in New York and I can't emphasize strongly enough how much he affected me. He would fast for days at a time and then become terribly prolific in the studio. I really related to that.

"As for de Kooning, he had just moved into his black-and-white street, or streetscape style, and had pushed a piece of newspaper right onto a canvas and left it there! It seemed a pre-Pop-art kind of thing to do, in retrospect. It had a big impact on me. You could use mixed media—even in clay. You didn't have to be truthful to materials. And it helped me clarify that the object was more important than its use. The act of doing it was more important than how it was used."[2]

With his evenings spent downtown and his days uptown at Columbia, Leedy commuted between the distant past and the urgent present of New York in the 1950s. He became fascinated with two aspects of Chinese art which, combined with Action Painting, were major influences on his oeuvre: the ancient black pottery culture (ca. 2500 B.C.) and Shang-period bronzes with their tripod legs. Thus his covered jars and expressionist plates from 1955 onward mix the bright spattered color of the New York School with the blackened surface and blunt, hand-built modeling of the ancient Chinese pieces. His triple-legged teapots employ the curved supports common to Chinese bronzes.

Leaving Columbia, Leedy embarked on his M.F.A. at Southern Illinois University, Carbondale, in the fall of 1957, and at the same time, he undertook the university's one-year degree program in art restoration. While there, he found a mentor in the visionary architect and philosopher R. Buckminster Fuller. By the end of the academic year Leedy received both his M.F.A. and an M.S. in art restoration. He set off for Montana briefly (where he met Rudy Autio for the first time) before spending six weeks in the graduate program in art history at Ohio State University (meeting Howard Kottler), and then returning to New York for the balance of the summer.

In the fall of 1958, he accepted a teaching fellowship at Michigan State University, East Lansing, and began another master's program, this time in art history, under Martin Soria. It was significant for Leedy's subsequent art, that in his Michigan State thesis he attempted to prove links between the arts of indigenous Siberian tribes and of North, Central and South American peoples, based on a theory of Siberian migrations through Alaska and southward. Leedy's universalizing and synthesizing tendency, coupled with the preoccupation with primeval myth of some New York School members—in particular Mark Rothko, Barnett Newman and William Baziotes—would lead his own work to a fusion of ancient and 20th-century art that I call Prehistoric Modern.

For the academic year 1959–60, Leedy accepted a position at Northern State College in Aberdeen, South Dakota. However, thanks to his contacts in Montana, a better job materialized. Leaving South Dakota behind, Leedy went to Missoula to become professor of art history and studio art at the University of Montana. He had come home.

The period Leedy spent with Autio and Voulkos in Montana, from 1959 to 1964, was formative and influential—for all three. Though Voulkos had moved to Los Angeles in 1954, he made frequent and extended visits back to Montana to see his mother—and to keep in touch with Autio. This is when Voulkos met Leedy, too. Contrary to what is generally thought, Autio's and Voulkos's familiarity with advanced, or modernist art was limited. Voulkos did not see major examples until his first trips to New York and Los Angeles in 1953 and 1954.[3] Autio is on record as not having seen Abstract Expressionist paintings until his visit to the 1962 Seattle World's Fair.[4]

Leedy brought to them thick paint surfaces and shaped canvases. Large bulky works, these paintings drew from New York School material indulgences, yet retained remnants of figures. In return, as Leedy has written, Autio and Voulkos "gave to me the total acceptance of clay as on completely the same level as painting and sculpture. . . . Because of their geographical isolation, they didn't have as rigid a view, or were concerned or conscious of the fact that there was a separation. Pottery and sculpture were taught in the same room. That was a big surprise."[5] Voulkos also provided an example of exuberant hand-building in vertical forms, while Autio, with his more European sensibility, offered the painted image wrapping entirely around the vessel. As Leedy wrote later, Autio's "attitude clarified my own endeavors and had a monumental impact on me. Only then did I know that my torn and ripped pots of the early 50s sculpture."[6]

With his scholar's grasp of ancient pottery forms, Leedy affirmed the historical legitimacy of the container status of their pots and, in Autio's case especially, Leedy brought first-hand the chromatic abandon and mark-making proclivities of the New York School painters. In a review of Leedy's work in 1981, Autio recalls Leedy's years in Montana: "Abstract Expressionism was the strongest influence then, and much evidence of these roots is still seen in the directness of process and fluidity of clay, with a fresh injection of spirit and maturity."[7]

So strong and individual were the three talents, that each developed into a giant in his own right after the halcyon Montana years. With Voulkos now in Berkeley and Autio ensconced in Missoula, Leedy left town in 1964 after a figurative painting of his, *Birth*, in a university art exhibition was censored. Leedy found a more liberal environment at the Kansas City Art Institute, where he was invited to become professor of sculpture in 1964. He has lived in Kansas City ever since, except for sojourns in Japan and New Zealand, and, in 1982, a visit to Finland with Autio and Voulkos, where they were hailed as founding geniuses of postwar American ceramics.

In Kansas City Leedy moved beyond his affinity for Chinese black pottery and Shang bronzes and into a darker realm of shamanistic effigies, horses and ritual platters. He has created objects for an ancient Leedy-land, in which bright colors, sparingly employed, drip from rough slabs or join trails of gold luster on brooding brown surfaces. Leedy's works masquerade as ancient artifacts—their refreshing small scale is another quality setting them apart from the work of Voulkos and Autio. Writing on Leedy's sculpture, *Kansas City Star* critic Donald Hoffmann refers to a "relaxed and rumpled feeling" and "irrepressible energy." He rightly argues that Leedy "condenses color and a sense of comic energy into an extraordinarily intense experience."[8]

Vessel with Hat, 1980, is the quintessential Leedy sculpture. Whereas Leedy early on revived ancient Chinese clay and bronze vessel forms, and more recent works revert to the flat canvas-like surface of his Abstract Expressionist paintings or are taller tripod forms, the middle years, 1972–82, brought forth abstracted figures, up to four feet high, which recall ominous guardians or sentinels. *Vessel with Hat* suggests an archaic idol. The exquisitely modulated firing of the stoneware surface is punctuated by black and brown strokes across its "chest."

In his insightful essay on Leedy's sculpture (part of which was published in *Ceramics Monthly*), the critic Michael Cadieux points out that as "the receptacle relinquishes its functional utility . . . the primordial impulses of grasping, holding, tearing, and shaping maintain precedence over the eyes as the sensuous link to the essence of the work."[9] This touches on the doomed-culture, preconscious aspect Leedy evokes through the figures, how he creates anew relics of a dead civilization that remind us of our imminent mortality and that of our culture.

Discussing *Whinny*, 1981, Cadieux distills exactly the sobering, apocalyptic dimension of the artist's achievement: "Perhaps Leedy is directly confronting these instinctual darker forces by materializing them in totem-animistic form. In addition some of them appear to be decaying or collapsing in on themselves, perhaps subject to a disjunctive or regressive force, a prelude to death."[10] It is this inner collapse of forms and the "sense of regressive natural force" that ultimately remove Leedy from the worn-out idealism or utopianism of modernist art and thrust him into the current uncertainty of our postmodern condition with its feeling for the fragmentary, the entropic and the discontinuous.

With color fainter than ever before and the return to a blasted-out sense of firing, Leedy's raku slabs seem to be remnants found in the aftermath of nuclear war. In their allusion to the Japanese example of raku and their imperfect shapes, these works bring Leedy's art full circle from his first outdoor experiments in the backyard in Virginia many years ago. They unite the automatist, chance operations of Abstract Expressionism to the deeper sense of art history Leedy has always maintained, and which he consciously typifies. In this way, Leedy's art links us to our prehistoric past through fire and simultaneously reminds us that the factor of such a reunion is the interaction of a critical mind and the human hand.

RICK DILLINGHAM AND
THE REPARATIVE DRIVE

> We are intact only in so far as our objects are intact. Art of whatever
> kind bears witness to intact objects even when the subject-matter
> is disintegration. Whatever the form of transcript, the original
> conservation or restoration is of the mother's body.
>
> —Adrian Stokes[1]

Rick Dillingham is an artist of challenging character although his
work has been widely underrated and misunderstood. He has been
working steadily as an artist for many years. Included in many major
craft art exhibitions and cited in several recent historical texts about
ceramics, his work nevertheless remains largely unexamined for its
implied meaning or deeper content. Part of this is due to his emerging
status as an artist; not enough art critics know about his work. Part
of it is due to a continually reiterated explanation about the origins of
his work; he is a leading authority on and dealer in Southwest Native American pottery. An early job restoring pottery in a museum is
swallowed whole as an explanation for why his current work appears
as it does. And another part (as if our understanding of him, too, has
grown in bits and pieces like his work) is due to his own ambivalence
toward such sources, processes and results.

What is required in order to place him in context is a brief review of
the heretofore largely mystifying explanations of his work, an even
briefer examination of his own confusing intentional statements, and
a fresh, non-historical explanation of why his art looks as it does. Psy-
choanalytic theory, chiefly certain ideas of British theorists Adrian
Stokes, Melanie Klein, and Hanna Segal, holds the key to unlocking
the true mystery of Dillingham's pots. In its application, as we shall
see, a basis for understanding the complexities and seeming contra-
dictions evident in his pots will be gained.

Too much emphasis has been placed on the influence of Dillingham's
museum-conservator work on Anasazi and other examples of Southwest Indian pottery. As author, curator, conservator, and connoisseur,
Dillingham's contributions have been significant but they threaten to
overwhelm the recognition of his own artistic achievement. When the
artist acts as dealer, as Dillingham does with his Mudd-Carr Gallery
in Santa Fe, he always runs the risk of confusing the issues. Still,
the bare bones facts of his background have taken the place of more
substantive efforts to appreciate his art.

Rick Dillingham:
Round Vessel, 1987,
raku-fired glazed
earthenware,
9 x 9 1/2" dia. Stephen
and Pamela Hootkin
Collection, New York.
Photo: Noel Allum

The two standard texts to have emerged on American ceramics during the 1980s, Elaine Levin[2] and Garth Clark[3], are, as is becoming increasingly the case, disappointing with regard to currently minor figures like Dillingham. Although she places him prominently in her section of low-fire vessels, Levin merely rehashes biographical information about his volunteer tenure at the University of New Mexico Maxwell Museum of Anthropology:

> Using one of his own broken vessels, Dillingham accented these lines with glue which had been dyed black. Experiments with shards refired and restored developed into a study of random surface patterns. The subtle interaction of clay shards and fire-flashed marks on Dillingham's early work changed in the late seventies when he added glittering enamels, gold leaf and lusters, a sophisticated contrast to the primitive quality of a smoke-blackened surface.[4]

Content with that concise and compressed summation, Levin leaves it at that.

Even less satisfying, Clark carefully rehearses the craft process of Dillingham's pots in excruciating detail, as if this were sufficient attention from a "leading" ceramics critic:

> Breaks are carefully "drawn" into the pot before firing...the act of reassembling the pot from a number of pieces allows a variety

of discrete elements on which to paint. Each shard is treated separately and painted with line and pattern out of a palette that is a mixture of bright primary colors and earthy hues. . . . When they are reassembled, there is a compositional unity that places Dillingham's surface painting among the most complex and sophisticated work of this type in contemporary ceramics.[5]

Approval, validation and acceptance are Clark's critical tools of empowerment but rarely has he ventured into realms of analysis, content, meaning or theory, all the areas in which the criticism of American ceramics—and Rick Dillingham—is sorely in need. Clark's entry on Dillingham's *Vase* (1981) in *American Ceramics: The Collection of Everson Museum of Art* is comparably terse and reiterative.

Without examining in depth the existing scant literature on Dillingham, two examples are worth singling out to set the stage for a more daring approach. In a discussion of his premature 1984 retrospective at St. John's College (New Mexico), Deborah Phillips proposed a modernist/formalist template to use in evaluating Dillingham. This was a good start. Although she alludes to the "Anasazi artifacts" they echo, she also revealed the artist's debt to abstract painting of the late 1970s and early 1980s as a source for his surface decoration and patterning, as well as insisting that "African, Egyptian, Greek and Spanish" forms reverberate throughout his early oeuvre. Speaking of the earliest, "quieter pots . . . in pink, gray, and tan," Phillips regrettably exacerbates the historicist mystification so prevalent by invoking "silent, totemic forms" which "seem to hold the secrets of centuries past in their hollow interiors."[6]

Further intensifying the miasma of mysticism now surrounding Dillingham, Jan Adlmann's 1990 catalog essay for his Linda Durham Gallery exhibition in Santa Fe last summer presents the most acute and confusing case yet for an understanding of Dillingham in "madly contradictory" terms redolent of promotion, validation, and, once again, ancient pre-Columbian history. Now, Dillingham is a "master of earthenware":

> A palpable sphere of silence seems to envelop each [object]...casting a spell of sorts; as happens with great vessels of . . . the ancient Orient, the Aegean, or the American Southwest.[7]

Adlmann does touch one astute note, that "fractured vessels of Dillingham are 'about' the process of making—and remaking—earthenware," but fails to pursue this any further. As we shall see, the "process of making—and remaking—earthenware" is a basic level of content in Dillingham's art but one that must be transcended or understood in other, more psychological terms.

JOURNEY TOWARD DESTRUCTION

Another way of describing Dillingham's art is as a cycle of destruction and repair. Its assembly, disassembly and reconstruction are more to the point when seeking keys beyond the historic. As Adlmann pointed out, the process is important. What most writers have overlooked, however, are the thoughts we might have as we inspect the final results, the restored, the repaired. One works backward in time, re-imagining the initial breakage, its specific circumstances; the reassembly of the shards; and the decoration and completion of the final object. If process is paramount to the content of Dillingham's art, then new devices for interpreting the process must be found.

An early vase included in Dillingham's 1984 retrospective provides a key. With a long neck and two bulbous protuberances, the vase has a decidedly erotic, feminine impact. Like the sculpture of Louise Bourgeois, it contains troubling yet satisfying psychological implications. What are the two plump forms? A double Adam's apple? Vertical breasts? In their very ambiguity, they foretell a future relation to such forms.

Like much other American ceramic vessel sculpture of the 1970s, Dillingham's forms had strong ceremonial and ritual associations. Curved and arching handles accompanied some of the pots. Bone-like side handles complemented others. Far more revealing, the cone forms which had emerged by 1979 and were smoke-fired, also may be seen as stylized, upright breasts. Within a few years, in works like *January 1982–2*, the conical shapes were crisscrossed with black intersecting lines which acted as grid-like supports for the broken parts. Seemingly whole and constructed rather than broken because of their full base and upper point or "nipple," these works built upon the double-rounded vase's physical and anatomical qualities.

When one inspects the step-by-step process of Dillingham more closely, a primal or unconscious strategy is unwittingly revealed. The entire space of activity parallels a destructive/creative cycle which has interested the British wing of psychoanalysts like Melanie Klein and her followers, art critics Adrian Stokes and Peter Fuller, and another psychiatrist, Hanna Segal. They argue that the direction taken by the creative artist resembles an infant's early love/hate relationship to its mother—and her breast. Stokes argues that the rebuilding or restoration process in creativity "remains a paramount function in art."

What is being restored or reconstituted? The "object" in the form of the mother. Drawing upon Fuller's summary of Klein's ideas in his book *Art and Psychoanalysis*, one could posit the hand-building, slip application, and bisque-firing of Dillingham's early stages of construction as analogies to the infant's first warm and cuddling relationship to the mother. The nourishment of the breast creates a bond between mother and child which falsely lulls the baby into thinking he is still part of mother.

The traumatic revelation that, after breast-feeding time, mother goes away unleashes an angry and destructive phase in the infant's development as he realizes that mother is an "object," a separate being and that he is, too. Screaming, kicking, crying and hitting might be the Kleinian parallels for Dillingham's next steps: tapping the bisque-fired pot near the rim on a hardwood board to begin the breaks which result in dispersed cracks that are "pulled apart with a controlled randomness."[8]

RETURN TO THE MOTHER

As Baby grows and becomes used to the routine of feeding and separation, he becomes used to seeing things in parts and, alternately, aware of the "whole" of his reunion with mother. Hanna Segal wrote:

> . . . the infant lives in a world of part objects: the mother's breast, eyes, holding arms. . . . The very young infant always sways between states of blissful satisfaction. . . and states of hatred.[9]

Once broken apart, Dillingham painstakingly glazes each piece separately. Some pots are largely homogeneous surfaces, some are disjointed color schemes, and some pit geometric, angular patterns against circular and spiral ones. Here we may imagine the beginning of the reparative drive, the other half of the destructive/constructive Kleinian cycle.

Next, the glazed shards are refired, still separate or "wounded" from their gentle tap of the hammer. After the firing, they are cleaned and cooled before metallic silver, copper, or gold leaf might be added.

The baby's recognition (if so conscious a term may be applied to such an early learning stage) gradually accepts his and mother's connected separateness and further fuels a sense of frustrated sadness, the hypothetical phase in Dillingham's case, when the broken parts are as unyet reassembled.

It is after this awareness that the "reparative impulses" are begun, "an overwhelming desire that what has been destroyed must be recreated, reconstituted and regained."[10] The artist's unconscious memory of this experience is among the most powerful impetuses to creativity that can be experienced.

When Dillingham next begins reassembling the refired shards into whole pots, this stage is underway. Once the surfaces are sealed, the process of making the pots is complete but the psychological journey from destruction to re-association with the mother is repeated over and over, renewed again with the making of each pot, becoming profoundly buried within the creative mind.

In the later work, color has been the other healing, ameliorative element at work repairing the breakage. Partially accentuating the breaks at first, it has served to conceal them with bright, sunny patterns. Dillingham skillfully juxtaposes earthy tones with the garish metallic leaf so that each pot is not confined to any one single mood. When the colors are excessively cheerful, one suspects that they are concealing the record of destruction each piece embodies. Color, too, then acts as part of the reparative drive. Rather than single moods, the vessels now resist the pat historicization of the quick-look critics and inhabit a completely individuated universe. Every bit as all-encompassing a world as the baby in the crib's, Dillingham's created universe ultimately repels most enforcements of exterior cultural or art-historical analogies, so deep is its subjective origins.

The persistent globular forms, flattened saucers, and peaked cones are abstracted breasts if one adopts my Kleinian analysis. But apart from such a proposal, they retain a convincing sensuality and startling originality entirely independent of criticism. It is a tribute to the intuitive, unsystematic impulses inherent in Rick Dillingham's creative identity that such works of art have both concealed and revealed their potential for deep meaning.

MICHAEL LUCERO DISCOVERS AMERICA

The new ceramic sculptures of Michael Lucero are his intervention in the past, his rescuing of pre-European civilization from the onslaught of the Christopher Columbus quincentenary. Ironically, his family background is Hispanic-American with relatives having settled in New Mexico in the early 17th century.

Michael Lucero:
Untitled (Pre-Columbus Series), 1991, earthenware with glazes, 22 x 12 x 5 ½". Collection of Stephen and Pamela Hootkin, New York. Photo: Noel Allum

From the beginning, as in much ceramic sculpture, Lucero has created a unity between form and surface. The dazzling landscapes he paints onto the various forms are windows into a subconscious world of memory. The forms have developed from self-portraits, figures, animals, insects, hearts, and other anatomy. Taken together, form and surface comprise the departure-points for meaning in the work of the California native.

The *Pre-Columbus* series (1990–92) and *New World* series (1992) touch on a number of contemporary art issues: multiculturalism; appropriation; revisionist history; and the new materiality being intro-

duced into the art world by artists of craft background. By using the
Mesoamerican devotional forms, he has abruptly brought up to date
ancient forms which invoke a pre-European civilization and remind
us that the Americas' origins are steeped in native culture. By lifting
motifs from early Modern artists like Joan Miró and Sonia Delaunay,
he continues his strategy of accentuating the aspects of twentieth-
century art which lend themselves to his purpose: circular, involving
patterns which reinforce the curved ceramic form. By mixing and
matching older forms, modern art motifs, and contemporary imagery,
he revises revisionist history itself that recently has downgraded the
positive results of Columbus's journey; to Lucero, pre- and post-Columbus America form a seamless thread. And finally, by his delightful material overkill, pattern upon pattern, imagery piled on imagery,
he exemplifies the renewed materiality in contemporary sculpture
emphasizing the artist's hands-on activity, downplaying the cold con-
sumerist mentality of much eighties art.

Far from retro, craft art is in, a crossover from function to sculpture,
a blurring of function and figure, a challenge to the cold emptiness
late 1980s art which elevated mass media, photography, and consumerism to the status of grand theory and scolding concepts.[1] The
personal and the material were anathema to the neo-Calvinist taste-
makers of 1980s social and political art who saw every studio strategy
as subject to a politically correct litmus test.

Refusing to be swayed by such hostile pressures on handmade
achievement, Lucero has pursued his own subjective vision and material indulgence since the day he arrived in Manhattan in 1978. Widely exhibited in the U.S., Europe, and Mexico, he recommitted to clay
after a two-year hiatus (1987–89) working in bronze and the turning
to the tall assembled ceramic-segment *Totems* (1989–90). Never one
to shy away from the delicious dangers of complicated composition
or material overkill, Lucero practices an art of historical reference,
strong physical and tactile qualities, in short, a kind of sculpture
which refutes recent developments in favor of new directions which
are driven by his view of the world and by his chosen medium, white
earthenware clay.

Context rather than consumerism, clay rather than Plexiglas or Formica, passion rather than the overrated irony of the 1980s, these are
the forces at work in the recent sculptures. Since he works continuously in his Alphabet City/East Village studio in lower Manhattan,
ideas are discovered more through direct action on the ceramic material—handbuilding, throwing, glazing—instead of elaborately pre-
conceptualized PC strategies. This is the residue of Surrealism—im-

mediate unconscious "automatic" artmaking—and it is worth noting that Surrealism also has its Spanish roots in artists like Salvador Dalí and Joan Miró (the latter whom Lucero frequently "quotes").

Paradoxically, the subjective, stream-of-consciousness imagery is tempered by the extensive, step-by-step building, glazing, firing, and refiring processes inherent in ceramics. The final effect may be instantaneous and dazzling; its genesis can take days or weeks. The failure rate is high: breakage, accidents, temperamental kilns.

Our purpose here is not to rehash craft techniques but, before that is dismissed, Lucero received a young lion's share of acclaim from the craft world including a "Young Americans" show at the American Craft Museum in 1978 and their more recent "Aesthetic of Excess" exhibition curated by new ACM director Janet Kardon in 1990.[2]

More to the point, he is contributing to a discourse about the Hispanic presence in the Americas after 1492. Radically conflating in terra cotta the achievements of pre-existing native populations and later modern developments of artists like George E. Ohr, Joan Miró, and anonymous African-American slave potters, Lucero offers a uniting vision of multiculturalism blurring "la différence" and gathering together conflicting cultures in the haven of his art. At a time when certain ethnic community leaders are stressing separateness, a kind of new consensual de facto segregation, Lucero 's *Pre-Columbus* and *New World* series draw on the best of all heritages and blend them together without sacrificing their autonomous cultural individualities.

Thus, as seated figures from Olmec, Chimu, Mochica, and other pre-Latin American cultures are used as jumping-off points, the artist draws, paints, and glazes the surfaces of his freely adapted historical models in order to simultaneously accentuate their allusive historical references and negate our prior, stereotyped convictions about such art: somber, primitive, violent, backward.

Beyond merely revering the playful but often impassive or stolid poses and expressions of the Pre-Columbian originals, Lucero completely reinvents artifact as mirror of his own subjective memories. Though it would be possible to create an autobiographical iconography based on Lucero's own experiences by looking at all the surface imagery in his work, for our purposes it is more important to see such images as triggers to our own memories. Gazing onto a Lucero surface, the animals, landscapes, modern art fragments, and arcane symbols release the viewer into a free-floating world of three-dimensional reverie.

Nature, culture, and heritage are used as a palimpsest for excursions of fantasy, wit, and humor. Using contrasts of shiny and flat glazes (or glossy and matte, to use craft jargon), he sets up a textural tension on each piece that further confuses the viewer's expectations of flatness and depth. No stranger to illusion, another Surrealist trick, Lucero constantly undercuts the volumetric stability of each sculpture by painting them with landscapes that make us look through the piece as well as onto it.

This activity of gazing into and onto is our metaphorical re-experiencing of the discovery and exploration of the New World. Lucero's revision of the Columbus myth insists on our accepting the subsequent mélange of European and native cultures rather than fruitlessly regretting it or assigning 500-year-old blame. Just as each piece competes within itself for our attention, so the many cultures within the U.S. compete for recognition, status, acceptance, and—assimilation?

Delving back within recent ceramic history, one may tie Lucero's art to the exuberant humor of Robert Arneson, on the faculty at University of California-Davis while Lucero was there, and to the equally outrageous let-it-all-hang-out sensibility of his graduate school mentor at the University of Washington, Howard Kottler (1930–1989).[3] Both artists were responsible for raising the fine-art status of ceramic sculpture through their personal, not to say narcissistic, visions.

Before that, one could note a decorative arts precedent in an 1880 earthenware vase by Christopher Dresser in the Dorman Memorial Museum collection in Middlesbrough, England[4] that incorporates an incised Indian head on a Pre-Columbian style vessel with connected top handles. This piece also relates to the New World series, Lucero's excursions into "face jugs" made by anonymous plantation potters.

With some of Lucero's *Anthropomorphic Jug Forms* having African-American features, it is also important to note his Hispanicization of the form elsewhere. With its flat-topped hat, high cheekbones, and (smallpox?) pockmarked face, *Anthropomorphic Jug Form #2—New World* (1992) could be Peruvian or Mesoamerican in reference.

Through his symbolic repopulating the Americas before and after Columbus, Lucero is stressing the solidarity among enslaved native populations and enslaved plantation workers from West Africa. He is paying tribute to the crafts of both populations, indigenous peoples and exported peoples, both of whom reached high levels of cultural development before, during, and after periods of European oppression.

The cluttered, crowded quality of surface covering on the sculptures emerges out of our current polyglot, image-saturated society. Lucero includes supermarket bar codes, faces on faces, animal heads, explicit sexual parts, and references to other ceramic artists like the "mad potter of Biloxi," George E. Ohr (*Lady with Ohr Hair—Pre-Columbus*, 1991), passages from Miró paintings (*Miró Mother; Miró Man—Pre-Columbus*, 1991), or French Orphist painter Sonia Delaunay (*Seated Man with Balancing Vessel with Eye—Pre-Columbus*, 1992), another favorite artist. In the case of Delaunay, the bold utopianism of early Modernism is reduced to a pattern on clothing.

Throughout, Lucero conceives of sculptures as a union of painting and sculpture, something clay is uniquely suited to serve. Our spatial experience of the work demands circumambulation of the figures so that, for example, the "back" of *Lady with Ohr Hair* is just as interesting as the "front".

The recurrence of crying or shouting faces nestled in the flesh folds of the seated figures suggests bawling infants and, when Lucero moved on to the post-Discovery New World series, the first figures were indeed babies. Now, Lucero is recasting ethnic heritage even more radically, combining thrown jug forms (such as the slaves and early white Appalachian potters made) with vessels of varying sizes to form the baby's head, body, arms, and legs.

Anthropomorphic Vessel Form with Slippers—New World (1992) is a symbolic expression of how even figurative clay sculpture first proceeded from the making of humble useful pots.

The entire question of plain pottery's fine art status is under open discussion today with many vanguard writers like Rob Barnard and Kevin Hluch arguing for its equal place. Lucero addresses these trends by creating sculpture out of the very basis of all clay forms, the pot. Richly decorated and glazed repeatedly, he draws our attention to the parallel evolution of functional and devotional forms made of clay. That is to say, when we examine the world history of ceramics, it becomes clear that sculptural (devotional) and functional purposes occurred simultaneously. The open question will always be, "Was the clay religious figure made first in order to assure crop growth, or was the pot made first in order to contain the harvest of the crop?" In this sense, he is investigating the historical underpinnings of ceramic art more than any other sculptor at work today in the U.S.

Big Feet—New World (1992) and *Zoomorphic Bottle Form—New World* (1992) point toward even more imaginative facets of his theme: cultural coexistence in a society increasingly divided along ethnic lines. Oversize and clunky, *Big Feet* are covered with an extraordinary range of images, redolent of urban existence, ancient worlds, and contemporary reassessments of the human body. Always viewing the body as a sum of parts, Lucero has finally gotten around to addressing the pre-requisite for any travel or exploration, feet. Plopping themselves down on the beach, so to speak, they are not only announcing the arrival of European Man but, typically with Lucero, conflating historical time, pre- and post-Columbus, into the unified time of the artwork.

Bottle Form is haunting, disconcerting, and prophetic. The eyes of Christopher Columbus are gazing at the New World. With the shape of tiny dog for a body, a graceful Scandinavian-style vase for a head, and a curled blue form for a tail, *Bottle Form* is human and animal, ancient and modern-looking, functional and sculptural. Further conflating his plea for cultures to survive together 500 years after the Columbian intervention, Lucero now proposes interspecies dependency, the bonds between humans and animals.

Deeply humanistic, entrenched in the culture of the handmade object while addressing the contemporary art world, Michael Lucero's work not only raises issues of current social and historical significance. *Pre-Columbus* and *New World* are potential paragons of how ideas and materials may be combined without sacrificing the sanctity of either. Despite their pictoriality, the three-dimensionality of sculpture is reasserted in these works and, in the process, our ways of looking at the world—and at art—are challenged, disoriented, and renewed.

Viola Frey: *Family Portrait,* 1985, ceramic and glazes, 84 x 70 x 29 1/2". Photo: Courtesy of Rena Bransten Gallery, San Francisco.

VIOLA FREY'S FAMILY PLOT
(For V. and V.)

> The family is the first grouping...
> The mother-figure becomes reduplicated.

> —D.W. Winnicott[1]

The ceramic sculptor Viola Frey (1934–2004) has gone to great lengths to create figures of anonymous character, intimidating physical scale, and seemingly impersonal gazes. Now averaging nine feet high, the standing men and women have been discussed by critics as representatives of our society, as blown-up figurines influenced by her frequent flea market scavenging,[2] as self-portraits[3] and even as "linguistic meta-structures."[4]

Only Susan C. Larsen and Cheryl White have hinted at the most fruitful path to understanding the art of the Oakland, California artist: approximating psychological encounters between individuals as a result of scale discrepancy between the object and the viewer. As Larsen states:

> drawn into the psychological orbit of these massive figures, the viewer experiences an odd feeling of familiarity while also becoming aware of the heavy textures and unnatural coloring of the figures. . . .[5]

Getting closer to the hidden core of meaning in Frey—parent-child relationships—she adds:

> We gladly grant their heroic scale but
> find in their anti-heroic emotional
> life an unsettling resemblance to our
> own half-hidden fears and inadequacies.[6]

The bubbling anger below the surface of jarring primary colors, the top-heavy broad-shouldered men, the reversal of scale in the smaller groupings, all these become signs pointing toward a theory of meaning which draws upon the British school of object relations psychoanalysis, originally formulated by Melanie Klein and D. W. Winnicott. These are ideas about child development which explain the mystery, resentment and guilt between small children and their parents. As Cheryl White implies:

> Frey's experiments with formal elements test the effects of
> proportion, color, and distortion on the psychological
> engagement of these figures.[7]

Indeed, it is precisely the psychological engagement between Frey's sculptures and her audience of viewers that concerns us here. It is my contention that the parent-child scale disparity—Mommy is big; I am small—is repeated over and over in an obsessive but knowing ritual of revenge, atonement, and ultimately a reversal of power relationships between parent and child, viewer and sculpture, object and artist.

As works of art, as effigies, these curiously inert sculptures both re-enact a family plot of aggression and appeasement and turn it to a reassuring end: though the viewer is tinier, temporarily humiliated, he or she eventually "towers" over the sculpture as surrogate maker, spectator, and determiner of meaning for these "giant strangers," as White describes them.[8]

Beginning with the taller figures in 1983, Frey nonetheless also works in smaller sizes including some tabletop bronze figure group-ings. The seemingly stark disparity between very big and small makes sense when seen in the light of object relations theory.

To the infant, the mother's breast is the first object. Gradually sepa-rated and made aware of his or her separate physical status as a human being (and another object), the baby then "reduplicates" the mother figure in other relationships with people including the father, "someone who can be feared and hated and loved and respected."[9]

The toy or doll can become what Winnicott calls "the transitional ob-ject" and, seen this way, Frey's smaller works function as intermedi-aries between the sense of loss of mother's breast and the subsequent power contained in the satisfaction of making other objects, the "giant strangers." According to Winnicott:

> If the infant could speak, the claim could be, "This object is part of external reality and I created it."[10]

If as Winnicott holds, "the transitional object is the first symbol,"[11] Vi-ola Frey's smaller individual figures and earlier piled-on assemblages of cast flea market finds also merit greater interpretive scrutiny than heretofore allowed.

For our purposes, though, the tall figures may be read as a later phase of object relations, what happens when a baby becomes an art-ist. After years of acquired technical prowess, advanced instruction (under no less than Mark Rothko at Tulane U.), and an insistent vi-sion that has remained stubbornly unique and strangely intractable, Viola Frey confirms English child development theory. Instead of the doll easing the pain of childhood, her big mothers, fathers, and grand-mothers repay with a vengeance the parental generation which, in any family, may treat the child as an object rather than as a person.

Building up, designing, hollowing out (with assistance) the additive stacked clay sections, Frey re-enacts the "reparative drive," Klein's and Hanna Segal's concept of how the infant atones for temper tantrums after reunited with a parent.[12] Bit by bit, little by little, a gift is made to express love and attain approval. In a startling reversal, the artist "gives birth" to parents, objects which are generalized images of families.

Not the Bride of Frankenstein, but rather Dr. Frankenstein himself, Frey has gleefully made her golem out of clay, not robots, scarecrows, or statues, but animated beings made alive by gesture, posture, and the manic patterning and modeling of color. Although Jean Dubuffet may have been an early paradigm for her painted figurative sculpture, Frey has gone beyond Dubuffet while retaining his anti-art aggression. Fernando Botero might be another analogy. Improbably obese, Botero's figures are also ridiculed, often collapsing into cartoon status. Benign rather than aggressive, though, Botero's sculpture is unthreatening, more the focus of amused condescension than fear or revenge.

Generalized into family-member types so the viewer may also undergo the result of the "reparative drive," Frey's sculptures become the putative subjects of a playwright, a Gothic novelist, and a choreographer as well. Whether assembled together in a museum or gallery, or on their own at home, the gingham-dressed women, blue-suited men and, recently, reclining nudes, confront the viewer in a garish blaze of orange and blue. As in a family, trauma-fraught interactions can occur between the figures without words.

With mother's or father's gaze pointed straight ahead away from us, any intimate reunion is impossible. The viewer is shrunk to the status of the eternally ignored or neglected child. Looking upward, we find ourselves pleading and penitent observers alternately reminded of how grownups can be oblivious of children and how children can "get back" by easily igniting the creative imagination and fantasies of escape and retribution.

Granny can thus be belittled, too, with her silly print dress, absurdly tilted hat (*Largest Grandmother*, 1987), and absent-minded glare. And Mommy rejects the reparative cuddle with her raised yellow hands (*Woman in Blue and Yellow*, 1983). And even Daddy, ever disapproving with arms akimbo (*Mean Man*, 1986), can forever be locked into a frozen state of stupid male aggression.

It is part of the greatness of Viola Frey's art that her figures are constantly re-enacting primal dramas of family conflict. Psychological readings of her work need not obtrude other levels of meaning but, when applied, they reveal more clearly what Larsen discussed as "an unsettling resemblance to our half-hidden fears and inadequacies."[13]

The revenging power of the child might also be seen in the figure groups, often four-to-five-feet high. In *Roman Market Woman and Big Hand* (1988), business-suited Daddy is perpetually in danger beneath the fingertips of a giant red hand upon which is a nude sup-plicating figure. With the prospect of emotional support and physical cuddling always out of reach, Daddy is ridiculed and belittled over and over again. Behind him, the "market woman" is unaware of his dilemma. Seen as a domestic melodrama by Tennessee Frey (starring Anna Magnani?), this sculpture depicts a truly dysfunctional family. Any ameliorating qualities, like the comforting big breasts of Gaston Lachaise's women, are ruled out in favor of Frey's cold, self-centered mothers. Even the Venus sculptures of Jim Dine seem more inviting even though they are sometimes over 20 feet tall.

Made in an age when one in two children are raised in single-parent families, the art of Viola Frey raises significant social issues as well and it is on this level that her art may appeal to future generations. The family as we know it may disappear and the superior/inferior scale relationships which I have proposed as a metaphor for parent-child relations may devolve to symbols of social power and authority.

Kneeling Man with Hammer (1991–92) and *World Man* (1993), in this sense, may be read as the American Worker and the American Au-thority Figure—President Clinton. With his spiky grey hair and blue suit with padded shoulders, *World Man*, like President Clinton, ap-pears at a loss when staring at the enormity of problems before him. Instead of "putting the fat back on space," as Bill Berkson suggested Frey is doing,[14] *World Man* seems slimmed down, perplexed but ready for the giant tasks at hand.

Characters in Frey's cinematic family plot, the sculptures remain am-biguous, enigmatic, and provocative. After our humiliation as view-ers, intimidated by their cold scale and resistance to warmth despite the tactile appeal of the pitted glaze, we, too, undergo a reparative drive, piecing together our experiences of the artist's achievements. After forgiving her repetitive, impersonal presents to the world, one can only "repair" to a state of gratitude.

As Winnicott concludes "The Child in the Family Group," a 1966 ad-dress to the British Nursery School Association:

> The family leads on to all manner of groupings, . . . that get wider and wider until they reach the size of the local society and society in general.[15]

Successfully evoking many levels of psychological development—infant, toddler, child, adult, parent—the art of Viola Frey challenges us to contemplate both our own family dramas and, more significantly, our relations to the greater world of objects, society as a whole.

Doug Jeck: *Sculpture*, 1994, ceramic and mixed media, 70 x 20 x 13".
Private collection. Photo: Mark Van S.

DOUG JECK:
MONUMENTS TO UNCERTAINTY

Since the death of Robert Arneson, the fate of figurative ceramic sculpture has been in limbo. True, plenty of candidates for succession abound. Viola Frey and Michael Lucero continue to sustain impressive achievements. Less well known, Eva Stettner and Judy Moonelis propose darker visions. Overlooked until recently, Doug Jeck shows signs of not necessarily assuming Arneson's mantle but of pushing figurative ceramic sculpture in an entirely different direction: realism, fragmentation, dismemberment, and defeat followed by a poignant and unsentimental optimism.

The Florida-born artist is now professor of art at University of Washington. Educated in Tennessee and at the School of the Art Institute of Chicago, Jeck is the first important postwar American ceramic sculptor not to have emerged from the West Coast. The difference is striking. Forget the humor and kitsch of Funk art, the beloved clay liberation movement of the 1960s so dear to the Arnesonites. Try the cold embattled condition of men in a postfeminist world, and add a fantastic modeling ability that matches—and explodes—the western European sculpture tradition from the archaic Greeks onward.

Jeck is abetting tradition, subverting it, and mending it at the same time. In a 1995 survey at William Traver Gallery in Seattle, viewers were astounded by the damaged realism of his handbuilt figures and the attendant undercutting of conditioned West Coast expectations for figurative sculpture. For once, Surrealism plays no part in this chapter of American clay sculpture.

Instead, the entire history of Western sculpture is invoked, questioned, and supplemented. While his earliest critics strove to distance him from the tacky illusionism of Duane Hanson and John De Andrea,[1],[2] realism per se has never been a goal for Jeck. As the work confirmed, the cultural tradition of male figure sculpture is under the gun here. With their poses alluding to Greek and Roman statuary, Jeck lops off arms and hands, attaches the bodies to freestanding tree stumps, and then uses the plinth or support convention to play with the ideas of how we perceive heroic sculpture.

In the process, we question how that entire tradition has been used to instill socially conditioned responses to gender, politics, power and history. Late in the twentieth century, far from being terminally exhausted and emasculated by feminist art historians, the male as subject was being reinvigorated by Jeck, dusted off and reclaimed without apology.

Portraiture or individuation are not the point. Although the heads seem to depict particular beings, no models are used, nor is there any of the sense that the heroic tradition uses the male nude as a means of reinforcing patriarchal power. Far from it, one cannot imagine these figures summoning anyone to action, or hurting anyone, let alone being welcomed into other (right) wings of realistic sculpture, say the bronzes of Seward Johnson or Frederick Hartt. The blank anonymity of George Segal might be closer but, because Jeck's are made of clay, his figures exert a substantial and absorbing material presence in their pale coloring, surface variety, and constructed hollowness.

At the other pictorial extreme, Frey's reclining male nudes are giant, if vulnerable, color cartoons. While Jeck shrinks the size to deny grandiosity of purpose, Frey balloons up her men, rendering them even more naked, targets of assault or ridicule. Both artists are commenting on the gap between the postures of masculinity and the reality of uncertainty and doubt felt by many men today.

Jeck's earliest works, like the six-figure tableau executed for his master's thesis in Chicago, played up authenticity, skin color, and lifelike qualities. By 1995, the works have been drained of most life thanks to the extraordinarily morbid gray skin tones. With each figure composed of mismatched body parts, any sense of traditional anatomical verisimilitude is impossible. No one is ever going to do a double take over a Doug Jeck sculpture.

Mocking marmoreal paradigms, Jeck uses clay to remind us, as one critic pointed out, of the body's ties to earth, the shared link between humanity and dirt.[3] If there is any illusionism, it is a mock-archeological specimen appearance. As if just dug up, the figures comprise an ancient world of their own. What culture, what artisans, what craftsmen made these strange beings? Look a little closer, however, and the trick is subsumed within a growing awareness of their complex construction. Even the *Venus de Milo* received proposals for prosthetic limbs or "improvements" in the nineteenth century after her discovery but Jeck's sculpture look so "repaired" that one wonders where the "original" ended up.

Precisely. If there is no "original," then there is no heroic paradigm and, thus, all such efforts to imply one are completely social (and studio) interventions. Extrapolate that to a revised notion of masculinity—fabricated, compartmentalized, battered, yet bizarrely optimistic—and you arrive at one corner of meaning in Jeck.

The fragility and breakability of clay could not be more perfect foils to such a view and Jeck demonstrates an astonishing virtuosity at stretching the materials' limits to serve this purpose. By joining body fragments to heads that seem life-like, the artist stresses how men's identities are not the result of monolithic corporeal confidence (expressed in Nazi sculptor Arno Breker or Vichy carver Aristide Maillol) but rather of an accrual of painful experience, setbacks, learning, and a determination to go on anyway. In the age of AIDS, no one has a monopoly on suffering and a consciousness of mortality.

Jeck's project is vast. First, he has broken with the Arnesonian pop humor that strangled American clay sculpture for so long while siding with Arneson's extraordinary narcissism. As a result, all of a sudden, the wrecked Egyptoid relics of Stephen De Staebler look a lot more prophetic: segmented, gray, morbid and undaunted (Could De Staebler be Arneson's heir as the greatest living American clay sculptor?).

Next, he is detonating the tradition of public statuary and its political use. For example, *Stopping Man* (1993) stands on only one foot; some pose of power! *Exponent* (1994) not only misses arms and a leg, it is reduced to resting upon a post.

Thirdly, Jeck has rescued the male figure as an object of devotion and potentially serious subject after the demonization of masculinity by feminist art historians throughout the 1970s and 1980s. Sharing their disenchantment with patriarchal control exuded by classical figure sculpture, Jeck still refuses to jettison the male as a symbol and image in art.

Unlike Judy Moonelis, he has not resorted to androgyny but held fast to a gender-specific identity at once recognizable and discussable. The genitalia alone in his sculptures are often an obsessive focus of carving. One is not encouraged to generalize all humanity from a headless and limbless torso (à la Moonelis) but rather is forced to realize that gender identity can reposition the male—and male-imaged sculpture—in a worthwhile setting open to examination and grief.

The reception history of Jeck's sculptures often says more about each critic than about his art. Many of the same sculptures elicit widely differing reactions from "passionate"[4] to "clinical." Women critics like Catherine Fox of the *Atlanta Journal and Constitution* and Regina Hackett of the *Seattle Post-Intelligencer* have taken projective, empathetic approaches with the former ascribing "a life within" expressed by the "posture, facial expression . . . and . . . the disposition of the hands." Hackett reads in "pomposity" when looking at the facial expression in *Mith* (1995), adding that the reassembled body parts seem "remade with indifference or even malice." Reviewing the range of responses, it is easy to see how such enigmatic art could stimulate contradictory readings like Hackett's.

Laura Lieberman, writing in *American Ceramics*, keyed in on how "acknowledgment of artifice is central to the emotional force of Jeck's aesthetic vision."

Among men, Atlanta art critic David Ribar extrapolates from "the lone male as a symbol for the labyrinthine passions of human nature," and compares Jeck's work to late nineteenth-century American marble sculpture of Hiram Powers and Randolph Rogers. He could have added America's first marble sculptor, ex-tombstone carver James Frazee. Ribar notes how "the indignities of the body have seldom been so ruthlessly scrutinized."

In conclusion, it appears that Jeck's art is indeterminate enough to evoke many eloquent reactions yet specific enough to raise issues commonly agreed upon: meticulous fabrication, exquisite modeling ability, rejection of overt humor and popular culture as content, and an examination of male identity and masculinity as constructions in and of themselves rather than universal or timeless qualities.

Down deep, at their base, lies one final aspect, how Jeck manipulates the plinth, pedestal, or support. Each is completely different. *Ornament* (1995) is an armless and legless youth seated on an upright wooden crate-like form. *Sculpture* (1994) rests on two bases, a smaller square perched above a rectangular base. *Archaism* (1993) stands atop three stacked bases. *Stopping Man* (1993) ludicrously raises one amputated leg while resting the other on three graduated-size low supports. *Blind Man* (1993) plays with the convention cruelly. The figure stands on two separate blocks near a third above a long rectangle supporting all. We know the next step will be a disaster.

What Jeck's next step will be is eagerly awaited. The female figure? A Laocöon grouping? Just torsos or heads? Whatever his future critics may say, the use of clay is crucial to his overall meaning. Its plasticity, earthiness, potential for realism and illusion, and its status as a downbeat stand-in for marble all stand firm. With the distant tie of narrative linking him to West Coast achievements, Jeck has added another brick, albeit moldy and suspiciously cracked, to the house of American ceramics.

RYOJI KOIE: NEW CONTEXTS

Of the many Japanese ceramics artists working today, Ryoji Koie is the one who occupies the most critical interface with contemporary art. His five visits to Seattle in 1999 put in motion a body of work that merits comparison to other international artists and to Pacific Northwest artists who have drawn inspiration from Japanese art.

Koie's response to non-Japanese art has always been a two-way street, reinforcing his own vision and background, which dates from the 1960s and 1970s, an exciting period in postwar Japanese art, and taking into consideration those works by American and European artists that challenged prevailing assumptions about taste, propriety, and attitudes toward traditional materials.

Widely traveled, with a string of guest residencies, and exhibitions in museums and galleries in Australia, Belgium, Germany, Great Britain, Italy, South Korea, and Spain, and the United States, Ryoji Koie always responds to the specific environment in which he finds himself. Thus, several stays in the Catalonian village of Olot, near Barcelona, Spain, led to a variety of works that utilized local clays and also distantly echoed the ceramics created across the border in Vallauris, France, by Picasso.

As Shingo Mori remarked in the preface to *The Works of Ryoji Koie* (Kodansha, 1994), Koie has always been open to experimentation and learning from amateurs. Whether seeking different types of clay to replace the facility of manufactured pottery clay or setting up some kind of material resistance that may be "conquered" in the firing kiln, Koie has diverged widely from hallowed Japanese traditions, even though he was born in Tokoname, one of the six ancient clay sites associated with Japanese ceramics.

He has among other things variously combined clay and glass in some pieces, created installations that hug the walls or floors of contemporary art museums, and incorporated other materials that radically transform the appearance of the clay body.

While much of the spontaneous appearance of Koie's clay sculptures, vessels, and plates is a result of his restless personality and desire to innovate, it is important to note correspondences in Western art, as well as in Japanese ceramics history.

Thus, as Mori mentioned in another essay "Murmurings of a Large Urn," (in the catalog for the 1995 retrospective exhibition at the

Museum of Fine Arts, Gifu), one dominant European sensibility with which Koie came into contact as a young man was the French *art informel* group (which included Hans Hartung, Georges Mathieu, Jean-Paul Riopelle, and Pierre Soulages among others) whose works were shown in postwar Japan and extensively discussed in print by the art critic Michel Tapié. The drip, splatter, splotch, and other generally animated gestures in postwar French painting were in turn influenced by American abstract expressionists such as Jackson Pollock, for whom Koie has expressed admiration. Koie may be closer to the French artists, however, in terms of the comparatively intimate scale in which he works, balancing an exuberance of attack with a powerful evocation of form. Whether tea bowl, vessel, open-mouthed cylinder, tray, of bottle, Koie's chosen shapes are instantly identifiable as pottery, yet they become departure points for an extraordinary range of surface treatments, from the indulgent to the austere.

Thanks to the combined cooperation of the faculty in the fire arts department at the University of Washington School of Art in Seattle, and the careful coordination of Bryan Ohno of the Bryan Ohno Gallery, Koie's five visits to Seattle in February, April, May, June, and August 1999 were highly productive and meaningful for students and teachers alike. In addition, the satisfying cultural exchange among the Japanese, Professors Doug Jeck, Akio Takamori, and Jamie Walker, and the numerous undergraduate and graduate students in ceramics was reinforced by the artist's insistence upon active student participation in the undertaking.

As he had done in Spain and in his other residencies, Koie located natural deposits of clay in a variety of sites in and near Seattle, including the shores of Puget Sound at Point Defiance Park in Tacoma. In addition to the events at the University of Washington, Koie also spent several days with art students at Charles Wright Academy, a Tacoma preparatory high school. Once again, he learned from amateurs.

While in the Pacific Northwest, Koie created a profusion of vessels, trays, footed plates, and "stretched" plates, each subject to the artist's freewheeling imagination as he altered, threw, ripped and tore, and applied glaze and slip, or liquid clay. Along with the adapted local or "found" clay, commercially available stoneware clay was also used in some cases, as well as colored and clear glazes.

Untroubled by divisive aesthetic issues prevalent in the United States surrounding the assignment of art or craft status to objects using traditional materials such as clay, or those with functional forms, Koie simply extends the definition of pottery to embrace objects that may appear useful but are elaborated upon so highly as to render them less functional. Although Koie never met Robert Sperry (the late professor emeritus of the University of Washington ceramics program), Sperry evidenced certain aspects of Koie's art in his own: altered and torn forms, animated slip, and an affinity for abstract expressionist brushwork.

The visibility of the human hand is another crucial element that contributes to the meaning of Koie's art. Whether they bear fingertip impressions of violated lips, rims or feet, each object is the repository for a variety of aggressive interventions that recall the dynamism of the studio.

One way of dividing the objects created in Seattle for the purposes of our discussion is to separate flat surfaces from rounded ones.

The rectangular trays or plates present brick-red surfaces that act as backdrops for a range of colored glazes and slips. *One Green Circle* balances the symbol of the throwing wheel, the circle, on the flat red surface. *Two Blue Spots* summons up references to the California artist Sam Francis, who had his first show anywhere at a Seattle gallery, Zoe Dusanne, that specialized in Japanese-American artists. The flat tray surfaces also resemble other Western artists such as Robert Motherwell (born in Aberdeen, Washington in 1902) and Mark Tobey, whose works are frequently compared to Japanese Zen calligraphy.

The stretched plates are actually thrown pots that are removed from the wheel and unraveled into a single, continuous flat surface. They resemble wood bark or the sandy rivulets in a coastal tidepool. Seen this way, the plates may ascend to the metaphorical realm of Nature. However, a few determined thumbprints in strategic places remind us again of the hands of the maker.

Each tea bowl has a thoroughly individual identity. The dark brown and dark red clay bodies proclaim their earthy sources yet have been transformed into elegantly curved forms. Koie uses the white slip as a high-contrast design element, sometimes pooling it at the base, sometimes immersing a tea bowl halfway in slip to create an interior of great interest. These works are the artist's most traditional from his Seattle sojourn and are most open to the Asian art connoisseur's scrutiny. The fine points of bowl form, surface decoration, and fortunate imperfections or "lucky accidents" all apply to Koie, but these objects stand on their own in a Western context, too, comparable to the small ceramic, cuplike sculptures of Ron Nagle and Kenneth Price.

Most adventurous and unconventional, however, are the altered cylindrical vessels. Here both form and surface treatment are pushed to the limits of legibility. As Jim Leedy and Peter Voulkos have often done, Koie scratches inscriptions around the pot, with either signatures or locations written in English and Japanese lettering. Such markings do more than identify the vessel; they claim it as a focus for expressive intervention, lifting it out of function and designating its dedicated purpose as a work of art. Seen in the round, the surfaces of the vessels expose enormously dynamic brushwork, with the white slip dragged across the curving surface, spattered or adjacent to numerous small gouges or indentations. This puncturing or pocking of the surface recalls another postwar European artist, Lucio Fontana (1899–1968), an Italian painter, sculptor, and ceramics artist born in Argentina. In Fontana's *Concetti Spaziale*, the artist first violated the surface of the canvas, and, later, the tile surface, thus emphasizing the physical nature of the object and recording the aftermath of his own hand.

Nature, tradition, expression, revolution—all are aspects that operate as emblems of meaning in the art of Ryoji Koie. One other aspect, sex, awaits interpretation. Male and female symbols coexist in Koie's art. From the phallic, pipelike tubes that act as "legs," to the flat plates, through the semen-like filmy white slips and glazes, to the fissures resemble female orifices that split the centers of plates and vessels, gender is represented as a deeply subjective yet active component in the meaning of Koie's art; such readings render his work more humanistic. Unconscious perhaps, but present nonetheless, the sexual dimension enriches the overall meaning and places Koie's art into yet another new context.

Because Koie is so international in his outlook, his art will inevitably be seen in many settings, enhancing and underscoring its individuality. Koie's stay in Seattle was important for this reason, not to mention the development of warm friendships among colleagues and new acquaintances.

When they are encountered on their own, one at a time, each Koie pot, tray, or vessel has its own straightforward identity as something specifically Japanese. When they enter into other worlds—Australia, Europe or the U.S.—they must be seen in relation to the art of each area. With the free coming and going between Asia and Seattle these days, such analogies are sure to add to an understanding of an art that is assertive, open-handed, and welcoming to the world at large beyond Japan.

Ryoji Koie: *Untitled Vessel*, 1999, ceramic, slips and glazes, 24 x 20 x 20". Courtesy of Bryan Ohno Gallery, Seattle. Photo: Michiyo Morioka

Lawson Oyekan: *Untitled*, 2003, terra cotta, 52 x 24 x 24". Courtesy of the artist, London, England. Photo: Garth Clark Gallery, New York

LAWSON OYEKAN: ORIGIN AND EXILE

One inadvertent side effect of the so-called "globalization" movement is the attention paid to artists at the margins or periphery of major geographical centers rather than just those at the metropolitan centers. English-born Nigerian sculptor Lawson Oyekan is a good example. Born in England but taken back to Nigeria by his parents when he was six years old, Oyekan later returned to London to study and develop as an artist. Today he lives with his wife and three children in London but also maintains a studio in Denmark where he takes advantage of larger kiln facilities for his large-scale handbuilt terracotta sculptures.

South Korean readers may already be familiar with Oyekan because he won the 40 million Korean-*won* (US$60,000) grand prize at the First World Ceramic Biennale 2001 Korea International Competition. That sculpture, *Healing Being* (2000), was on the cover of the beautiful catalogue published by the Korea Organizing Committee and exhibited in the new Ichon World Ceramic Center where I first saw his work and met him at the time. Recently I met with him in his London studio where we discussed the issues of origin and exile and saw new work for his exhibition in December 2002 at Garth Clark Gallery in Long Island City, New York.

The physically vigorous and powerful work Oyekan creates in clay has attracted worldwide attention including recent exhibitions in Denmark, Germany and Austria as well. Tall, vertical objects with rounded tops, Oyekan's sculptures are comprised of numerous individual flat pieces of clay that are pushed together. Each individual flattened piece has a handprint on it, then set in as part of the sculpture's outer wall, and then incised with a variety of linear images including words, letters and abstract and geometric designs. In one way, they are very contemporary objects, recalling the work of Peter Voulkos, especially in their use of loosely assembled clay slabs with frequently punctured sides. In another way, they emerge out of the ancient origins of the continent of Africa, birthplace of the human race, according to the most recent archaeological discoveries. In still a third way, they resemble sacred East Indian *lingams,* rounded tall shapes that suggest sexual organs and symbols of male fertility. It is part of Oyekan's power as an artist that the cultural references in his work point in many directions rather than just specifically making narrow national references. After all, he is a man of the world, born in Great Britain, raised as a child in Africa, today equally at home in

England, Europe, Asia and the United States where he also has close family members living.

As the chairman of the International Academy of Ceramics, Tony Franks, wrote about Oyekan when he won the Grand Prize at Ichon:

> Oyekan's terra cotta carries hint of both organic forms and the vernacular architecture of his homeland. Its title, *Healing Being*, however, suggests other more bodily references in this large but delicately built piece, for the piercing and scratchings with which it is adorned lead the viewer and the light through the surface to its cavernous echoing rib cage. This sculpture has an intense presence both physical and mystical and provides an appropriately impressive introduction to the exhibition.

Speaking with Oyekan in London, he mentioned other equally important aspects of his intentions when making his monumental clay sculptures: "I believe my work expresses a sense of the human spirits, it is also about the balance of tensions as well as the spirit of it."

The scratching of the surfaces may suggest allusions to the intensely linear patterns one finds in West African textile weavings, usually done exclusively by male members of a tribe. The aftermath of the appearance of knives and other cutting tools is also an important African cultural reference. Historical precedents of ancient African, specifically Nigerian ceramics, also exist in the work although not consciously so on the part of the artist. For example, in some of his other sculptures one can see the reoccurrence of the three-face pots of the Nok culture, or the double-sided figures on pots by the Dakakari people.

"Aspects of human construction and the nature of the human condition—building, creating, cutting, improving—enter the studio of my mind when I am working," the 41-year-old artist noted about his working methods.

Although most of the work is unglazed terra cotta, in recent works splashes of white clay slip are applied and in others touches of red are used. The presence of the earth (symbol of Africa—and humanity's—origins) is never far from the source.

Exile has forced Oyekan to remember Africa as well as go beyond it into the 21st century world of England and Europe. One of the most important and evocative of contemporary artists at work in the world today, Lawson Oyekan has successfully combined and evoked images of primal origin and cultural exile in his large clay sculptures. He is among the artists of this century worth watching closely because he epitomizes the merging of the developing world's art and that of the better-known traditions of Europe and the New World.

PICASSO'S CERAMICS:
A LIFELONG INTEREST

Not only did Pablo Picasso revolutionize 20th-century ceramics by bringing them back into the respectable realm of fine arts, he did a lot to rescue the sleepy little town of Vallauris, France, where, on July 21, 1946, he wandered into the Madoura pottery works after viewing an annual local potters' show. In the "valley of gold," (as Vallauris translates), Picasso undertook a long and fruitful, if sporadic, period of working in ceramics that now appears inextricable from his other myriad activities as an artist.

In its only North American venue, the Tacoma Art Museum exhibition, "Picasso: Ceramics from the Marina Picasso Collection" attracted thousands of visitors until its closing on January 10, 1999. Thanks to a sensitive installation and a fully translated catalog from the original exhibition at Fundación Bancaja in Valencia, Spain, this Picasso ceramics exhibition brought forward treasured family heirlooms for the first time and presented them in a way that offered dignity, context, good lighting and, most important, plenty of space so that, in many cases, top, bottom, front and sides of each piece could be seen clearly.

Since Picasso's death at Mougins, France, on April 8, 1973, interest in the seriousness of his ceramic oeuvre has grown substantially. While his tributes to other artists—Delacroix, Velázquez, Rembrandt, Poussin, and others—have been hailed as antecedents to the postmodern practice of appropriation, Picasso's ceramics now appear to tie him to an ancient Mediterranean past. After all, ceramics are the only art medium that can be traced back that far.

Remembering that Spain has been the crossroads of many civilizations—Carthage, Phoenicians, Celtic, Greek, Roman, Moorish, and others—the subjects of much of Picasso's surface decoration now appear to allude directly to not only the examples of Greek terra cotta vase painting but to Greek myths as well. Satyrs, flute players, laurel-crowned dancers, wine-drinking revelers, owls and bulls all have their places in a variety of ancient Mediterranean coastal and island cultures. It is as if Picasso was able to escape to his cultural roots through clay and reinterpret artifacts of the past, updating approaches, and bringing them into the mid-20th century.

To be sure, he was not alone, nor was he the first European artist to do this. But he was the most famous and thus the most influential.

Kosme de Barañano, the independent curator who organized the
exhibition and wrote the catalogue, has finally exploded the myth
that Vallauris was the debut point for Picasso's ceramic undertaking.
In fact, it was his first artist-mentor in Paris, Basque artist Francisco
Paco Durrio who showed the 25-year-old Spaniard Paul Gauguin's
ceramics in 1906 and encouraged him to explore hand-built clay
figures. Another artist, André Metthey, lent him a kiln the following
year and, after World War I, Picasso met Catalan clay artist Llorens
Artigas who would later build all of Miró's ceramics, and also work in
clay for Marc Chagall and Raoul Dufy.

Add to that the fact that clay pitchers, bowls and vases were crucial
subjects in both Picasso's youthful still lifes done in Barcelona and in
the breakthroughs to Cubism with Georges Braque between 1904 and
1912. In this way, ceramic images at least were part and parcel of the
early 20th century's most important artistic advance to abstraction,
Cubism. Their solidity and simplicity of shape were the perfect proving ground for challenging optical reality.

Paco Durrio's influence on Picasso has been vastly undernoted. It was
he who gave Picasso his own studio in the Bateau-Lavoir building in
Montmartre. Thus, a ceramic artist's studio was the first important
studio for the most important artist of the first half of this century. It
was also Durrio who showed his young countryman how ceramic jugs
and vases could be turned into figurative sculptures. Although they
were not included in Tacoma, Picasso's *Woman Combing Hair* (1904)
and *Man's Head* (1907) are considered Picasso's first ceramic works,
long before the visit to the Madoura workshop of Georges Ramié.

In between, clay played a crucial role for the artist's bronze sculptures which were often modeled in clay before casting. And the hefty
solidity of ceramic objects found its way into the dimensional round-
ness of his Neo-Classical paintings of the 1920s and 1930s where the
chubby male and female figures seem little more than painted still
lifes of giant ceramic figurines.

So that, when Picasso spent that fateful afternoon settling himself in
a quiet corner of the workshop in Vallauris, the artist, now 65, was
more than ready to return to ceramics. However, it wasn't until the
following summer of 1947, after seeing the same annual pot show,
that Picasso showed up for more. This time, he had hundreds of drawings and studies from which to work. The point is, Picasso's ceramics
were not just dashed off spontaneously. He took the medium just as
seriously as the other materials he had used. Almost 2,000 pieces
were created in the 1947–48 period. In the following years, especially

1950, 1953, and 1963, additional bodies of work were made in editions of 20, 25, and 50, or, as in Tacoma, in completely one-of-a-kind sculptures, plates, and vases.

The introduction of an electric kiln on January 21, 1953, turned Picasso and his colleagues at Madoura away from the time-consuming wood-fired firing process to an approach more rapid and modern. The necessary brevity of execution when painting on glaze decorations also suited Picasso perfectly.

As with everything else he touched, Picasso broke rules of technique, approach, tradition and taste. Often the Spaniard would deliberately mismatch or reposition handles or spouts in order to ingeniously create facial or anatomical features (*Large Jar (Woman with Sunflower)*, 1952). Other times, he would pick up discarded scraps of unfired clay to make seated or standing female figures (*Seated woman with Crossed Legs*, 1950). This was in keeping with his open attitude toward found or recycled objects that he transformed into art with a few deft strokes. Along with Ramie's indispensable technical tips (and thoroughly professional backup on all production and firing), Picasso used unconventional tools for surface patterning such as kitchen knives or perforated cooking utensils.

Pitcher (Nun and Faun), c. 1954, seems innocent enough and clever with its upper handles acting as wings of the nun's headdress. Actually, it is a dangerous scene of potential rape and violence. With the two opposite Mediterranean symbols of chastity and priapic obsession, the nun and the satyr (in this case, half man, half faun), Picasso placed the faun (with widely spread human legs) above and behind the nun in a position of sexual dominance. This is a key foreshadowing of Rudy Autio's later vivacious female nudes also often caught with accompanying aggressive animals like horses, wolves, and dogs. Similarly, the huge phallus on *Goat*, 1957, belies its innocent 2 5/8-inches-high size.

Besides his widely accepted influence on Autio, Peter Voulkos, Robert Arneson and Michael Lucero, and other less well-known American ceramic sculptors, Picasso's example in clay stands as a beacon for many reasons. His absolute integration of clay into his sculpture output rehabilitated the medium, one hopes, for all time. His forays into plate, bowl, platter and tile decoration (*Large Oval Plate (Bull Fight and Spectators)*, 1952; *Tile (Musician and Dancers)*, 1958; *Large Bowl (Self-Portrait)*, 1958; *Floor Tile (Face)*, 1965) proved that everyday objects can also become the focus of great art.

Ceramics allowed Picasso to reclaim his Spanish heritage while still in France. The persistent, historically allusive surface imagery of ancient Mediterranean cultures along with his encounter with terra cotta, earthenware, chamotte, and even porcelain (which entered Europe through Mediterranean trade routes) reconnected him to the earth and the earthy. Now, when we look at the paintings and sculptures of Picasso, instead of asking again, "How did the paintings and sculptures influence the ceramics?" the more pertinent question must be "How did ceramics influence the paintings and sculptures?" Thanks to "Picasso: Ceramics from the Marina Picasso Collection," we are much closer to knowing the answer.

NORTH AMERICAN
CERAMIC SCULPTURE NOW

INTRODUCTION

In 1989 at the opening of the Shigaraki Ceramic Cultural Park in Japan, I discussed American ceramic sculpture in crisis. I noted that the retirements and deaths of senior university ceramics professors, combined with an aggressive return to art pottery in the galleries, suggested a reactionary turn for American ceramic art that imperiled the advances of ceramic sculptors centered chiefly on the West Coast.[1]

Since the death of Peter Voulkos in 2002, an era has indeed come to an end: the Age of Voulkos. Not only is Abstract Expressionism a faint historical memory, but its gestural spontaneity and claims to contemporaneity have long since dissipated. Voulkos's best achievements will definitely last and his contributions will be debated for many years. For our purposes, however, we must look beyond Voulkos and fast-forward to the present.

Figurative imagery, social-political art, isolated individual vision, and installation art characterize contemporary North American ceramic sculpture today and tie it to the broader international contemporary art scene. Although many of the artists included in this section attended prominent university-based ceramics programs (Alfred, Kansas City, Cranbrook, University of Washington etc.), others came out of graduate programs like the School of the Art Institute of Chicago where advanced ideas share space with material concerns or were self-taught.

Gender, ecology, consumerism, genocide, sexuality, agriculture and animal rights are but a few of the themes of content in this art. They join concerns about the nature of the object, manners of fabrication, surface decoration and ornament but, today, the latter two aspects alone do not suffice to interest younger artists, many of whom seek ties to the world we live in and hope to reflect the temper of their times in art made of clay that may occasionally allude to traditional, historical aspects of ceramics—form, function, surface, pattern—but transcends such overworked details in favor of the more thoughtful object, the ceramic sculpture that has been renewed and renovated by the intervening rise of conceptual art in international art circles.

As we shall see, North American ceramic sculpture is now at another crossroads: the burden of art history confronting the historical moment of the Now. History and the Now compete for attention in contemporary ceramic sculpture with historical tradition taking second-place. Art of the Now takes ceramic sculpture to a different place, an area where younger and older artists take Voulkos's breakthrough to freedom as a given, an area where, more pertinently, in sculptor Patti Warashina's words, "clay can be any thing, do any thing." To put it more bluntly, contemporary North American ceramic sculpture has arrived at a point where it need not resemble clay.

REWRITING POSTWAR AMERICAN CERAMIC HISTORY: JIM LEEDY

The first world ceramic biennale in Korea, 2001, showcased artists like Warashina along with Voulkos and Rudy Autio. However, one artist of that generation whose role was crucial in transmitting the ideas of the New York School or Abstract Expressionism into pottery, Jim Leedy, was not included. Part of the 2003 invitational, he was the subject of my monograph, *Jim Leedy: Artist Across Boundaries*.[2] The artist was not only in New York long before Voulkos's 1953 first visit, but he personally met or knew several of the major figures of the movement, including Willem de Kooning, Franz Kline and Jackson Pollock.

Leedy's work in the 2003 biennale sustains a vision of material spontaneity that predates Voulkos in every way (not to mention Autio who, by his own admission, did not see his first work by de Kooning until 1962) and deserves corrective status in the pantheon of American clay sculptors. Hand-built and wood-fired, Leedy's abstract sculptures, such as *Tree Vessel* (2003), *Stilted Vessel, Baroque Vessel* and *Space Vessel* (all 2002) offer an alternative to Voulkos that is both painterly and redolent of violent surface texture. Leedy is the last American Abstract Expressionist ceramist, restored to significance, and already revered in Japan (where he has completed architectural tile mural commissions) and the People's Republic of China (where he will soon complete an architectural commission).

As time passes, the Age of Voulkos will be further analyzed—and perhaps dismantled—but in the meantime, Leedy's critical pioneering role must not be overlooked. His long teaching career at Kansas City Art Institute also has had a huge impact over the years as many of his students have gone on to careers of their own.

NORTH AMERICAN CERAMIC SCULPTURE AFTER VOULKOS AND ARNESON: ANNABETH ROSEN AND ALLAN ROSENBAUM

With the death of Voulkos in 2002 and Robert Arneson in 1992, my predictions at Shigaraki about a vacuum in American ceramic sculpture seemed to be coming true. We have seen how, as in the case of Leedy, establishment histories of American ceramics by Garth Clark[3] and Elaine Levin[4] were far from adequate or complete and omitted or overlooked many key figures. If anything, when Leedy's accomplishments are examined, Voulkos's importance seems overstated.

As for Arneson, his acceptance by the contemporary art world far outstripped Voulkos's and, since Arneson's death, has resulted in at least two museum retrospectives, one dealing with his self-portraits[5] and another with his preparatory maquettes.[6] His replacement at University of California-Davis is Annabeth Rosen. Interestingly, her work—vigorous, tactile, abstract, unbalanced—seems more indebted to Voulkos than Arneson. For example, in *Cinctus I* (2002), dozens of small tubular shapes are roughly stacked in a vertical form, casually glazed white, and fired to form a top-heavy, tottering form.

Although craft-sensitive critics have tied her to tilemaking traditions, it is not necessary to connect Rosen's work to decorative arts history, the methodological matrix of writers like Clark. Instead, Rosen's work spins off other contemporary sculptural precedents for multiple groupings in matching materials, like Tony Cragg, Josiah McElheny, Anish Kapoor, Louise Bourgeois and Jeffry Mitchell. Sinister, visceral, chaotic, and obsessive, Rosen's art emphasizes the expressionist side of Voulkos's legacy without his masculinist strategies of massive volume and violent, puncturing attack. She has a great future if she can balance central studio concerns with the confines of academic and administrative responsibilities. Her 2003 show in Manhattan received a glowing review in *The New York Times*.[7]

Also a professor, Allan Rosenbaum has taught at Virginia Commonwealth University in Richmond, Virginia since 1986. Although he studied at University of Wisconsin and not with Arneson at UC-Davis, Rosenbaum's art pays tribute to Arneson's breakthrough—combining humor with seriousness in figurative ceramic sculpture—but extends it to a more intellectual end. Symbols play an important role in Rosenbaum's assembled vignettes that use books, buildings, furniture, and other handbuilt shapes in combination with anatomical body parts, heads, hands, feet and fingers.

Tale (2002) is a good example. With the head emerging from an open book, the sculpture is an image of knowledge acquisition, thoughtful and profound. Other works, like *Book Man, Groundscraper* (both 2002) and *Ram* (2000), continue the idea of referential images in relation to human figures. In the process, Rosenbaum has accumulated a body of work that comments on urban affairs, the built environment, and mankind's responsibilities toward our freedom and community. To the extent that Arneson's final works dealt with current events like war and the military, Rosenbaum's art is less newspaper-headline-driven, more introspective and, in the long run, possibly more psychologically compelling.

UNCOMFORTABLE TENSIONS: SOCIAL AND COMMUNITY ISSUES IN LEOPOLD FOULEM, CHARLES KRAFFT, LIFE IN GENERAL, AKIO TAKAMORI AND LEE STOLIAR

Building on the sociocritical content of late-period Arneson, as well as responding to numerous artists associated with postmodern practice, these artists represent a clear rejection of the Age of Voulkos in favor of pushing North American ceramic sculpture closer to international conceptual art that addresses social and community concerns. In some cases, the associations or analogies may make us uncomfortable (challenging taste, social proprieties, and tolerance of difference), but they put ceramics on the same level as other contemporary art, proving its power to participate in a broader global dialogue that transcends nationality while at the same time paying attention to local or parochial issues.

American sociopolitical art made of clay has a long history, dating as far back as souvenirs made in post-War of Independence Britain where facsimiles of President George Washington were used as decorations for tea mugs sold back to the U.S. More recently, the 1930s and World War II served as the impetus for sculptures ridiculing both Allied and Axis political leaders. Viktor Schreckengost's *Apocalypse '42* (1942) sets (according to Levin) "a terrified horse carrying the Four Horsemen portrayed as caricatures of Hitler . . . Hirohito . . . Death dressed in a German military uniform . . . and Mussolini."[8] And Russell Barnett Aitken's three statuettes of President Franklin D. Roosevelt, Prime Minister Winston Churchill, and Chancellor Adolf Hitler satirize three men who shaped the twentieth century.

Sixty-one years later, Charles Krafft, a self-taught artist with a prior background in pseudo-Asian-style painting and a reputation for Da-

daist pranks and outrageous publicity stunts, made a blue-and-white porcelain effigy of Hitler in the form of a teapot. One hopes a series savaging Josef Stalin, Mao Tse-Tung and Pol Pot will come soon.

Recipient of support from the prestigious George Soros Foundation, Krafft traveled to Central Europe in 1997 and visited Sarajevo, Serbia with a performance/rock group. Later, for an exhibit at the defense ministry of Slovenia, Krafft created a display of blue-and-white porcelain machine guns, fragment grenades (on view in Korea), and pistols that received substantial and admiring attention from European critics. Taming weaponry through art, Krafft has extended Arneson's political caricatures into the realm of the neutralized weapon, a gesture reminiscent of the flowers set into the muzzles of Russian rifles by citizens during the Velvet Revolution of 1988 in the Czech Republic. Krafft was the subject of a double-museum retrospective in southern California in 2002, accompanied by a monograph, *Charles Krafft's Villa Delirium*.[9]

Life in general is a family in Woody Creek, Colorado engrossed in the creation of an imaginary ancient civilization quite similar to our own. If Krafft makes threatening objects like guns seem dangerously attractive, the LeVan family (Brook, Rose, Cooper and Shepherd) makes attractive everyday objects like small appliances seem ancient and grotesque. Actively involved in the construction of an alternative reality through the dozens of found objects covered in clay, fired, cracked and painted, the LeVan family shows us how "life in general" can be a mirror of our own extravagant consumption of commercial goods. Playing off sociologists' notions of "planned obsolescence" and the American "throwaway culture," this group applies decorative motifs of one of the continent's first ceramic cultures, the Anasazi and Mimbres potters of the Southwest, to create an uncomfortable and perplexing tension between vanished indigenous cultures and our own. Could they be implying that, one day, our own electric steam irons, handheld dust vacuum cleaners, children's toys, and gardening tools will be excavated and American society will be judged by such implements?

The Colorado family's art has clear historical links to other recent ceramic art such as the elaborate archaeological excavation sites (using phony clay bones) by the California artist Clayton Bailey who even has his own fake museum. In addition, their work on view in Korea, *Snow Shovel with Mimbres Men and Mythic Beings Hunting Bowl and Mohave Man Effigy Pattern, A.D. 1050* (1997–2003) recalls a significant icon of 20th-century art, one of the first Dada projects, *In Advance of the Broken Arm* by Marcel Duchamp. Truly an "altered readymade," to use Duchamp's term, *Snow Shovel* builds on Duchamp's absurdity and unexpected juxtaposition of object and title. Also, like the artists Jeanne-Claude and Christo, the family's collective artistic undertaking often involves elaborately planned public appearances and community involvement through residency art projects in often remote geographical areas.[10]

Popular culture in the form of consumer household appliances and tools drives the art of life in general; the everyday world and the humdrum are rediscovered with a touching and humorous pathos. After all, their imaginary culture is lost—and yet it resembles ours. The oldest art material of all, clay, is perfectly suited to masquerade as a player in this enormous spoof of American consumer society.

That loving send-up is continued with a Gallic twist of irony and analysis by Léopold Foulem. Among the most widely recognized of Canadian artists, Foulem has long attacked art pottery head-on with his hilarious unusable vases and teapots. In a telling shift, Foulem now employs the human figure—like Rosenbaum and Krafft—to comment upon the intersection of art, myth, culture and mass-produced kitsch. With regard to myth, the Christian symbol of Saint Nicholas (linguistically corrupted to Sant'-a-claus) is combined with Hindu sacred devotional imagery. *Santa Claus in Ecstasy* (2002) both ridicules Christian iconography and turns it to a pseudo-devotional end. St. Nicholas became the popular Christmas-gift-giving folk hero in western and central Europe: "Santa Claus." Foulem associates the gift-giver with the unending consumer conditioning of the Christmas holiday season. Adding a Hindu *lingam* or phallus, however, Foulem eroticizes the aged character so beloved by children in dangerous and provocative ways. In another bicultural face-off, the gold luster covering the aroused Santa references both divine Asian manifestations of deities and cheap western fake-gold mass-produced kitsch souvenir objects.

While space does not permit a full discussion of Foulem's art and critical writings (he is the subject of numerous museum exhibitions and essays)[11], it is worth noting that, when one contemplates Foulem's serious aesthetic projects addressing ceramics, along with his lectures, interviews and published writings, it is no exaggeration to say that he is not only one of the leading intellectual figures in North American ceramics today, he is the only intellectual in the field, the one whose oeuvre and influence are sure to grow in stature.

With Foulem turning religious figures into "high" kitsch and Krafft taking political subjects and trivializing their potential horror with

troubling implications, Akio Takamori executes a comparable operation on two of the last century's leading figures, General Douglas
MacArthur and Emperor Hirohito. *General and Emperor* (2001) is a
smaller, pedestal-size version of slightly less-than-life-size effigies of
the two, but with no less power or provocation.

The Japanese-born artist who came to the U.S. in 1972 and who is
a professor at the University of Washington addresses the issues
of both the American's controversial role in postwar Japan and the
desacralized Japanese leader's recently disclosed greater role in the
military planning of the catastrophic conflict. Takamori preposter-
ously places a golden pillow or block of wood beneath Hirohito's feet,
raising him closer to the old soldier. With one such gesture, Takamori
speaks volumes about the Japanese and American "special relationship:" interdependent, delicate, yet open to discussion, comment and
even ridicule.

Lee Stoliar's sense of community and social involvement emerges directly
out of her experiences in New York's East Village of the 1980s. Like Michael Lucero who also emerged there at that time, Stoliar is both involved
and aloof, immersed in the urban fabric of ideas—feminism, sexuality,
art, labor—and yet cut off in the cluttered confines of her studio.

Her sculptures are as crowded as the New York subway at rush hour.
Moving from low- to high-relief carved terra cotta, Stoliar's sculptures
deal with community through an imagery of individuals, couples and
multiple figure groups. All unglazed, all cartoonish and indebted to
popular comics, they have specific activities such as lovemaking, as
in *One of the Ways IX* (2002), or prayer and supplication, as in *Empty
Hands* (2000). Somewhat comparable to Mary Frank (who also makes
unglazed earthenware female figures), Stoliar's obsessive, repetitive
approach attains an hallucinatory and highly expressionistic level.
Over and over, the viewer encounters a mysteriously intimate moment laboriously constructed to be on public exhibition, its privacy
undone by handmade spectacle.

THE LONERS: MICHAEL LUCERO, DOUG JECK AND JEFFRY MITCHELL

Since Stoliar is the transitional figure between the social commu-
nitarians and the loners, Lucero becomes the most sociable of the
loners, another New Yorker's trait. Another candidate for inheriting Arneson's mantle of "greatest living American ceramic sculptor,"
Lucero's odyssey has been one of constant searching, material transformation and radical experimentation.

His current interest, yarn-covered molded garden statuary, may be shocking at first, but it is perfectly in keeping with this artist who has always followed his own path. Answering Foulem's glittering Santa surfaces with a masking, mystifying tangle of colored thread, Lucero is able to re-concentrate the viewer's focus of attention on surface pattern, form and profile. Pioneer in the use of additional materials with clay, Lucero, at 51, is too young to take on senior status yet his achievements are so huge and varied, they bear comparison to Voulkos and Arneson. Where he will go next is unclear but it will undoubtedly continue to influence North American ceramic sculpture. His influence on contemporary art in general has already been noted.[12]

Poet of the solitary soul, Doug Jeck, who teaches at the University of Washington with Professor Takamori, is the only major American ceramic sculptor not to emerge from the West Coast. His art bears none of the overly familiar hallmarks of California clay: humor, puns, vulgarity, illusionism and caricature. Instead, artists like Rodin, Epstein, George Segal and Stephen DeStaebler are more appropriate precedents with one major difference: Jeck is making anti-humanist figurative sculptures that shrivel classical nobility and physical perfection.

Mismatched anatomical parts of old and young people are combined into absurd bodies that cannot possibly be alive yet, strangely, appear conscious. Uncanny and powerful, Jeck is the dark poet of American ceramics, closer to DeStaebler but also to the withering pathos of Jack Earl, the savagery of Viola Frey's unsuccessful businessmen, and the postwar alienation of Giacometti's bronze figures.

Forced Study (2001), shown here in Korea, combines machine-like steel plates with ceramic undergirding in a foreshortened, fragmented head that compresses Jeck's general dismantling of the human body into one intense and compelling image. Working so against the grain, Jeck is indeed a loner but one with a brilliantly promising future. His art chronicles American loneliness.

Even though Jeffry Mitchell once apprenticed with a Japanese teabowl master and makes art that obliquely comments on Asian ceramic conventions, he never became a potter. Instead, he has used clay, along with wood, plaster, paper and other materials, to create multi-part assemblages that border on installation art. In that sense, he is the transitional figure to our final group, the installation artists.

Mitchell's *The Holy Family a.k.a. the Green Light* (2003), like Foulem's *Santa Claus in Ecstasy*, appropriates Christian iconogra-

Lee Stoliar: *Completer (Zooming to Cythera)*, 1988, waxed terra cotta clay and
wood, 9 1/4 x 21 x 6". Stephen and Pamela Hootkin Collection, New York.
Photo: Noel Allum

Jennifer A. Lapham:
Untitled (detail), 2000,
slipcast and glazed
ceramic and wood. 36 x
26 x 36". Courtesy of the
artist, Bloomington, Illinois.
Photo: Kevin Strandberg

phy (Jesus, Mary, Joseph) and grafts it onto an Asian platform: the shrine. Small animals of indeterminate species comprise the "holy family" enshrined in a dense green and black glaze, complete with hierarchical composition and accompanying adornments. The extraordinary amount of filigree and frills are muted by the somber, near-monochrome, of the glaze covering. Rejecting the unitary object in favor of the new postmodern paradigm—the multi-element display—Mitchell sets the stage for the other installation artists.

REORGANIZING SCULPTURAL PRESENCE: NANCY BLUM, JUAN GRANADOS, SADASHI INUZUKA AND JENNIFER LAPHAM

If the chief advance in recent contemporary North American ceramic sculpture is the addition of different materials and the expansion to multiple elements, the installation artists named above represent both a culmination of a decade-long trend and a refreshing retort to mainstream art pottery advocates like Clark. Because their art must exist in a public space, these artists embrace and confront community, too, but often with ambiguous results.

Nancy Blum's *Flower Wall* (2000) precedes her special project for this exhibition, *Lotus Pond(2003)*. A compressed wall-mounted display of porcelain-and-bronze floral elements that nod to the Asian religious and cultural significance of the lotus, this assemblage also evokes symbolic representations of female anatomy. Delicate yet brittle, Blum's art has attracted the substantial attention of museum curators who have commissioned several larger presentations.

Juan Granados's *Implement #4* (2003), seen here in Korea, is but one element in a normally larger installation. Granados manages to retain the integrity of the individual object while also multiplying it into installations that, as in *First Harvest* (1999), recall the artist's childhood as one of a migrant agricultural labor family. Now teaching at Texas Tech University, Professor Granados stresses ceramics' origins in the earth and comes close to the abstract organic nature of some recent Japanese and Korean clay sculpture.

Sadashi Inuzuka created *Memory* for the Canadian Embassy in Tokyo in 2000. He now teaches at the University of Michigan in Ann Arbor. Exploring every material and process phase imaginable for ceramics, he has also used metal, wood, and even rice in temporary installations that interact with architecture and often change appearance over time. His recent debut at a gallery in New York City brought his work to the attention of a wider, more informed audience.

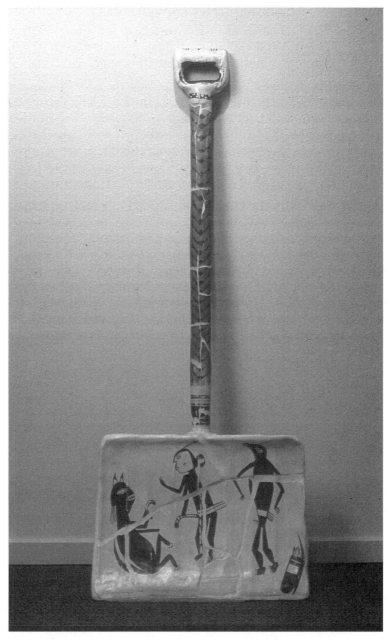

life in general: *Snow Shovel with Mimbres Men and Mythic Beings Hunting Bowl and Mohave Man Effigy Pattern, A. D. 1050*, 1997–2003, clay, glazes and found objects, 48 x 15 x 4". Photo: Courtesy of the artists, Woody Creek, Colorado.

Inuzuka's interventions address the fate of the object—alone, together, assembled, combined, dismantled?—and call into question prior formal assumptions of presentation, display, time and space. He, too, has created a special mini-installation for "Now and Now."

Finally, Jennifer Lapham's installations (some done in collaboration with her artist husband, Paul Sacardiz) point toward an optimistic and open-ended direction for North American ceramic sculpture. Ecology, especially the fate of animals and birds, is a central theme in her art, but one with metaphorical implications. Rooted in community, Lapham's installations toy with the bird as a decorative motif, both as kitsch figurine and target of American sports hunting enthusiasts.

Untitled (2000) is part of a larger installation but stands on its own in Korea. Two young fawns are positioned atop a brutally cut-off log. They are painted in military camouflage pattern both to "conceal" them from hunters and also to comment symbolically on innocent victims of military power. Lapham's manipulation of clay is put to conceptual use. She places clay within the world at large, not at the margin. Like the other North American artists in "Now and Now," Lapham has expanded clay's possibilities and integrated it into the international conceptual art community so prevalent in the early 21st century.

PART III
GLASS

Fritz Dreisbach: *Creamy Lemon Yellow Flaring Fluid Mongo Compote with Four Waving Ferns, Polychrome Filigree Inlays and Cast Foot,* 1994, blown glass, 14 x 16 x 22". Courtesy of William Traver Gallery, Seattle. Photo: Roger Schreiber

AMERICAN STUDIO GLASS SINCE 1945: FROM COLD WAR TO HOT SHOP

I: COLD WAR, COLD GLASS

Before World War II, American glass was primarily created in a small industrial factory setting. A visit to the Museum of American Glass at Wheaton Village in Millville, New Jersey, quickly demonstrates the splendors and achievements of glass manufactured in the U.S. from the 18th to 20th centuries. Cast, pressed, cut, carved, engraved, and colored, most American glass was useful rather than sculptural and was created in much the same way that European glass was made: one person designed; another group of men executed the finished product, from mold-making or blowing, to finishing and polishing.

For example, the Fostoria Company was founded in 1887 in Fostoria, Ohio, and later moved to Moundsville, West Virginia, where it remains today. It was joined by other U.S. companies such as Blenko, West Virginia Glass, Fenton, Pilgrim, Tiffin, and Owens-Illinois-Libbey. These are the firms that create practical, mass-produced items for the middle-class American home. Very few unique art pieces were made.

One company, however, Steuben (since 1933 a division of Corning Glass), prepared the way for both the triumph of glass art in an American factory setting and, later, for its elevation and appreciation in the private studio environment. In a way, Steuben became the official glass company of the U.S. government after World War II. Between 1946 and 1958, for example, Steuben created numerous special presentation pieces in lead crystal for the U.S. State Department to use as gifts to foreign dignitaries visiting the White House, heads of state approved of by the U.S., and others including H.R.H. Queen Elizabeth II of Great Britain. President Dwight D. Eisenhower was given a large Steuben vase by his cabinet members in 1954. In return, he commissioned a similar vase for retiring Secretary of Treasury, Miss Oveta Culp Hobby.

After the shift from colored to clear glass at Steuben in 1933, the design process was set in motion for the artistic glass triumphs of the Cold War period. The war was "cold"—and so was the look of the glass: crystal-clear, icy, imperious, with massive curved walls. Designer Sidney Waugh (*Merry-Go-Round Bowl*, 1947) was a distinguished artist for many years and was responsible for the largest-scale glass sculpture yet produced at the time, *Atlantica* (1939), for the Steuben pavilion exhibition at the 1939 New York World's Fair. He was joined by others like George Thompson (*Genesis*), James Huston, Eric Hilton, David Dowler, and, by 1972, James Carpenter who collaborated with Dale Chihuly on an elaborate and amusing series of functional vases, bowls and decanters.

Before and after the 1933 takeover of Steuben by Corning, Frederick Carder was the significant design figure and an important artist in his own right. A brilliant colorist as well, he specialized in pâte-de-verre reliefs and sculptures such as a portrait head of President Abraham Lincoln. Maurice Heaton was another important glass artist at Steuben in the late 1930s and early 1940s who fused colors onto glass plates and platters.

As Jane Spilman and Susanne Frantz wrote in their 1990 book, *Masterpieces of American Glass*, of the exhibition, "Glass 1959" (the first international survey):

> Though barely reflected in the inventory of "Glass 1959," the post-World War II period was a time of revitalization for handicraftsin the U.S. Soldiers returning from the war received scholarships from the federal government to continue their education. . . . While other craft media flourished, the age-old technical difficulties of working with glass caused it to lag behind in development.

This state of affairs—the retarded development of postwar glass—would not change until after 1962 but, in the meantime, a few men and women were already attempting studio- or small-kiln-based work. One French model, Maurice Marinot, was a painter who made glass until 1937 but had a lasting impact on American studio glass artists because of his appreciation for the properties of the material. The Americans long remained unable to equal his level of artistic excellence.

Similarly, Edris Eckhardt made cast-glass faces and other objects in the Cleveland, Ohio area. She first worked in ceramics, like many of the glass artists. Claire Falkenstein, on the West Coast, was embedding small colored bits of glass into metal-wire web patterns such as her commission for the gates of Peggy Guggenheim's villa in Venice, Italy. Frances Higgins and her husband, Michael, fused bits of glass into plates and platters that became highly prized in the Chicago area.

Other Americans went directly to Venice in the 1950s, long before Dale Chihuly's watershed Fulbright Fellowship year at the Venini factory in 1968. For example, Robert Willson was on Murano, designing objects that were made by various hot shop crews. Thomas

Stearns came to Venini in 1960 and created a series of vases based on the facades of Venice palaces. He also collaborated with Fulvio Bianconi on a group of cylindrical vases. *The Sentinel of Venice* (1962) by Stearns is an important sculptural slab with many colors. In 1962, the 31st Venice Biennale exhibited six works designed by Stearns and completed at Venini on Murano Island.

While the Cold War period began with the severe clarity of lead crystal at Steuben in Corning, New York, the late 1950s saw the signs and omens of the more open and experimental attitudes of the 1960s. Stearns and Willson were in strong contrast to the strict hierarchy of authority in the Venini hot shops. As Americans, they wished to observe and make, not just design and give orders to the workers.

More importantly, Harvey K. Littleton, a university-trained potter teaching ceramics at the University of Wisconsin-Madison, traveled to Europe in 1958 and met French glass artist Jean Sala. Littleton was searching for a way to make glass outside the oppressive industrial environment of the American factories. Perhaps without knowing it, he sought a path out of the cold carving and clear color of the Cold War period, into the suffused color, organic forms, and hands-on character of studio glassblowing.

By 1962, a fortuitous set of circumstances would result in the single most important moment of historic change for American glass art. It would change from cold to hot, away from the stuffy smug achievements of the Cold War aesthetic of Steuben, over to the individualistic and sensual models of the sexy, psychedelic 1960s.

II: FROM TOLEDO TO SEATTLE: STUDIO GLASS IN THE CONTEXT OF AMERICAN CRAFT

Why is it that within 25 years, American studio-based glass art not only supplanted ceramic sculpture but also surpassed all other activity in American craft? Not every critic or historian would agree. Janet Koplos, for example, former Tokyo art critic and current senior editor at *Art in America*, believes ceramic sculpture is the most important medium of achievement within American craft art. But increasingly, glass has stolen the limelight from clay culminating in its strong showing in the special collection of American craft assembled by Smithsonian Institution curator Michael Monroe for the White House residence of President Bill Clinton and his wife, Hillary Rodham Clinton.

It did not happen immediately. And one cannot overstate clay's significance in pioneering acceptance of craft materials as fine art in

museums, galleries, private collections and art magazines such as
Artforum and *Art in America.*

After all, as Spilman and Frantz pointed out, "the post-World War
II period was a time of revitalization for handicrafts in the U.S."
The delayed development of glass, however, due to greater technical difficulties, changed in 1962 at two workshops held at the Toledo
Museum of Art in March and June of that year. Michiaki Kawakita
and Shigeki Fukunaga have discussed this pivotal event in their 1982
book, *Contemporary Studio Glass: An International Collection.* They
point out how Professor Harvey Littleton of the University of Wisconsin sculpture department sought funding for the two workshops from
Mrs. Aileen Osborn Webb, the founder of the American Craft Council.
Before Toledo Museum of Art Director Otto Wittman agreed to host
the workshops, Littleton unsuccessfully approached the Corning
Glass Co. (where his father had been head of research and development) and Alfred University, America's oldest university training
institution for ceramics.

With the approval of Wittman and the help of Norman Schulman
(who taught ceramics classes at the museum), Littleton planned and
built a furnace similar to a ceramics kiln and brought it to the Toledo
site. Dominick Labino, a glass chemical engineer, suggested a few
changes to the furnace and later brought over a supply of small glass
marbles that could be melted at a relatively low temperature. As it
turned out, other, cheaper sources of meltable glass were available
close by: soft drink beverage bottles like those used for Coca-Cola!
Nevertheless, Labino's contribution is important and his subsequent
artistic work is not to be denied.

The second workshop in June, 1962 attracted a variety of artists,
mostly university ceramics professors and students, including Tom
McGlauchlin and Howard Kottler. Labino began blowing his own
glass, something he learned for the first time at this session. Official
photographs were taken and the state of American glass art was
never the same again. Remember, now the artist was freed from the
supervisory nature of the factory floor; alone in his or her studio at
home, the artist was now free to create in an unfettered manner, to
do as the rock 'n roll song said, "Express yourself!"

As Dan Klein stated in his 1989 book, *Glass: A Contemporary Art,*
glass became so popular in the 1960s because of a "general preoccupation with self-expression" in all of American culture at that time.
"Question Authority" was another slogan of the day. At the same,
ironically, because the majority of the Toledo participants were aca-

demics, the machinery was also put into motion for the institutionaliza-
tion of American studio glass within a university setting. Yes, the new
glass artist would be alone in the studio and free—but not for long.

It is not our task here to trace every step of the path that led to the
international primacy of American glass by 1995. Rather, let us take
a detour around the nation and visit briefly a few artists who were
pursuing sculptural and artistic creations in textiles and fibers, ceramics, metals and wood.

As Kimpei Nakamura has clarified in his writings, West Coast ceramic sculpture of the 1960s and 1970s caught America by surprise.
Bold, brash, erotic and unconventional artists like Robert Arneson,
Peter Voulkos, Patti Warashina, Howard Kottler, Robert Sperry and
Anne Perrigo embraced popular culture in all its energetic vulgarity
and violated traditional limits of European traditions still prevalent
on the East Coast at schools like Alfred University.

Voulkos and Sperry, among many others, turned to Japanese models
such as Bizen ware for inspiration that incorporated accident and
surface imperfection to liberate their imaginations and attain "self-
expression." The startlingly fresh results were welcomed gradually
by museum curators, critics, and prescient collectors such as Mr. and
Mrs. Fred Marer and Drs. R. Joseph and Elaine Monsen.

With the experimental permission already established in 1960s
ceramics, certain clay artists went even farther by encountering the
fire and greater uncertainty of glass. Among them were Littleton and
Schulman, Marvin Lipofsky, Benjamin Moore, William Morris, Fritz
Dreisbach, Henry Halem, Dan Dailey, Ann Gardner, and Richard
Marquis. Besides their prior familiarity with a medium of great potential, flexible and plastic properties, these artists brought to glass
the desire for even greater technical challenges, more evident qualities of fragility and transparency, as well as a pride and conviction
that glass, just as easily as clay, could be a material to embody the
highest aesthetic content and levels of quality.

Within textiles and fiber art—cotton, wool, silk, linen, burlap, sisal,
hemp, jute, goat hair, horsehair, nylon, rayon, acetate, acrylic and
metallic thread—the artists involved emulated the same liberating
approaches to clay and glass. To push the material to its limits; to
suspend traditional European expectations of system and process; to
veer toward the subjectivity of self-expression, all these desires found
voice within fiber art. Lenore Tawney and Claire Zeisler are important senior figures, comparable to Voulkos and Arneson, or Littleton
and Labino. Unlike the exuberant physicality of the male artists,

however, Tawney stressed a feminine, meditative approach to the manipulation of thread. With many American zoned out on stimulants in the 1960s that relaxed the user, her quiet, spiritualized art found many admirers. The "flower power" culture of San Francisco was the perfect match for the delicate frailty of her weavings.

Zeisler, on the other hand, confronted masculine monoliths by creating freestanding "soft sculptures" like her 1967 *Red Wednesday* in the American Craft Museum (now Museum of Arts and Design) collection.

In the ensuing 30 years, fiber art has not reattained the considerable interest it had in the 1970s, the age of Women's Art. Although the accomplishments of artists like Ed Rossbach, Katherine Westphal, Lia Cook and Rebecca Medel have been substantial, there has not been a market or museum enthusiasm comparable to what has happened to American clay and glass. In certain ways, textile art lends itself to narrative or social and political subject matter (current contemporary art trends) even more easily than glass because of cloth's flat surface but, except for a few, art critics have played down fiber art or been unable to appreciate its broad embrace of processes and images borrowed from developing areas of the world like Asia, Africa, and South America.

Metals are divided into jewelry and sculpture. Here there are many signs that metal arts are catching up with glass. Artists like Albert Paley, Robert Ebendorf and William Harper are attracting attention through major public art commissions, successful New York gallery and museum exhibitions, and institutional acquisitions. With textile artists having to settle for second-rank publications like *FiberArts*, *Ornament*, and *Surface Design Journal*, metal artists are closely and articulately commented upon in *Metalsmith* (the Journal of North American Society of Goldsmiths) and *Sculpture* magazine. Most of the prominent figures are still tied to university teaching positions, however, and only Paley has been able to support a large fabricating headquarters and staff in Rochester, New York. There he creates his limited-edition furniture and large outdoor architectural commissions. No matter how large they become, they still retain the sense of delicate filigree and baroque compositions of his earliest jewelry.

In wood, Wendell Castle's technical innovations of laminating pieces of hard wood together which are then sawn into curved forms for furniture were a crucial breakthrough for American studio furniture. Closest to glass in market success, luxury studio furniture like Castle's and other works by Peter Pierobon, Garry Knox Bennett, John Cederquist, and Judith Ames, are rapidly attracting the interest of art critics like Arthur C. Danto, as well as the praise of the curator-in-charge of the Renwick Gallery of the National Museum of American Art, Kenneth R. Trapp. He once stated that American studio-built furniture was the most important area of excellence within American craft at this time. This could presage substantial U.S. government endorsement and acquisition comparable to the Cold War support of Steuben Glass.

That may be so but few high-style furniture makers have reached the sculptural expressions of Wendell Castle. Most recent art furniture is either dependent upon lavish use of inlaid rare woods (often ecologically endangered) or tend toward the excessively whimsical.

As we have seen, American craft has moved forward on all fronts with each decade seeming to wax enthusiastic about a different medium: clay in the 1960s, fibers in the 1970s, furniture in the 1980s, and glass in the 1990s. It is my belief that glass will remain at the top well beyond the 1990s. Nearly 70 university-based glass programs are now in place. Specialty magazines like *GLASS* and *Glass Art Society Journal* are regularly joined by coverage in national art magazines. Substantial private collections of glass far outnumber those in clay, jewelry, fiber or furniture with the expected gifts and bequests to major U.S. museums to come. Most important of all, younger artists like Walter Lieberman, Charles Parriott, Nancy Mee, Hank Murta Adams, Therman Statom, and William Morris, have built on the breakthroughs of Littleton, Labino and Dale Chihuly. With no end in the sight, American glass has traveled from its Cold War role as political bribe to its current role as the most exciting area in all of American art at this time. The temperature within the studio hot shop is always hot; at this time, it appears as if it will never cool down.

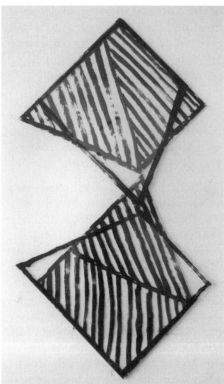

Peter Millett: *Glass Drawing (Girl Before a Mirror) I*, 1981, glass and enamel paint, 34 x 19 x 1". Photo: Courtesy of Greg Kucera Gallery, Seattle.

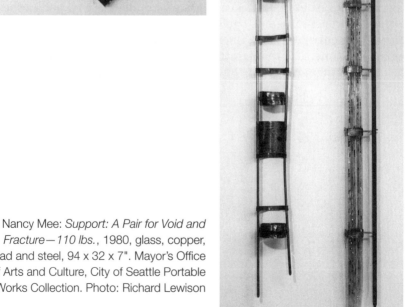

Nancy Mee: *Support: A Pair for Void and Fracture—110 lbs.*, 1980, glass, copper, lead and steel, 94 x 32 x 7". Mayor's Office of Arts and Culture, City of Seattle Portable Works Collection. Photo: Richard Lewison

GLASS AS ELEMENT: FIVE ARTISTS

Patti Warashina's dictum about clay being able to "do any thing, be any thing" might be updated by Buster Simpson's comment on his early introduction to glass:

> My eyes were opened to the potential of glass at the Rhode Island School of Design because of my background in ceramics. I realized there were just as many gimmicks. But I looked at glass as a skin. I liked the phenomenon of its being heated, molded, and cooled. But I thought maybe I could take it a little further.

Five artists, Charles B. Luce, Nancy Mee, Peter Millett, Buster Simpson, and Therman Statom, all use glass and embody the immense variety of expression available with that material. Though not all are craftsmen by training, each has benefited from the freewheeling attitude toward sculptural materials such as wood, glass, and clay that has been present in the U.S. since the early 1960s. They represent a new generation of artists, Post-Crafts we might call them, who take artisanship into consideration only insofar as it leads to artistic achievement.

Today glass is the most important sculptural medium in Seattle. This fact undoubtedly has something to do with the advent of Pilchuck Glass School in Stanwood, Washington, 80 miles north of Seattle. Only two of the artists under discussion here (Buster Simpson and Therman Statom) ever worked there, however. Simpson's influence has been strongly felt by younger Seattle artists more as a result of their coming into contact with him in the city's Belltown neighborhood than at Pilchuck (he left under fire in 1973 after a tenure as co-director). Pilchuck's emphasis on artisanship instead of art has served as a negative example to young Seattle artists using glass as a route to meaning rather than as an end in itself. The chief difference between Dale Chihuly, William Morris and Benjamin Moore—the Pilchuck "masters"—and Luce, Mee, Millett, Simpson and Statom is that the latter have turned to glass as a component or *element* of their sculpture; not as a seductive, mesmerizing challenge to be conquered by bravura craftsmanship. In this way, their work is not *about* glass per se. It is about, in part, the literal and symbolic properties of glass—and much, much more.

Peter Millett, for example, is also a Rhode Island School of Design-trained painter and sculptor who only turned to glass three years ago. Sharing an invitational exhibit with Chris Jonic at the Seattle Art

Museum in 1980, Millett debuted five sculptures of painted wire-reinforced transparent "vandal glass." This adaptation of an industrially produced material immediately associates him with Marcel Duchamp, the early 20th-century artist who first used glass in that way, chiefly in his controversial *Bride Stripped Bare By Her Bachelors, Even*. Yet Millett's work is more post-modern than modern: it strives for breakdowns between traditional categories of art—as did Duchamp—but is concerned with the retinal activity painting affords, something Duchamp eschewed vehemently.

Night and *Day* (1979) have two versions, large and small. The diminutive models or maquettes each consists of two adjacent diamond shapes, like the final versions, but allow for a closer inspection of their vitreous character. Both *Night* and *Day* studies are composed of pieces of "vandal glass" sandwiched together and painter over with enamel. *Night* has one diamond shape painted red and yellow, another thinner one beside it, is painted purple, blue and black. The hatchings created by steel wire within the second glass remind one of black tile in a Matisse interior scene. They present not only compositional order for the painting but also, given their industrial origin, have associations to the world about us. Whereas Chihuly's glass baskets allude to primitive cultures, Millett's severe geometries allude to our own. *Day's* maquette has a lower diamond painted over with mustard yellow and green that has been scratched irregularly then covered with transparent glass. This, too, is a far cry from the intimate wedding of color and material so assiduously sought by the Pilchuck vesselmakers. The point here seems, again, to use glass as a see-through shield to accentuate a different material, in this case, paint.

Fragility is a tantalizing quality of glass and Millett's flaunting of that is obvious in his large-scale pieces. As if they might come tumbling off the wall at any moment and yet remaining constant there, they use glass' fragility to create a sense of drama. The positioning of the panels at angles to one another also implies to some a sense of motion across the wall, again, seemingly at odds with the delicate medium.

This contradictory aspect, fragility versus strength, the "whole" versus the "fragment," is extended even farther by Nancy Mee. Dating from her 1977 incorporation of small pieces of found glass into collages, California-born Mee praises what she calls the "double quality of glass, its grace and elegance, versus its fear and brutality." Introducing a heavily symbolic interpretation of her own "much more interesting than the material itself," Mee now concentrates on glass as the major element in her sculptures of steel, copper wire, and gold leaf.

Working in cooperation with Seattle glass wholesalers like Belknap Corporation and Washington Glass Company, she builds on her seven years' experience as a picture framer to give her a complete sense of ease with the daunting material. Nancy Mee's art centers on the adolescent women's disease scoliosis or curvature of the spine. Her sculptures (seen in her 1979 solo debut at Linda Farris Gallery and 1980 invitational installations at the Los Angeles Institute of Contemporary Art and the University of Washington's Henry Art Gallery) are stylized representations of spines in various stages of illness and health, braced and unbraced. Cutting all her own glass, she begins by cracking a large half-inch-thick sheet into three-inch columns. These columns are then cracked into shards and laminated with silicone glue that cures in a week's time. Next, she further "pounds, cuts and shapes" the shafts to attain the unique, dangerously sparkling appearance of her "supports." To bind the shafts permanently, copper bars are made by hand and secured around the glued columns and tiny handmade copper pins are set in holes that have been precisely drilled through the stacked, shattered glass.

Nancy Mee has battled what some conventional glass artists embrace. Wanting instead to set up an irritating dichotomy, she admits to the difficulty of balancing the "overwhelming beauty of glass and the harsh quality of my meaning." What is that meaning? Affecting what Buster Simpson has called a more "holistic than crafty approach," Mee seeks to use the durability of glass as a metaphor for good health. While her earlier work contained X-ray phototransfers of girls' contorted backs in various stages of scoliosis enmeshed in "green" glass panels, her current art has dropped literal photographic references almost altogether and depends on the sculptures' strict formal qualities to express her ideas.

Given this shift, her use of glass as element to convey meaning works—for the most part. In *Support—A Pair for the Braced and Wrapped*, iron wire is randomly wound around an inner "spine" of vertically stacked glass shards. The tight packing of windowpane fragments simulates a spinal fluid chamber and functions as vehicle for a commentary on clarity and health. In the right-hand segments of each piece, Mee has constructed elaborate braces attached to glass fragments, suggesting a straightened spine. All the other materials used have a further medical analogy in that they are assimilable by the human body and used variously in orthopedic surgery. Finally, the fluidity of glass provides a general metaphor for the unstable nature of the body, too.

Returning to the functional heritage of glass, but in a quirky postmodern way, Charles B. Luce uses glass as a building material for
installations and small props related to a complicated mythology for
his persona, Osawa. It was Luce who introduced the "vandal glass" as
sculptural element in 1976 that Millett would use later with such ef-
fectiveness. The former's *Green Wall (Mer)* incorporated green-paint-
ed plywood, bamboo, stone and "vandal glass" in a sculptural wall
installation. Following that, the artist experimented with mirror and
neon in his *Imagined Inverted Staircase* (done at <u>and/or</u>), an intriguing set of wooden steps surrounded by glass-like materials.

His first major use of transparent glass plate was at the Seattle Art
Museum in his 1978 *Reconstruction of the Aether House, Part I*. All of
Luce's art has revolved around the notion of "informed objects," usually, functional objects rendered useless by an aestheticization which
presumably replaces utility with private meaning. Put another way,
Luce's "informed objects" are for another's use: Osawa's. In the SAM
piece, the original "aether house" was "destroyed by an earthquake
because it was too near a mountain; it contained an inverted staircase." The "reconstruction," therefore, was an act by the artist's alter
ego to restore order to the serenity of the "aether house," a container
for air. At this point, glass is not a building material (though indeed
the structure consists of glass sheets placed on a wooden frame) but
rather as with Nancy Mee, a metaphor. Glass is, as Luce puts it,
"frozen liquid." Like ether, it is still in the process of "moving, giving
off energy, becoming informed." The large eight-foot-square installation was also built of pine and glacial schist. All the panes in *Aether
House* and a companion piece, *Holding Device for Aether Pains*, are
acid-etched which gives the effect of wind moving over a transparent
surface.

Buster Simpson's tenure at Pilchuck (1971–73) came to an abrupt
end when patron and founder John H. Hauberg reportedly viewed
the artist's *Hot Glass on Plate Glass* videotapes (done in collaboration with Toots Zynsky) and summarily dismissed him. Those tapes
occupy a place within the history of Northwest glass art akin to
Duchamp's readymade snow shovels and urinals. They outraged, they
influenced, they captured the medium's essentials in a new way and,
in my opinion, they will one day appear as prophetic of a new way of
thinking about glass. Simpson, the major sculptor to emerge from the
Pacific Northwest since Robert Maki, has been associated with glass
long before Pilchuck was. Before Zynsky's tapes of his laying crosses
of hot molten glass on solid plate and allowing it to crack and shatter
on camera (thereby pointing up the simultaneously fluid and stable

nature of glass), Simpson trained as a ceramist and sculptor at the University of Michigan. His earliest work with glass was not so much anti-craft as conceptual craft. Just as Howard Kottler's decal production souvenir plates poked fun of American culture, Simpson's *History of Urban Window Repair* (1969–1973) provided the first thorough documentation of an American vernacular approach to working with glass. Storefronts, homes, automotive repair shops, and other unwitting scenes of glass' beauty from New York to Seattle form the subject of this witty artwork.

After a 1970–71 residency at the Rhode Island School of Design with Dale Chihuly, Simpson came to Pilchuck as video documenter: "I was interested in a use of the material as it made itself available. I did a little bit of blowing, but I decided if I were to become a proficient blower, it would take more time."

Instead, he took infra-red flash stills of nighttime "drawings" with glass (*Half-Minute Infra-Red Performance*, 1972) and made videotapes with *New West* magazine food critic Ruth Reichl of bacon and eggs cooking on hot glass ladled from the furnace (*Video Hot Glass Breakfast*, 1972).

Simpson's first Seattle sculptural projects also involved glass in an unusual way. *Selective Disposal Project and Manual* (1972)—done in collaboration with Chris Jonic—included an untitled installation in an abandoned loft (85 Yesler Way) of two six-by-four-foot glass plates held by two wooden wedges in front of an exterior window and a collected pile of pigeon droppings. Once again, the use of glass combined a flaunting of inherent qualities ("invisibility," reflection of light) with a spurning of them (not dusting the glass, setting the droppings nearby). An angry response, in some ways, to the refined craft mania of Pilchuck, it equaled the Stanwood Fellows in elegance of execution all the same.

Cone Cups (1979–1981) were shown at Simpson's Seattle Art Museum exhibition with Andrew Keating in the "New Ideas" series organized by curator Charles Cowles. A cone cup consists of a rolled, hollowed-out, hot glass cone shoved into a chromed, recycled bedspring to serve as a cup holder. A newer version of this functional art object was done in Mt. St. Helens glass, a greenish-black shade made from ash of Washington's latest volcano.

Continuing in the recycling vein so important to this environmentally conscious artist, *Glass Chair* (1978) takes a child's aluminum-tubing kitchen chair of the 1950s and replaces the original cushions with small sheets of one-inch-thick plate glass. This simple act also sums

Buster Simpson: *Crowbar Bottle Trap Shoot (Ninety Pine Street)*, 1983, steel, glass and rubber, 19 x 8 x 22' [destroyed]. Photo: Free Advice Consulting Co.

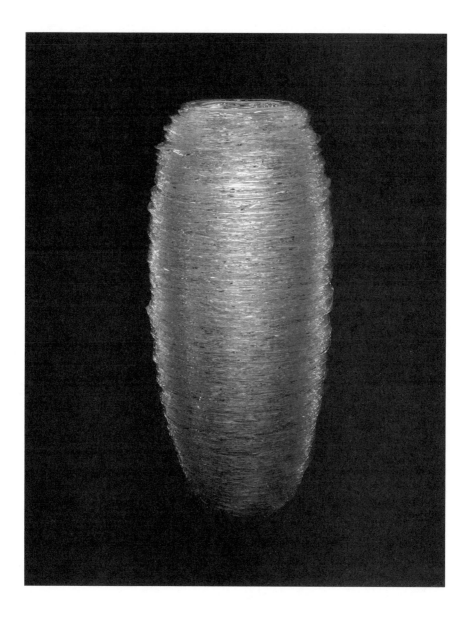

Toots Zynsky: *Waterspout #9*, 1979/94, fused glass filaments, 19 1/4 x 8 3/4" dia.,
Dan and Linda Rocker Silverberg collection. Photo: Rob Vinnedge

William Morris: *Antler Stack*, 1992, blown and sandblasted glass, 42 x 36 x 36".
Courtesy of William Morris Studio, Stanwood, Washington. Photo: Rob Vinnedge

up what is distinctive about Simpson as a glass artist. He has mixed modernist roots (Duchamp) with crafts heritage and come up with an art that is singular among American sculptors today, but one also tied to a functional history of the medium.

Therman Statom, also a RISD graduate, moved to Seattle in 1980. Briefly director of glass at the City of Seattle's Pratt Fine Arts Center, he embodies the newest use of glass on a "heroic" or large-scale level. His untitled small cast-glass houses have become a signature shape and act as symbols of simultaneous domestic security and chaos. By sticking colored shards into them and melting wax crayons on them while they are still hot after casting, Statom has created objects of great spontaneity and beauty. Although he is now working in a glass-related medium at the Wilkerson, Washington Sandstone Quarry, Statom's major sculptural works thus far have been room-size installations of nine-foot-high transparent glass sheets.

At Portland State University's Littman Gallery and at Seattle's Traver Sutton Gallery, the Washington, D.C.-born artist shoved aside issues of fragility or breakage and moved closer to monumental glass. To be sure, Charles B. Luce's Seattle Art Museum installation and DeWain Valentine's 1979 Los Angeles County Museum of Art installation already set the pace for such work. Statom, however, has avoided the geometric and minimalist character of Valentine's art and offered an approach more akin in appearance to Abstract Expressionism. The scribbled gesture, by both crayon and glass rod, has extended the medium's possibilities and turned it into a *tabula rasa* for the artist's ignited and activated images. Like Simpson, he has not relinquished the internally fluid properties of glass but twisted them to an end at once more theatrical and conceptual than refined or elegant.

Such an extension of the medium, though anticipated by Simpson, has been echoed by Luce, Mee, Millett and Statom. Together, they suggest the unlimited potential of a medium heretofore generally thought of as suitable for functional or decorative use. The controversial ambiguity between art and craft, beauty and function, is still an integral and propelling force in American art. These artists represent but a fragment or shard, if you will, of a larger mosaic.

BUSTER SIMPSON:
THROWAWAY GLASS

One of the lesser-known co-founders of the Pilchuck Glass School, Buster Simpson, did not last long there but the shadow he has subsequently cast on Pacific Northwest art and, now, art in public places across America, has become long indeed. Brought in by Dale Chihuly in 1971 and politely ushered out by John Hauberg in 1973, Buster Simpson set up a dark room for Pilchuck, taught theory, assembled video equipment, planned temporary housing, and worked with hot glass.

He is a good example of an artist who was initially attracted to the Puget Sound area because of Pilchuck but who stayed on to do great things. Among the many others in this situation are Charles Parriott, Paul Marioni, Walter Lieberman, William Morris, and Benjamin Moore.

"Reflectivity, transparency, fragility and breakability" are the four properties of glass Simpson most admires. Buster Simpson's use of glass is experimental, improvisatory, disposable, interchangeable, and subversive of traditional craft aesthetics and expectations. His aversion to authority and his playful transformation of that into open-ended, unfinished-looking mixed-media objects is the antithesis of high craft. With good reason, his works have stressed their social context over their aesthetic object status, often at great expense but, more usually, to the benefit of art, craft, and content.

Born in a sawmill town in Michigan in 1942, raised as a Boy Scout in Frankenmuth, Michigan, and educated in ceramics and sculpture at the University of Michigan, Buster Simpson blended a Midwest Protestant moral pragmatism with the wild and wacky values of American college campuses of the 1960s: community is better than individuals; cheap is better than expensive; people matter more than big companies.

Eyewitness observer and occasional participant in the shenanigans of the Ann Arbor performance-art gathering, ONCE Group, Simpson early on amalgamated street theatrics, social missions, and subversive attitudes toward the mastery of art materials into his own studio practice. "I never really blew glass but I was interested in it as a hot medium—I cooked breakfast on heated glass plate at Pilchuck," the artist recalled in his Yakima Street studio in Seattle's Mt. Baker area.

Expressing a very different view of the Pilchuck Glass School's origins and possibilities, he mentioned how, after participating in the epoch-making 1969 Woodstock Festival, he became convinced art needed to become more integrated into life. He helped design and build the original dwellings at Pilchuck using recycled French doors and tree houses. These, in turn, were the inspirations for architect Thomas Bosworth's award-winning designs for the school.

Black Mountain College, the celebrated and short-lived multi-media summer camp college near Asheville, North Carolina that flourished in the early 1950s, was more a model of Simpson's dream Pilchuck School than Dale Chihuly's sense of a Haystack School on the West Coast.

Settling in Seattle in 1973 on lower Western Avenue near Pioneer Square in the first of seven separate studio spaces, Simpson took full advantage of nearby Perkins Glass Co. when it moved to new facilities and left behind hundreds of pieces of glass. Thus began Simpson's first Seattle period, his "urban archeology and excavation" phase which tracked down and mopped up after an extraordinary downtown building boom of the 1975–85 period. Thirty high-rise buildings were erected, 60,000 low-income residents were displaced, and the city's greatest artist quarter, Denny Regrade or Belltown, flourished, faded, and was disfigured by real estate developers.

From the beginning, Simpson was there to photograph, chronicle, make art on the spot, and gain great inspiration from the battle and, as we shall see, the bottle. Glass became an essential tool and symbol of changing Seattle. It reflected the cloudy and rainy skies; it was the eyelid on each building about to be torn down; it was the container for the cheap fortified wine which numbed many of the down-and-out inhabitants; it was the new material for the Pilchuck refugees who left the countryside and rushed to a livable city with cheap studio space, cheap hydroelectric power, and a palpable sense of community.

Whether a repair in a cracked window of an auto-repair garage using a real wrench (1974), a recycled kitchen aluminum-tubing chair "padded" with thick plate glass and a truck windshield (1975); or the placement of old glass sheets on a dusty floor to accumulate surrounding dust (1978), Simpson's archeological-phase works took into consideration the changing aspects of a city in flux. They redeemed the environment as he found it in the alleys and gutters. The far side of technique, his method involved discovery, alteration, and documentation, in short, 1970s Process Art—using glass.

When he moved north of the Pike Place Market in 1975, Simpson joined the City of Seattle's design review commission for the market historic landmark district and began a series of on-site art projects within the main artery, Post Alley. These were barely perceptible to the average passerby but still radiate a glow in the memory today that far outlasts their temporary nature. For instance, transparent glass plumbing pipe was used to create a see-through downspout filled with limestone fragments that "purified" polluted rainwater and then provided water for nearby plants clinging to an old brick wall.

Later, *Ninety Pine Street* (1983) was the best and most important of the Pike Place Market projects. Glass was an essential metaphor on every level of meaning. First, the plate glass windows of the abandoned tavern at 90 Pine St. within the Market acted as observing sites for pedestrians to gaze in on an elaborate and mysteriously beautiful tableau. Next, by creating a complicated wine- and beer-bottle recycling site behind the old tavern, Simpson drew attention to alcoholism, a sensitive side effect of downtown development.

Galvanized aluminum daubed with black tar was the material for silhouette windvanes of the Northwest's ubiquitous crows and ravens, also potent Native Northwest Coast symbols of transformation and adaptation. Simpson set up the crows as targets for the street population to toss their empty beer or cheap fortified wine bottles at. The bottles dropped down and accumulated in 55-gallon drums, were separated into green and brown glass, and sold to a local recycling company for $90. The money was given to the non-profit Pike Place Market Community Clinic.

On the roof, Simpson placed full-length hatted figures made of flat steel and attached to revolving poles that ran through the roof into the old tavern below. There they were connected to matching figures placed behind the counter that was covered with empty Mexican brown-glass beer bottles. When the wind turned the silhouettes up top, the figures below would shift and knock off beer bottles onto the floor.

Simpson drew attention to the city's growing migrant worker Hispanic population and to the paradox of Mexico's having a thriving commercial glass industry manufacturing, among other things, beer bottles.

Archeologist, activist, chronicler, and conscience for a city rebuilding itself into a Pacific Rim megalopolis, Simpson left Belltown in 1989, driven out by disappearing cheap studio space and, with his marriage to Laura Sindell, the need to find a environment more suitable to raising a family.

A few other discreet objects using glass bear mentioning. For a 1980 installation at Western Front in Vancouver, British Columbia, the artist evolved a plumb-bob shape in glass suspended below a silhouette of a crouching surveyor-engineer figure. Filled with water, it reflected the rest of the exhibition upside down.

A later work, *Crystal Ball* (1989), filled a spherical vase with water and inverted it over a Styrofoam cup to seal in the water. Once again, the "future" foreseen by this purported psychic's tool was seen upside down.

Inverted forms, mirror images, and distorted symmetries have become repeated formal elements in Simpson's art and it is important not to pass over these aspects in a zeal to recognize his sincere social message. Lacking the artist's convoluted language and often unwittingly confusing explanations, the viewer is left with a panorama of unexpected configurations of familiar objects.

Joseph Cornell, Marcel Duchamp, Robert Smithson, and the Canadian sculptor Jerry Pethick are all people Simpson has acknowledged as influences but, parting company with them, he has always insisted on a practical dimension to his art, as if aesthetic qualities alone were somehow suspect.

A 1991 Seattle Art Museum exhibition, "The Effluence of Affluence", organized by chief curator Patterson Sims, brought together a medley of the more palatable Simpson projects. Four bathroom-corner sinks were separated by mirrors creating an especially striking set of illusions. Half of each mirror was de-silvered so that one museumgoer standing at a sink would be seen through the half-mirror by another. This slivering of the figurative image bluntly implies a psychological metaphor of "split personality" and has great untapped potential for further investigation.

After nearly 30 years of using what he calls "just another material", Simpson plans to install the four-way sinks and half-mirrors in a Seattle public men's restroom. That project and whatever it may lead to will definitely merit close critical scrutiny. At a time when glass is being used beyond the craft world, Buster Simpson's contribution appears to have been prophetic.

TOOTS ZYNSKY: THE CLIMATE OF COLOR

INTRODUCTION

> Éclat, coupure, fragilité, transparence,translucide et
> transplendissant, leverre est toujours en transe.
>
> —Jean-Pascal Billaud on Toots Zynsky, 1990

The art of Mary Ann Zynsky, known since childhood by the family
name Toots, is a result of restless experimentation, deep subjectivity
of intent, and a profound affinity to glass as an art material. Using
glass as a vehicle for her expressive ideas, she has created her own
vision of its rigidity and fragility, its opacity and transparency, its
power to convey suggestive meanings of memory, its power to carry
line and color.

Now an accumulation of over 30 years of achievement, revision, development and success, the art of Toots Zynsky emerges out of the triple
fountainheads of the American studio glass movement: the Rhode
Island School of Design, where she turned from painting to glass in
1969; the Pilchuck Glass School in the Pacific Northwest which she
co-founded with Dale Chihuly and others in 1971; and her relationship to Italian glass, starting in 1983 when she traveled to Venice
searching for materials, and continuing to the present day with her
use of solid-colored canes manufactured there for her.

As we shall see, her stable New England roots and Polish-Lithuanian
background (her grandparents came to the U.S. in 1917) gave her the
confidence to travel widely and to feel at home in Europe. Her art has
developed as a result of three other factors: an openness to experiment, innovate and act intuitively; the freedom to travel in the U.S.,
Europe, Africa and Asia and to assimilate those experiences into her
art; and the claiming of western Europe as a home base for her career
as artist, teacher, designer and lecturer.

Connecting together such diverse yet related strains is like the way
Zynsky has connected both the diversity of her life—artist, traveler,
parent—and that of her artistic background—painter, rebel, innova-
tor, professional, master glass artist.

Toots Zynsky is among the most important American artists living in
Europe because she has adapted European materials and the inspirations of European painting to a completely original end. She has built
upon the elevation of individual subjectivity in early 20th-century
European art (what Sir Herbert Read called the "art of inner neces-

sity") and, indeed, even exhibited in 1989 with Russian Suprematist Kasimir Malevich at the time of her retrospective exhibition at the Stedelijk Museum in Amsterdam. Given such European affinities, she has also consistently favored American-style innovation and exploration over the strict observance of decorative arts traditions within conventional art history.

The fact that her Russian grandmother was a master weaver adds another European link, the passing down of family traditions of craftsmanship that are transformed in the process. Not repairing tapestries (as did Louise Bourgeois's family), Zynsky makes three-dimensional tapestries out of glass thread: intricate, linear, yet dependent upon spatial form for their being and beauty.

In addition, her travels brought her into contact with the purity of color in medieval religious painting (as in Fra Angelico) and was responsible for her shift from primaries to a broader palette once she was in Europe for good.

As was so often true for the Generation of 1968 (*les soixante-huitièmistes*), her rebellion and questioning were informed and inspired by prior family traditions. In the process of her education and subsequent studio activities, she has responded to those family legacies as well as to the spirit of '68.

The evolution of Toots Zynsky's work is a result of many years' experience amalgamating her knowledge with her experience and artistic sensibility. She has assimilated and transposed many different techniques at the same time: glassblowing, pâte-de-verre casting, slumping, and fusing, along with the issue of how to use color in glass in the most compelling way.

THE EXPERIMENTAL YEARS 1971–1983

The crafts or decorative arts in the 20th century have often been defended as shadow movements behind greater artistic style shifts. For example, Art Déco followed Purism, modern design emerged out of the Bauhaus, and postwar American ceramic sculpture supposedly parroted the abandon of Abstract Expressionism. The work that Toots Zynsky created throughout the 1970s and early 1980s was related by critics and commentators to Process Art, Italian Arte Povera, and Minimal art but it had its own parallel development, quite independent of New York or Milan. As she told Mary Blume of the *International Herald Tribune*:

> People said, "You're doing process art"but it had nothing to do with that. I did itbecause I wanted to know why sometimes glassbreaks

and sometimes it doesn't because itisn't really logical. We attached contactmicrophones to glass and learned it canbreak without your even seeing a crack, youjust hear it. Also, I am fascinated by the sound of glass because I love sound and music.[1]

Thus, as she began her undertakings in glass, Zynsky's interests were not strictly attuned to art-world developments, or even art, but sound. This roots her in an aural world, like the music and theories of American composer John Cage ("There is no such thing as silence."), as well as a visual one.

Her earliest glass at Rhode Island School of Design, untitled blown pieces of white glass, were traditional vessels despite their extravagant handles. During freshman year at RISD, she turned to glass rather than painting after visiting the glass studio in 1969 and was attracted to the fun-loving, open-ended attitudes in the program under Dale Chihuly. As she told Jean-Claude Bester:

> We were looking for alternative answersto established institutions, lifestyles, and philosophies. . . . Anything was possible.[2]

One "alternative answer to established institutions" proved to be the Pilchuck Glass School in Stanwood, Washington, to which she was invited by Dale Chihuly in 1971, the summer he was trying to set up a summer craft school similar to Haystack in Maine, or Penland in North Carolina. Over 35 years later, the school itself is a respected "established institution," but in the early days, from 1971 to 1974, Zynsky was part of an extraordinary assembly of people who not only built the buildings and facilities to make glass, but who changed the face of glass art permanently.

In experiments like *Hot Glass/Plate Glass* and *Thermal Shock Sculpture* (both 1971) with Buster Simpson, Zynsky stretched the limits of glass and art. The videotaping of the four square glass plates in *Hot Glass/Plate Glass* while molten glass made them crack and was related by others (in retrospect) to classic Process Art pieces like Robert Morris's *Box with the Sound of its Own Making* (1969) but, unlike Morris, Zynsky obliterates the sanctity of the object itself, an even more subversive act. The explosive sounds accompanying the breakage and the chance elements of how the glass broke differently each time were highly appealing to Zynsky. Differing rhythms and volumes of the breaking sounds seemed like a form of music to her, much more important than the visual results.

During the subsequent years, while living in Seattle and Pownell, Vermont, Stanwood, Washington, and New York, other works also violated the purity of the vessel, commenting on the violent times more than the hallowed vessel tradition. One artist, Mary Shaffer, further developed the ideas she discussed with Zynsky and represented by Zynsky in *Wall Piece* (1973) and *Thermal Shock Sculpture*. Shaffer's own slumped clear-glass sculptures demonstrate the impact of their conversations. Zynsky's "Breaks and Relocation" series (1979) applied broken shards to the insides and outsides of clear blown vase shapes. This work and others like *Promises and other Misinformation* (1980) built upon the Pilchuck experiments with Simpson and had a further impact on younger Seattle artists like Walter Lieberman and Michael Burns. With the defiant inclusion of jagged shards, Zynsky was redefining beauty and reflecting the bitter social realities of American cities and society that made more openly beautiful objects seem superfluous.

Promises and other Misinformation keeps the clear vase intact but fills it with spiky, cut pieces of glass, the forerunners to her later glass threads, and an important component of line quality that would also dominate her later work. By omitting color at this point, Zynsky was letting the viewer see into and through the container whereas in later works, exterior and interior "sides" of the bowls are read separately as colored surfaces.

By the time of her first New York show at the Theo Portnoy Gallery in 1982, Zynsky had accommodated beauty (through monochrome hues of red, black and green) and remained true to the expressively violent shard module she developed. Building on her *Cocktail Party* (1981) and *Dust Collectors* (1979), a four-part work, *The Queen, The Decoy, the Pawn and the Joker* (1982) presented to New York audiences a radically different approach to the short-stemmed cup or fluted glass form. With painstakingly hand-pulled long threads set on each glass, Zynsky created a kind of vicious lace that was similar to the New York punk sensibility of the early 1980s. The whole work takes on a board-game-like character both in its composition and card-like colors. When the pieces are upside-down, they even resemble the chess pieces and card-pack images of the title.

The Guardian, Keeper of the Trap and *Longing* (1982), all in the same exhibition, were individually conceived breakthroughs that were completely unlike anything in the art world at the time. Even so, *The Guardian's* corner placement recalls Richard Serra's spattered-lead *Splashing* (1968). *Absent Without Leave* and *Clipped Grass* moved away from corner and wall-mounted works to the bowl form that Zynsky would perfect in the coming decade.

Besides the unusually innovative examples of her New York debut—placement, material, a sense of the aftermath of violence—the most important outcome of the exhibition was a meeting with Dutch artist Mathijs Teunissen van Manen. As Zynsky told Shawn Waggoner, he

> saw us pulling the glass by hand.He thought the method was "medieval" and within 24 hours, had jerry-rigged together a marvelous contraption that pulled glass continually from cane. There have been four machines since then, and the one I have now is a brilliant, wacky, eccentric device loosely based on the process Corning used to pull fiber optics.[3]

Once Teunissen van Manen devised the first thread-pulling machine, Zynsky quickly developed further methods, with help from Lithuanian glass artist Albinas Elskus. The pieces are, as she told Waggoner, "laid out flat on a bed of compressed plaster. . . . They are slumped into one of a series of four or five different stainless steel molds, some of which are found and some made to my specification by a local metal spinner."[4]

With all the new techniques falling into place, Zynsky realized that, like parts in a jigsaw puzzle that are assembled from the outside in to attain the overall image, she had to begin by working backwards towards the "solution," laying down what will be the threads of the outer wall first, then working toward the central void. Though her current work is extraordinarily varied in color, the first *filets de verre* (threads of glass), like *Clipped Grass* were monochrome, like the other works in the 1982 Portnoy show.

When the breakthrough occurred, a whole new world opened up for the artist. Newly equipped technically, with a well-received New York debut and a Corning Museum of Glass acquisition of *Clipped Grass* to her credit, Zynsky moved to Europe in early 1983, at first in search of the materials in Italy that she now uses extensively. Not expecting to stay for the next 15 years, she gradually realized after one month in Italy and then in the Netherlands that Europe was the place for her. The move there would usher in a decade of travel—Africa, North America, Europe, Asia—which would, once again, change her work profoundly and coincide with a new mastery and artistic maturity.

After her first trip to Venice in 1983 researching materials sources, Zynsky returned the following year, invited by the de Santillana family of the Venini Glass Company who had learned of her work through a former RISD classmate, Tina Aufiero.

Originally invited to create unique sculptural pieces, she eventually had an opportunity to work informally with blowers on the hotshop floor. The pieces she created with them were so well received that the company asked her to edition them for sale.

Although her stay at that time was only two months long, she not only inadvertently created two series of designs for functional pieces to go into production ("Folto" and "Mulinello," both of which are still in production) she also ended up creating a number of sculptural works at the same time.

After Raoul Gardini acquired the Venini Company in 1986, the new owner asked Zynsky to return to Venini as art director. Declining the offer, Zynsky made a crucial decision to stay at the Amsterdam studio and avoid further ties to industry for the time being. However, in 1991, she returned once more to Venice and executed a limited edition of pieces for E.O.S. Long after Venini, her ties to the de Santillana family remain stronger than any relationship to the company.

THE NOMADIC YEARS 1984–1994

> Africa was one of the most profound and enduring experiences of my life. I knew that the challenge of assimilating an entirely different set of cultural values was essential for one at that point in my existence and career.
>
> —Toots Zynsky[5]

The impact of Toots Zynsky's six-month stay in Ghana in 1984 was only felt after her return to the Netherlands where she had settled in 1983. When she and Teunissen van Manen both received a Klankschap Foundation grant to travel to west Africa to experience and record popular and folk music traditions, little did Zynsky realize that the residue of visual experiences—the birds, sunsets, water, land, and ethnic fabrics—would seep into her art in a way that would transform it remarkably. Once she resumed making art again back in Europe, roughly three months after returning, it was the memory of kente cloths and striped silk fabrics that was felt in series like the "Silk Bowls" and "African Dreams" (1985).

These works signal the first fully mature phase of Zynsky's oeuvre. The avid interest of museum curators in Denmark and elsewhere affirmed the sense that, beyond the radical experiments of her New York and Seattle-Pilchuck periods, the "Silk Bowls" and "African Dreams" were responding to experience rather than reacting against it. Leaving behind the barbed wire, shattered pieces, and omission of color, the new work was dazzlingly colorful, intact, and closer to painting. With newfound freedom, a greater wealth of materials thanks to the thread-pulling machine, and the inspiration of the

Ghana trip, Zynsky used the threads and the molding-and-slumping process to echo the informality of natural growth in the upper edges of the bowl. Each work became a three-dimensional metaphorical fragment of memory. The irregular shape of the "Silk Bowls" also mimicked the soft curves of pliable cloth yet were rigid and unfoldable.

Combining a number of guest teaching appointments throughout Europe and the U.S., in England, the Netherlands, Ohio, and Switzerland, Zynsky jockeyed her studio activities into a further fertile remembrance of Africa in "Exotic Birds" (1984–1987); "Birds of Paradise" (1984–1987); and "Angry Birds" (1986). Feathers were the material metaphor the glass simulated in these and, for the first time, multiple colors appeared within single pieces. A stunning contrast to the quiet, placid monochrome colors in the earliest "African Dreams," the "Birds" ignited the artist's dormant color sense.

Like the 17th-century English poet Andrew Marvell's poems "Bermuda" and "The Garden," Toots Zynsky's art recaptured "a green thought in a green shade." That is, she transformed the specifics of her memory of tropical climates into generalized works of art, like poems. The extent of the artifice, the elaborate and lush color, and the repeated rhythms of pattern are shared by both Zynsky and Marvell.

As for many other artists in the 20th century (Paul Valéry, Henri Matisse, Andre Gide, Paul Bowles), Africa proved to be a way for Zynsky to release her imaginative attraction to intense visual phenomena, both natural and manmade. The "exotic birds" of the bowls each take on the character of individual animals joined by a common species. The American-born artist created separate creative entities that are tied together by the overarching theme of the birds.

Zynsky's homages to cloth cannot be underestimated during this period, both its pliability and its basis for repetitive decoration. The influence of cloth and the potential of glass with its own draping quality should be considered, too. Harkening back to the artist's experimental slumped pieces of the late 1970s, the new work built upon that but took it several steps farther.

Kente cloths, the ceremonial and everyday fabrics of the Ashante people of Ghana, made their influence felt in the extraordinary patterns. As she told Bester:

> Inevitably, however, the impact of the kente fabrics, the countryside, the indigenous architecture and the strong character of the people left an indelible mark on my work.[6]

Zynsky's approach to color changed gradually, shifting from little or no color during the experimental years to monochrome or bicolored pieces shortly after the African trip. With a limited yet multiple range of hues in the "Exotic Birds," Zynsky simultaneously altered the nature of the bowl lip, folding it inward or crimping it irregularly to add more interest to the overall profile of the bowl.

Both color and form intensified in the next series, "Tierra del Fuego" (1988–1992), works which set vivid reds and oranges against black areas. Never having visited the Tierra del Fuego region of southern Argentina, Zynsky's use of the term is an imaginary "land of fire."

Glass and all its territory are a "land of fire," the fire of the hot shop, the flames of the oven and the heat of the kiln. In addition, the chromatic shift was a transition away from cooler hues like blue and green and an echo of her first New York show at Theo Portnoy where in many of the pieces used bright red.

It was not until the advent of the "Chaos and Order" series (1992–1997) that the artist began a full investigation of color and line within the same piece. When the Musée des arts Decoratifs, Paris, acquired *Blue Moon, Total Eclipse, Isla Bella* from the "Tierra del Fuego" series in 1987, the expatriate artist felt honored and confirmed in her new direction. Other museums followed suit in Germany, New York, New Jersey, Australia and elsewhere around the world.

Considering how orderly many of the colored stripes in the "Chaos and Order" series are, it's hard to analyze the series title short of imagining how all glassmaking involves a certain chaos. Zynsky is literally bringing order out of chaos, however, and making some of her most beautiful pieces in the process. She is responding to the night lights of Paris in many of these pieces, afterthoughts and inspirations of her many nightly walks around the city with its street architecture, bright lights, and brightly lit areas and shadows. Like Robert Delaunay's responses to Paris early in the twentieth century, her pieces use curves, lines, and color to evoke the magic of Paris.

With strictly regulated stripes resembling wide plant leaves in works like *Italian Chaos* (1994), for example, or blurred edges of color in *The Paradise Piece* (1992), the artist demonstrates how potentially inexhaustible both her technique and imagination are. *Sunrise Chaos* and *City Lights* (both 1993) reintroduce black as a linear element that offsets the colored background but also adds structural divisions to the circumference of the bowl's surface. As Jean-Luc Olivié put it, she achieved a "symbiosis of drawing and color. . . a synthesis of decoration and form."

Africa is far away now, with the bowl surfaces seeming much more
urban than rural, their colors more sophisticated than merely intu-
ited or rooted in the natural world.

THE CLIMATE OF COLOR: 1994–1998

She reads the universe in splashes of color.
—Jean-Pascal Billaud on Toots Zynsky[7]

Just as the "Tierra del Fuego" series alluded to the fiery reds of the
Theo Portnoy Gallery pieces like *Red Curtain* and *Corner Piece,*
Zynsky's clear "Waterspouts," commissioned by Cara McCarty of the
Museum of Modern Art, New York, (and later of the St. Louis Art
Museum), reintroduced the pale or no-color pieces of the experimen-
tal years. These cylindrical and bulging forms using horizontally
wrapped clear-glass threads were an important hiatus from color.
Later, the Corning Museum also acquired one of the "Waterspouts."

Another prestigious commission came from Susanne K. Frantz, curator of the Corning Museum of Glass, who asked Zynsky to create a
pair of works, *Pagaritos en la Cabeza* and *Cabellos de Angel* (from the
"Tierra del Fuego" series) to honor two of the museum's patrons, Dr.
and Mrs. Leonard S. Rakow.

Comparisons to Color Field painter Morris Louis (1912–1962) come to
the fore with works like *Italian Chaos IV* (1994) and the two "Chaos
and Order" pieces acquired by the North Norwegian Decorative Arts
Museum in Trondheim. Louis worked in diluted acrylic paint on un-
gessoed canvas of great size but, like Zynsky, he favored overlapping
bands of color that interacted with one another. Intensified and more
materially focused in the medium of glass thread, Zynsky uses color to
trigger such experiences on an intimate material scale. Rather than the
huge environmental feeling of Louis's canvases, Zynsky's bowls elicit a
touchable, near devotional, feeling on the part of the viewer.

After the expatriate artist settled down with homes in Paris and
Amsterdam in 1990, her nomadic pursuits slowed somewhat, despite
continuing international interest in her objects. According to Olivié,
Zynsky shares her "preoccupations as a painter and as a sculptor-pot-
ter" combining both aspects in each work.

Color acts as line in Zynsky or, as Olivié continued, "each thread is a
line of inner tension, a gesture that is color." Given her complete mastery of the threading technique, it appears that Zynsky can use color
and line in just about any way she wishes. This is not the same as a
painting that is restricted to a flat, two-dimensional plane. Zynsky's

work operates fully in all three dimensions and it is its existence in space that distinguishes it from wall-mounted paintings.

We revolve around a Toots Zynsky bowl, rotate it, and contemplate its chromatic narrative in the same way we turn a Greek vase to tell its story. Line and color become event, not in the sense of her early video performance timed events, but in the optical sense that the viewer is engaged and confronted by chromatic and linear events.

In the process of looking, the viewer steps into a climate of color no less environmental than a Morris Louis painting but experienced imaginatively in the eye, not the body. From the public demonstrations of the limits of glass during the experimental years, through the advances of the thread-pulling machine, Toots Zynsky has evolved into an artist of intimate sensations. Her art attracts the viewer into an interior world where color sets an emotional tone, and shape enacts a visual rhythm that enhances and reinforces an overall aesthetic experience unique to each individual work.

WILLIAM MORRIS: PALEOGLASS

William Morris (b. 1957) has created a fully peopled and furnished imaginary world, his vision of prehistory. It is an idealized culture of men and women hunting, gathering, cooking and building shelters. Executed in glass, it has brought forth a variety of reactions. This essay briefly examines Morris's critical response and offers its own theory of meaning for his work: how the making of objects can accumulate into a freshly imagined vision of human history; how art immersed in an imaginary past can counter the relentless pressure to create art reflecting current political problems; how art dealing with aggression, violence, and an untamed world can contribute to a reassessment of masculinity in the 1990s.

Nostalgic? It wasn't so long ago that the early Abstract Expressionists were alluding to the collective unconscious of Jung, the oedipal dreams of Freud, and the petroglyphic conundrums or "pictograms" in caves in attempts to attain "tragic and timeless" subject matter to replace the tired and tendentious social-political art of the 1930s.[1] Barnett Newman (*The Song of Orpheus*, 1945), Adolph Gottlieb (*Forgotten Dreams*, 1946), Mark Rothko (*Vessels of Magic*, 1946), Jackson Pollock (*Wounded Animal*, 1943), and Theodoros Stamos (*Movement of Plants*, 1945) all sought visual analogies to prehistory in efforts to de-verbalize American art, rendering it more philosophically profound and able to transcend immediate social context. Maybe William Morris is presenting his own version of Abstract Expressionism's "formative years."[2] Like them, he is seeking enduring alternatives to forms of contemporary art steeped in cynicism, irony, and the humiliation of the handmade object.

Morris's art steps back from the tendency toward blurring the figurative and the nonrepresentational that the early New York School favored. In his case, images and objects are definitely identifiable. All the same, he shares with them a fascination for archeology, preliterate artistic expressions, and the possibility of art that honors the ancient past by pushing a response toward it based in today's world.

Sculptor rather than painter, though, William Morris has used glass to embody such pursuits. With the advent of figurative imagery on his vessel surfaces around 1988, Morris came close to meeting painters on their own ground. Like ceramist Rudy Autio, he has managed to create substantial independent objects that become the ground for imagery that sets up narrative implications. In this sense, his art also resembles the Finnish concept of art, *taide*, wherein painting and sculpture are fused.

In a key insight, arts journalist Roger Downey claims viewers are always conscious of the surface.

> Sometimes it's because the surface is articulated into . . . patterns. . . . Sometimes you're aware of the surface because it demands to be read, bears quasi-totemic imagery.[3]

Less willing to go along for the ride, art critic Ron Glowen expressed a deeper, but widespread, prejudice about glass:

> [Morris's] grand idea of a meditation on mortality and life is hampered by a medium that is still too elegant, too glamorous, to make his statement seem real.[4]

And apparently it's all right for Nancy Graves (for whom Morris has made work) to create bone installations in bronze, but not acceptable for Morris to do it in glass, according to Ben Marks:

> sadly, there wasn't a hint of any underlying content, such as, in Graves's case, the rejection of European art culture in favor of a more pure aesthetic of the organic primitive and mystic (not to mention careful choice of bones)[5]

Why the double standard? Could it be that many art critics are uncomfortable with Morris's work or the deeper-content potential of glass because they despise its simultaneous decorative potential?

Even a co-author of *William Morris: Glass Art and Artifact*, Patterson Sims, could not resist condescending to the artist, accusing him of "picturesque escapism," allowing that in the new work (the artifact still lifes, installations, and petroglyphic surface decoration)

> for the first time, . . . ideas have made an appearance . . . vague concepts of history and time. [6]

Leaving it at that, Sims makes no further effort to interpret or unravel such purportedly "vague concepts," remaining content with a regrettable reference to "Jean-Paul Sartre and Indiana Jones" as an interpretive catch-phrase. In the same volume, Henry Geldzahler is closer to the mark when he uses Morris's *First Fruit* (1988) as a departure-point. One black skeleton reaches toward a clear one, becoming for him, the "ultimate paradigm of our national tragedy [racism]."[7] He also sagely points out a crucial difference between the younger artist and his ex-mentor Dale Chihuly. Morris's art is rooted in the earth and forest while Chihuly's emerges out of air and sea.

Most damaging, the third contributor to *Glass Art and Artifact* doubts whether Morris is an artist at all. Narcissus Quagliata claims

> Morris's work does not ask the viewer for an intellectual and studied response. . . . [He is] bypassing words, concepts, or thoughts

and confidently presumes that Morris "probably would object to being called an artist."[8] With friends like this, who needs critics?

Nevertheless, the art of William Morris cries out for interpretation. It may operate on many different levels of meaning. For example, are the installations and surface imagery allusions to a lost male culture or one so idealized that even its residue—death—sparkles and gleams? Or is his art a Romantic meditation on the ruins of early prehistoric cultures, an expression of the yearning to make contact with our human forebears? Embracing a decorative, i.e., beautiful, response to death may be too hard for many to take but the mesmerizing qualities of glass can actually act as shills or lures to the viewer, entrapping him or her in a voyage of discovery.

Or perhaps it is the doggedly masculine subject matter that repels others: hunting, trapping, killing. Yet a close reading of the surface imagery in *Suspended Artifacts* and the *Petroglyphic Vessels* reveals a co-existence of men and women in the artist's ancient world. Imagine for a moment a primeval Europe where women not only hunted but were a revered and extended focus for goddess worship. The writings of the late Marija Gimbutas proposed just such controversial theories and have found great favor among feminist art historians.[9] Why not place Morris's female imagery in that setting instead of consigning it to what Roger Downey derided as "little-nude-bimbo-with-black-stocking drawings that used to infest the margins of *Playboy*."[10]

In fact, women are empowered in Morris, wielding battleaxes, scouting animals, and acting as predators toward men as well as other dumb animals. Despite the repeated references to Morris's acknowledged influences (cave drawings at Lascaux, France, Stonehenge, etc.), his work always carries a different look, as if emerging from an as yet unknown culture he has personally excavated.

Long-time collaborator Jon Ormbrek does most of the drawings, themselves a technical innovation based on glass-thread and crushed-glass drawings done by Flora Mace in 1974 and taught to Morris and Ormbrek soon thereafter.

Beginning with the *Petroglyph Vessels* in 1988, Morris has extended both his vocabulary for meaningful surface decoration and for evocative forms. Perhaps initially limited to his vessels' flattened surface

as a focus for his and Ormbrek's drawings, Morris gradually expanded into bone still lifes, suspended "artifacts," and his most impressive
recent achievements, temporary museum and gallery installations.

I call such environments paleoglass. Paleoglass involves imaginary
excavation of materials, imagery, and theories of meaning. Paleoglass can act as an unraveler of coded visual symbols without being a
literal explainer. The paleoglass installations are a breakthrough in
a number of ways. As for Nancy Graves, they provide an "extended
field" for sculpture (to use Rosalind Krauss's term), a disparate, non-
monolithic collection of discrete objects that nonetheless assemble
into a whole. Not nostalgic but strangely bright and shining and new,
their sheen startles us into accepting the artist's "discovery" of a
paleolithic site.

But how dare death be so pretty, so glamorous? West Coast art has
long had fun with death. And Morris's background in ceramics with
Richard Fairbanks at Central Washington University surely provided
a context for such disjunctions. Arneson, to be sure, is a possible
influence but another is Clayton Bailey who pioneered mock-archeological installations as early as 1971. Morris has extended a West
Coast clay sculpture convention into glass. His scavo technique, a
chemical treatment that gives some of the bones a dusty surface, acts
as a glaze might in Arneson or Bailey. The point is, Morris must be
granted the latitude of humor for his paleoglass. Now his art must
carry the weight of wit as well as the weight of deeper content. Too
much to ask? Again, Arneson carried it off brilliantly—and Morris is
still young.

Death, humor, beauty, a new male culture—an impossible task for
any art to contain? Not at all. In fact, once one allows the possibility
of spoof (paramount in Bailey), Morris's art seems to breathe fresh
northern California air. This was the case with his Renwick Gallery
installation, *Garnering* (1990). Mastodon-like bones, antlers, human
skulls and tools were all found together, as if in an uncovered cave.
With death as the great leveler, Morris reminds us that regardless of
advanced weapons technology (millenia beyond the bow and arrow)
and extravagant efforts at national defense, we will all end up like
the figures in *Garnering*.

Situated in a city of museums, the Renwick installation in Washington, D.C, also summoned up another art-historical analogy: 17th-cen-
tury Dutch and Flemish vanitas still lifes with their symbolic skulls
and material possessions side by side. This is the same northern European, Protestant warning that comes through in Morris contrasting

with any California hedonism. Yes, Morris is a moralist, too, like his namesake, 19th-century Socialist and founder of the Arts and Crafts movement. But the younger artist concentrates on filling an art-viewing environment instead of the senior Morris's highly controlled living environment. This way, Junior Morris's warning, his Wordsworthian "intimations of immortality," must be placed in the context of our culture that more often than not resists such reminders. Through the seductive material appeal of glass, Glowen's unease notwithstanding, viewers are roped into contemplating the implications of his carefully assembled "excavations."

Cache (1993), the American Craft Museum installation in New York, further reinforced this dichotomy—beauty and death—much to the approval of critic Holland Cotter. He accepts Morris's "sacrificial altar and poacher's camp filled with animal and human remains" and concludes how Morris's and co-exhibitor Steve Tobin's "ideas could not have been embodied so effectively in any other medium."[11]

A freestanding sculpture made of multiple elements, *Antler Stack* (1992), suggests a future direction halfway between the earliest *Standing Stones* (1982) and the recent dispersed installation pieces. Powerful, evocative, and composed to the point of appearing casual or accidental, *Antler Stack* symbolically intertwines the trophies of violence (antlers) with their prior tools of destruction (spears). Visually stunning, this work also encapsulates the artist's growing power over composition, his gradually more complex approach to content, and most significantly, it offers a focus for his virtuosity that is equal to the profound content he earlier strove for but was unable to achieve.

Art-meaning resides in craft when it can invoke comparably poetic and metaphorical layers of meaning. William Morris embodies this when critics are active interpreters, taking notice of his twin heritages of early Abstract Expressionism and West Coast clay sculpture. With its ties to earth and the birth of human societies, his art is socially engaged as well, affirming the need for community as well as co-existence with the animal world. Add to that the possibility some of his art is chronicling a dying male culture of today, hunting.

In this sense, William Morris is a regional artist (Northwest ecological concerns) and an international one (his ample European exhibition record attests to this). By being reminded of the ancient past, we are confronted by contrast with our troubled present. By avoiding the scolding character of political art, he proposes relief, an escape into the past that is really a window onto the present, a present that sidesteps systems and elevates custom, ritual, and a masculinity under assault.

These issues and others comprise the content of the art of William Morris. They indeed border on the "tragic and timeless" Newman and Rothko longed for as artistic impulses.

Executed in glass, these works join an international culture of glass art, able to transcend one culture's hierarchical prejudice against craft and effortless travel about in a welcoming world.

Therman Statom: *Antarctic Novella*, 1994, sheet glass and paints, 90 x 84 x 84".
Photo: Courtesy of William Traver Gallery.

THERMAN STATOM: INSTALLING SPACE

Therman Statom is one of the most significant and prolific of American experimental glass artists. His museum, gallery, and contemporary art-space temporary installations using glass comprise a highly important (if subsequently destroyed) body of work. Born in Florida, educated at Rhode Island School of Design and Pratt Institute of Art and Design, Statom spent his formative years after school in Seattle and New York prior to moving to California and, after that, to Omaha. where he now maintains a studio.

The progression of over a dozen separate installations between 1980 and the present constitute perhaps the most important art he has done even though glass collectors may know him better from his numerous gallery shows of glass sculptures in Washington, D.C., Seattle, New York, Chicago, as well as in Sweden and France.

Like the title of two early Seattle installations, Therman Statom is a "tornado" and "hurricane" of activity. The exhilarating and often frightening exuberance of his temporary installations is compressed and confined into his unique objects but none can contain the explosion of energy present in the many installations.

The installations of Therman Statom create a pathway to freedom of expression, a journey from the stark white-cube minimalism of his art student days to the not so subtle mixtures of order and chaos evident in recent projects at the Toledo Museum of Art and at William Traver Gallery in Seattle.

Briefly, prior to the breakthrough Seattle installations at Rubin/ Mardin and Traver Sutton galleries in Seattle in 1981, Statom's art dealt with the pristine nature of tinted plate glass. Shades of Larry Bell, DeWain Valentine, Robert Smithson, and James Carpenter, these works, too, were dependent upon architectural framing for their status. In *Untitled* (1974, 1976, and 1977), geometry and stacking were dominant strategies for relating the glass to a wall, window, or corner.

Recessive in the extreme, they were a stark contrast to the abandon and anarchy of the later work. One key to what was to come along may lie in *Untitled* (1974–75), a thesis project at Pratt Institute in which found objects like lawnmowers and rakes were cast in cement. Definitely arranged like a three-dimensional still life, they were colorless and unadorned.

Untitled Study (1980) is another Ground Zero point for the later work: two tall plates of clear, colorless glass were angled at 90 degrees to enclose a corner in a white-cube room. It is as if Untitled Study were the *blanc* slate the artist was about to embellish.

Once in Seattle, the exploratory works encouraged by artists like Buster Simpson and restaurateur-turned-dealer Ben Marks began to take an aggressive, more painterly and, hence, personal approach. Statom's individuality as a glass artist rests partly on his ability to retain a fresh improvisatory appearance in all his work despite elaborate processes beforehand in some cases. In Seattle, Statom was the vibrant hothouse atmosphere of Belltown, a downtown artist's quarter inhabited by many glass artists who, like Statom, had stayed on after teaching or studying at Pilchuck Glass School.

Before the scattered, disparate look of the Rubin/Mardin installations, *Tornado* and *Hurricane* (1981), and the sleek scribbling of *Untitled* (1981) at Traver Sutton, Statom participated in "Four Leaders in Glass," a seminal exhibition at Craft and Folk Art Museum, Los Angeles.[1] According to Statom, *Untitled* (cat. #29, #30, #31) in Los Angeles were the last of the highly prefabricated and preplanned assemblies and the first of the installations where painting extended from the Pittsburgh Plate Glass panels onto the walls. Violating the white cube at last, then, Statom struck a chord of disorder and brash expression.

Being given permission to "deface" by Craft and Folk Art Museum program directors Edith Wyle and Sharon Emanuelli opened up worlds for the artist, allowing him from then on to anchor the glass objects in an hospitable environment and freeing him periodically from the necessary but commodity-driven pressures of his growing number of gallery commitments.

Blown glass objects were now broken. Fragments were glued to the clear walls. The structure in L.A. was like a see-through, freestanding Japanese screen. The viewer had to navigate through the space as Statom acted upon it, installing space for the purposes of personal expression and, later, encoded meanings.

The viewer is given free admission by Statom to locate his or her body in relation to the glass. Delight and danger underscore the hall of mirrors effect, disorienting and entertaining the viewer at the same time. Bruce Nauman may have made his corridors first; Statom let the viewer see where the maze leads by rendering the walls transparent.

Subsequent installations at Thorpe Intermedia in New York State, in New Jersey, and at Scripps College introduced signature shapes that would act as symbolic codes of memory and reference for the artist. The blown glass vase, the glass chair (another idea borrowed from Simpson), the giant deck of cards, and the dominoes became symbols of, respectively, work, rest, chance, and inevitability.

An interlude of collaborative installations with friend and colleague Richard Marquis occurred in Cincinnati at the Contemporary Arts Center, in Washington, D.C., at the Branch Gallery, and at the San Jose Museum of Art. These were a giant step forward in terms of adding elements. With Marquis an inveterate collector of cheap and tacky Americana and Statom moving full tilt at painting walls and now floors as well, these projects represent one excessive extreme in the younger artist's oeuvre.

Untitled (1984) in Ohio assaulted the white cube space, filling it with objects like metal coffeepots and glass sphere snowmen, accompanied by the introduction of neon.

As Statom readily admits, color came to the fore for the first time thanks to Marquis and their work together on these installations.[2]

In 1989 and 1991, Statom had come back down to earth temporarily in additional assemblages at the now-defunct Los Angeles Institute of Contemporary Art (LAICA) and at the city's Municipal Art Gallery. The latter project, *L.A. River Travel* (1991) was suggested by Simpson and was to have been based on a canoe trip down the Los Angeles River. Arrested with a warning ticket early on in the trip, Statom had to jump ship, so to speak, and settle for images suggestive of L.A. seen from the concrete-conduited river, a popular area for the city's homeless.

Part of the exhibition "Art and Urban Resources," *L.A. River Travel* contained a silhouette of a canoe made of wire suspended from the ceiling. More than the Marquis collaborations which emphasized surface planes and discrete, often found, objects, *L.A. River Travel* seemed to use geographical space as a totality and as an inspiration for the first time.

At LAICA, the tower was introduced as an element. This would become the central image for *Novella*, his 1994 William Traver Gallery installation. With LAICA inspired by the 1994 Olympics, Statom's project also used two giant dominoes, symbols of inevitability, chance and order.

In *Northern Tide* (1995) at the Dorothy Weiss Gallery in San Francisco and *Forgotten Saints* (1994) for the Studio Museum of Harlem, Statom demonstrated how far from the minimalist abstraction of his youth he has traveled. Polar opposites of excess and restraint, the West and East Coast projects suggested how the artist's decisions are based on the nature—and limits—of the site.

Relatively benign and object-oriented, *Forgotten Saints* used a giant black-and-white pinwheel on the wall to punctuate an extended field of giant playing cards, cast and plate glass houses, and painted images of birds. With the hardwood floor untouched, it was Statom's most well behaved (and least successful) installation since *Untitled Study* (1980).

The floor of Dorothy Weiss Gallery, on the other hand, looked like a bleeding Clyfford Still painting. At home in a city that spawned its own gestural painting movement, the exhibition was about Statom's 1983 visit to Iceland. It included images of Viking art painted on plate glass walls of a house. Statom added tall glass snowmen made of spheres, images of sea life and fauna, as well as landscape paintings. The viewer's encounter with *Northern Tide* necessitated reading journal-like entries on the walls while passing through the structure.

For a peripatetic artist like Therman Statom, it could be the only time he can stop, slow down, and access personal memory is while he is making the installations. Although temporary, they serve as a focus for recollection and reminiscence. Unlike the object sculptures, little remains after the show comes down. At the Renwick Gallery, for example, it took days to remove, smash, and destroy the elements.

Novella (1994) and *Hydra* (1996) comprise a recent cycle of installations in Seattle and Toledo. Supervision and escape are dominant themes in *Novella*. With its tall, half-black, half-white tower suggestive of a penal institution, *Novella* was a manically cheerful presentation of otherwise troubling or horrifying images: Luminous Path leader Abumel Guzman, jagged glass edges, giant toys as symbols of childhood or willful immaturity. It was also Statom's most ambitious and beautiful work to date.

Hydra was the most straitlaced and organized. Given access to the entire museum collection at Toledo, the artist borrowed a Cézanne and van Gogh which were encased in Plexiglas vitrines before the artist began his wall paintings. An interior building using arches that allude to periods of art history and architecture was the centerpiece. Inside it, a huge historic Libbey Owens punch bowl was placed. On the walls were painted images of Asian artworks and other examples of the global art tradition.

Severe, austere and well mannered, *Hydra* was more constrained than restrained. In his most traditional museum setting yet, Statom was unable to violate the sanctity of the white cube in quite the same way as in his earlier achievements. Neither gallery nor contemporary art space, Toledo Art Museum offered an opportunity for a dialogue with past art and Statom definitely rose to the occasion. It could be a new direction or, backtracking on himself as usual, it could lead him straight back to a sheet of plate glass, a loaded paintbrush, and a hammer.

Ginny Ruffner: *Mind Garden,* 2000–2001, glass, bronze and mixed metals, dimensions variable, Seattle Art Museum installation. Photo: Paul Macapia

CONTAINING SPACE:
GINNY RUFFNER'S INSTALLATIONS

In the midst of a highly prolific and publicized artistic career, Ginny
Ruffner's installations may have been lost in the shuffle. For an artist
with so many ideas who has also seized the moment to embody so
many of them in her more widely familiar unique-object sculptures,
installations have been a parallel, overlapping activity. In fact, since
roughly half of her ten major installations since the first in 1985
have been in galleries, viewers (let alone critics) may not have realized what they were witnessing: no less than a concerted, consistent
effort to reconfigure and reframe the viewing space for highly crafted
objects made of glass, steel, fabric, paint and, eventually, bronze. Examined more closely on their own terms (extensively planned, plotted
and acted upon art spaces), Ruffner's installations share credit not
only with her earlier achievement of establishing serious aesthetic
purpose for glass sculpture, but for expanding the limits within contemporary art viewing context.

Maybe the reason people did not realize Ginny Ruffner was becoming an installation artist to be reckoned with was that her version
of installation art is so different from the one she grew up with: the
bleak white cube of carpentered Minimalism or the dry, text-illus-
trated scholastics of Conceptualism. Ironically, both movements have
affected her art at the same time she was reacting against them and
seeking a physical province for the expression of her considerably different ideas about sculpture.

For example, *Seven Stations of Intimacy* (1985) combined Plexiglas-
covered banks of colored neon lights (shades of Dan Flavin or Keith
Sonnier) with tattered backdrop curtains with diagonal glass sheets
attached (last echoes of 70s feminist fiber art?). Devotional, experiential and site-related, this 1985 Fay Gold Gallery installation in
Atlanta attracted attention and might have seemed at the time to
foretell a whole different direction for the artist.

Instead, indefatigable worker and thinker that she is, unique objects
continued alongside additional installations, sometimes including
glass sculptures but, eventually, bringing up their scale with the
help of steel structural reinforcements. Subjective in the extreme, as
well as suggestive in the way a disassociative Surrealist painting can
be, Ruffner's installations throughout the past decade bolstered her
position as an artist capable of honoring the individual object and at

the same time placing it in an inhabited space, contained by exterior elements of wood, steel and gallery or museum walls.

Not yet entirely there as site-related installation, the 1990 Renwick Gallery grouping, *The Possession of Creativity*, introduced painted wood murals of realistic flowers and fruits accompanied by a giant, swirling clear-glass tornado-shape in the center of the room, and recycled female torsos from a 1989 Traver Sutton Gallery exhibit mounted on walls. This was still too much about individual elements coexisting in an ordered formal space.

Before her first fully successful installation, *Yours, Mine and Ours* (1995) at Linda Farris Gallery in Seattle, Ruffner created an outdoor public art piece, *Machan Oasis* (1993) for an elementary school in Phoenix that helped her draw together disparate physical elements and images into a site that became bigger than the sum of its parts. With upright metal "pencils," floor maps, chessboards and, most importantly, interactive schoolchildren, *Machan Oasis* was the catalyst for the artist's reconceptualization of physical space. Even outdoors, her elements framed the space, claiming for aesthetic undertakings. The Farris collaboration with Steve Kursh introduced the steel container baskets full of jewel-like glass spheres and treated the surrounding walls as a totally painted environment. The results were fanciful, beautiful and warmly glowing and enveloping.

Thus, with the ensuing invitations to create multiple-element environments at the Varberg Museum in Sweden and at the Bryan Ohno Gallery in Seattle in 1997, Ruffner was better able to draw upon features of each site and adapt the idiosyncrasies of her vision to them. What are those idiosyncrasies? An imagery of generative growth, as in flowers, vines and fruits, to be sure, but also a sense of spatial reality and perception that involves see-through structures that puncture conventional expectations of sculptural mass and volume. Both in Sweden and in Seattle, viewers gazed through huge empty gilt frames to the elements beyond, themselves replete with smaller frames, glass appurtenances and more gold-framed paintings that, by now, emphasize an extreme sense of theatrical display and organic spectacle.

Beautiful Ideas, at Varberg, accentuated the museum's gilt-capital Ionic Neo-Classical columns beside a giant gilt frame for her caryatid-like figure holding a basket of glass balls. Beauty personified, the combination of the female figure, the winged urn above and the candy-sweet colored glass balls foreshortened space more than any of Ruffner's other installations but did so with great economy and conviction.

Mind Garden at the Seattle Art Museum and *The Beauty of the
Creative Process* for Laumeier Sculpture Park Gallery (both 2001) are
tentative culminations of the artist's decade-long assault on the once-
sanctified white cube. Introducing millions of preserved rose petals
(first seen at Bryan Ohno), Ruffner pushes sensory overload in these
works along with optical and physical perceptions. More than before, the presence of the body comes into play. And if the high-flying
stainless steel and glass conglomerations briefly bring to mind Judy
Pfaff, Ruffner's solutions are always more rooted in representational
imagery, away from the New York installation artists she's otherwise
closest to, like Pfaff, Eva Hesse and Dennis Oppenheim. The sculptural nodules are now widely entangled mixtures of steel and glass,
ornate and baroque, perhaps reminiscent of Frank Stella but with
none of his faux-street-graffiti sensibility; instead the pure wandering
line of Ginny Ruffner.

With the extraordinary distance covered since 1985, it appears that
the current direction of the installations may prove to be Ginny
Ruffner's most enduring and influential body of work.

METAMORPHOSIS:
GLASS SCULPTURES BY LYNDA BENGLIS

The glass sculptures of Lynda Benglis, done between 1971 and
2000, constitute an important but rarely commented upon aspect of
her oeuvre. The distinguished American sculptor has persisted in
her exploration of different materials in the face of an overbearing,
anti-material conceptualism that ran parallel to her own development. Indeed, part of the first movement she was associated with,
Postminimalism, was said by the critic who coined the term, Robert
Pincus-Witten, to involve "substance and eccentric materials," specifically with reference to her work.[1] Yet as we move further away in
time from the intoxicating atmosphere of New York art in the 1970s
and early 1980s, it is necessary to take another look at the artists of
that period and question some of the critical shibboleths surrounding
them. With all her subsequent interest in ceramics and glass, is it
time to re-categorize Lynda Benglis as a closet craft artist? With all
the current interest in craft materials in contemporary art, this operation could be fruitful. And Carter Ratcliff recently pointed out that
cotton, fabric, chicken wire and bronze also interest her.[2]

Process was another buzzword of Postminimalism. Not just the appearance of process but actual making was considered important.
Benglis told Erica-Lynn Huberty in an interview last year "I have
a hands-on technique with everything I do. . . . Now I want to make
very small works that have an intensity."[3] Given such startling ad-
missions that contrast with, for example, the take-out attitude of the
Minimalists, Benglis deserves credit for following her own vision, one
frequently opposed to Minimal and Conceptual Art and increasingly
seen as one of the strongest and most individual of sensibilities associated with American sculpture in the final quarter of the twentieth
century.

What is the overall meaning of the art of Lynda Benglis? How has it
been revealed in the 100 or so glass sculptures she has made since
1971? It is the fundamental nature of change, becoming and metamorphosis, the shift from one form to another. Although her newest
glass works, the *Hot Spots* series (1999–2000) concentrate on "very
small works that have an intensity," thereby accentuating a concentrated objecthood, these, too, signify metamorphosis, resembling cells
dividing at the earliest stages of life. *Hot Spots* comes full circle, in
a way, from her undertakings at the Pilchuck Glass School in 1984.
Colored blown spheres with overlapping double-leaf or tendril forms,

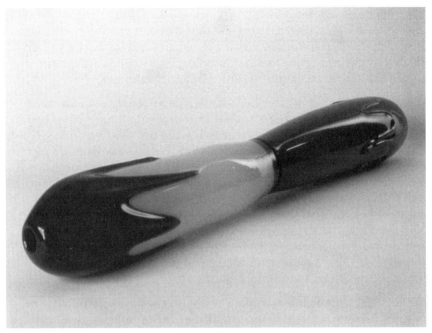

Lynda Benglis: *Blansko*, 1997, blown glass, 5 x 24 x 5". Novy Bor Glassworks, Czech Republic. Courtesy of the artist. Photo: Fred Dorfman Projects, New York

Chloe, Niobe and *Maera* suggest bulging growth forms about to sprout or shoot off additional natural appurtenances.

Given all Benglis's craft-friendly material pursuits (poured plastic; slathered and cut ceramics; gilded and bronzed or coppered cloth), the word process should finally be changed to craft. Thus, Postminimalism was really heralding the rise of craft art! Metamorphosis of forms was closely tied up with metamorphosis of material states: liquid plastic or latex to solid floor and wall constructions; messy clay to rigid and sinuous, fired stoneware; blobby, boiling glass to transparent opaque and crusty solid glass. Her next encounter used molten glass poured into molds that was then altered and twisted into knots (*Chi; Taf; Ksi; Ni; Pi*; all 1984).

The next year, 1985, saw the artist turn to underwater species as inspirations or additional images of metamorphosis. *Golden Top Minnow, Atlantic Wolf Fish* and *Snubnose Sculpin* (all 1985) bring her brilliant color sense to elongated, twisted forms made of black glass with bronze, copper and powdered pigments added. Regardless of the marine naturalist titles, they all appear as slimy, colorful eels. What

is an eel but something metamorphosing from fish to reptile? Benglis
also admitted in a recent interview that while at the Pilchuck Glass
School in 1984, the work of visiting Swedish sculptor Bertil Vallien
had an important impact on her, considering the see-through qualities of the sandcast sculptures she made that summer.[4]

A little over ten years after her scandalous appearance in an adver-
tisement in the November 1974 *Artforum* (posing nude with sun-
glasses and a dildo), Benglis returned to the provocative dildo shape
with *Slender Madton* and *Bourbot* (1985). With the surrounding
stripes covering the bi-colored, curve-ended forms, metamorphosis is
again evoked: bulging, expanding rings shifting from a flaccid state to
erect.[5] True, the elongated lozenge is a form that Benglis was already
using in her molded wax paintings shortly after she moved to New
York in 1964, but the *Artforum* ad forever associated her with the
aggressive sexual appliance; the 1985 works are closer to real dildo
proportions (Has anyone ever thought of the dildo as a functional
object, tying Benglis even more closely to primal craft?).

Yet another decade later, while working in the Czech Republic,
Benglis further refined the shape, although she referred to *Blansko,
Praha, Litvinov* and *Bratislava* (all 1996) as "double nipple forms."[6]
If all of Benglis's art is a search to "express bodily aspects in other
materials,"[7] the Czech sculptures suggest a metamorphosis from male
genitals to female secondary sex characteristics, a kind of omnisexu-
ality akin to the breasted and blinded prophet Tiresias in the Greek
tragedy of Sophocles, *Oedipus Rex*. Benglis has moved from the dildo
empowering women to beautiful forms implying worship of male and
female sexuality. With transparent colors and a bulging, provocative
form sheathed at one end like a foreskin, *Blansko* is the artist's most
open embrace of craft aesthetics: an openness to beauty; a pushing of
material limits; an acceptance of process as craft; and an exaltation of
color as referential and reverential studio practice.

"Eva Hesse hated my color," Benglis mentioned in an interview.[8]
However, as the glass sculptures prove and the new *Hot Spots* demonstrated in a 2002 exhibition at Bryan Ohno Gallery in Seattle,
Benglis has transcended and outlived her critics. For this artist, so in
command of "eccentric materials," glass became a crucial vehicle to
transformation and heightened expressive power. As in the legendary
ad in *Artforum*, male and female are now one in the *Hot Spots*, not
battling but merging on a deep, compelling level.

Daniel Clayman: *Bracht*, 1998, cast glass, graphite and copper, 60 x 9 1/2 x 10".
Courtesy of the artist, Rumford, Rhode Island. Photo: Jessica Marcotte

DANIEL CLAYMAN:
THE OBJECT IS THE IMAGE

Now that Daniel Clayman is a young veteran of the American glass
art movement, it is worth stepping back both to look at the work
anew and to disentangle it from a learned string of commentaries
that emphasize process, a tendency toward metaphor as meaning, a
woozy spirituality, and a deep subjectivity. Are his sculptures really
that complex and multi-layered in meaning?

Clayman's 1998 solo exhibition at Elliott Brown Gallery in Seattle
was his 14th such survey since 1989. Despite Clayman's comments
about "many hours of grinding, hand honing, [and] sandblasting," he
has been extremely prolific. Looking back to the years following his
1986 graduation from the Rhode Island School of Design and beyond,
Daniel Clayman has created an extraordinarily varied number of
sculptures, often combining other materials such as copper, pewter or
bronze with laboriously wrought kiln-cast pâte-de-verre sections.

Putting him in the context of West Coast glass for a moment (what
might be called the Seattle or Pilchuck sensibility), Clayman is not a
blower, nor is he really a colorist. Additive ornament or surface decoration are not aspects of his work either.

Instead, by his own admission, he strives to identify with Post-minimalist artists such as Jackie Winsor, Christopher Wilmarth, Martin
Puryear, and Michael Singer. Perhaps more pertinently for our purposes, he was a studio assistant between 1987 and 1989 for metal-
and-glass artist Michael Glancy. A resident of the Providence, Rhode
Island area since 1983, it makes more sense to set Clayman briefly in
the context of other glass artists associated with RISD: Howard Ben
Tré, James Carpenter, and Jack Wax. All favor a hefty casting process, largely symmetrical compositions, color in a less than primary
role, and, at best, imagery that seems restrained yet referential, cool
rather than hot, frequently suggestive of residual function.

Given such a powerful lineage, then, it is to Clayman's credit that he
may be the most interesting and innovative sculptor of the lot. Is he
the "reductive Minimalist" he claims to aspire to be in artist's statements, or really an additive Post-minimalist? Clayman is also starting to pay more attention to color. By adding metal parts, he alludes
back to Wilmarth's and Glancy's examples, but has found his own
way toward a sensibility that seems more immediate, less contemplative than theirs.

Clayman's early work might have had more to do with, by way of analogy, the art of glass blower William Morris. Both artists sought to recreate a mock-antique object, "survivor" of a bygone world of ritual, intensely nostalgic for old musical instruments or cave-man weapons, what Clayman once called his "useful objects." Whereas Morris applied mock-paleolithic surface decoration of Lascaux-like cave drawings, Clayman achieved a quiet, hushed atmosphere of the recently excavated Near Eastern or Egyptian tomb.

William Luecking pointed out the dangers of this approach in a 1994 *American Craft* review when he mentioned the "risk of . . . generic classicism." That is, by evoking ancient tools or musical instruments, permission was granted to adapt a different kind of "found object," a paradoxically constructed "found object," light years away from anything with a more contemporary, let alone Post-minimal, feeling.

Faburden, Kithara and *Life's Work* (all 1994) were the high end of this undertaking, tautly strung lyre-like objects that could furnish an imaginary temple or cave. Put William Morris's bones or clubs in one corner and Clayman's silent stringed instruments in another. *Voilà*, a highly imagined yet retrograde living room for an ancient world.

Whether or not they evoked what William A. Fields called a "primal echo" is debatable. His 1999 essay in *RISD Views*, an alumni magazine, projects an entire sound or "resonance" spectrum onto all the stringed pieces. "While there is no sound, we are disposed to imagine sound by their form and composition." Or, put more obtusely, "the viewer is free to initialize the form with private sound."

Early on, Karen S. Chambers, writing in *Japan Glass* in 1992, gave the Massachusetts-born artist credit for graduating to an art at last "completely divorced from function," yet Clayman has returned time and again to forms that recall functional objects, a familiar recourse for craft artists. Only occasionally and with great success, as in *Kita* (1994) and *Echo* (1996), do the sculptures attain complete aesthetic autonomy. The oblong simplicity of *Kita* cancels out most metaphorical possibilities while the roughly octagonal, stringed and striated niche of *Echo* dates back more to Barbara Hepworth, Henry Moore and Amédée Ozenfant than to the permutations of the Post-minimalists.

Conceptually, Clayman seems to want to have his cake and eat it, too. Sympathetic critics have accorded elaborate metaphorical constructs of meaning for the sculptures ("vulnerability and protection," "fertile terrain of the in-between," "reliquaries for unseen spirits,"—all Marsha Miro in *GLASS* #66) yet the shapes have become simpler, farther away than ever from the "useful objects," closer to a Minimalism that requires no exterior meaning at all other than the physical status of the (repeated) object.

Why not approach Clayman purely as a formalist for the sake of countering the heretofore-heavy projections of meaning? Push the Constructivist legacy, stress the Minimalist links, and, with the new installation piece, *Layers / Tiers* (1998), connect to recent developments in contemporary art. This may be Clayman's only escape route from an atmosphere of sentimental rhetoric that verges perilously close to New Age hokum.

First, resist and sever the deep subjectivity of Clayman's intentional statements such as "Each piece stems from a story in my life, perhaps a fleeting moment as a child or a vignette of my mood yesterday." Once such "personal nostalgia" is vacuumed away, the objects remain in a clear and cold, free-floating space of independence. Do they then stand up as fully abstract sculptures? Yes and no.

Inference and *Bract* (both 1998) may obliquely allude to lutes, but their combination of line (copper wire) and mass (blue glass) gives them an adequately salutary integrity of their own. And the double-drawing, *Object / Shadow Plumb* (1998), plays a real drawing of a plumb bob off a companion that creates a ghost image of the same shape by sandblasting everything around the central shape floated above a white piece of paper. Looked at this way, older works like *Kita* take on greater significance, too, devoid of surface markings, pristine and plain in the extreme.

At Elliott Brown in Seattle, two works suggested a fertile new direction with greater, austere formal strengths. *Flourish* (1998) is a reddish-brown blown rod beside a copper bowl at its base. Stark and barely referential, *Flourish* is like a drawing in space.

Most interesting of all, *Layers / Tiers* adapts Minimalism's repeated elements as a method of composition and stretches sculpture's definition to something on a wall with very little depth. Since Clayman's works all have hollow interior spaces, mass and volume have never been defining criteria for him as a sculptor. With the dozens of flattened shapes in *Layers / Tiers*, Clayman goes one step farther away from traditional sculpture to the positioning of a painting on a wall. The effect is shimmering, indeterminate and beautiful. Also as in painting, color matters more now. Pale blue and white ovals of glass are joined by matching pewter shapes.

In fact, such a development leads one to reconsider all the earlier work not in terms of its intentional aspirations to sculptural status but as instantaneously readable images. What was a weakness as sculpture—their wholly symmetrical design and composition—becomes a strength in this new re-iconicizing reading.

Unlike most forms of sculpture which stress three-dimensionality (volume, mass, deep materiality), in Clayman's art, the object has become the image. Blank, blunt and forthrightly two-dimensional as in *Layers / Tiers, Object / Shadow Plumb, Flourish, Bract* and *Inference,* the object is the image. Freed of the necessity of metaphor, the works operate on a more visual, purely phenomenological plane, dependent upon the viewer's perception of the image and, as in Minimalism, the relation of the body to the object.

Moving in this direction, away from the deep subjectivity of "personal nostalgia" and generative anecdote, over toward multivalent optical and physical encounters with the object, the art of Daniel Clayman occupies a new position beyond his teachers and mentors, one still indebted to process and material but more likely to transcend studio limits in favor of a primacy of vision and response.

James Carpenter: *Light Tower*, 1998, 45' h. x 6'8" dia.
Photo: James Carpenter Design, New York.

GLASS IN PUBLIC ART TODAY: PRESERVATION, RENOVATION, INNOVATION

> We are embarking on a wonderful period. We are privileged to sail this ship on its maiden voyage. Though it is stormy, we are sailors now, and it is a great honor.

—Ed Carpenter, 1990

The idealism of Ed Carpenter's statement in 1990 about the future of glass in public art was somewhat qualified by his own admission that concepts like "artistic integrity" and art status did not matter to him, so tightly meshed were his projects with pleasing the architect in question. With 26 commissions completed at the time, craftsman Carpenter has gone on to complete over 30 works in this collaborative vein using glass, and symbolizing one extreme of public art, total subservience to architectural design. As we shall see, his approach has some merit, but any problems or issues he has had have been technical, not aesthetic.

When Carpenter was quoted by Susan Stinsmuehlen-Amend in her talk "Glass Goes Public" at the 1990 annual conference of the Glass Art Society in Seattle (abstracted in the conference proceedings document), public art using glass was just coming of age. Fifteen years later, the issues are not those of sustaining artistic integrity in the face of complex administrative structures but rather three other aspects: preservation, renovation and innovation.

A thorough analysis of American glass artists subsequently involved in public art is not feasible here given the limits of this essay, but it may be possible to get a feeling for how generally successful art in public places programs have been in recruiting glass artists to work on such projects, and to mention a few examples of how glass projects require special needs for maintenance, construction and preservation. Without dwelling unduly on commercial or corporate public projects, it is necessary to mention how Dale Chihuly, more than any other glass artist, has straddled public and private commissions, completing over 200 residential, institutional and publicly accessible commissions since 1990. The overhead aquarium-like frieze for the Rainbow Room at Rockefeller Center in New York in 1987 proved to be just the beginning of a variety of large-scale, highly innovative uses of glass by the Seattle-based artist. The opposite of Ed Carpenter, Chihuly never makes pieces that are architecturally recessive or quietly cooperative; his stand out and, indeed, usually dominate the setting.

PRESERVATION

So successful have glass artists been that, with the breakneck pace of publicly funded buildings in the past two decades, some projects are already in danger of being supplanted, removed or destroyed. Public art administrators need to be aware of such potential pitfalls in order to head them off or have in place procedures for preservation, alteration, removal, re-siting and/or return to site after repair or reconstruction are completed. There have been wins and losses.

Using the Seattle Arts Commission and the Port of Seattle's Seattle-Tacoma International Airport as examples, the reader can get an idea of how increased public art using glass sets up unique assets and liabilities for the given patron. Paul Marioni's scene of young boxers in a ring was the first cast-glass window for a publicly funded commission in the U.S. Already published widely, the Seattle Arts Commission-funded work was recently removed permanently from its original municipal host-site, Delridge Community Center, which made a transition from disadvantaged youth center to women's health clinic (when its subject matter was deemed inappropriate). Now in storage, the 1980 window has yet to be relocated.

Two large-scale leaded stained-glass windows by Dick Weiss at Sea-Tac Airport, respectively at the south and north ends of the ticket level concourse, are also being removed as part of a ten-year expansion project at the airport but, unlike the Marioni, they will be expanded and resited near one another at the new northern end of the area. Also at Sea-Tac, William Morris's 1993 *Northwest Garnering*, a mock-archaeological installation of glass "mastodon bones," has been removed as well pending construction plans. A new site has not been decided.

In New York City, Manhattan's largest publicly funded contemporary stained glass project, at the Mid-Manhattan Public Library branch on Fifth Avenue and West 41st St., is due to be removed soon for reconstruction and expansion of the library. Artist Richard Spaulding, now of Seattle, is lobbying for a return but it is currently uncertain as to whether he will succeed. Spaulding began his career as a public artist in 1975 with a series of CETA-funded windows in neighborhood branches of the Seattle public library system. Twenty-five years later, one window has been lost, one removed and returned in half, one rehung in a windowless basement, and two retained intact. After an important and well-received 11-part window project for the Scripps

Miramar Ranch Library Center in San Diego in 1990, the artist now concentrates on private commissions.

Preservation of glass has not been fully addressed by public arts commissions or agencies but, as America's late 20th-century art in public places projects age, this must become a top priority.

RENOVATION

In lieu of completely new public projects being funded, monies are often allotted for per cent for art commissions fitting into existing civic structures, such as Ellen Driscoll's monumental glass mosaics at Grand Central Terminal in Manhattan (See *Public Art Review*, Fall/Winter 2000). Her sensitive and complex cultural grounding for *As Above, So Below* (1993–99) helps demolish absurd theories separating craft from art, such as those claimed by Bruce Metcalf, wherein concepts supposedly cannot coexist with handmade art. Drawing upon the cultural backgrounds of New Yorkers as inspiration for her imagery, Driscoll represents an admitted advance for glass in public art. Pretty or decorative—but with content, too! (Richard Posner's vestibule lobby piece for the Veterans Administration Hospital in Seattle, with its references to the Vietnam War, would be another).

Chihuly's 1994 multiple-element, permanent installation at Union Station in Tacoma, Washington, also took full advantage of a renovation project, in this case, a conversion of a railroad terminal to a justice center and courthouse. With a massive suspended blue "chandelier" in the old waiting room, the Tacoma native also placed individual glass "flowers" in both lunette windows on either side of the room. The setting is visited by over 100,000 people each year.

Ed Carpenter's close collaboration with architects found its most successful site thus far during the renovation of Seattle's largest church by the architects Olson Sundberg Kundig Allen. The St. Mark's Episcopal Cathedral expansion (1995–2000) now has Carpenter's clear, 21-foot-diameter window on its western wall behind the main altar. Nearby is a 28-foot-diameter clear glass "rose window" of 184 panels. Dichroic laminated glass panels are used above a glass altar screen and around the rose window. Clear, rather than colored, glass enhances light in the often-cloudy Seattle climate. It won the 1998 national design award for art and religious architecture given by the American Institute of Architects.

INNOVATION

James Carpenter (no relation) is, after Chihuly, probably the most
innovative among glass artists undertaking large-scale architectural
projects on a civic level. Unlike Chihuly, however, Carpenter has
worked with architects of national and international stature, notably
Richard Meier in *Lens Ceiling* (1996–2000) for the new federal building and courthouse in Phoenix, Arizona. Like Ed Carpenter, he favors
clear glass but, instead of lead lines, he has developed elegant laminating, clamping and cable support structures along with other uses
for dichroic, spectrum-emitting glass. *Fresnel Ring* (1995–96) at the
Rhode Island Convention Center in Providence is a stunning addition
to the entry lobby ceiling. It dwarfs another work in glass just outside
the lobby by Howard Ben Tré.

James Carpenter has also been effective with renovations, namely
the creation of a glass scrim wall (1996–99) for the exterior wall
surrounding an outdoor sculpture garden at the Scottsdale Museum
of Contemporary Art in Arizona. The area the wall surrounds is a
former movie theatre and Carpenter's addition indeed resembles a
curving movie screen. Another project, *Light Tower* (1998), at the
San Francisco Civic Center makeover offers a transition structure
between the old courthouse building and the new state office building.
His most sculptural work thus far, *Light Tower* suggests that even
with a giant firm like Skidmore, Owings and Merrill to contend with,
the canny public artist using glass can be effective and innovative.

Although they were both co-founders (with Chihuly) of the Pilchuck
Glass School, Carpenter and Buster Simpson could not be more different in their approaches to public art using glass. Much of Simpson's
earliest art was provisional in the extreme, more sketches for a
possible public art than the real thing. Yet his influence as a clever
subversive within public art projects has been substantial. Glass was
important to him early on (*Hot Cross Glass* video, 1976; *Selective Disposal Project*, 1978–79; *History of Urban Window Repair*, 1980) but
few of his numerous public art commissions across the nation have
used glass. A recent long-term installation in the Jon and Mary Shirley sculpture court of the new Gwathmey-Siegel-renovated Henry Art
Gallery of the University of Washington, *Shard Cornice* (2000) uses
colorful shards obtained from Chihuly's nearby Lake Union studio
and turns them into a parody of a viciously topped security wall. With
jagged glass at its top, *Shard Cornice* is a freestanding 45-degree-
angle concrete cinderblock wall that may yet end up influencing other
public art projects, if only bringing something new or ameliorative to
the booming business of state prison décor.

Cappy Thompson's forthcoming *I Was Dreaming of Spirit Animals* (2000–02) is one of the new artworks commissioned for the Sea-Tac airport expansion. It uses dozens of nine-by-four-foot, reverse-laminated and leadline-free glass panels constructed in Taunustein-Wehen, Germany, to tell a story of night skies, viewing towers, and animal star constellations in the northern hemisphere sky. Images of trees and birds will also be part of the 33-by-90-foot-long exterior glass wall. A smaller, interior glass wall at Sea-Tac by public art veteran Linda Beaumont was also constructed in Germany.

Finally, it is worth looking backward and forward once again as we complete this rapid journey surveying recent public art made of glass. Robert Willson, who died at the age of 88 in San Antonio in 2000, completed *Everybody Come Play* (1994) in Venice, Italy, at the age of 82. It was among the last large-scale works (8 x 4 ft.) designed and completed by this overlooked pioneer of American glass art who worked on Murano Island every summer from 1956 until shortly before his death. Commissioned by Texas Military Institute in San Antonio, *Everybody Come Play* uses petroglyphic figures scattered across 8 steel-frame-mounted blown-glass flat panels. For a man who began his public art involvement with Diego Rivera and Jose Clemente Orozco in 1935 (when he assisted them on their murals), Willson made art for far less explicit and ideological reasons than Rivera or Orozco but still retained an identifiable imagery and readily accessible content: community and athletic teamwork.

Another flat work also points forward and backward in terms of technical innovation and ancient, paleolithic imagery. William Morris's *Artifact Panel* (2000) was commissioned by Portland Art Museum patrons Lois and Leonard Schnitzer for the Oregon museum's new contemporary art wing. At 32 feet in height and 15 feet in width, *Artifact Panel* employs an ingenious studded steel panel backdrop for suspending hundreds of colored glass bones, weapons, vessels and fragments at equidistant points.

In place of the past twenty-five years' themes of preservation, renovation and innovation, it could be that glass in public art in the twenty-first century will involve, like Thompson's, Willson's and Morris's, aspects of fragmentation, dispersal, historicism and an uneasy continuity between past and present conditions.

PAUL MARIONI: THE VISITOR

One thread that goes through the extraordinarily varied oeuvre of Seattle glass artist Paul Marioni is that of "the visitor." This spirit, figure, character and alter ego appears and reappears like a ghost over a 35-year period, floating, flying and connecting the multifarious achievements of the Cincinnati-born artist. Paul Marioni, in his own journey as visitor-artist to the American studio glass movement, has become one of its most important figures. Long before most glass artists, he has pioneered the equal status of craft and concept.

The indeterminate identity of the visitor and its ambiguous function within the long narrative strain Marioni's art comprises are keys to its success as an underlying image that typifies this uniquely talented artist's work. With one brother, Joseph, a noted painter and another, Tom, a conceptual artist, Paul Marioni became a fusion of both influences: a painter on glass involved with concepts that transcend and overshadow technique.

With a background in philosophy at the University of Cincinnati, Paul Marioni is a largely self-taught artist, steeped in art history, widely traveled, and an eyewitness participant to the development of the Pilchuck Glass School. Marioni not only first taught there in 1974, but went on to become part of an inner circle of experimental artists who included Dale Chihuly, Fritz Dreisbach, Marvin Lipofsky, Toots Zynsky, and Buster Simpson.

His gradual evolution into an acclaimed artist of art in public places projects and public and private architectural commissions is not our subject here. Rather, his evolution as a West Coast Surrealist (or Funk artist heavily influenced by Surrealism) better explains the tightly individual and original nature of his achievement. Neither completely comfortable as a brilliant craftsman nor as an object-obliterating conceptualist, Marioni is an historical by-product of both trends, sometimes paradoxically so. Craft and concept have long appeared inimical foes within contemporary art yet, along with certain other artists who emerged out of the early Pilchuck experience, Marioni fused both seemingly contradictory trends.

His aesthetic always has mattered more than techniques. As he told Michelle Gyure in 1989 in *Glass Art* magazine, "I always look for a way to achieve my vision regardless of what the purists think." This has been his saving grace in an era when elaborate ornament often overwhelms sculptural form (see Chihuly) or when technical bravura overwhelms purported content (see William Morris).

Set apart, Paul Marioni may be the real visitor: to Pilchuck, to Seattle, and, above all, to the land of much of his recent creative inspiration, Mexico, where he has spent increasing periods of time with his partner and collaborator on architectural projects, Ann Troutner, since 1991. Paul Marioni, the visitor, is many things: an outsider, an observer, a borrower, a visionary.

For an artist who wrote "art is a reflection of the human spirit," Marioni is sufficiently vague about his own intentions or motives. Indeed, he added in *Telling Compelling Tales: Narration in Contemporary Glass*: "I prefer to leave the meaning in my work somewhat vague so that viewers can see into it what they want."

With such liberating permission, let us explore the paths and permutations the visitor has taken, from Surrealism to Conceptualism and craft, from flat to blown and cast glass, from private subjectivity to public openness.

An early flat glass work, *Dalí* (1972), sets a tone of homage to one of the most subversive and conflicted artists of the twentieth century, Salvador Dalí (1904–1989). Like Dalí's own art, Marioni's portrait of him straddles high and low worlds. Constructed, damaged in transit after an international tour in a USIA exhibition, and wholly reconstructed in 1975, *Dalí* took on a narrative of its own as an object, just like the fabled Catalan-Spanish artist's reputation: up, down, destroyed and currently rehabilitated.

Dalí's disjunctive juxtaposition of unrelated images became a dreadfully reiterated formula not only for him, but for much of West Coast Surrealism of the 1960s and 1970s. The sheer simplicity and predictability of placing one thing next to another thing that had nothing to do with it became conventional in the extreme both in Dalí's own work after 1940 and in that of the hundreds and thousands of American and European artists he influenced.

In one way, *Dalí* (1972) is the first visitor to Marioni's oeuvre. Glaring eyes confront the viewer while the window's clear background implant him in the strange and alien world of northern California.

In Marioni's case, however, what he called "stark realism" really had more to do with the darker implications of Surrealism: the divagation and fears of the subconscious mind; the obsessions with sex and death; the dream-like difficulties of perceiving psychological identity. Thus, in certain key works created between 1972 and the present, the former San Francisco Bay Area artist used painting on glass, blowing and casting glass as vehicles for expressing the uncertain side of Surrealism, rescuing it and reviving it in ways that were hitherto unseen.

For example, the elongated "cone head" of *The Saint in Repose* (1981) proposes a new hagiography of alien beings, a burning red-skinned figure asleep during time-travel on his way, perhaps, to Earth. Once arrived, as in the two cardinal versions of 1984, both called *The Visitor* (a cylindrical vase and a blown-and-flattened sheet), the mystery figure trudges out into a new world.

The two *Visitors* of 1984 serve as poignant symbols on many levels. Building on an earlier work, *The Premonition* (1981), that foretold the perils of nuclear holocaust, the 1984 *Visitors* are roughly identical images in two- and three-dimensional formats. With a white disc above that may be an "unidentified flying object" (or apocalyptic moon) and a triangular igloo-like dwelling nearby, the horizontally striated figure floats slightly above the ground.

Reminiscent in one way of the Michael Rennie character in the 1953 film, "The Day the Earth Stood Still," Marioni's Visitor arrives with a warning and a plea for world peace. Saying not "klatu beradu niktu," (the movie character's mantra), but more likely, "Humanity, unite or perish," the Visitor communicates in its own "language," circular clouds of smoke emitting from its mouth. The exact meaning of the verbal clouds is up to the viewer.

Nine years later in three works, *The Come-On, My House of Dreams*, and *The King & The Queen* (1993), Marioni extended the notion of the Visitor into new expressions. *My House of Dreams* alludes to the Surrealist dream-state, the fount of inspiration, in this case, pictorialized into female genitalia. With the Visitor now presented in cocoon-like form, the house contains the dream, a pink screen of involuted, curving female anatomy. Never precisely medical or clinical, the Visitor's dream-vision looms high, potent with generative power and implied fecundity. With the yellow of dawn beyond the other window, both the sense of potent imagination and imminent transformation (and waking) are strong. Enigmatic because of its unspecified character, *My House of Dreams* also recalls the work of fellow Seattle Surrealist painter Andrew Keating.

The Come-On and *The King & The Queen* are a pair of double images, twin figures, as if the fate of the Visitor had led to a companionship and a new, if bizarre, peopling of its adopted world. Matched in the colors red, orange and black, with gold-leaf accents, both works posit figures that are more illusionary than corporeal, more suggestive or symbolic than psychological.

The long-nosed figure in *The Come-On* operates as a comic, misplaced phallus directed toward a headless companion with a pink, uterine spiral hovering over her head. Marioni uses gold leaf to create a surrogate or shadow self for these Visitors, locked into a courtship ritual of approach, encounter and penetration. The empty eyeholes and long nose of the male figure also recalls masks and costumes of the Italian *commedia dell'arte*; humorous but, as usual, with sinister overtones.

The saga of the Visitor continues with *The King & The Queen*. With clear casing over the faces and orange crowns on their heads, both figures have the royal gravity and impassiveness of masked actors in Greek tragedy. If the Visitor arrived lonely from another planet, in *The King & The Queen*, it has found a mate. After the abortive courtship of *The Come-On*, the two figures are not so much united in procreative urges as ceremonially installed as literal figureheads. The gold leaf acts as a sacralizing agent, symbol of an unknown hierarchy with precious and intimidating status. Far from voicing royal utterances or edicts, neither monarch has a mouth.

In *The Journey* (completed with Ann Troutner, 1997–99), the Visitor has finally attained a degree of domestic stability. Surrounded by elephant-like household deities within a brick-like home, two masked figures greet the viewer. Again, narrative is flexible and open to the viewer's imagination. Having donned animal masks, the aliens are still outsiders; not human, not only animals. Posing in another connubial gesture of carrying the bride across a threshold, the two figures confront and greet the viewer.

Seen another way, however, the Visitor is cuddling a smaller being, perhaps the offspring of *The King & The Queen*. Not only assimilating into the planet's dominant species but also proliferating when interpreted this way, Marioni's Visitor has come a long way from uneasy alien to domesticated dweller with residual outsider status, humanoid but not quite human. Within the grand narrative of Paul Marioni's art, *The Journey* is about the galactic trek completed, begun long ago but not yet THE END.

Paul Marioni: *The Visitor,* 1984, cast glass, 20 x 24".
Photo: Courtesy of William Traver Gallery.

Robert Kehlmann: *Fort Wayne*, 1992, sandblasted glass with charcoal on board, 12 x 15". The Oakland Museum of California. Photo: Richard Sargent

ROBERT KEHLMANN:
ASPECTS OF MEANING

In lieu of adequate critical commentary on many contemporary glass
artists, curators and writers have understandably fallen back on the
artists' written statements as a guide. Robert Kehlmann is a case
in point. Artist, critic, stained glass historian and former graduate
student in English literature, Kehlmann makes flat glass panels that
have been the focus of numerous Japanese, European and American
commentaries. The only problem is, most of it is based on interviews
with the artist. Little, if any, analysis or interpretation has occurred.

Taken visually, then, and adapting an empirical, skeptical, and
ultimately formalist reading, Kehlmann's glass constructions have
alternated between mind and hand, eye and heart, feeling and form.
Shown in depth in a 1996 retrospective exhibition at the Hearst Art
Gallery of Saint Mary's College in Moraga, California, they were accompanied by a full-color catalogue complete with essays by Corning
Museum of Glass curator Susanne K. Frantz and independent critic
and philosopher William Warmus.[1]

Therefore, if we are to take the artist at his own word, does it ring
true that Kehlmann's stained-glass art "was and continues to be rooted in the art of this century. . . . Abstract Expressionism has always
been an important influence"?[2] Or is it clearly evident that "there is
a definite Japanese influence in both the 'calligraphy' and scale of my
recent work"?[3] Other aspects of meaning claim literary narrative or
allegory, that is, sequential stories or tales in which particular elements (e.g., characters, moral qualities, virtues) are encoded.

As is true for many craft artists, intentional statements in interviews,
catalog essays, profiles, letters and elsewhere stand in for critical
analysis where little or none has appeared, or where writers have
been unable to exercise vigorous interpretive powers.

On top of it all, a few meetings with the late art critic Clement Greenberg led to no essays or articles by Greenberg but have been inflated
out of all proportion. In letters, interviews, and conversations, Greenberg told Kehlmann "glass artists have not yet done anything in the
way of major art" and predicted "the first steps in that direction are
two-dimensional, pictorial. I make this statement based on what you've
done."[4] Later in 1984, after another studio visit, Greenberg wrote Kehlmann, "Also got a more vivid idea of what a serious 'painter' you are.
So stay warm and even hot in color & suppress light-&-dark drawing."[5]

To be fair, there are New York School artists with whom Kehlmann shares certain affinities. Like Kehlmann, Robert Motherwell had a humanities background with little or no art training and was a voluble writer and translator, comfortable with international connections. Motherwell's gestures find an echo in Kehlmann, though both may owe a greater debt to Japanese calligraphy as an image source than has been heretofore admitted. Along with a third West Coast artist, Mark Tobey, both Motherwell and Kehlmann are greatly admired in Japan today.

Thus, it is necessary to temporarily pare away the artist's intentional statements along with highly cooperative catalog essays by Frantz and Warmus. This leaves the art in a state of free-floating meaning, unattached to elaborate verbal constructs, closer to a free-associative state of mind similar to Surrealist automatism. No symbols, no stories, no allegories; just marks, strokes, drawings, and images remain.

Demolishing the intentionalist aura further, is his art really even "painting on glass"? A case could be made that drawing is the operative aesthetic strategy in the art of Robert Kehlmann, not painting. Line is what activates each image. Just as Peter Voulkos was gerrymandered into abstract expressionism by Rose Slivka in order to shoehorn a maverick West Coast clay artist into the New York canon, so Kehlmann and his apologists have attempted to legitimize a very different kind of art—drawing with and without lead on glass—by associating his inspirations with the indisputable aesthetic status of postwar American gestural abstract painting.

Instead, let us examine the flat glass of Robert Kehlmann as a series of reductive strategies to use line and color in a way to elude, exploit or even escape the reflective glassiness of glass. Despite the highly unconventional and untraditional appearance of the leaded panels of the 1970s (e.g., *Composition XXVIII*, 1976), in retrospect, they seem to be about drawing rather than painting. The meandering lines, curves, and squiggles surround pale areas of color. Kehlmann was transferring the informality of drawing to the normally formal and strictly regulated compositions of stained glass.

By 1979, the dimensionality of the metal line was rising above the glass plane in works like *Quartet*, and the demarcation of space in the vertical forms was also drawing-like: curves, arcs, straight lines, often above faintly gridded areas of glass.

An ensuing body of work, sandblasted pieces from 1980–89, like *Palais Royal II* (1981) and *Red Tablet, Blue Tablet* (1981), are purportedly inspired by Color Field painters like Mark Rothko, New-

man, and Morris Louis yet, unlike Greenberg's favored postpainterly
abstractionists whose works depended upon the thin layers of paint
and an evanescent touch, Kehlmann's works seem blunt unadulter-
ated sheets of brittle color.

Edge is a stand-in for line in many of these works with their irregularly sided, overlapping planes. Upright like windows, their inner
shapes seem more like tilted window shades, settings for subtle
juxtapositions of varying shades of the same colors, red and blue.
Nor, at barely three feet high, do they emit any of the environmental
wraparound effect common to Rothko and Newman (see *Vir Heroicus
Sublimis*, 1950–51). The sandblasting mutes the glassiness yet inhib-
its any painterly sense of touch.

Only in 1985, when he added an underdrawing in acrylic-on-board to
a sandblasted oversheet of glass, did the works take on a painterly
density. Line is still the dominant activity throughout works like *Pelt*
(1985), *Interior* (1987), *Falling Angel* (1988), and *Fort Wayne* (1992).
This approach was inadvertently echoed a decade later by Robert Ryman in a series of untitled works shown in 1996 at Pace Wildenstein
Gallery in New York. Roughly the same size as Kehlmann's two-by-
two-foot works, Ryman's paintings also placed a piece of glass an
inch or so above a painted piece of paper beneath. While Ryman used
nonglare glass, both artists accept the frank object status of the work
of art as a priority over elevated aspects of meaning.

More significantly, it is the surface of each work that was changed
materially at this time. The artist placed a piece of sandblasted glass
with various linear effects or bubbled areas above the mixed-media
painting on board. Drawing over drawing, then, the Greenbergian
"integrity of the picture plane" is violated, completely to the benefit
of the work's power. In fact, the more Kehlmann disregarded Greenberg's helpful advice, the stronger his work became.

Flat glass is not a subset of modernist painting but a genre based on
tradition constantly being reinvented. With the viewer's physical and
optical encounter mattering more than ever, Kehlmann's glassworks
of the 1986–96 are his strongest, most varied, and most exploratory
work.

Interior (1987) and *Fort Wayne* (1992) favor a black palette with the
fogged, sandblasted sections of the overglass acting as the color white.
Here and in *Falling Angel* (1988), Kehlmann complicates the material
structure of the work by adding layers of process for the eye to unravel. Meditation, not manic, macho abandon, is a more likely aspect
of meaning in these and ensuing works. As the viewer stares into the

layers, a paradox of concealment and revelation occurs, all related to the interaction of drawing, process, and material fabrication. Ironically, it is through the aggressive physical nature of the art object that any route to spiritual or metaphysical introspection is mapped.

The *Stations of the Cross* (1982–1996) are the artist's most extended series and, taken together, a culminating masterpiece of his middle period. Meeting Barnett Newman's *Stations of the Cross* (1958–66) on their own ground—black and white, abstraction, and rejection of narrative—Kehlmann countered Newman's heightened verticality in favor of intimately meditative projection. Naming and numbering provide adequate references to the agony of Christ, allowing the viewer to experience each artwork individually and in a compounding sequence. Like Newman, Kehlmann removed the series from a religious site, using the white-cube environment of the museum or gallery to sanctify the production of art in a secular setting. However, Kehlmann's advantage over Newman is the use of glass itself, a medium tied to the history of devotional stained glass in architectural and liturgical settings.

Disregarding Greenberg's advice to avoid "light-&-dark drawing," Kehlmann lends strong symbolic force to the interplay of lightness and darkness in each station. The viewer may guess at residual pictorial references to the fourteen stations—cross, path, figures, crowds, veil—but is ultimately left alone with the line, the mark, and the muted reflective power of the glass. Meaning is internalized by the viewer, a result of prior experience or religious belief, not any panoply of written discussions, but a confluence of materials, studio intervention, and the deft manipulation of subdued colors working with black. Seen in one final light, the Stations parallel Kehlmann's own journey with glass. Stumbling along the way, he has reinforced the human over the divine, arriving not at Golgotha or Calvary but triumphantly at the Parnassus of art.

Marvin Lipofsky: *Untitled* (California Loop Series), 1970, glass, paint, and rayon flocking, 11 x 20 x 13". John and Colleen Kotelly collection, Washington, D.C. Photo: M. Lee Fatherree

MARVIN LIPOFSKY:
CONCEALING THE VOID

Regardless of where they were made—and Marvin Lipofsky is perhaps the world's most itinerant glass artist—all his glass sculptures
are about concealing an inner void. China, Poland, the Soviet Union,
Italy, Finland, California, Seattle, and the Czech Republic are all
sites where Lipofsky has traveled to make glass but the subject of
this essay is not a travelogue. Rather, it is an analysis of the formal
properties of his work—color, line, form, texture, translucency, opacity—that radically disregards the geographical and temporal contexts
of their making in favor of an appreciation of them as works of art for
their own sake.

Nor is this a biographical profile of the ex-California College of Arts
and Crafts professor. Those have appeared in abundance.[1], [2] In the
ensuing literature on Lipofsky, much has been made of his status
as a "roving ambassador of glass" (to use Cheryl White's term,[3] or
as a "bad boy" (as he told Robert Kehlmann in an interview in *GAS
Journal*,[4]). All this detracts from the art itself, one of the most extraordinary and impressive bodies of abstract sculpture created by an
American glass artist.

Developing in the San Francisco Bay Area during the 1960s, Lipofsky's art was influenced by that weird hybrid of Surrealism and Dada
on the West Coast, Funk art, assembled and chronicled by curator
and critic Peter Selz in an exhibition at the University Art Museum
in Berkeley in 1967[5]. Distended anatomical forms like intestines,
breasts, stomachs, brains and sexual organs found humorous expression in both Lipofsky's art (which was not included in Selz's pathbreaking survey) and that of his friends and colleagues William T.
Wiley, Robert Arneson and Peter Voulkos.

Coming shortly after the Funk show, Lipofsky's *California Loop*
series (1970) seems much of a piece with other droopy, loopy art of
that time and place. With its cheesy flocked surfaces, an untitled
yellow and green glass sculpture from the series traverses Funk into
the realm of Jean Arp but with a sunny, non-threatening disposition.
With the inner void completely sealed off at first, Lipofsky posited a
sense of comic mystery that would be literally cracked open in later
years, for example, while in Yugoslavia. *Fragments Jugoslavija
Stakla* (1980) is yellow and green, too, but "broken open" into three
separate but related shards. At only seven inches high, this work also
demolishes our expectation of sculpture being a single, autonomous

object. Here, as elsewhere, Lipofsky was breaking new ground for the possibilities of glass sculpture: the allowance for accident and imperfection; the multiple-part piece; the abolition of strict translucency of the colored wall.

The Illinois-born artist's first trip to Italy was in 1962. Lipofsky began a relationship to Venetian glass then that proved fruitful but was not as crucial for him as for other Americans. Subsequent visits to Murano Island in 1972, 1975, 1977 and 1978 led to a collaboration with various master blowers like Gianni Toso who blew Lipofsky's striated *Split Piece* (1978). Red and white and black, this candy-striped piece continued the artist's two-part or multi-part compositions and, as usual, took advantage of the special skills available to him wherever he was working. Lipofsky has an amazing ability to seek out the special techniques at each foreign factory and turn them to his own end. No matter where they are made—Mexico, Bulgaria, Serbia—they still are unmistakably Lipofskys.

From the process point of view (which we shall dip into only briefly), Lipofsky's sculptures employ a wide range of effects to get his desired appearance: blowing, molding, cutting, hand grinding, and sandblasting, to name a few. What matters more is the uniquely individual and individually unique appearance each work has. Like Professor Harold Hill in Meredith Willson's 1957 "The Music Man," Marvin Lipofsky has an acute sense of possibility and charitable exploitation for each town he visits. Not River City, Iowa, but Penland, North Carolina, Meisenthal, France (where Gallé worked), and Novy Bor in the Czech Republic are among the many places where Lipofsky has worked his magic.

Difficult people always manage better in a foreign language they don't speak because they must be more polite and they are dependent upon the kindness of strangers. For Lipofsky's prickly sensibility, his overseas ventures have been the perfect escape into a different personality, the one that became "Marvin Lipofsky, American Artist Abroad."

Looking at the results of nearly 40 years of such undertakings (since his 1970 arrival at the Royal Leerdam glass factory in the Netherlands), the formula has worked brilliantly. Lipofsky's color sense has developed in tandem with an exploration of blown forms that alternately conceal and reveal the inner void. That space, surrounded by walls of transparent or opaque color, is a light transmitter as well as a surrogate for sculptural mass or volume. Without requiring recourse to the vessel or basket shape à la Dale Chihuly and his followers, Lipofsky's status as a sculptor is not open to question.

Though he may have been influenced by the brightly glazed ceramic surfaces of some of his colleagues working in the medium of clay, Lipofsky's translation of them into glass has a conviction all its own.

It's tempting to try to assign national characteristics to each series made overseas but, is it really necessary? Yes, the colors of the Finnish flag are present in the blue-and-white *Suomi* series (1990–93). The vivid imperial vermilion seems appropriate to *China Group #2* created at the Dalian Glass Factory in 1993. However, seen in the context of a lifetime's achievement, they add up to an ongoing experimental investigation of all color, not just those summoning up souvenir memories. Like the greatest paintings we admire for their command of color, Lipofsky's greatest sculptures encompass the widest spectrum possible. So *Pilchuck Group #4* (1997) is a sumptuous array of primary colors with supplementary pinks, oranges, and purples. And *Czech Flowers #2* (1992) uses one end in white to offset an intense sequence of red, black, blue and green at the other.

When the colors verge toward one hue or are monochrome, as in *Seattle Series #3* (1990), the sculpture's form or baroque profile matters more. In this piece, Lipofsky took advantage of the intricate glass caning skills of Fritz Dreisbach.

Wherever they are made and whichever colors they use, the forms of Marvin Lipofsky's sculptures always appear to be evolving, in the process of becoming whole. This is the secret as to why his work still appears so fresh after all these years. Everything is irregular and asymmetrical in Lipofsky; nothing is perfectly shaped or abruptly finished. Given all that, the inner void is like the expanding breath of the blower, enlarging the sphere to the correct limit, with the right amount of color (never too much) so that each piece exudes a dynamic, life-filled radiance of its own. The walls protect the inner void, the area of the blower's breath, its residue and symbolic source of vitality. Seen this way, the art of Marvin Lipofsky has come home to the land of the artist's interior imagination. Far from exotic lands and overseas friendships, the inner void has opened up, welcoming the world.

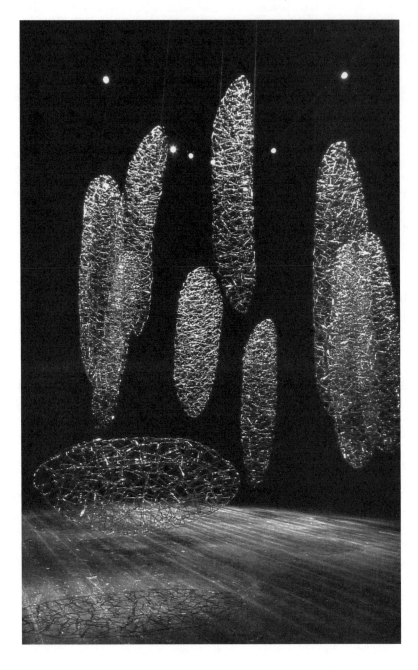

Anna Skibska: *Untitled*, 2000, lamp-worked glass of variable sizes averaging 48" h. each, Courtesy of William Traver Gallery.
Photo: Russell Johnson

FEMCLUSTER: A NEW PARADIGM

Have recent women glass artists created a new sculptural paradigm? When the work of Masami Koda, Jocelyne Prince, Kait Rhoads and Anna Skibska is examined closely the likely answer is yes. In a fascinating interface with contemporary sculpture in general, these artists are doing more than re-introducing multiple-element sculpture after a time of arid conceptualism, often so hostile to the object. They are collectively (and quite independently of one another) pushing sculpture closer to a new possibility, one of shifting centers, massing, disembodied volumes, and intricately translucent compositions. Coming in the wake of Neo-Conceptual art, however, their work nods to content, but only on the most primal, subjective plane.

Since craft art is often about the nature of its own making or assembly, these four artists working in glass allude to construction and process but, by virtue of their chosen techniques (blowing, lampworking, casting, etc.), use such approaches as metaphorical stand-ins for broader references. Claiming the additive sculptural process as a feminist strategy (as in Louise Bourgeois, Louise Nevelson, Judy Pfaff, and others), Koda, Prince, Rhoads, and Skibska are all creating images of generative growth, protective forms, open linear networks and clusters of circular, feminine forms.

Femcluster is a term that might describe this cumulative effect. Each artist in her own way contributes to the private terrain of Femcluster: by gathering and piling up pieces of glass that result in open-ended forms redolent of outward growth and open visibility. Leaving behind the opaque, volumetric units of Minimal art, for example (as in the masculine architectonic structures of Ronald Bladen and Robert Morris), the Femcluster artists present the viewer with fragility strengthened through intertwining, and delicacy enhanced by the inherent properties of glass.

To be fair to at least one male artist—the chandeliers of Dale Chihuly (1992 to the present)—provide a very substantial precedent for the massive clustering of individual, related glass elements yet, their size is so overwhelming as to remove them from the intimate realm of Femcluster. Similarly, the lucid transparency of James Carpenter's glass and metal architectural constructions anticipated the connectedness of, say, Rhoads's glass igloos but, again, is so overscaled by comparison as to cease attaining any sculptural, or feminine, potential.

With *Megapathogen* (1994), Jocelyne Prince posited her own, dense vision of Femcluster. At once preposterous, humorous, poignant and beautiful, this work combines duct tape, real pumpkins, and blown glass blobs into a strange science-fiction, off-kilter sphere of imposing presence. Here and in the low-to-the-ground *Thaw: A Wasting Disease* (1997), Prince employs extreme informality of construction. The clear and frosted glass plates and silvered blown elements piled atop one another reject the confident, finite size of conventional sculpture, not to mention leaving any decorative arts legacy of the vessel a million miles behind. Instead, Prince at least retains a sense of reflective finish common to much glass art while avoiding color altogether.

Like Robert Smithson's prophetic mirror sculptures, *Eight Unit Piece* (1969) and *Alagon* (1972), Prince's *Thaw: A Wasting Disease* is downbeat, messy, dirty and shiny, all at the same time. Its juxtapositions of shiny and matte, grungy and glitzy are also oblique spins on what Donald Kuspit once referred to (in writing about 1970s artists Rodney Ripps, Lynda Benglis and John Torreano) as "cosmetic transcendentalism." The viewer is jolted into another state of consciousness by the shiny surfaces but, in Prince's case, dragged back to reality by the dingy glass plates or, in *Megapathogen*, by the startling mundanity of the pumpkins.

Even more dismissive of masculine scale and the macho density of foundry-cast volume, Masami Koda adapts lampworking techniques to feminine clusters redolent of flowers, female anatomy, and, delicate insect chrysalises and seedpod forms. *Sunflower* (1997) is an icon of Femcluster. Carefully assembled of clear, pale green and angry red "petals," *Sunflower* is a mesmerizing work that sidesteps the dainty in spite of its revelation of delicate, time-consuming process. Part sunflower, part sea anemone, part vagina, its vivid red center seems slightly predatory in appeal.

Orbit (1998) is even more assertive, a cluster of bunched, pale pink "new blooms" hovering above a clumped-together group of dessicated husks or podlike forms. Part pseudo-science, part ceremonial offering, *Orbit* uses glass, paper and copper to convey metaphors of nature, community, death and rebirth.

Extending the cluster idea to one of mock architectural construction, Rhoads falls short of betraying the sculptural object into the area of building arts. While some of her "huts" are pedestal-size (*Doublehut*, 1999), several larger works (*Blue Dome*, 1995; *Pas de Deux*, 1999), have been shown in installation settings in Seattle, and Astoria, Oregon. In these works, the clustering is activated by assembling colored pieces of glass into ice-blocklike stacked rows underconnected by diagonal patterns of steel wire. Realms of protection, places for nestling or contemplation, the "huts" or "shelters" expand the scale of glass sculpture through feminist studio strategies similar to knitting or sewing. The casual, diagonal wire networks undercut potential fragility or collapsibility. Volume is avoided by the emphasis on a central surrounded void.

In these ways and others, the Femcluster artists are redefining glass sculpture and contributing to a broader contemporary art dialogue that challenges the macho monolithic legacy of large-scale Minimal sculpture. Polish-born artist Anna Skibska is making her own substantial contributions. Since her widely hailed U.S. debut in 1996, Skibska has extended her meticulous forays into more intimate glass networks, accentuating see-through forms alluding to nature, microscopic structures, and ways that glass can be used to attain scale and presence.

The former Soros Fellow from Wrocław has completed recent temporary installations in Seattle; New York; Portland, Oregon; and St. Louis. Her earliest American works, such as *Tympanum* (1992), were done in New York on a Kosciusko Foundation fellowship. Purportedly inspired by New York, its streets and skyscrapers, Skibska did not fully come into her own as an artist until she arrived in Seattle. Coming into contact with other women artists, Skibska's art became less jagged, more rounded, more graceful and colorful.

Her sense of form led to groupings of objects as in *One* (2000) wherein irregularly hung oblong shapes of lampworked glass networks are suspended in "crowds," like ghostly figures gathering on a darkened moonlit night. As with the other three artists under discussion, Skibska has arrived at a Femcluster sensibility through a gradual and growing technical evolution of her own ideas rather than drawing on any group-think, theory, or even loosely knit women artist's support group. Independent yet acutely aware of the advantages of community, Skibska's use of interconnected glass filament networks and her glowing, transparent effigies shift her work from nature to figure, from singular to effective multiple-element compositions. Femcluster may inform or describe her work, as with the others, but it does not define or direct its future. Those possibilities are solely in the hands of the artists.

Robert Willson: *Mirage*, 1992, solid glass, 16 ½ x 8 x 4 1/2", signed Robert Willson and Barbini/Murano, Collection of The Corning Museum of Glass, gift of Margaret Pace Willson, 2001.3.28. Photo: Ansen Seale

ROBERT WILLSON:
IMAGE-MAKER

The art of Robert Willson (1912–2000) spanned eighty-eight years of
the twentieth century and touched upon dramatic cultural, social, and
political events: the Mexican Revolution, the Great Depression, World
War II, the Cold War, and the computer age. Robert Willson's artistic
vision sprang from his parents' nineteenth-century agrarian roots,
was baptized in the Mexican mural movement, intensified during the
postwar phase of American regional and abstract modernist art, and
culminated in the fusion—the first and most sustained by an American artist—of those strains and the Venetian glass tradition. Willson's nearly five-decade-long contact with the artisans and masters of
the island of Murano, by Venice, not only is unique in twentieth-century art but became strangely reciprocal. His demands for larger and
larger solid (not blown) glass sculptures stretched the abilities and
outlooks of three generations of makers on Murano, where today solid
glass sculpture is accepted.

Like other artists of the modern movement in the past century,
Willson embarked on a roving, geographically displaced career. But
unlike a war refugee transplanted from Europe to America, Willson
moved, ceaselessly for a time, in the other direction, away from the
United States: first to Mexico from 1935 to 1941, next to the South
Pacific for a distinguished military career, then to Arkansas, and on
to Miami for twenty-five years as an art professor. Finally, continuously from 1956 to 1997, he worked in Venice, serene fountainhead
and realizer of his dreams.

Over the years, Willson's geographically diverse formative experiences turned him into an artist and intellectual at home anywhere in
the world. He benefited from his at first periodic and later sustained
expatriate life. The eclectic blend of influences that define his work—
Maya culture, modern art, and the Venetian glass tradition—renders
his achievement singular in twentieth-century art.

Despite an actively exhibiting professional life, Willson is not as well
known as he deserves. Perhaps a generation too early to be fully accepted by the homegrown American studio glass movement, and a
generation too late to be grouped with American regional artists such
as Georgia O'Keeffe, Grant Wood, and Alexander Hogue, Willson has
slipped through the cracks of American art history, as artists who
exhibit outside mainstream population centers often do. However,
when we examine his breadth as an artist—painter, ceramist, water-

colorist, photographer, and glass sculptor—combined with his parallel roles of art professor, writer, curator, amateur graphic designer, and publisher, his contributions to American culture become undeniable. Robert Willson led many lives—cowboy, adventurer, soldier, academic, artist, lover, husband, father, grandfather—but they all impinged upon an art characterized by a driving urge to create visual images of an easily identifiable nature.

Born in 1912, a crucial year of geometric abstraction in Europe, Willson grew up to accept only certain aspects of modern art. He got to know giants of modern art—Diego Rivera, José Clemente Orozco, David Alfaro Siqueiros, Frida Kahlo, Rufino Tamayo—and his art, like theirs, would remain figurative, symbolic, and narrative. Following the example of the ancient Maya artists, whose works he encountered in Mexico in 1935, his annus mirabilis, Willson evolved a pictorial language of simplified figures, shapes, and petroglyphic signs that communicate directly with the viewer. Ancient Mexican indigenous art was a far greater influence on Willson than Mexican mural art, but his exposure to the murals makes his own art unusually accessible. It is the refinement of that pictorial language and its embodiment in solid glass sculpture (fashioned by, in some cases, thirteenth-generation glass furnace artisans) that makes Willson's art so unexpectedly enjoyable.

Like younger American glass artists—William Morris, Harvey Littleton, Richard Marquis—Willson arrived at glass through ceramics. Suspecting that his ideas were better suited to glass than clay, in 1956 he approached legendary former Steuben Glass designer Frederick Carder; that contact led him to a Corning European study travel fellowship, and to Venice for the first time.

Unlike a Henry James hero—Christopher Newman in *The American*, for instance—who is crushed by the older civilization of Europe, oppressed by the weight of its tradition, the man from Texas embraced the European tradition, even bent and expanded it. As Willson explained in an exhibition-related video:

> I want a simple form of symbolic meaning much as primitive people do. . . . It's always an experiment. With each piece, I'm learning something. . . . Sometimes they will tell me we can't do it but usually I can overpersuade them and we do do it.[1]

Such a combination of gentle persistence and seemingly modest goals belies decades of trust and challenge between the American gentleman and the Murano masters and their assistants. Small wonder they grew to adore him by the time of his final visit to Murano in

1997. Indeed, as a very young man, one of the now highly respected Murano masters begged Willson to adopt him and take him to the United States where he could become Willson's full-time assistant.[2]

Willson rambled around Venice, picking and choosing hot shops and masters to suit his needs on a given summer stay. As a result, his oeuvre is a visible biography of Murano glassmakers in the last half of the twentieth century. All the big names—Alfredo Barbini, Fratelli Toso, Pino Signoretto, Licio Zuffi, Loredano Rosin, Giordano Guarnieri, Ercole Barovier, Egidio Costantini, Roberto Moretti, Elio Raffaeli, Renzo Vianello—worked for and with Willson. The extent and duration of these collaborations varied from year to year, but the purpose of each personnel decision was to find the best and most simpatico master to execute the artist's increasingly complex demands. Willson began by sketching white spiral footed bowls, but ended by supervising the construction of eight-foot-high steel-framed multiple-panel glass sculptures. By observing the hot shop skills available on the island, Willson matched his wishes to those he thought most likely to fulfill them. Though he commented that there was little or no decent glass sculpture being done in Venice when he arrived in 1956, glass masters and others today pay greater attention to the possibilities inherent in glass sculpture.[3]

Willson's influence is not only found in the island's workshops and galleries. He became the first American glass artist to have not one but two solo exhibitions in Venetian museums: in 1968 at the prestigious Correr Museum on St. Mark's Square, and in 1984 at the Ca' Pesaro Museum of Modern Art, the birthplace of Italian modern art. In both instances, the substantial testimonials and tributes from Italian colleagues, curators, artists, and critics were effusive. The art of Robert Willson was acclaimed in a city, country, and culture that have not always singled out American art for approbation.

Willson's experiences in Latin America and Europe had far-reaching curatorial implications while he was teaching ceramics in Coral Gables, Florida, at the University of Miami. Two exhibitions he curated there represent the artist's apogee as a cultural world statesman and low-profile diplomat, much in the mode of André Malraux, Paul Valéry, and Octavio Paz. Sociable and personable, Willson was able to marshal U.S. oil interests in Colombia to pay for three trips there, culminating in "3,500 Years of Colombian Art" in 1960 at the Lowe Art Museum on the Coral Gables campus. Thirteen years later the same museum mounted "International Glass Sculpture," the first such survey in the United States. Many of the artists in the exhibition became the leading lights of the studio glass movement in America and Europe.

Willson's indefatigable correspondence—friends wrote him letters in English, French, Spanish, Italian, and German—made possible his open-handed internationalist approach. Part Southerner, part Euro-expatriate, and all-Texan, Willson brought people of different nations closer together, especially important during the postwar period, but also throughout the Cold War when American artists were less respected in Europe. Willson's rock-solid support of the Murano masters, and his lifelong commitment to the fellowship of artists, set an international model that prophesied the glass world today.

Willson should be examined as a modern artist who lived into the postmodern world. Modern art has been criticized, first, as too tied to the colonization of the Third World (Cubism and African Art)[4] and, second, as too responsive to American foreign policy (Abstract Expressionism and the U.S. Information Agency touring group shows in the 1950s).[5] But Willson's sensitivities to indigenous art and his championing of American regional subject matter were deeply rooted in his own background. By growing up on a Choctaw reservation, being the son of a Christian missionary and itinerant minister, and spending extended periods in Mexico at archaeological sites and folk-art villages, Willson absorbed Native American imagery as a natural and wholly defensible outgrowth of his environment.

This gift of multicultural influences was particularly appreciated by the Italians.[6] Transformed into glass via his detailed workshop drawings, the petroglyphic, hieroglyphic, and diagrammatic imagery existed on immediate as well as symbolic levels. Mustang, serpent, coyote, armadillo, Earth, dog—all had both autobiographical and indigenous meanings for the artist. As the imagery gradually became more peopled and schematic and spread across the glass surface, Willson approached a form of ideographic writing that could be tailored to the hot shop workers' three-dimensional fulfillment. The closer the rapport and the longer the working relationship (as with Barbini and Raffaeli), the more clearly realized the artist's complicated ideography became.

The humor in Willson's art, its simplicity, and the sense of a child's dream world of animals drew on popular culture as seen in comic books and cartoons. Seemingly at odds with higher cultural aspirations during the modern period, such direct influences came easily to the proto-postmodernist Willson, who believed that, even in a largely illiterate society such as the ancient Maya, carved picture stories on the temples communicated with the population. The bracing interface of modernism and populism in Willson's art relies on a visual language he created from first-hand experience with the ruins and relics of pre-Columbian societies. Add to that his responses to art by the Mexican muralists, and one begins to see how Willson adapted the symbolic character of ancient Mesoamerican languages to a variant of the visual images used by Rivera, Orozco, and Siqueiros.

Willson's resolve in 1956 (some twenty years too early?) to use molten glass as an art material now appears prescient. After mainstream media such as oil paint and bronze were discredited by postmodern theorists as too traditional, ironically, craft materials (clay, wood, metal, cloth, and glass) came to be seen as radically unconventional and marginalized, and hence, as desirable aesthetic tools. If many of the younger glass artists included in "International Glass Sculpture" went on to gain considerable status (Richard Marquis, Marvin Lipofsky, Joel Philip Myers, Stanislav Libenský), it may be because of the older artist's earlier efforts to break down prejudices against glass and claim for it a high seriousness of purpose.

Although my book on Willson is not a biography, I have drawn upon the artist's journals, letters, and published writings to give a voice to this American tale. The man who the young Italian glassblower wanted for an adoptive father, comparing him to the actor James Stewart, had a magnetic personality. In lieu of a full biographical study, we fortunately have the written and videotaped legacy of this charismatic artist. He was also an English major as an undergraduate, and a contributor to literary journals. Perhaps more than the utterances of other twentieth-century masters, his voice rings with a true authorial tone.

Robert Willson traveled from Oklahoma and Texas to Mexico and Florida, and then throughout Europe and the Mediterranean, all the while jotting notes and observations. Reading his words adjacent to the images of his remarkable art, the reader may begin to understand this outstanding artist and cultural figure.

Bertil Vallien: *Head 1*, 1995, sandcast glass, 7 ½ x 5 x 6 1/2". Courtesy of William
Traver Gallery, Seattle. Photo: Goran Ørtegren

BERTIL VALLIEN: SOMNA VAKNA

Swedish glass sculptor Bertil Vallien's most recent body of work, *Somna Vakna* (2000–2006) (*Sleeping / Waking*), is the current culmination of a long career that has remarkably close ties to American art. Yet despite this, Vallien is not as widely known in the United States as he deserves to be. His exhibitions have tended to be in art galleries that specialize in glass and these do not always come to the attention of contemporary art enthusiasts. However, set in the context and perspective of this essay, the art of Bertil Vallien may be seen in relation to recent American art from the 1960s on and to postwar European existentialist/humanist cultural and artistic strains. The question, besides the ubiquitous "How Swedish is it?" should really be a series of questions including "How European is it?" or "How global is it?" Critics and commentators[1] have repeatedly stressed how the cast-glass abstract and representational forms alternately epitomize and transcend their original cultural context of production—a Swedish glass factory where Vallien has worked since 1969—and extrapolate from there poetic and metaphorical references for extremely simplified imagery that has impressively accumulated over the years into a broad and deep vocabulary of recognizable imagery signs.

Dividing his time between at the Orrefors/Kosta Boda factory in Åfors, Sweden, between design tasks and personal studio activity, Vallien is far better known outside Sweden for his narrative-figurative sculptures than for his tableware designs. Long before that, however, as a young man traveling on a postgraduate fellowship funded by the King of Sweden for promising young Swedish artists, Vallien went to Los Angeles in 1962 where he was an eyewitness to the California ceramics explosion at Otis Art Institute and the Funk art movement in clay sculpture coming out of Berkeley in the mid-1960s. Both the swagger and scale of Peter Voulkos's art and that of his cohorts and the wit and erotic fantasies of Robert Arneson and others in northern California had an important impact on the young artist.

Over the ensuing years, after his return to Sweden where he accepted the offer of a job as head of design and artist-in-residence at Orrefors/Kosta Boda in 1969, Vallien populated a dream world that not only built on the breakthroughs of figurative American ceramics but transferred the wide-open studio sensibility he encountered in America to the expansion of European figurative glass sculpture.

For Vallien, storytelling is allusive and connotative, suggestive and poetic. The cast shapes with people in them may have originally followed from his clay sculptures—people in boats—as has been noted[2] but their manifestations in a series of objects captured a wide variety of elements including men, women, houses, bridges, boats, stair steps, maps, stars, crosses, pyramids, rings and circles, heads, torsos, faces and bodies. Smaller elements are often set into the molten glass so that, after cooling, they remain visible through the clear glass. Embedded thusly, they propose an imaginary opening for the viewer who peeps into a lost, yet retrievable, world of ancient settlements, archaeological sites, sunken Viking ships, and fragments of memory that are often disconnected yet logical, as in a dream. Prior to and including *Somna Vakna*, the unconscious or dream state has been a potent metaphor for appreciating the vast realm of Vallien's art.

With periodic exhibitions in the U.S. largely shared between Seattle and New York galleries, enthusiasm and recognition for Vallien's art gradually grew[3]. At the same time, positioning and site became extremely important aspects; how the sculptures are perceived and experienced by the viewer. Whether heads set on tall narrow pedestals all in a row, as in the "Four Acts in Glass" exhibition at the American Craft Museum in New York in 1997, or sculptures set on lower, longer tables wherein the viewer gazes down into the see-through boat forms[4], Vallien continued to experiment with maximizing the intimate encounter between object and viewer.

In addition, unusual settings such as medieval towers,[5] 10th-century French dwellings, or the Museum of History in Stockholm,[6] helped Vallien face the architectural context of displaying his art head-on. Part of this development relates to American artists like Fred Wilson, or the Polish artist Krzysztof Wodiczko, who seek to critique the very institutions—museums—noted for protecting and legitimizing art. Another aspect of historic sites, however, has more deeply European roots. There simply are so many more such venues there that it makes sense to take advantage of them. Much Postminimalist and conceptual sculpture in Italy, for example Mario Merz and Iannis Kounellis, is unthinkable without a solemn, highly contrasting sense of architectural context surrounding the contemporary art spectacle.

Far less theatrical than the Italians', Vallien's installations always draw the viewer into a meditative inspection of the objects, the way one might examine specimens in a natural history museum. And since many of the embedded elements—coins, heads, houses, metal fragments—are open-ended in their symbolic potential, the viewer becomes the spectator of a miniature fantastical world. As a result, the juxtaposition between historical setting and faux-artifact sets off an uneasy but still aesthetically satisfying dialectic.

Unlike American artists who rarely allude to national history, European artists like Vallien have millennia to draw upon, analyze and refresh into contemporary statements. Instead of history being a burden of tradition, it becomes an asset for contemporary content and comment. Vallien's predominant theme with more outward connotations has been Sweden's maritime history. The long ships of the Vikings, the heavily loaded trade cargos (some of which sank), and the ties of transportation and communication are all summed up in the boats and map series, reminding us of the preceding generations of adventurers and risk-takers (and nascent global capitalists) that are part of Sweden's past. With the clear glass sometimes taking on a foggy character, the viewer's perspective is clouded, too, just as our grasp of the ancient past is obscured, too, filtered and conditioned by intervening time and colored by opinionated commentators. Vallien is not passing judgment on Sweden's checkered yet impressive past; he is materially reminding us how subjective the reading and writing of history can be. Similarly, our appreciation of his art—and art in general—wavers between an encounter with materials facts (the glass, the pedestal, the interior elements, the lighting) and an emotionally driven response based on our own prior experiences, enthusiasms, and prejudices.

Beginning with the humorous ceramic figures, evolving his control over the studio mechanics of glass, and balancing referential images with private meanings, Bertil Vallien has arrived at a point where his art operates on many levels: the public, the private, the historical, the contemporary, the realistic and the symbolic. As we shall see in the *Somna Vakna* series and other related works, the combination of specific and general, local and universal, can lead to an art of deeply satisfying visual experience, one that resonates in the eye and the mind long after the initial viewing experience.

Iciness is a key to the beautiful, yet contradictory, appearance of Bertil Vallien's more recent sculptures of the past decade. Seen in the context of northern Europe and Sweden, the icy quality is immediately evident. Figures are encased in ice, the transparent yet solid medium the glass pretends to be. This quality, partly related to the extraordinary purity of Swedish crystal, also has earlier roots in Italian glass history. As early as 1564, the Venetian ice technique, or *ghiaccio*, is mentioned as being represented in the Venetian glass collection of Philip II of Spain. With those works, however, rather than transparency, the irregularly crystalline or fractured surface of cracking ice is emulated. Vallien's variant stresses a cloudy, filmy character, partly revealing, partly concealing the submerged representational elements.

Furthermore, Vallien gradually sought out or "collected" stories about people being buried in ice by accident (as with the Swedish woman Karolina Olsson who emerged from years in a coma after a childhood incident involving ice) or deliberate (as in the case of a Mr. Moro or Portland, Oregon who experimented with cryogenics in the 1930s). The artist may have overstated such inspirations as specific clues to subject matter and content but they do provide a backdrop for the numerous sculptures that proceeded throughout the 1990s and early years of the present century.

Set right to the edge upon wax-treated steel pedestals roughly a meter high, many of the works in the *Somna Vakna* series appear elevated as if on funeral biers or similarly ceremonial supports. Transformation and transition are two themes for the current work: from liquid to solid; from water to ice; from life to death; from female to male; and from sleeping to waking. This quality of change from one state to another, a kind of suspended animation, is crucial to retaining the viewer's interest in the work. It can never be completely experienced as a fully confident perception but rather looms in and out of our optical field, now static, now fluid, now rigid, and now permeable.

A few works, like *Passage, Mr. Moro I, The Barn* and *Horn* use an elongated house-roof shape spanning the length of each piece and reinforcing an illusion of domestic enclosure. With primitive tools visible, Sweden's agricultural past is invoked, reminding us that, with Sweden's entry into the European Community, unique aspects of its past are not so much endangered as set up for potential nostalgia.

Several other works, like *Funnel, Somna II, Mr. Moro II* and *Corridor I* and *II,* have a faceted edge on top that resembles a coffin lid. The full-length figure in *Mr. Moro II* is improbably dressed in a coat and tie, absurdly capturing a formal dress style of the 1930s that is embellished with a top hat in another work. *Idol* also has a coffin lid, one revealing a stylized, truncated body with a tinge of red, as if archaeological remnants of paint still adhere to a devotional figure.

Vakna and *House* share a circular porthole area near one end, along with, in the cast of the latter, a phallic protuberance at the opposite end, as if the figure, whose face is glimpsed through the porthole, is partially arising from the solid glass.

Very different from the boats crammed full of detritus, cargo and booty, the *Somna Vakna* figures are completely alone, experiencing the solitude of eternity yet somehow oddly alive to their surroundings despite their frozen state. Vallien has compressed the imagery of all his earlier work into one extremely powerful and quiet image per sculpture. In the process, he allows for potential interpretation to occur more spontaneously and also permits the iconic power of the raised glass oblong shape to command space more clearly than before.

Provenance, Singular and *Mr. Moro I* are male nudes in all their naked vulnerability. Here Vallien is addressing contemporary issues of gender and masculinity, as if to suggest that these qualities are not completely determined by social circumstance and conditioning. With the anatomy of *Provenance* slightly more chubby and stylized, another idol is posited, one revered by a culture long past but somehow regained through memory and the artist's making. In *Claude Cahun*, the artist goes one step farther in addressing gender, from female to male. The American poet and artist, Claude Cahun (1894–1954) dressed as a man frequently and had herself photographed as one. This strong urge for gender transference is rendered iconically through the use of a specially staged photograph commissioned by Cahun. It also stands as an emblem of erotic ambiguity and sexual ambivalence, another central preoccupation of artists in the late 20th (and indeed, late 19th) century.

Set together in a grouping as at the William Traver Gallery in October, 2000, the *Somna Vakna* sculptures were reinforced as installation art through dim, artfully placed lighting that further underscored the sleeping/waking dichotomy or twilight world. Vallien is insisting on the necessity of imaginative engagement for the full appreciation of his art, always retaining poetic license and effortlessly manipulating the material of glass as a vehicle for imaginary journeys. Sleeping is crucial to the operation of the imagination and the fertile unconscious, repository of the seeds of creativity. Waking is necessary for the recognition of consciousness; the objective claims of reality that always impinge on the individual who awakes from the sleeping state. Although the viewer is awake while inspecting the sculptures, he or she may identify with the effigies of the sleeping figures in many of the sculptures. Seen together as in Seattle, they are a dormitory of cultural memories echoed in the half-light of the gallery, embodied in the meeting of glass, steel and other materials.

Craft *becomes* concept in *Somna Vakna*, as in all the most interesting contemporary art employing traditional materials or methods. Both craft and concept work in tandem toward an apotheosis of meaning, combining the process of making with the workings of the mind. In this sense, Vallien stands beside many of the most challenging artists of our time, those who do not spurn the handmade or retinal but who turn them to a new end, one embracing a content that is inextricably tied to the nature of construction, fabrication and the resurgent power of the object as a work of art.

Joe Feddersen: *Cinder Block*, 2003, sandblasted blown glass, 16 x 11 1/4 x
11 1/4". Courtesy of the artist, Olympia, Washington. Photo: Froelick Gallery,
Portland, Oregon.

VISION QUEST:
NATIVE AMERICAN GLASS

Well established in the Northwest, Native American glass art is
poised to become a national phenomenon. When the touring exhibition, "Fusing Traditions: Transformations in Glass by Native
American Artists" came to the Mashantucket Pequot Museum in
Mashantucket, Connecticut, in 2004, East Coast residents saw for
themselves. The show featured four of the most prominent Native
American glass artists living in the Pacific Northwest and British
Columbia, each working with traditional imagery and forms in the
relatively contemporary medium of studio glass. Tapping into their
rich heritage, they boldly explore new forms and take on the challenge of balancing tradition with their personal artistic visions.

Joe Feddersen, Marvin Oliver, Susan Point and Preston Singletary
all have extensive gallery and museum exhibition records both in the
contemporary fine arts world and the narrow, but lucrative, parallel
realm of contemporary Native American art galleries. Indeed, none
of these artists has had to choose. Their individual approaches bring
up a provocative question that is central to the entire movement: how
to reconcile traditional heritage with contemporary art sensibilities?
The way each of the four has answered this question—through their
interviews, writings and art—offer insight into artists with a unique
cultural heritage. The pluses and minuses, the advantages and disad-
vantages, the pleasures and challenges are considerable. And the re-
wards mean a new dimension for North American art made of glass.

Marvin Oliver is a good example of a minority artist who has had
to play many roles: professor, curator, panelist, juror, lecturer, and
maker. The recipient of a 1986 fellowship from the National Endowment for the Arts, Oliver's work is included in numerous corporate,
museum, and municipal art collections from the People's Republic of
China and Japan to Rhode Island. Oliver has also acted as a graphic
artist and book illustrator and designer, all the while maintaining an
active exhibition schedule in both traditional Native American museums and contemporary art galleries.

With a Quinault heritage from the tribes originally present on the
Olympic Peninsula northwest of Seattle, Oliver's transition to glass
has been a natural one given his wide-ranging interests in other materials. As curator of contemporary Native American art at the Burke
Museum of Washington State History at the University of Washington, Oliver comes into contact with classical heritage objects in the

Burke's permanent collection and the art being made today by the living artists who have been inspired by them.

A series of cast-glass faces with undersheets of dichroic glass has attracted close attention and critical scrutiny. Using Oliver's mastery of the vocabulary of Pacific Northwest "formline" design—the abstract, linear style of totem poles—he has emulated the refined, low-relief carving of coastal tribes' facemasks. Sun and moon faces summon ancient mythological presences but also cast an eerie, colorful glow due to the remarkable qualities of the dichroic spectrum.

More ambitious, the life-scale, freestanding *Raven Kachina* (2004) won the top prizes in two categories (glass and sculpture) at the 2005 Heard Museum Indian Market in Phoenix, Arizona. At over seven feet high, *Raven Kachina* combines aspects of Northwest and Southwest Native art. This is appropriate since Oliver has family ties to the Isleta-Pueblo people, too. With the flattened out, conjoined panels of colored glass for the body sections, Oliver uses black formline drawing to augment the rounded sheets. The head is another dichroic, cast-glass face, surrounded by a red halo. Oliver has been able to answer the larger scale of Northwest totems by using glass but also to allude to the Southwest Kachina dolls through bright colors. A series of smaller Kachina figures continues his explorations.

Joe Feddersen's background is in painting and printmaking. Part of the revival of Indian Modernism in Seattle in the early 1980s at the Sacred Circle Gallery of American Indian Art, Feddersen is not turning to abstraction as an option; he is simply inheriting a cultural given.

Feddersen's work was seen in New York in 2003 in a small solo survey at the National Museum of the American Indian of the Smithsonian Institution. "Continuum 12: Joe Feddersen" debuted the Okanogan/Colville tribal member's glass in Manhattan. Because of his heritage rooted east of the Cascade Mountains in the drier, Plains-style part of Washington State, it makes sense that the artist's chosen format for glass is the woven basket. Although he has learned to weave actual baskets, the works executed in glass bring a strong contemporary design flavor to traditional forms and further explore Feddersen's interest in reconciling figurative and abstraction through referential form.

Tire, Cul-de-Sac and *Cinder Block* (all 2003) set patterns from everyday objects or sights onto the sandblasted surfaces of cylindrical, white basket shapes. Mall culture, suburban housing developments, automobiles and even computer circuits and street maps serve as identifiable background images within the overall object. With a red lip-wrap atop each, the baskets are part of The Evergreen State College art professor's ongoing Urban Indian series. The glass baskets operate with abstract patterns for their own sake but also as subliminal subjects of consumption and ecological environment.

Canadian artist Susan Point is a member of the Coast Salish tribe in British Columbia. Widely honored, her ventures into glass have been numerous and are documented in the 144-page book *Susan Point: Coast Salish Artist*, edited by Gary Wyatt (University of Washington Press, 2000). Besides various design projects, including the Governor General's Academic Medal, Point's vision as an artist has closely hewed to the myths and images of her heritage.

Point's use of glass has been supplemented by other projects that use or combine ceramics, bronze, ceramics, stainless steel and wood. *Return* (2003) is a good example from the Spindle Whorl series, enlargements of her grandmother's wool thread-spinning apparatus, a large shield-like disc of glass perforated by a cedar stick. Symbol of the creation of the world, the Spindle Whorls function as symbols of the origins and transformation of natural materials like wool (or wood or fur or whaleskin) into art. When one recalls that it is ritual alone that ignites aesthetic content in traditional Native American religions, Point's Spindle Whorl series posits its own postmodern self-consciousness as an engaged and artificed object.

Operating in her own way as a highly organized and productive design atelier owner, Susan Point is not that different from Dale Chihuly or even Jack Lenor Larsen. In the glass pieces, especially, sizes and degrees of adventurous execution are often tied to special commissions or editioned pieces. *Wind Dried* (2003) is unique, however, and symbolically represents village methods of hanging salmon up to smoke in the open air over an alder wood fire. Instead of grades of the color orange denoting various degrees of smoking, Point uses four shades of blue. Each of the four inset cast blocks is a different formline representation of a salmon.

Perhaps more than her male colleagues under discussion here, Susan Point has had the greatest success at combining a surprising range of materials (including Texada marble). The extension of her "protected heritage" of Indian imagery into contemporary expression is one of the artist's greatest achievements.

Youngest of all, Preston Singletary brings a second-generation studio-glass artist's grasp of the material in ways that none of the others have. Mastering and understanding glass before he turned to his heritage, Singletary is among the greatest beneficiaries of the Pilchuck Glass School revolution.

Trained and apprenticed with some of the greats at Pilchuck, from Chihuly and Tagliapietra to Benjamin Moore and Tony Jojola, the Seattle artist is the Native American glass movement's current poster child and cover boy. But, as with Chihuly, to dismiss Singletary's high profile would be a grave mistake because what he has brought to Native American art has been more than equaled by what his rediscovery has done for him. After a successful, respected career making Swedish Modern-style glass (filtered through a Melrose Avenue retro sensibility), Singletary's transition to Native themes and formline imagery at least provided potentials beyond period-style replays.

As the museum exhibitions, public and private commissions, and growing awards mount, it's important to note that, of all the artists under discussion here, Singletary has done the least to relate his art to any other contemporary art attitudes. Perhaps that is part of his appeal.

Lifting the shape of the cedar gift box (*Never the Same Twice*, 2003) or the flat spread of a Chilkat blanket (*Wall Screen Panel*, 2003), Singletary's Tlingit ancestry brought him the ultimate readymade: an entire cultural language of visual myth and ritual that the early Abstract Expressionists would have cried their eyes out to have inherited. With traditional, preset images, though, "all" Singletary has to do is translate them into glass as perfectly as possible.

Despite the results and growing respect for his work, Singletary must still be set in context at the deep end of tradition with the smallest degree of any radical innovation (unlike Point) or any solid modernist-abstract core (drawn upon by Feddersen). The perfection of Singletary is also the greatest trap awaiting him. How can the Native American artist respect tradition and add to it? Maybe the artist inheriting pure Northwest Native formline drawing, as does Singletary, simply has a bigger room to live in than others. The narrative compression so admired by Adolph Gottlieb in his Pictographs, or the self-contained room-size mural borrowed by Barnett Newman, were only the first cross-transmissions from the Northwest to modern American art. What will remain crucial for Singletary and, to a lesser degree for Oliver, Point and Feddersen, is the ratio of give-and-take between the chaos and uncertainty of the contemporary world and the still pulsing, evolving world of Native American art. One thing is certain: the introduction and adoption of glass by these artists is making an enormous difference in both areas.

Benjamin Moore: *Palla Set (Yellow and Clear, Blue and Clear, Black and Clear)*, 2004, blown glass, 19" h. , diameters up to 20". Courtesy of Foster/White Gallery, Seattle. Photo: Rob Vinnedge

BENJAMIN MOORE:
THE TRANSLATOR

The Italian influence on American studio glass is one the most significant cross-cultural exchanges of the past century. Benjamin Moore—
glassblower, designer, ex-Pilchuck creative and educational director—has been at the forefront of the Murano-Pilchuck interchange of
ideas, techniques, and talent. After Dale Chihuly and Richard Marquis, Moore was "the third man" to have an impact in Venice and the
only one of them to speak fluent Italian. And just as with the Orson
Welles character Harry Lime in the 1946 film of Graham Greene's
novel, *The Third Man*, an aura of ambiguity and uncertainty about
Moore's role has long colored his reputation among the Italians, some
of whom have voiced concern about just how effective Moore has been
at decoding the language, culture and craft he came to study. Moore's
skillful performance as diplomat and educator has also brought with
it suspicions in Italy that, intentionally or not, he had served as a spy
and facilitator of technology transfer.

To the Americans, Moore is a hero. To the Italians, he brings to mind
the old saying, "Il traduttore è un traditore," the translator is a traitor. Situated right at the center of an international cultural phenomenon—the rise and fall and rise of Venetian glass due to American intervention—Moore's profile may now be seen as much more complex.
His art must be seen in the context of his other activities that may
have distracted attention from his uncanny powers of observation. As
he says today with characteristic modest understatement: "The art of
making glass? You can learn everything you need to know by watching. Speaking Italian was not as important."

Yet speaking Italian clearly did matter. Though it may not have
seemed as important at first, Moore was to become the person responsible for translating the comments of Lino Tagliapietra, Checco
Ongaro, Loredano Rosin, Pino Signoretto and Mario Grasso, and the
one outsider privy to the intense discussions of the Italians when they
first arrived in America. "When Lino first came [to Pilchuck,]. . . he
didn't speak any English whatsoever," Moore told Victoria Milne in
an interview in the Summer 1994 issue of *GLASS*. "After the second
or third year, [Lino] said, 'Murano is very different now. It's really
America where exciting contemporary things are happening and
that's where I want to be.'"

Such a *pronunciamento* changed Murano glass over time, and Moore
was indirectly responsible. Perhaps that is the reason his prototypes

were omitted from the Venini catalogue raisonné. Founder Paolo Venini's daughter, Anna, expressed the widely held discomfort with the American invasion in her introduction to the *Venini Catalogue Raisonné 1921–1986* published in 2000: "At first I looked favorably on this exchange. Now, however, I wonder if we were a little too generous since that openness perhaps entailed losing our heritage of experience and knowledge. . . . The benefits had been heavily in favor of those who had come, that they had effectively taken away more than they had brought."

Anna Venini's remarks must be set alongside the long history of Venetian ambivalence about outside influences and the fierce protection of materials and technology which date back to before 1291 when Murano became the chief production site for Venetian glass. Would Moore or Tagliapietra be tracked down today and killed for their cultural perfidy? That hasn't happened since the 17th century although one especially bitter published account in Italy compared Tagliapietra to a procurer offering his wife for sale.

While dramatic, all this discussion of espionage actually neglects Moore's own background and evolution before and after his initial 1978–79 guest residency at Venini. Even prior to his exposure to contemporary art and design at Rhode Island School of Design, his ceramics studies with Richard Fairbanks at Central Washington University were significant in that Fairbanks had been a pupil of Swiss Purist master Paul Bonifas at the University of Washington and of Kaj Franck at the Arabia china factory in Helsinki during a 1956 Fulbright fellowship. Like Fairbanks, Moore learned to draw the pot before throwing it. So Moore's approach was largely contrary to the prevailing, spontaneous mode of American craft even before RISD or Venice. "No surface embellishment, a use of subtle color and of simple forms" is how Moore describes the legacy of his pottery studies, further fueled by his admiration for Korean and Japanese ceramics.

Moore's ceramic apprenticeship has been examined in depth in another essay (Kangas, "Turning Points" *GLASS*, Fall 2002). After Fairbanks, he went on to complete clay studies with Viola Frey at California College of Arts and Crafts in Oakland and, while there, blew his first glass with Marvin Lipofsky.

By 1978, Moore "had reached a plateau. I had to go to Italy so I wrote to fifteen factories and only Venini responded." Continuing his Italian-language studies that he had begun by auditing classes at RISD, Moore progressed from auditor and observer at Venini to visiting foreign designer. Venini's son-in-law, Ludovico Diaz de Santillana, who had taken over the company after Venini's death in 1959, "paid me under the table between 1978 and 1979," according to Moore, " but I was back in Pilchuck each summer and, in fact, for the next 14 summers when the Italians continued to come over."

During those years, Moore's Italian apprenticeship continued, but in America. "Lino and his peers had very deep discussions about the history of glass" which Moore was able to follow in Italian. "At first, while I was in Italy, it was starting to happen—the evolution of my vision. I learned how to cane and reticello, but that was not my voice. The forming of the glass at the furnace, though, that was where it all started for me."

Some of Moore's *Tessuto* series, reminiscent of stripes of cloth, are still in production at Venini but omitted from the catalogue raisonné. Was this payback for Moore's amazing feats of cultural technology transfer? It's hard to say, but soon thereafter, in 1980–81, Moore left Venini for good and embarked on a design career beyond Venice. Lobmeyr of Vienna hired him for two years but for all Moore's immersion in and admiration of Secession glass, none of his designs ever went into production there.

After the inauguration in 1985 of his own hotshop, Benjamin Moore, Inc., in Seattle, other production lines and commissions followed, including glasses and tableware for Neiman-Marcus and Nordstrom. Repeating the Murano routine, however, proved not to be as satisfying for Moore as he had expected. "In Murano, it's all commercially oriented and I saw it could be a rut. We'd do a prototype, make it, receive an order for five hundred and then, wait a minute, I'd think, 'Is this what I want to do the rest of my life?'"

Instead, Moore invited others to come in to work for and with him and to execute designs by other glass artists, including Dan Dailey, Chihuly and Fritz Dreisbach. A series of lamps and lighting fixtures done in collaboration with RISD professor Louis Mueller also was developed, along with a separate series of smaller lamps commissioned by Pilchuck co-founder Anne Gould Hauberg and done with metals artist Walter White.

Residential and corporate commissions virtually flooded in from Los Angeles, New York, Florida and the affluent high-tech enclaves east of Seattle, Bellevue and Redmond. Among the larger projects have been the Grand Hyatt Regency, Hong Kong, the Port of Seattle headquarters and the Two Union Square branch of Home Street Bank in Seattle.

For better or worse, this has meant a diminution of Moore's art glass. Over a 26-year period, barely three separate series have emerged besides the Venini prototypes, the department store series and the architectural collaborations. *Interior Folds* (1982—), *Exterior Folds* (1983—) and *Palla* (1983—) are masterfully beautiful objects that have been made available at select art galleries around the nation.

Maybe it is a mistake to limit Moore to maker status. Theorist, critic and manager might better explain his multi-faceted pursuits. Looking toward the future, he mentioned more lighting designs as fertile, unexhausted territory. And he threw down the gauntlet, challenging U.S. glass artists in general: "I don't think there's ever been a design sensibility in American glass. Before, everything was mass-produced, like press ware. It's always been a free-for-all. There have never been any specific design schools in any areas geographically. And all the big figures—Chihuly, Littleton, Lipofsky—are all non-design-oriented. There are a few young kids in New York and Seattle now but otherwise? Nothing."

Were it not for his unassailable achievements leading to the internationalization of American studio glass, such comments might be considered too tart. From his bicultural viewpoint spanning Italy and the U.S., however, Moore is speaking with authority. The translator may not be a traitor but something even more to be feared, a prophet.

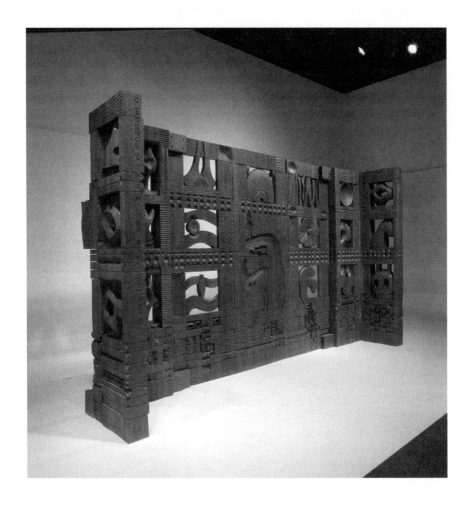

Leroy Setziol: *Freestanding Screen*, 1972, Teak; 84 x 148 x 27". Collection of the
Salem Public Library, Salem, Oregon. Courtesy of the Jordan Schnitzer Museum of
Art, University of Oregon. Photograph by Jack Liu

PART IV

WOOD, FIBER AND METALS

LEROY SETZIOL:
SYSTEM AND SYMBOL

Just the way a thicket of thorns and underbrush often bars entry to a forest of grand old trees, so the legend of Oregon wood sculptor Leroy Setziol (1915–2005) obscures his art and any deeper effort at determining its roots and meaning. Alternately called a folk artist and a Modernist, Leroy Setziol is an enigma, an original, and an unheralded genius of American craft.

Musician, lapsed Protestant minister, doctoral candidate in philosophy, homespun carver, and beloved regional character: these are all masks the Sheridan, Oregon resident has donned, developed, and discarded over the years. Many were placed there by well-meaning admirers. As the 1991 University of Oregon Museum of Art retrospective exhibition organized by curator Tommy Griffin revealed, however, there is far more logic and system to Setziol's art than the loquacious direct carver has conceded; in addition, there are heretofore undetermined levels of meaning which his articulate but anti-interpretive statements have not allowed.

This essay is a walk in the forest of Leroy Setziol's art. It begins with the well-worn paths but shortly takes off into barely marked byways, the territory of subject matter, content, and meaning which unveils itself once one gets more deeply into the woods and away from the comfortable path so treacherously set out.

Leroy Setziol was born to Polish-American parents on December 4, 1915 in Bristol, Pennsylvania near Philadelphia. His father was a retail store window display designer whom Leroy helped after school. The family soon moved to Buffalo, New York where the children attended public schools.

Setziol remembers visiting the Albright Art Gallery as a youth and seeing a painting where "the artist left his tool marks. This affected me greatly."[1]

Young Setziol's interests were not directed toward art for long, however, but rather toward theology and philosophy. By 1938, he had graduated from Elmhurst College in Illinois and pursued an additional bachelor's degree in divinity at Eden Theological Seminary at Webster Groves, Missouri. In 1940, he married his wife, Ruth, the child of missionary parents in India. Their daughter, Monica, was born the following year and was joined by her brother, Paul, in 1946.

Shortly before World War II, Rev. Setziol was assigned his first con-gregation in the Evangelical Reformed denomination at Bennington, New York. He soon was sent to chaplain training school at Harvard and sent with an infantry company to the South Pacific islands.

It was there that Setziol, in an idle moment, completed his first wood carving, *Icon* (1944), made of mahogany. It would be eight years be-fore Setziol would realize that wood was meant to be his material and direct carving his métier in life.

Until then, Setziol would remain embarked on a spiritual quest, seek-ing an answer to the question, "Why was I placed on this earth by God?" and pursuing through advanced studies in voice at the Peabody Institute while reassigned to a congregation in Baltimore, Maryland. He also undertook further graduate work in philosophy at Johns Hopkins University. Somehow, all these experiences would affect his art: the familiarity with the symbolic pictorial language of Christian-ity; the appreciation for the multiple levels of sound in music; the order and logic of secular analytical philosophy. All this would lead to a world of system and symbol in Setziol's art, its uniting factors, and seeming reconciliation of conflicting forces in his life.

Once he and his wife moved to Oregon in 1950, Setziol had realized "I wasn't going to become part of anything; I was going to stay home and work." Nevertheless, economics forced a re-enlistment in the U.S. Army with another assignment as chaplain, this time to West Ger-many. Though the stint lasted barely a year—until he resigned and returned to Portland—it exposed him to the carving of Ernst Barlach (1870–1938) who combined influences of Russian folk art and medi-eval German church sculpture, all filtered through Cubism. A similar mixture describes Setziol's first figurative carvings in fir, walnut, maple, and myrtlewood completed between 1952 and 1959 after his return from Europe.

Without any real training in art, Setziol still knew he wanted to be an artist working in wood. First, he was still under the spell of the South Seas. "I have a very intimate and direct relationship to all the master carvers like the Maoris, those in Africa, and the Pacific Northwest. You see, I don't recognize the distinction between primitive and so-phisticated."

Though this would come to describe his own mature style—primitive and sophisticated—the early figurative reliefs and church commis-sions do not rise above the primitive to the sophisticated. *Family Group* (1956) and *Head of Christ* (1958) are small and stylized with-out being abstracted, caught in a netherworld of spiritual sincerity, inadequate mastery of craft, and greater attention to mark-making or chipping away at the maple or myrtlewood surface than to the overall image.

Curiously, Leroy Setziol did not become a mature artist until he abandoned the figure. Though he continued sporadically to work with the figure (again, mostly for ecclesiastical clients), it was his shift to a composition based on drawing, rough clearing away of the top surface of wood, and the residue of excavation left on the wood which brought Setziol his own original style.

Looking back, it makes sense that the *First Grid Relief Carving* (1962) was a turning point. Nature, rather than humanity, became the correct focus for this artist so obsessed with the inherent character of wood. Coming upon a grid system of pictorial organization by chance while simply attempting to "rough clear" the top layer of wood in order to begin relief carving, Setziol realized that the saw lines and chipped-away areas had a considerable beauty of their own. Instead of circular tree trunk rings marking the tree's age, for example, Setziol stratified vertically the plan of a given piece of wood. Using a variety of tools—gougers, planes, electric saws—he further altered the surface to reveal a mixture of simple grain and manually arrived-at new structures. *First Grid Relief* introduces both the system and symbols which would dominate Setziol's art for the subsequent 30 years.

The vertical division of space in varying widths anchors and orders the composition like a Cubist painting. The vocabulary of natural forms—knotholes, seeds, buds, and blossoms—acts as collector of symbols for life and growth without requiring recourse to the unsuccessful depiction of the human figure. In short, he had happened upon a way of being a figurative artist without using the figure. Without realizing it, he had become a Modernist or abstract artist without formally studying the dominant style of mid-century American art.

Scott Landis carefully chronicled all phases of Setziol's career in the catalogue accompanying the University of Oregon Museum of Art exhibition but, following the artist's preference for a nonverbal response to his art, offers no real guide for interpretation.[2] In fact, a critical appreciation of Setziol's achievement has long been obscured by his insistence on open-ended unspecified meanings; his disdain for Modernist poetry like Auden and Eliot, for example; and his stubborn streak of yearning for transcendent experience beyond words.

Leaving that aside and trudging past the entangling undergrowth of his rhetoric, one must literally see the forest for the trees, that is,

catch the overall plan in his work which combines system and symbol. The aborted career as spiritual counselor led to a later suspicion
of efforts at concretizing aesthetic meaning. His thwarted academic
adventure in philosophy at Johns Hopkins imprinted an admiration
for systematic thought and logic. As he admitted about the non-figu-
rative works, "Actually, the so-called meaningless pieces are loaded
with meaning."

Fusing both possibly contradictory strains—the spiritual and the
systematic—Setziol broke through to a clearing, so to speak, his
large-scale relief carvings completed over the past 30 years. Within
five years of the 1962 relief, he was awarded a carver's dream, a carte
blanche commission at a new Pacific Coast resort, Salishan Lodge.
His first major accomplishment in an architectural context, Salishan
was a situation where the developers, Grayco Resources, "let me do
whatever I wanted. They trusted me though I was not well known."
The task ended up including 14 vertical carved panels; the Cedar
Room entry area with panel, door, and sign; four space dividers for
the Gourmet Room; and redwood locator signs throughout the complex, all done in close cooperation with architect John Storrs.

The success of Salishan led to other commissions which, while not
nearly as extensive in scope as the resort, benefited from Setziol's
newfound mastery and interest in pairing natural and geometric
forms. The side-by-side wall and door at Salishan used stylized scal-
lop shells, starfish, tideflat rivulets, rocks, and sandpiles as seemingly
random motifs created in Oregon black walnut. Swirling elliptical
horizontal areas like aerial views of a beach are balanced by three
upright lines separating one wide and one narrow wall panel from the
large door.

Five relief panels made in 1968 out of teak for the First Interstate
Bank of Salem further extended the close relationship of system and
symbol in Setziol's art. With each panel divided by an irregular vertical band suggesting Oregon rivers flowing west to the coast, Setziol
balanced the meandering "river banks" with strict grids recalling Oregon's rich agricultural Willamette Valley seen from the air. "I love the
small Oregon villages and farmlands in the wilderness," he muses.
"They're not planned but from five thousands feet up, they take on an
order all their own."

The other successful public commission done for Salem in 1972 is the
freestanding screen in the public library's children's section. Simultaneously dignified and playful, Setziol's screen at the Salem Public
Library expands his symbolic vocabulary to include stylized animals

like rabbits as well as tree branches and dogwood blossoms. Scaled
for children, the lower part has richly tactile surfaces with a building
block appearance rising to a massive central panel of a riverbed surrounded by a wagon wheel. This is flanked by negative-space niches
containing inset wavy branches. Perfectly indeterminate in its imagery, the screen provides children with a protective nestling area leaving open the precise nature of the elements, all the better to embrace
young readers comfortable with a suggestive, nonverbal world of early
childhood.

Though teak was his favorite wood, Setziol warmed to a variety of
hardwoods throughout the 1970s and 1980s. Besides his beloved Oregon black walnut ("It's a better color than East Coast walnut") and
Oregon native myrtlewood, he chose elm burl, redwood, koa, Mexican
purple heart, iffala, Alaska yellow cedar, African zebra, and Hondu-
ras mahogany. An avid treeplanter at home on the many surrounding
acres in Sheridan, Oregon, he is also sensitive about the fate of the
rainforests and has abandoned using any endangered woods. "My
woods are from Africa, like teak and zebra. Teak is not a rainforest
tree. It grows in southeast Asia like fir—plentiful—though Thailand
has declared a moratorium on exports. Saving the rainforests is crucial but I don't have any guilt feelings about having used these woods
in the past. . . and I definitely won't use rosewood."

Given the artist's interplay of system (the grid) and symbol (natural
forms), it is also necessary to hasten to add that, despite any system,
there is always a sense of spontaneous composition in the major wall
reliefs. The zebrawood relief of 1985 in the Sorenson collection begins,
like most, with detailed banding or "fringe" at the left margin and is
immediately followed to the right by the panel's largest image, a kind
of nine-pointed starfish. With the severe contrast inherent in zebrawood, Setziol risked a compositional battle between grain and grid.
Wildly fluctuating in pattern, the work is saved from formal collapse
by a central circle or contemplation point. For an artist with no formal art training, Setziol's grasp of complicated nonrepresentational
compositions is astonishingly secure.

Panels of the past decade have become more ambitious in pictorial
complexity, if not size. Now the grid is often overlapped by a single
swooping shape, like the "fishnet" in a 1991 relief. And vestigial faces,
if not figures, have returned to inhabit niches usually containing
seeds or blossom shapes.

In one work, the artist seems to have come full circle, returning to the
use of a full-length figure abandoned nearly 40 years ago. *Untitled*

(1991) is also a turn away from the grid system. On a tall (96 inches) oak plank, Setziol incised a slightly curvaceous female form in profile. All that remains of a geometric organizing principle is a rectangular pegged area at the base. Breast and buttock are gently nudged onto the undulating curve of the plank and the garment is decorated with a loose graduated series of carved stripes.

Untitled (1991) represents both the triumph of longevity and the reconciliation of his earliest yearning to master the human figure. By omitting the head and arms, Setziol symbolically freed himself as well as his Venus in oak. Setting aside his grid system which was so necessary to his self-taught technical growth, he fully embraced the wholly symbolic. *Untitled* (1991) captures the essence of the female form.

Brian Gladwell: Cabinet with Cabriole Legs, 1992, wood, MDF, lacquer, 52 1/2 x 17 x 7". Collection of Mendel Art Gallery, Saskatoon, Saskatchewan, Canada. Photo: A. K. Photos

BRIAN GLADWELL:
TWELVE WORKS

Tell all the truth but tell it slant,
Success in circuit lies—

—Emily Dickinson

INTRODUCTION

The art of Brian Gladwell raises a variety of issues, all of which
merit critical scrutiny. He is part of an international movement using
furniture designs as departure-points for sculpture. As a Canadian,
he takes his place in a long and honorable tradition of handcrafted
furniture which includes Québec country furniture, Hutterite blanket chests, and Doukhobor cabinets. He also has roots in the North
American studio craft movement which began after World War II and
flourished in the 1970s when Gladwell was developing as an artist.
Without conveniently fitting into any of these categories, however,
Brian Gladwell has arrived at an enigmatic, unnameable niche of his
own. How he got there and how his considerable achievements elude
pinning down easily are the subject of this essay. In the process, we
may gain a view of him as an articulate theorist as well as maker. In
addition, we may examine his works and—better understand them—
in the special setting at the Mendel Art Gallery that Gladwell created
for their presentation.

How did these unusual works come to be made in Saskatchewan?
Born in North Battleford and raised in the northern part of the province, Gladwell grew up surrounded by prairies and vernacular farm
architecture. Not formally trained as an artist, he shares much with
the province's folk artists, inventing himself along with the distinctive objects he creates. Some of his works are influenced by Canadian
ethnic furniture and lift and borrow styles from other art sources in
the way folk artists often have.

Available wood, timber, lumber, and wood-pulp products like the
corrugated cardboard he uses, are also a part of his Canadian environment. Ready availability of the latter, and the proximity of the
supplier, Macmillan Bathurst, has provided one context of creation.

Stretching the definition of wood and wood products as he does,
Gladwell concomitantly stretches the definitions of chairs, tables, and
desks as well. As is the case in so much of his art, things are seldom
what they seem. Veils, masks, screens, and scrims find their meta-

phorical equivalent in his art of playful concealment. By challenging our notions of what is real and what is fake, Gladwell makes us more attentive to the world as it is, rather than the way we choose to see it. Just as the pioneer artists painted wood to look like metal, or tin to look like wood, Gladwell teases our optical and tactile expectations of materials, forcing us not only to look more closely but, crucially, to touch and caress as well.

Within Saskatchewan art, he is the odd man out. At one end, the Emma Lake Artists' Workshops elevated landscape painting to a late-modern, abstract enterprise endorsed by American art critic Clement Greenberg during successive visits. At the other end, indigenous prairie art and European immigrant folk art express immediate material responses to ritual, agricultural settings, and survival in a harsh climate. In between, Funk art, the West Coast Pop Art of the 1960s and 1970s, took hold in Gladwell's chosen city, Regina, where it still dominates a segment of the university-based art community and is shown by Gladwell's hometown dealer, Susan Whitney. Though closest in spirit to Funk and its playful humor, Gladwell is not really a part of any of these three groups.

Instead, it is necessary to see his work in a broader continental and global context to appreciate its power. Better, perhaps, to consider the American sculptor and art critic Scott Burton whose massive corporate seating area at the Equitable Life Insurance Co. headquarters in New York shares Gladwell's witty impersonality. Or to consider former Workbench, Inc. modular-furniture designer-turned-sculptor Richard Artschwager whose use of monochromatic plastic Formica covers areas in a table which would be a spatial vacuum otherwise. He echoes Gladwell's "filling in" of similar empty spaces with lacquered cardboard (*Table with Cabriole Legs*, 1990). Or Swiss sculptor John Armleder whose large comical tables and chairs resist use but remind us of their central role in our daily lives, the way Gladwell's elaborate conceits on simple furniture shapes defy us to use them for everyday purposes. Or American metals artist Albert Paley whose bent steel plant stands, bookshelves, and dining tables impart a sense of grand ceremony or sinister ritual, the way Gladwell's *Alcove* (1988) creates a monumental space over five feet tall to contain some unknown special belongings.

Though its energy as an architectural movement is largely spent, postmodernism within contemporary art remains a helpful term to explain work which resists a conventional sense of stylistic "progress" in favor of stylistic retrievals or reappraisals of the past. In this sense, Gladwell is a postmodern artist. Far from modernism and Emma Lake's "truth to materials," Gladwell is lying to us all the time, teasing us, fooling us into realizing that the bulky shapes and shiny metallic surfaces are really very cosmetic and superficial, much closer to theatre props than to the "integrity of materials" so revered by Greenberg's followers.

Not only that, within the tradition of the crafts or decorative arts, lifting prior historical styles (the way Gladwell borrows from Art Déco, folk art, or granary architecture) has always been acceptable and even desirable. Instead of rejecting the past and invoking the *dernier cri* of the avant-garde, Gladwell transforms the past without unduly revering its models. True postmodernist, his work is eclectic as well as eccentric.

GLADWELL'S RECEPTION

Considering the Mendel Art Gallery exhibition was Gladwell's fifth solo exhibition since 1987 (others were in Regina and San Francisco), written critical and curatorial response to his art has been carefully considered. It is worth summarizing briefly to regain insights into his work before launching into any new theories about it. Not surprisingly, opinion seems divided between viewing his work as furniture or as sculpture, something Gladwell vacillates about, too, in his own published statements and interviews. This sets up a fruitful ambiguity and captures what is provocative about his art.

Indeed, Gladwell is an articulate critic of his own work although, in general, we should be skeptical about accepting on face value what artists say about their art. Setting out a general area, Gladwell commented on his interest in "content which goes beyond the object itself."[1]

Helen Marzolf first established him as a postmodernist in 1987 mentioning how his aesthetic "became more and more a cribbing of motifs, strategies, and solutions from architecture and engineering."[2] She also pointed out how cardboard challenges our notions of permanence with its "associations of . . . fragility and industrial or commercial use, to build forms laden with connotations of domesticity, permanence, and durability."[3] On a psycho-perceptual level, she pointed out how his furniture "directs attention to the subconscious reliance we have on illusion."[4]

W. P. Morgan places Gladwell in a figurative context in his catalogue essay for a survey of Saskatchewan crafts. He quotes Gladwell admitting he "uses the human body as an organizing principle . . . [and] shares with us opportunities for mystery and fantasy."[5]

Elly Danica, in a 1986 article in *The Craft Factor*, first raised the
issue of unexpected or "long shot color combinations" in Gladwell's
work and reported that the first cardboard furniture began as maquettes for commissioned projects in wood. Tellingly, she elicited a
confession of deception from the artist:

> I'm interested in contrast and contradiction and things that are
> something more than they seem to be at first, with a strong sense of
> personality.[6]

Franklyn Heisler reinforced the sculptural status of the cardboard furniture in his comments for an exhibition concentrating on furniture-as-
sculpture. To him, Gladwell "makes banal materials. . . into sculpture,
relegating the purpose of the object to a secondary position."[7]

As a key to understanding his own work, it is helpful to see how
"fashion . . . visual arts . . . [and] industrial design" are the "new
paradigms for the crafts" Gladwell constructs in his introductory essay for *Beyond the Object*, the 1987 exhibition of Canadian craft art
he curated for the Saskatchewan Craft Council. Applied to his own
art, we can ask of *Table with Cabriole Legs*, "does it look like a big
pink skirt?" *Cabinet* (1987) is as sleek and intimidating as a Philippe
Starck bookcase with its severe metallic presence.

Outlining his general philosophy of craft in *Beyond the Object*,
Gladwell describes his own working attitude:

> The object's reference to traditional convention or to function
> provides us with a context within which to approach the object.[8]

Stressing Marzolf's psycho-perceptual angle, he says the artwork can
"trigger other associations with our individual experiences and fantasies" and comments on work that is

> concerned with interior space . . . created . . . or implied . . . or
> divided . . . and with its associations of mystery, hope, and fantasy.

Most importantly and poetically, he asks:

> What is contained within the cabinet? What is contained within
> ourselves?[9]

CONCEALMENT AND REVELATION

The emphasis by Gladwell's critics and himself on a broader and more
abstract reference is understandable if the work is to be taken as
more than functional craft. But this equation will not work without
a more engaged, attentive viewer. We need to free up our own imaginations when looking at his objects and allow a healthy interplay of
memory, fantasy, and risk-free enjoyment.

Just as important as our imaginations is the presence of our bodies
in relation to these furniture-sculptures. Because we cannot explicitly use them in a museum setting, we must content ourselves with
a vicarious state of use. As we stand before them, our awareness of
our own physical stature becomes a central factor in our appreciation. This, however, is true for the experience of all sculpture. Where
Gladwell's work differs from traditional sculpture is in its concentration on a concealed interior space rather than on the opportunity
for walking all around a piece to experience it in three dimensions.
Fronts tend to matter more than backs in Gladwell, especially for the
wall-mounted works and this, in general, limits or constrains their
sculptural status, reinforcing their furniture status.

The cabinet doors may remain closed within the exhibition space
but, once at home, may be opened at will. In this sense, the museum
setting can narrow our full experience of his work. Here, it is unquestionably art but, as Gladwell and his critics have suggested, it is
much more. Yes, the "more" is dependent partly upon our willingness
to interpret but, equally significantly, the "more" rests on owner-ig-
nition of use in the privacy of one's home. That dimension remains
purely imaginary in the museum setting.

By way of illustration, let us examine some of the specific works.
Alcove is grand and imposing, not at all tied to what is placed in its
shallow shelf area. One of the first works with pigment rubbed into
the cut cardboard edges, *Alcove* fuses painting and sculpture. The tall
shape may suggest a home entertainment center but, as sculpture,
it is a rigid interplay of horizontal and vertical planes pierced by the
central presentation space.

Console Table with Drawers (1988), *Table with Cabriole Legs* (1990),
and *Cabinet with Cabriole Legs* (1992) seem feminine in gender,
evocative of ladies' leisure symbolized by a make-up vanity table, a
curvaceous boudoir sidetable, and a baffling contrast of a mysterious blue "blouse" above four horse-like legs. Gender has its place in
the history of furniture, too, and Gladwell has invoked the legacy
of women's furniture and how those objects mimic the bodies of the
women who use them.

House Wall Cabinet (1988) and *Tall Cabinet* (1990) relate most
directly to the Canadian environment. Slightly skewed off the wall,
the peaked roof and triangle "window" in the former are echoes of
prairieland granary architecture. The latter uses diamond-point
paneling which emerges from early 19th-century French-Canadian
furniture. It is Gladwell's most sumptuous work, at once regal and
practical. Gold powders mixed into a lacquer base cover the tip-edges

on the cabinet's "crown" above three prominent relief areas on the door. Each has two concentric elongated diamonds around an inner flattened one. With warm red, purple and blue coloring, the sides are green. Gladwell is both honoring Canadian folk artists and, through the use of cardboard, satirizing them.

Wall Shelf (1991) recalls provincial public-utilities administration architecture of the 1930s and 1940s with its stark stone-like blue coloring, recessed blind-wicket shelf, and jutting drawer. Inward-leaning sides stress height and summon up visions of cold bureaucrats.

Cabinet #2 (1989) combines male and female qualities with graceful exposed corrugation sides forming matched arabesques around a severe upright container area. The curves are repeated in *Pedestal* (1991), an unusual work which exposes support structure more than any other Gladwell work. Horizontal wood slatting climbs up a sinuous curve with corners left open so that the inner void of this intimidating plant stand is left open to view. Unlike the other works, the interior mystery space is revealed. In silhouette, *Pedestal* also suggests Asian ceramic ginger jars.

Cabinet with Wavy Panels (1993) and *Mirrors* (1993) may point toward the future: issues of function versus the question of identity. While the new cabinet relates to *Cabinet #2* with its surrounding curves, *Mirrors* literalizes the human body "as an organizing principle" by reflecting the viewer's image. Here, Gladwell is reminding us, none too subtly, that our choice of domestic appurtenances casts back upon us the sense of our own taste, and hence our own personality.

Dangerous territory, worthy of Oscar Wilde who sought to "live up to my blue-and-white china," *Mirrors* conflates the functional and the sculptural into a symbolic realm where both co-exist.

Building upon his earlier examinations of how useful furniture may attain sculptural status, Brian Gladwell how appears ready to further explore his new hybrid object with scrutiny, wit, and skill. In the process, he stands as an example of how today's artists are expanding the boundaries of both areas—art and craft—and how new ways of looking at and discussing such art need to be applied.

Using individual objects in the installation at Mendel Art Gallery, Gladwell presents an imaginary or idealized fantasy realm to the viewer. Walking through the Gallery, we engage our sense of humor, most importantly, and, in the process, we are forced to re-examine our prior expectations of what both furniture and sculpture can be—and have become—in the late twentieth century.

ALBERT PALEY: ORGANIC FORM

How have major public commissions of large-scale sculptures and architectural projects affected Albert Paley's smaller-scale freestanding sculptures? With much of his time devoted these days to numerous monumental art-in-public-places projects, Paley's other sculptures may have gotten critical short shrift—what with all the attention focused on public and corporate projects for Asheville, North Carolina; Houston, Texas; and the Bausch and Lomb headquarters in Rochester, New York.

When they are examined on their own, however, the freestanding museum-, gallery- and domestic-scale sculptures reveal an integrity and stylistic development all their own, definitely worth pursuing as keys to Paley's other multifarious studio activities.

As far back as 1971, Paley's forays away from jewelry (for which he first became known) extended into delicately forged and riveted steel constructions like *Wall Sculpture* (1971) and *Iron Form #101* (1974). Highly linear, they lacked the sculptural volume that he would redefine in subsequent works.

Before the flowering of sculptures in the early to mid-1990s, Paley continued to use forged and fabricated steel rods to extend sculpture out into space, as in *Steel Form #102* (1976) and *Sculpture* (1979), both of which explored, respectively, extreme horizontality and verticality. This upright composition became crucial for Paley's large outdoor compositions.

Another way of approaching the difference between the artist's autonomous sculptures and architectural commissions is in the area of planning, drawing and direct working. Necessarily, the art in public places require elaborate drawings, maquettes and small-scale models. With the other sculptures, there is often more of a sense of spontaneity, direct intervention, and, despite the frequent use of a team, hands-on alteration within the studio setting. As Stacey VanDenburgh wrote,

> When Albert creates . . . work for an exhibition . . . he frequently works in an intuitive, experimental fashion, with no formal drawings, working directly with the material and the highly skilled craftsmen . . . at the studio.

Thus, *Cardiff* (1988) and *Sculpture VII* (1989) are both roughly 90 inches high, they demonstrate two of the artist's attitudes toward

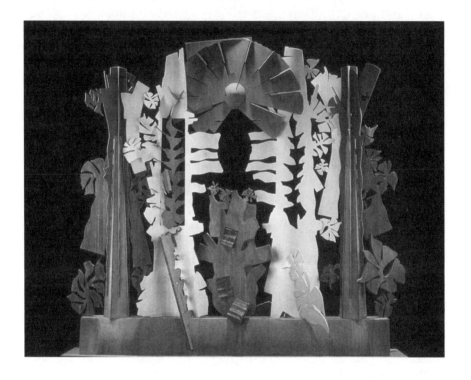

Albert Paley: *Apollo*, 1996, formed and fabricated weathering steel and stainless
steel, 190 x 209 x 36". Courtesy of the artist, Rochester, New York.
Photo: Bruce Miller

composition: irregularly balanced multiple-elements and symmetry. The latter may be a regrettable influence of the public commissions, as in the orderliness of the Willard Building commission in Washington, D.C., *Sculpture* (1985), as if the complexities of the site and context (a lobby with highly patterned marble walls and floors) dictated the piece's shape too much. *Convergence II* (1988) confronts a comparable dilemma.

Another work, one that survived an abortive public commission proposal but lives on to survive in its own state of sculptural independence, *Gate Section for the Central Park Zoo (Prototype)* (1987), is unique for another reason: the incorporation of representational imagery of birds, mammals and reptiles. Tall like a see-through panel, *Gate Section* has a narrative power of its own that is only implied in the artist's abstract works.

Paley's biographer Edward Lucie-Smith (Abrams, 1996) has compared certain works like *Zig Zag* (1991) to Minimalist sculpture but is quick to point out Paley's

> temperamental opposition to the Minimalist esthetic. His instinct, even when his shapes are at their very simplest, is always to find a way of animating them.

By the time works like *Periphery* (1991) were made, Paley seemed at his most spontaneous, closer to sketching in metal than to drawing up plans. The results appear fresh and innovative. Other abstract artists who were rejecting Minimalism at the same time come to mind: Michael Todd, Michael Steiner, and Michael Singer. Paley's contribution to this group involves a more delicate line, thanks to his technical forging abilities, and a rejection of simply compiling metal elements in favor of composing and altering them.

With his shift in the early to mid-1990s to unique and editioned furniture, Albert Paley created at least two major works that stand on their own despite residual functional aspects, *Mystery Table* (1993) and *Oasis* (1994). The cut-into edges of *Mystery Table* define its large frontal composition, anchored and centered by a marble slab yet claiming space forcefully on its own. *Oasis* uses weathering steel with clumps of bundled metal "tumbleweeds" or "palm leaves" at either end. Sculpture-as-landscape, *Oasis* is self-contained, autonomous despite its original introduction as a coffee table.

For an exhibition with Jim Dine and Therman Statom at the Toledo Museum of Art in 1996, Paley, like the other two artists, ransacked the museum's permanent collection for inspirations for a new body of work. The results included *Continuum*, *Apollo* and *Sanctuary* (all 1996), Paley's most complex and successful sculptures to date.

Continuum, with its central Doric column, relates to the notion of the museum itself as a repository of civilization. *Apollo* is a direct homage to Matisse's 1954 ceramic-tile mural of the same name in the Toledo collection. Borrowing the French master's flower and leaf forms, Paley left an inner, open area that outlines in negative space a figurative image that could be interpreted as the presence of the Greek god. Radiating above this area is a giant sun, the planetary body associated with the myth of Apollo, bringer of daylight.

Sanctuary completes the trio and, at its center, physically represents a mummy-like figure, alluding to Toledo's Egyptian holdings. Paley has adapted the beveled edges of *Zig Zag* to a sheltering backdrop for the elevated effigy. As with *Gate Section*, the incorporation of recognizable figures greatly enhances the sculpture's power, moving from the idealized abstraction of the bulk of Paley's art to a realm of suggestive and symbolic reference. *Sanctuary* may also portend a further evolution away from the uneasy modernism Paley has always employed and challenged, over to an area of allusion, figuration and heretofore untapped narrative content.

LIA COOK:
ARIADNE IN BERKELEY
(For Mary Rajala Kangas, 1880–1962, who spun her own wool)

INTRODUCTION

> Now, before Daedalus left Crete, he had given Ariadne a magic ball
> of thread, and instructed her how to enter and leave the Labyrinth.
> She must open the entrance door and tie the loose end of the thread
> to the lintel; the ball would roll along, diminishing as it went and
> making, with devious turns and twists, for the innermost recess
> where the Minotaur was lodged. This ball Ariadne gave to Theseus
> and instructed him to follow it until he reached the sleeping
> monster, whom he must seize by the hair and sacrifice to Poseidon.[1]

Although certain materials (abaca, a banana fiber), techniques
(thread painted prior to weaving), and processes (layering of images)
are Asian influences in the art of Lia Cook, a European, specifically
Mediterranean, context for her work has been overlooked. This essay
attempts to provide that context briefly and discuss a body of work
made since 1982, which culminates in works which underscore the
California artist's great achievements: expanding the limits of tex-
tile-art traditions; confounding medium-specific critics by combining
painting and weaving; attaining a profile and influence in western
Europe which puts her on a level with few other American artists;
and creating a subtle, complex and richly varied series of weavings
which radiate ambiguous yet satisfying levels of meaning.

A product of the American craft revolution of the 1960s, specifically
the fiber art movement in the San Francisco Bay Area, Lia Cook is a
major artist so prolific that the Oakland Museum of California exhibition alone cannot encompass all her shifts, transitions, and evolutions
in style. Nevertheless, it is the purpose of this essay, and those of the
curator Inez Brooks-Myers and co-authors, Chelsea Miller Goin and
Janis Jefferies, to create a context for understanding, appreciation
and enjoyment of her art.

Like Ariadne, daughter of King Minos on the Greek island of Crete,
Lia Cook has used thread (or yard) as line, as unraveler of meaning,
as basic tool for an elaborate path toward artistic realization which,
as in the mythical Labyrinth, has often crossed back on itself only to
eventually lead to a new departure-point or opening into the light of
day. Whether cotton, rayon, or abaca fiber, it has undergirded the images and reinforced the themes of Lia Cook's art.

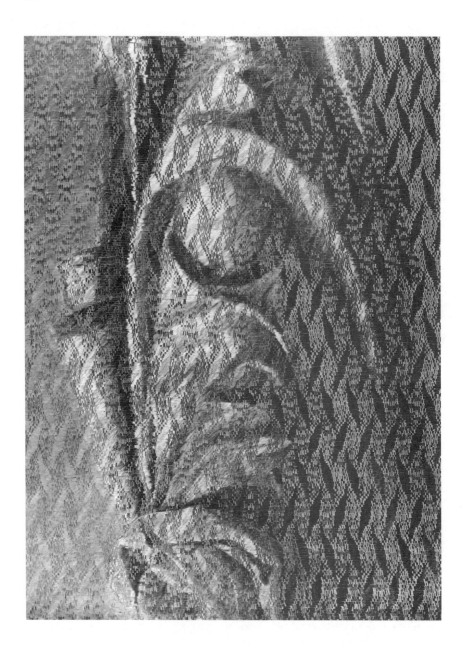

Lia Cook: *Leonardo V (New Master Draperies)*, 1991, woven and pressed linen, rayon, acrylics, and dyes, 66 x 51". Courtesy of the artist, Berkeley.
Photo: The Oakland Museum of California

What are those themes, those strands of meaning which have emerged over a twenty-year period? First, the tug-of-war between two- and three-dimensional art is one continuum that affects image, form, and content. Next, physicality, sensuality, and tactility are toyed with, exploited, and investigated again and again through the creation of the woven and painted object.

These lead to the realms of the veiled, the concealed, the mysterious—and the erotic. As a curtain may be lifted and dropped at will to reveal theatrical events, so Cook plays with the image of the drape or curtain as a symbol of display and presentation. While the curtain is usually the forerunner of event, in Cook it becomes event. This introduces the themes of edge, marginality, and detail which are moved to the forefront. By seizing on the detail of a drapery in an Old Master painting by Leonardo, Dürer, or Artemisia Gentileschi, Cook moves the marginal to the center thereby reversing a long-standing prejudice in Western art: the literal edging out of textiles. In a brilliant postmodern strategy, Cook centralizes the neglected, rescuing the "minor" arts of decoration and function, subverting the conventional wisdom that craft or decorative art cannot contain or express deep content.

Finally, devotion bordering on the ecstatic or spiritual is another key theme. Related to process and construction, the laboriously slow and precisely elaborate technical aspects of Cook's woven works are not a central part of this essay, but the attendant devotion involved in their execution is a highly important path to understanding. It is the result of her expressive response to materials on both an emotional and intellectual level. The intertwining (worthy of Ariadne) of complicated structure and image is the result of an absorption, a hardheadedness, which may only be described as devotion.

With her paternal grandfather's family coming from a village near Pordenone in northern Italy, Lia Cook gravitated naturally to an interest in historic Italian textiles and the handmade in general. Artisanship is also a part of her European heritage, her grandfather Luigi Polese, having built furniture according to his own designs. In addition, the satisfaction of complicated problem solving came naturally to the daughter of James Polese, who invented types of electronic tubes.[2] The combination of problem-solving powers and a craftsman's abilities made Cook a likely candidate for picking up the thread of textile arts which so flourished in the fourteenth through seventeenth centuries.

Eventually this scholarly interest led to extensive research at, among other places, the University of Washington Henry Art Gallery in Seattle where she examined samples of cut and uncut voided velvet woven in Italy between 1600 and 1625, as well as earlier fragments of Spanish damask weaving. Looking at them, her own interest in scale, repetition, and idiosyncratic abstract units of pattern was deeply reinforced. Confirming these links, recent Italian critics have commented on the analogies in her work spanning four centuries of tradition.[3]

And although her combination of Asian and European processes may seem jarring to some, it is important to remember that this was exactly the situation in fifteenth and sixteenth-century Italy: silk technology, original examples, and patterns from the Islamic world and China were the dominant factors which subsequently transformed European weaving and made possible the triumphs of Italian and French Renaissance tapestries.

Coming full circle, then, the *New Master Draperies* (1990-) and the *Material Pleasures* series (1993-) make cultural and historical references to both Medieval and Renaissance Italy, its textiles and paintings, its accomplishments, like Cook's, facing both east and west.

BEFORE THE CURTAIN ROSE

> A perfect rag-bag of odds and ends . . .
> the whole assortment shall be lightly
> stitched together by a single thread.
>
> —Virginia Woolf, *Orlando* (1928)

Just as Virginia Woolf's heroine spanned centuries wearing a variety of attire "stitched together by a single thread," so Cook developed her art through a combination of historical awareness and attention to the contemporary moment, all connected by Ariadne's ancient thread. Her studies with Ed Rossbach at the University of California at Berkeley grounded her in both the history of textile traditions and the possibilities of what textile art could become. Her own tribute to Rossbach (written for his 1990 retrospective catalog at The Textile Museum in Washington, D.C.) carefully analyzed the influence of this quiet yet towering figure in American craft. Cook's formal and informal sessions with the Cranbrook-trained teacher reinforced her sense of individual vision rather than any predetermined professorial direction:

> Doing anything in reaction to Rossbach was difficult because
> you never knew whereyou stood. I never knew exactly what he
> thought.Yet not knowing suited my way of working quitewell. I
> became my own critic.[4]

All the same, one can see traces of Rossbach's own art in Cook's—and vice versa. His use of photographic imagery, such as the one appearing in his *Handgun* (1975), may have led to Cook's taste for a subliminal image. In turn, his *Damask Waterfall* (1977) shares the same shape—square—and weave structure as much of Cook's work. Although Cook shied away from Rossbach's Pop Art imagery, she shared many other freewheeling attitudes towards textiles with him along with the idea that the artist will find the right material for the right idea regardless of its humble or unexpected source. Cook's 1967 weaving studies at Handarbets Vanner, in Stockholm, were the original inspiration to commit her life to textiles but, again, it was Rossbach who was the experimental, Americanizing influence on this artist so aware of European traditions.

Her frequent inclusion in museum exhibitions in Switzerland, the Netherlands, Germany, Spain, Norway and Belgium attest to her perhaps greater reputation abroad than in the U.S. and her three highly important solo exhibitions—in Oslo (1993), Liège (1989) and, most significantly, in Beauvais (1983)—the spiritual nerve-center of French tapestries—confirm the interest in her work on the part of European curators and dealers. The Beauvais retrospective at the Galerie Nationale de la Tapisserie et d'Art Textile was widely attended, enthusiastically reviewed, and accompanied by an extensive catalog essay by Rémy Prin which reproduced all Cook's major works to date.[5]

Rope (1974) and *Coming Through* (1978) remind us of the actual three-dimensional pieces which would later become spatial illusions. Relating to much Postminimalist sculpture of the day, like the work of Eva Hesse (1936–1970) and Robert Morris, *Rope* defies a monumentality of form, as does *Bedroom Fantasy* (1974), and offers instead a sequential linear shrinking of sculptural volume without recourse to the blocky somber masses of Minimalism.

Within the year, Cook had gone even farther, flattening the surface and imprinting it with photographic images of ropes rather than the real rope shape previously constructed (*Knot*, 1974). Her work at once became both more conceptual and more material-oriented—or craft-like. With the simulacrum of the three-dimensional object—a rope—twining its way across a bulging surface, Cook next addressed ways of heightening the tactile qualities of the surface. Here concept was sacrificed for physicality and many works of the late 1970s were either filled with polyurethane foam or turned the surface itself into an object through folding and twisting the heavy woven forms.

Recalling topographical maps, other undulating works like the *Land-forms* series (1978) alternately alluded back to Optical-Perceptual Art or forward to the Pattern and Decoration movement. Elsewhere, in *One and Twenty* (1978) and *Two Point Four* (1980), the grid predominated as image both accentuating the basic structure of weaving and playfully violating or altering it by setting up contrasting lines or poles which implied a shallow pictorial space reminiscent of Cubism[6]. Growing in size, Cook's weavings before 1982 constitute her earliest phase of maturity.

The basic themes of interplay between two and three dimensions; the rich tactility of the textile surface and its limitless possibilities; and the introduction of a mysterious, ambiguous picture plane are all laid out with cautious power and assured artistry. Armed with the confidence of the Beauvais retrospective, she refined the body of work featured in this exhibition.

LIFTING THE VEIL

Draped forms appearing from and
disappearing, into the darkness. . . .

—Lia Cook[7]

Although the first use of the drapery or curtain image appeared in *Fabric I* and *Fabric II* (1982), it was not fully explored for a few years. *Hanging Net* (1984) literalizes the fold again, this time using the wall as a support, as in *Rope*. It is typical of how Cook's art interplays volume and flatness, object and image. It also foreshadowed Cook's most important works to date, the weavings in various series that use the image of a folded drape or curtain emerging from a pressed abaca, rayon, or linen surface. Not only that, it was a harbinger of her large-scale museum installations using both flat drapery-image panels and real draped fabric.

Before those explorations began in depth, however, a trip to the People's Republic of China in 1984 had a different kind of impact. A pilgrimage to Mecca for any textile enthusiast, Cook's sojourn in the land where silk and the fine textiles tradition of Asia began resulted in her excursion into the "imperial" style. *China Stage Curtain, China Curtain II*, and *Through the Curtain* and *Up From the Sea* were all completed upon her return. Using repeated scallop-shape modules, each describes a graduated vertical "landscape" evocative of the abrupt frontality of Chinese landscape painting, executed without recourse to Renaissance perspective. The curves are repeated in the top and bottom edges of each "curtain," accentuating an illusion of billowing wing on fabric. Colors are rich as well, restricted to tones of red, yellow, and blue, all subtly and sumptuously modulated. Cook's pressing of the weaving once it is off the loom also mimics the effect of Chinese couched embroidery, another province of imperial style.

Within American decorative arts, one work by the nineteenth-century New York City luxury goods manufacturers, the Herter Brothers, comes to mind. An 1882 portière[8], or doorway curtain, by Gustave Herter (1830–1889) and Christian Herter (1840–1883) also uses a hierarchical banding composition, in this case, combining silk brocade and metallic thread but mixes floral and insect imagery rather than Cook's symbolic landscape which, in *Through the Curtain* and *Up From the Sea* even suggests mountain peaks seen in a colored mist.

Dolly's Crazy Quilt (1987), *Crazy Quilt: Royal Remnants* (1988), and *Framed and Draped: Material History* (1989) all share a broad palette and deep modeling. By now, Cook has added a border to each and settled upon a repeated triangular motif common to American folk art quilts. Besides intersecting irregular polygons in *Dolly's Crazy Quilt*, a swooping white grid or net pattern sways in the upper right-hand corner. (The work is inspired by a prize-winning quilt made by her great-grandmother, Dolly Boyes Hopkins, in the artist's collection.) This motion is repeated in *Royal Remnants* using a "royal blue" area extending across the upper half. Rather than lifting the veil, the veil or fabric image is the central figure. Among Cook's most visually complicated works, the series reaches a culmination in *Leonardo's Quilt* (1990) which, again, lifts pattern modules from fifteenth- and sixteenth-century Italian textile samples. Brighter, more reflective, this work's jagged diagonal movement animates the surface, drawing further attention to Cook's "material history," her postmodern invocation of prior traditions. In addition, she mixes the purported "high" and "low" cultural traditions of oil painting and folk-art quilts.

Switching to the banana fiber, abaca, in *Oil Cloth* (1988) allowed Cook a more supple painting surface after washing, shrinking, and pressing. This gave full rein to her interest in painting, both the act and the genre of Renaissance tableaux. As she told the Women's Caucus for the Arts in Chicago in 1992:

> I enjoy the irony of using the established"masters . . ." to confront our assumptions aboutthe hierarchies of subject matter, media, andother materials.[9]

It is my opinion that discussion of the precise sources for the images in the *New Master Draperies* and *Material Pleasures* has somewhat obscured analysis of the individual works. What matters more (and will be evident to viewers of this exhibition) is the way Cook has set tight chromatic limits for herself (a base of red/pink and blue/green) and mined them deeply within each approach. The color choice mimics black-and-white photographic reproductions in art history books, further distancing us from the originals and pointing out details of famous paintings: the role of textile as prop, appurtenance, afterthought.

Cook moved the marginal to the center, lifting the veil on textile history, and expressing devotion to both the European heritage of high weaving while critiquing painters—and art historians—who downgraded cloth's significance as a result of rigid academic conventions.

At first, in *Oil Cloth* (1988), *Sashay* (1989), and *Shadow Frieze* (1990), the curtain was given full play, approximating a covered window. In *Shadow Frieze*, the drape is accentuated in three groupings stretching to a width of nearly six feet.

With *Leonardo III* (1990), *Leonardo VI* (1991), and *Michelangelo* (1991), the *New Master Draperies* shift toward greater surface-and-shadow contrast with less emphasis on symmetry. Glaring light sources seem just off-stage, highlighting folds which may or may not cover anatomy or furniture. Varying the pattern module from piece to piece (triangles, lozenges, diamonds), Cook invokes the Mediterranean textile masterpieces as well as the painters to whom the weavings are dedicated. *Florentine Fresco* (1993), with its single towellike form is especially successful in this sense because its left- and right-leaning patterns seem directly inspired by the Italian originals. With less chromatic variation and a blunt frontal placing of the towel, Cook's strategy of appropriation and devotion emerges most clearly.

A major installation at the Museum van Bommel-van Dam in Venlo, Netherlands in 1993 returned Cook to the interplay of object and image which is at the heart of her oeuvre. *Material Pleasures* included *Dürer, Giulio R., Leonardo III*, and *Artemisia* from the series, positioning them on the wall between bunched sections of computer-woven jacquard fabric designed by Cook and made especially for this installation while artist-in-residence at the Müller-Zell Company in Zell, Germany, near Nuremberg.

With the weavings displayed salon-style, Cook created her own museum setting, lifting the veil on the overlooked, drawing back the curtain to reveal her responses to art history, old and new weaving techniques, all filtered through a creative imagination of extraordinary breadth. There was another purpose as well. The panels act as windows onto an erotic panorama of the body. Fabric is used in relation to human anatomy, a new direction Cook continues today.

In conclusion, the art of Lia Cook builds on a heritage and offers a critique of European culture. Equally important, however, it has done so through a subjective vision of that culture, elevating the personal and expressive to a level of meaning with subtlety and skill. Combining illusion with a paradoxical material presence, she has challenged the way we perceive and encounter the real world. Along with other major American craft artists of our time, Lia Cook has restored the independence of beauty and its relevance in an art of complexity, nuance and significance.

Wendell Castle: *Dark Secrets*, 1990, bubinga, mahogany and birds-eye veneer, 48 x 66 x 30". Photo: Wendell Castle Studio, Rochester, New York

WENDELL CASTLE: ENVIRONMENTAL WORKS

INTRODUCTION

Wendell Castle's latest work made for his 1992 Peter Joseph Gallery exhibition in New York signals a return to the growth forms of his earliest pieces and a step forward into more open-ended, looser imagery. More than any other American sculptor working in wood, he has pushed the material limits of what wood can do and used it to reinforce underlying meanings of organic evolution, development and decay. His is a paradoxical, contradictory art, one of entropic growth. As in nature, every leaf bears the imprint of its own demise; every tree ring reveals its own moment of extinction; every seed germinates toward its own flowering and harvest. So it is with Wendell Castle's use of the seed and pod forms.

Nearing the peak of his powers, Castle arrived at one more polar extreme in his long odyssey from Kansas to upstate New York. With the elaborate inlaid marquetry works and historicist-revival pieces of the early 1980s at one extreme (*The Lady's Desk with Two Chairs*, 1981), Castle rejects fine finish and strict ordered profiles in favor of the sprawling irregular line and the aggressive intervention of the chainsaw—as pencil—onto the darkened, laminated mahogany surfaces. Wendell Castle retains the freshness and improvisatory flair of his initial drawings. The overall presence of his work is one of becoming rather than being.

Beyond the uniting theme of growing and decaying natural forms, two other themes persist in the 1993 works: illusion and imbalance or asymmetry. As we shall see, all three themes reach a new culmination in the lamps, cabinets, desks, sideboards and tables at the Peter Joseph Gallery exhibition. How they have occurred and convened together in an art of deep subjectivity and great originality is worth exploring briefly before examining the individual works in greater depth.

BACKGROUND

> Things grow in an arbitrary manner.
>
> —Wendell Castle, 1993

Not enough has been made of the artist's origins in America's agricultural heartland, the Midwest. Born in Emporia, Kansas, in 1932,

Castle spent much of his youth on his grandparents' farm where wheat, oats and corn grew. Significantly for our purposes, his father taught vocational agriculture classes and his young son was fascinated by the students' seed-germination experiments that often produced bizarre results after as short a time as two days in the lab. When a seed is grown without dirt, strange things occur. In one way, Castle is doing the same thing in these works. Removed from the nurturing earth of Kansas, he created seed and leaf forms which take on unusual configurations of their own. His art is a series of seed-germination experiments in wood.

The tree root is another Castle signature image, acting as table legs, supports and meandering, life-giving counterpoints to the container form above. Castle recalls the fluttering maple tree seeds common to much of the Midwest and New England. The child's toy "helicopter", the maple seed configuration is a dominant support in the new work but its position is not merely undergirding a chest; it is leaning, adjacent and arranged to double as a figure's "legs."

All these shapes—the leaf, the seed, the root—first affected the artist while growing up in Kansas. They were thoroughly and painstakingly developed over two decades of technical refinement and intellectual distillation. The 1993 pieces are acts of memory as well as transformations of earlier inspirations and techniques. Castle is invoking the sturdy heritage of Midwest agricultural labor through the leaves but at the same time he conceals all but the final touches of the human hand—the gouging of the chainsaw into the surface to create the drawing. Thus activated, the sculptures have a strong energetic presence.

AMBIGUOUS OBJECTHOOD

> A table means does it not my dear it means
> a whole steadiness. Is it likely that a change. . . .
> A table means necessary places and a revision
> of a little thing it means it does mean that
> there has been a stand, a stand where it
> did shake.

> —Gertrude Stein, "A Table,"
> from *Tender Buttons*, 1914

Instead of belaboring art/craft distinctions, or worrying over sculpture/furniture categories, let us take a more direct route to understanding Wendell Castle's art: seeking aesthetic meaning based on interpretation, formal analysis and recurrent visual themes: growth and decay; illusion and deception; imbalance and asymmetry. He has created ambiguous objects which proclaim their own status of identity, regardless of external categories, in the same way Gertrude Stein forged her own poetry about objects in the everyday world in her poem, "A Table."

The persistent explorations of leaf, seed and tree-root images have now been extended to the surface decoration and are, for the first time, fully integrated with any support structures. The leaves shift from two to three dimensions as the viewer inspects the work. This reinforces the dynamic power of each work by conveying a sense of movement and growth before our eyes.

Illusion was paramount in the trompe l'oeil sculptures of the late 1970s (e.g., *Coatrack with Trench Coat*, (1978). Articles of clothing were carved into wooden furniture as if they had just been placed there. Rejecting Surrealism now, Castle takes his place near the Great Moderns, specifically Henri Matisse. The character of the wood is concealed by acrylic paint and oil pigments on the exterior but is allowed to shine through on the cabinet or desk-drawer interiors. Furniture itself is disguised as a wall-hung relief or painting which becomes a drop-front desk. The precious surfaces and pristine proportions of high decorative arts furniture are also rejected in favor of the expressionistic image, forever tilting or teetering with breathtaking vulnerability and uncertainty. Doubt and correction, as in Matisse, play a greater expressive role than before.

This shift from illusion to disguise is tied up with Castle's exalting of imbalance and asymmetry. Fighting gravity, the modulated leaf shapes barely touch the ground. The top of a cabinet seems wider and weightier than its base, sure to fall. The legs beneath a dining table create a forest of their own, implausibly supporting a vast upper curly maple surface. Virtuosic in the best sense, Castle's daring subversion of gravity and the expected order of things is willfully subjective, gleefully flaunting rigid "rules" of function in order to better convey his vision of natural growth—and inevitable collapse.

Three legs are always better than four and many of the works employ a tripod structure to tease the viewer into a spectator's sense of tension and imminent fall. This dangling of meaning between certainty and doubt, recognition and disguise, is reflected in the works themselves, underscoring their ambiguous objecthood, reinforcing their sculptural status.

The tripod is the central shape for the new lamps. Vacillating between floor and tabletop, they also vary shades of Fiberglas, bronze

and copper. When the shade is incorporated into the lamp, as in
Green Thumb (1993), the sculptural implications are strong with no
visible utilitarian purpose. Using opaque metals such as bronze or
copper, Castle is also satirizing American Arts and Crafts furniture of
the early 20th century that favored dark and metallic materials.

Stand-in (1993), *The Slightest Clue* (1993), *Jack and the Beanstalk*
(1993) and *Knowing How* (1993) represent another step forward for
Castle: they incorporate strong figurative elements which co-exist
with the leaf or pod shape. Tapered table legs now "stand in" for human legs. Stand-in is the artist's first self-portrait, a tall, relaxed and
lanky figure symbolically "supporting" the adjacent cabinet.

In *Knowing When it's Time to Go* (1993), the figure begins as three-
dimensional at the base but enters into a two-dimensional state in a
nearby painting above. The painting is actually the bottom of a drop-
front desk when closed. Castle has refused to let function subordinate
pictorial content in these works. Seen as figures instead of leaves,
the "arms" and "legs" recall Matisse's famous red-skinned figures in
Dance (1909).

Stand-in shows a black figure in profile lazily leaning against the
freestanding vertical form. Violating another rule, the figure serves
no structural purpose at all. Conversely, *The Best Laid Plans* (1993)
takes on an animal form with four feet extending beneath corners like
a turtle.

Two ambitious works complete the cycle and suggest fruitful future
directions. *Clock For All Seasons* (1993) is a four-part sculpture with
each freestanding element representing a successive season. All connected to a computer, the clocks are individually turned on at precise
moments when the new season begins. While continuing Castle's
long-time interest in time, *Clock For All Seasons* also extends the
artist's preoccupation with the effect of time on the growing seasons. *Fall* is painted with rich yellow, red, orange and brown. *Winter*
uses white, gray and blue. *Spring* exudes a vivid fresh green that is
supplemented by brown in *Summer*. The hands of each clock are a
seed and pod form.

Transformer (1993) suggests the artist's extension into installation
art or environmental sculpture. It embodies all three of the exhibition's themes: growth and decay, illusion and disguise, and imbalance. Lengthening table leaves are added to each end of the table
rather than inserted into the center. Thus the table itself appears to
undergo a growth process when enlarged. When the leaves are not in
use, they are arranged side by side upright at the back of the accom-

panying credenza. This creates both a sheltering environment for the diners and doubles as a decorative screen that may be rearranged according to the host's wishes.

Although the table surface is a rich and smooth curly maple, Castle has roughly carved the underside of the table so that, as in certain earlier works, every single wooden surface is acted upon. Normally not visible to diners, the undersurface grooves will be apprehended by touch only as the dinner progresses. Thin tapered bronze legs hold up the tabletop with incredible gracefulness and fragility.

CONCLUSION

Building upon many years which explored the entire range of sculptural possibilities for furniture, Wendell Castle is now free to allow sculptural properties—mass, form, volume, edge, profile—to dominate objects which are disguised furniture. He has arrived at his own dialectic of art and craft, function and decoration, sculpture and object, fully driven by a subjective vision expressed with impressive technical power and ease.

Drawing has replaced any intricate woodworking technique on the surfaces and this has, in turn, reinvigorated the works with a fresh and open-ended, even unfinished, character. Taken together, the desks, cabinets, tables and chests comprise a cycle of work that challenges existing limits of sculpture and extends the artist's lifetime vision of art as a symbol of nature that is acted upon by the artistic intervention of hands-on fashioning.

Ramona Solberg: *Tantric*, 1972, silver, leather and bone, 24 x 2 1/4 x 1 1/2".
Nancy Worden collection. Photo: Rex Rystedt

THE AGE OF SOLBERG

The art of Ramona Solberg (1921–2005)—artist, teacher, author, curator, traveler—not only changed Pacific Northwest metals, it changed much of contemporary American jewelry. Her necklaces are few in number (no more than 200 over a 30-year period) but their influence has been vast. Rejecting modernist purity of form and the preciousness of materials common to midcentury American studio jewelry, Solberg pioneered the use of ethnic and found objects in order to reintroduce personal expression in the widest sense of the word.

Ironically for a woman so self-effacing, much of the literature surrounding her has dwelt on her fascinating life. For our purposes, an analytical and interpretive, rather than biographical, approach may answer the question "What does the art of Ramona Solberg mean?" in order to determine why the period 1975 to 1995 may be called, in retrospect, the Age of Solberg.

Her students from the Seattle Public Schools (she taught junior-high originally), Central Washington University (Bill Ritchie, James Marta, Barbara Burnham, Pat Mahar, Robert Iverson) and the University of Washington (Robert Bruya, Flora Book, Elizabeth Chenoweth Palmer, Nadine Kairya, Cheryl Leo-Gwinn, Marilyn Ravanal) have been numerous but a few—Ron Ho (b. 1936) and Laurie Hall (b. 1944)—have not only been directly influenced enough to comprise, along with non-Solberg student Kiff Slemmons (b. 1944) an informal *école*, they have further transferred and extended her ideas about both the value of informal material construction and the global nature of American craft as a whole. International rather than regional or national, her cultural synthesis and unexpected juxtapositions of Third World souvenirs and mundane Americana have grown out of a lifetime of travel to every corner of the world including Antarctica. Solberg's vision (which has been communicated to artists as diverse as Robert Ebendorf and Thomas Mann) is one of inclusiveness rather than exclusion, of visual simplicity rather than complexity, of modesty rather than conceptual pretension.

Nevertheless, it is necessary to clear away some of the clutter of rhetoric surrounding the response to her work to see it more clearly for what it is, a forum for what she called, in another context, "limitless possibilities of life." Aspects of Solberg's life have been extensively chronicled by other writers[1], [2] but few critics have sought out possible meaning systems for her art or for that of her associates and colleagues. Before attempting that, let us revisit a few helpful observations about what constituted the Age of Solberg in the words of writers, the artists, and her enthusiastic fellows.

For a moment, if we take Solberg at her own word, "two thirds art educator, one third jeweler," then it is possible to see all her art as educational. But what are the lessons? In my opinion, no less than bringing humanity closer together is the educational and moral goal of her art. Active in the World Crafts Council as well as a craftsman fellow of the American Craft Council, this artist claims, "If people would travel more, there would be more world understanding."[3]

Firmly believing in a "united humanity through the crafts," Solberg has traveled so extensively that her experiences have accumulated not only as touristic forays but as low-key cultural diplomacy and informal statesmanship.

Pluralist in a time of resurgent nationalism, internationalist in a period of emerging cultural differences, Solberg and her art blur cultural and ethnic differences while preserving unique properties of each borrowed material. Thus, her worldview is rooted in the shared global unity of craft and extrapolates memory of place into the unique art object. Never a serialist nor production jewelry, Solberg approaches each work as a singular aesthetic entity using design, composition, placement and juxtaposition as organizing principles for an art which is immediately accessible on one level but also prone to wider and deeper appreciation and analysis.

University of Washington School of Art colleague Spencer Moseley codified her formal powers: "repetition of shape given extended meaning by the repetition of process or pattern of growth. Thus, repetition becomes allusion and illusion."[4] Referring to a key work, *Africa* (1973), Moseley added

> The title also identifies a formal relationship to another culture. That relationship however is one of assimilation not imitation. . . . [She is a] contemporary primitive.[5]

That may open charges 20 years later of colonialism, racism and cultural condescension given the recent controversies over the use of the word "primitive," but this would be an inaccurate accusation. Hugely respectful of the art of postcolonial nations, Solberg has spoken out against modernizing changes which delete indigenous cultural practices such as beading and jewelry-making and defends herself with humor: "I don't plunder but I sure do shop."[6]

In *Metalsmith*, Cindy Cetlin really began the first critical analysis of Solberg discussing *Mudra* (1983) at length and proposing "many levels of meaning," revealing the necklaces' deeply subjective origins:

> Solberg confesses that these necklaces are initially, secretly, made for herself which accounts for their consistently personal iconography.[7]

Less illuminating but on the right track of delineating Solberg's masks and veils, her aesthetic chador, Carolyn Benesh claimed an "anti-elitist, strong populist, and exuberant democratic bent" for the Seattle artist.[8]

Slemmons has hinted at parallels to linguistic structure in Solberg's compositions. On the one hand, the various elements may be read as plot or narrative chunks for the wearer to create stories out of (even if we now know these each had subjective, experiential roots). Comparably, each item might be seen as a word in a poem, an approach first stressed about other American craft artists by critic and editor Rose Slivka in her essay for the Renwick Gallery exhibition, "The Object as Poet."[9] The unexpected juxtapositions of found objects recalls Joseph Cornell, as Slivka holds, and Solberg's work, with its simple but sophisticated choices of elements, definitely sustains such a reading. She is making wearable haiku.

Slemmons stresses Solberg's "visual language," however, "how things look," and draws attention to how, in Solberg,

> the visual language comes first sincewritten or spoken language may not alwaysbe available. . . and visual language changes[depending on] different idioms withdifferent times [and] different cultures.[10]

Placing Solberg in the historical context of modernism, Slemmons reminds us that, as with most of the U.W. School of Art faculty of her day, Solberg's modernist pedigree was impeccable. Her links to modernism, besides her tutelage with Ruth Penington (1905–1995) and her postgraduate studies in Norway and England, include use of assemblage, collage, the grid as an organizing structure, the primacy of design, and an affinity for ethnic art that could be traced back to Matisse and the Cubists.

The younger artist also points out how courageous Solberg's use of representational imagery was "at a time when abstract pure form signaled 'higher' development along with intellectual detachment.[11] In this sense, Solberg along with J. Fred Woell, Ebendorf, and Donald Tompkins (1933–1982), was among the few American jewelers to anticipate representation and the cultural content of the postmodern condition: sensitivity to Third World and "marginal" populations; appreciation of popular culture; elevation of craft as an alternative to mainstream media such as painting.

The Age of Solberg traversed the modernist period into the postmodern. Another key participant in this crucial transition is Ron Ho. As Sylvia Kennedy wrote of him:

> He likes to use objects from differentcultures together in one piece. This maystem from his growing up in Hawaii wherefood, language, and friends from manycultures coexist.[12]

Also an educator, Ho sees the influence of children's art and the sense of play as a central element in Solberg. Giving her credit for his own shift to found object jewelry using ethnic art, Ho recalled: "She could see the beauty of ethnic designs and shapes."[13] And as Laurie Hall pointed out about him, "Ron did Ramona better than Ramona!"[14]

With much of his art now obliquely treating his Chinese-American heritage, Ho is indebted to Solberg for both her reverence of Asian art and her courage to use inexpensive materials. Thanks to her, he "gravitated to pendant shapes." Many would agree that Ho's Solbergian mixture of found objects, Asian artifacts and the evocation of travel and personal memories not only mirror the older artist's interests, they often go much farther in piling on elements redolent of the Pacific Rim.

Ho's forms and compositions are much more baroque, however, and in pieces like *Treasures of the Orient* (1974) and *The Rise of the Phoenix* (1978–80), entire screenplays seem evoked by the poetic and sensuous combinations. In addition, Ho's compositions are less frontal and grid-like than Solberg's.

With Solberg and Ho frequently traveling together, two other artists, Slemmons and Hall, adapted Solberg's principles to their own ends with comparable individuality. *Nanauq* (1984) is closest to Solberg's aesthetic among all Slemmons's metals. Doubling the polar bear head of the original Eskimo ivory cigarette holder, Slemmons used silver to echo the original ethnic image, something Solberg did with her bead necklaces, too, creating silver "doubles" of trade beads. Like Solberg, Slemmons's art uses found elements to retrieve memory and transform it into personal expression.

Hall's own retrieval deals more with American folk art while retaining aspects of nostalgia and cultural memory, adding them to a rich storehouse of humor and pragmatic American character.

My heritage is Northwest Oregon pioneer so I couldn't use all the same kind offound objects they did but I wanted tohave it be honest and real, whateverI was doing and Ramona was there encouraging.[15]

Hall warmed to the informality of Solberg's construction which tallied with her own interest in the looser fabrication of American folk art objects (e.g., *I Get a Kick Out of Champagne*, 1989).

Finally, if we recast our views of American art jewelry during the past 30 years, incorporating tolerance for the found objects, downplayed technique, and affinity to ethnic art, a definition of American metals becomes wider, more inclusive, and infinitely richer. What the Age of Solberg produced was significant for the artists discussed above. What its purlieu revealed was a large body of work by a number of artists, including Solberg, whose work deserves greater attention, analysis, and critical scrutiny.

Ken Cory:
Nancy's Buckle, 1988,
sterling silver, copper,
brass and enamel,
2 x 3 x 1/2". Nancy
Worden collection.
Photo: Lynn Thompson

Don Tompkins: *Pablo
Picasso (Commemorative
Medals Series),* 1969–72,
sterling silver, brass,
synthetic stones, 5/8 x 4
3/4 x 5/8". Collection of
Judith Whetzel, Seattle.
Photo: Rex Rystedt

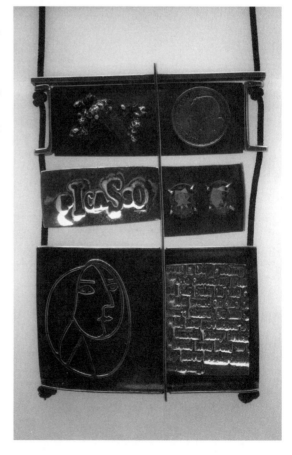

ELLENSBURG FUNKY

Central Washington University in Ellensburg, Washington, is ninety miles east of Seattle across the high Cascade Mountains range and a world away from the comparatively sophisticated cultural institutions of Puget Sound. At least two local variations of art movements got their start there—Funk Art and Found Object Jewelry—or were redesigned and retrofitted to suit the needs of the students and teachers.

While Davis, California may have been the fountainhead, the Athens of Funk, Ellensburg was its Alexandria, a willing provincial outpost with its own learned clutch of followers. The closer one looks at the oeuvres of the major post-1970 artists—Donald Tompkins (1933–1982); Ken Cory (1944–1994); Merrily Tompkins (b. 1947); Nancy Worden (b. 1954); and Ed Wicklander (b. 1952)—the easier it is to realize the differences between them and the California Funk artists like William T. Wiley, Robert Arneson, and Robert Hudson.

Institutionalized for the first time in a 1967 exhibition at the University Art Museum in Berkeley by director Peter Selz, the style was the subject of Selz's perplexed catalog essay, "Notes on Funk."[1] He agreed with artists who told him, "When you see it, you know it." Nevertheless, he pointed out several aspects that are pertinent to our discussion of the Ellensburg Funky style:

> Funk art is hot rather than cool . . . it is bizarre rather than formal
> . . . it is sensuous."[2] Selz, a leading authority on twentieth-century
> German art, traces its attitude back to Dada and Surrealism,
> updates it to the early work of Robert Rauschenberg and Jasper
> Johns to give it a fine-art sheen, but sets it in opposition to Pop Art.

Moving north by northwest, Funk art became all the rage in West Coast university art schools. Its irreverence appealed to the young; its adaptability and non-hierarchical attitude about materials appealed to craft artists. From Davis to Las Vegas; from Eugene to Boise; from Corvallis to Pullman; north to Ellensburg, and even to Bozeman and Missoula, Calgary and Regina, Funk art freed regional artists from the pressures of the dominant style of the day, Modernist abstraction.

At the same time, an earlier C.W.U. professor of jewelry Ramona Solberg (b. 1921) widened the net of possible materials even farther to incorporate references to ethnic art, talismans, and amulets. According to Worden, an artist and former student at C.W.U.,

> what always made Central different was that we were jewelers. Don,
> Ken, and Ramona knew how to forge but they never taught it. . . .

They were closer to anthropology than art, more cultural, interested
in how jewelry intertwines with people's lives[3]

With that appreciative ground, artists such as Worden, Merrily
Tompkins, Cory and Wicklander combined the love of found materials
with other aspects of Funk they found appealing: subjective content,
sexuality, and humor.

Although there were many other teachers and artists at C.W.U. with
similar affinities to Funk, a few concentrating on jewelry and metals
are the subject of this essay.[4]

An extraordinary figure long neglected in American jewelry history,
Don Tompkins studied art and art education at the University of
Washington after a strong high-school program under Russell Day
in Everett, Washington. He began graduate work in Seattle but also
studied at the School for American Craftsmen in Rochester, New
York and at Columbia University Teachers College where he received
an Ed. D. in 1973. His dissertation dealt with historical precedents
for jewelry as fine art.[5]

Strictly speaking, *Pablo Picasso, Jackson Pollock*, and *Richard Nixon*
(Commemorative Medals series) (1969–72), are pre-Funk, more New
York Pop Art. Living in Manhattan in the late 1960s and early 1970s,
Tompkins was an active participant in the nascent SoHo art scene
while he was a graduate student at Columbia. He owned a studio,
Jewelry Loft, where he sold necklaces and pendants based on current
events of the day. Other subjects commemorated were political fig-
ures like *J. Edgar Hoover, Martha Mitchell*, and *President Theodore
Roosevelt* (whom Tompkins was said to resemble, hence his nickname
"T.R."); musician Janis Joplin; writers Norman Mailer and Henry
Miller; *Playboy* publisher Hugh Hefner; and art-world luminaries
Pablo Picasso, dealer Ivan Karp and Claes Oldenburg. They comprise
an important body of work that satirizes American society in pen-
dant-necklaces of great linear delicacy, impeccable composition, and
withering wit.

Nearly ten years after his kid sister, Merrily, studied with him in
1968–69, she made *A Woman and Her Dog (Gov. Dixy Lee Ray)*
(1977). Borrowing her brother's commemorative-medal format, Tompkins celebrated and vulgarized in true Funk fashion the state's only
woman governor, Dr. Dixy Lee Ray, ex-director of the Atomic Energy
Commission and blatant apologist for corporate pollution sins.

With her love of folk art (and folk artist father) and its often unapologetically sloppy construction, the younger Tompkins chafed at the
small size of jewelry and quickly moved to larger objects. Washington

state's most eccentric and controversial (one-term) governor is honored in this kinetic piece. When the rabbit's foot is pulled, the silver
French poodle pet wags its tail and the marine biologist-turned-politi-
cian shakes a vial of polluted water.

Later works like *The Blemish* (1985) limit metals to a hammered copper face and depend even more upon allusions to self-taught artists.
More than her brother who lived in Ellensburg between 1964 and
1972, Merrily's art remains rooted in the comfy, homey, funky side
of Ellensburg, its ramshackle wooden buildings, its cowtown atmosphere, its sleepy college town mentality. With cozy junk shops and
abundant roadside attractions, Ellensburg is very conducive to quiet,
private fantasy.

With Don Tompkins's return to New York in 1972, Ken Cory took
over the metals program. A graduate of California College of Arts and
Crafts in Oakland, he arrived complete with Funk sensibility intact
ready to be adapted—or violated. Before that, he had studied jewelry
under Victor Moore at Pullman High School and continued at Washington State University in the same town, studying sculpture under
George Laisner.

Michael Dunas wrote a well-meaning but diffuse study of Cory in
Metalsmith. More a reverie or disquisition about Funk in general
than about Cory, Dunas even went so far as to second-guess Cory's intentions, claiming without documentation that the bordering images
in *Skunk* (1974) are:

> heroes of Cory's subconscious. They are there for no other reason
> than that Cory liked them. . . . They are the preemptive signs of the
> artist's free choice.[6]

That may be but so dense is the iconography of Cory's oeuvre and
so rich in potential symbolism is the rest of Cory's work that Dunas
seems to have cheerfully sidestepped any real interpretive effort in
favor of simply opting for "free choice." He stressed the arbitrary too
much in Cory's method. More troubling, Dunas persisted in a dread-
ful analogy to self-induced vomiting as a metaphor for Cory's and
Funk's methods of intuitive inspiration.[7]

Far more thoughtful than Dunas gave him credit for being, Cory
chose subjects which were erotic, both feminine and masculine. The
juxtapositions of rigid geometry and floppy organic forms repeated
over and over in his jewelry are a clue to this, as are his choices of
materials: plastic and leather; copper and silver; hammered and
stamped or smooth surfaces. A pioneer in men's jewelry, Cory was
strangely hermetic and withdrawn compared to Don Tompkins, his

predecessor. At the time of Cory's death, virtually his complete output was contained in a few compartmentalized suitcases. A full-scale retrospective and catalog are planned.

Again and again, Cory went far beyond the witty illustrations in his collaborations with Les LePere, the "other" Pencil Brother about whom Dunas wrote. The C.W.U. professor evolved an erotic vocabulary of male imagery: phalluses; auto parts; urinal traps; spark plugs; and batteries. These were executed in exquisitely intricate "feminine" techniques, however, like champlevé and cloisonné enamels (*Nancy's Buckle*, 1978). A late work like *Tent Brooch* (1988) retains all the mystery of Ellensburg Funky (insect? switch? vagina?) yet demonstrates a refined feeling for silver stamping, gold accents, and a single carnelian stone.

In 1974, 1975, and 1984, Professor Cory organized jewelry shows on campus so that budding talents like Worden could see first-hand the best work being done nationally. Among artists included were Jim Cotter, Lane Coulter, Richard Mawdsley, Gary Noffke, Linda Ross, and J. Fred Woell.

Worden decided to go to the University of Georgia to study with Nofke after working under Cory but his influence has stayed with her today. Though she would possibly deny it, her work, too, falls under the rubric of "Ellensburg Funky." After all, what else could one call using a toilet bowl brush in a brooch?

Worden took to heart the loose or informal construction of Nofke, added an anti-preciousness of materials, and combined them (in ways Merrily Tompkins did not) with feminine subjects. Grateful for Cory's inspiration in the same way Merrily was indebted to her big brother, Worden commented in a letter:

> What Ken created for me was an atmosphere completely lacking in pretense or convention. . . .Without inhibition, his imagery wallows in what a lot of men like: sex, cars, tools, being outside and getting dirty. . . . My work looks like an American woman designed it and I want it to.[8]

Her *Initiation Necklace* (1977) with its mixing of plastic pink hair curlers, chicken bones, copper and silver wire satirizes the tribal conformity of mall life. In that and other necklaces and brooches, Worden affectionately spoofs American rituals of beauty, mating, consuming, shopping, and romance.

Beginning her signature eyeglass-lens pieces in 1987, Worden created a series of pins both accentuating the roots of Ellensburg Funky—

found objects, mixture of "good" and "bad" materials, informality of construction, and bizarre or sexual subjects—and added a crucial yet important factor: personal narrative. Most acute, arcane, and rich of West Coast art characteristics, hermetic narratives are also most maddening to East Coast residents who view these artworks as self-indulgent, self-referential, and, hence, shallow and narcissistic.

Worden's later necklaces like *Broken Promises* (1992), which uses U.S. currency images of politicians in a mock-Victorian necklace, extend the cynical, inside humor of the tiny college campus to the wider social world. Her *Seven Deadly Sins* (1994) touches on current events even more and distantly echoes Tompkins's *Commemorative Medals* series.

Each of the seven sins—lust, gluttony, sloth, envy, avarice, wrath, and greed—is matched with a photograph (on the back of each metal section) of a prominent culpable celebrity, respectively, Woody Allen, Elvis Presley, Zsa Zsa Gabor, Bo Derek, Leona Helmsley, Lorena Bobbit, and Imelda Marcos.

Finally, Ed Wicklander, another artist who took Ellensburg Funky farther, into pedestal and freestanding mixed-media sculpture, had some salutary and insightful comments about the cowtown/college town phenomenon:

> Their sensitivity dealt with personal narratives in a three-D realm. Not only [Robert] Arneson, [William T.] Wiley, and [Robert] Hudson, but there were other influences there like Chicago artists H.C. Westermann, Jim Nutt, and Ed Paschke, along with giants like Kienholz and Duchamp.[9]

My Dad's Foundry Pin (1976) couldn't get much more personal. Using his father's Tacoma factory ID card, Wicklander fetishized a personal icon in close emulation of Cory. With a cast silver crucible and silver-soldered copper and slate bricks, the foundry kiln is evoked and, like the back of many Ellensburg metals, the reverse side is also deeply symbolic and visible. It shows his father's fingerprint.

Bile Torso (1992) blows up the intimate joining of Cory's and Worden's brooches into welded-steel sections comprising a headless human figure. Building perhaps on the Surrealist-inspired years of his graduate work at University of Illinois—Urbana-Champaign, *Bile Torso* nevertheless harks back to little Funkytown in eastern Washington state. Wicklander demonstrates how often, in Northwest metals, big things start out in small packages, small, enigmatic, and funny packages.

Ross Palmer Beecher: *Homage to Sylvia Plath*, 1983, perforated tin and wire,
19 1/2 x 14 1/5 x 3". Courtesy of Greg Kucera Gallery. Photo: Rob Vinnedge

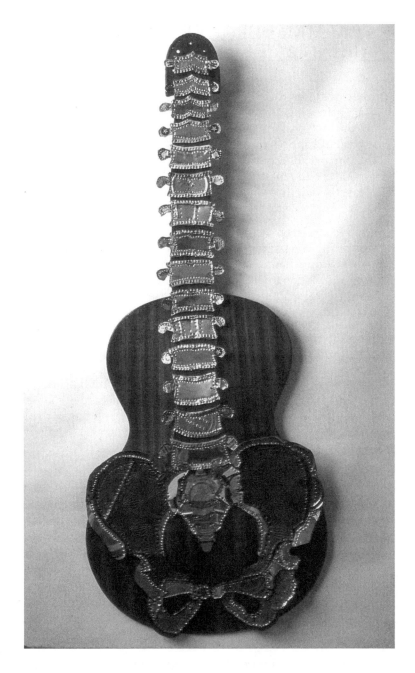

Ross Palmer Beecher: *Vertebrae/Pelvis (For Kurt Cobain)*, 1994, stitched tin, found objects and guitar, 33 x 13 1/2 x 3". Courtesy of Greg Kucera Gallery.
Photo: Rob Vinnedge

ROSS PALMER BEECHER:
EXPLORING AMERICAN MYTHS

The Yankee qualities Ross Palmer Beecher mentions in discussing her art—thriftiness, tradition, waste not/want not—are almost as mythic as the stories, forms or genres she invokes. Whether emulating New England churchyard gravestones, quilts, flags, or various types of tramp art, Beecher draws upon a wide range of aspects of American culture to make her point: simple is beautiful, we can get by with less, the handmade is the key to salvation in an increasingly materialistic, throwaway society.

Born and bred in Greenwich, Connecticut, Beecher comes from the wrong side of the tracks. Instead of country club values—snobbism, racism, sexism, anti-Semitism—she was imbued with older Yankee myths: work hard, don't borrow, and I-can-do-it-for-myself. Blue-collar rather than Peter Pan-collar, the artist left Rhode Island School of Design after two years in 1978 and headed west.

Once in Seattle, she undertook a series of odd jobs—"deli work, parking cars, and working in a laundromat"—and quickly realized that, although she had left RISD and "a lot of sophisticated equipment,"[1] her interest in making art was stronger than ever. Avidly riding her bicycle all over town, she frequently came across discarded materials like gas caps, bottle caps, auto tail light fragments, and empty soft drink cans.

Partly out of an urgent need to continue making art even in the cramped living quarters she still favors, and partly out of a desire to recapture the spell of her New England roots, she began a series of metal-and-mixed-media wall sculptures which today have gained regional and national attention in galleries, museums and private and public art collections.

Faux-folk art is a strong trend in Pacific Northwest art. For nearly 20 years, various practitioners besides Ross Palmer Beecher (Buster Simpson, Wally Warren, Alison Slow Loris, John Rice and others) have adapted their art school training to emulate the innocence and wisdom of untutored artists along with their fresh, nonhierarchical attitude toward materials. This is the milieu and context of Beecher's art.

By 1986, she was being invited to participate in folk art-inspired exhibitions in Texas, Illinois, Louisiana and California. Her early art does have a closer link to the work of unlettered artists but is still individually quirky enough (in technique and subject) to separate her from true Outsider or folk art.

Function is an oblique link between folk art and Beecher but none of her constructions is in any way useable. The quilts and flags operate as commemorative backgrounds for her over-the-top, obsessive material indulgences. Appropriately flat and two-dimensional, they proffer an image-ground that accumulates within each piece. As the social referents of the recycled materials are unraveled by the viewer (Coke cans, chewing tobacco tins, BIC lighters, olive oil cans), the meaning of each piece emerges as a fusion of fragment, detail and the whole.

Talking with Beecher reminds one of Emily Dickinson in logging boots ("I'm Nobody! Who are you?") but the poet Sylvia Plath (1932–1963) is probably a more apposite comparison. Beecher's 1983 *Homage to Sylvia Plath* uses only one material, perforated tin, and updates America's first real art form—carved stone headstones—to both pay tribute to and claim Plath's suicide as a warning and cautionary tale.

Using the same epitaph as Plath's real gravestone in England, "Even amidst fierce flames/The golden lotus can be planted," Beecher and Plath remind us that beautiful things can emerge out of turmoil. The aggressive punching of the metals is an expressionistic strategy that is obviated or balanced by the strict upright composition. Unusual among the artist's work because the text is so central, it marks a point where language became image. Words serve as fragments of ornament in later works, whether product logos or ad slogans, downplayed in favor of the greater evidence of workmanship and visually complicated, not to say cluttered, compositions.

Homage to Sylvia Plath is also inspired by examples of Mexican folk art Beecher saw in Seattle's many import shops. Rigged so that a candle may be inserted to illuminate the punctured letters, this work has distant links to Mexican Day of the Dead paraphernalia.

More Unitarian than Puritan, Beecher moralizes in ways that most New Englanders would recognize as an inescapable part of the Yankee conscience. Secular and humorous instead of religious and castigating, however, Beecher's works embrace myth only to deflate it or point out how fictional our memories of American heroes and heroines can be. Subsequent works dealt with Halloween, Washington Irving's *Sleepy Hollow* legends, Richard Nixon, Mickey Mouse, Willy Loman, T. S. Eliot, the Pilgrims, Abraham Lincoln and Uncle Sam.

Gradually, in works like *Green Heart* (1989–90) and *Rib Cage* (1995), Beecher began to address the human body. This interest in anatomy and mortality grew out her new part-time job as art therapist at an AIDS hospice, Bailey-Boushay House. The elements of *Green Heart* (leaves, beer cans, green grapefruit soda cans) may read symbolically as a narrative about love. Autumnal imagery suggests the ending of an affair. The valentine shape of the heart moves it away from a medically correct heart. The green cans may stand in for "green-eyed jealousy."

The exposed rib cage in *Green Heart* with its see-through center breaks any pictorial illusion and prepared the way for *Rib Cage* (1995) which may be about smoking and health. Disposable cigarette lighters are within the lungs behind the ribs made of metal and cut-up vegetable steamers. Far from polemic or partisan, Beecher presents the breathing organs as cluttered, crowded and possibly impaired. The flattened film cans surrounding the ribs may also allude to Hollywood's glamorization of smoking.

The artist's affinity to metal has only increased with the years. Its pliable hardness, especially tin, appeals to her as well as the "sensual feeling of pounding its hardness into delicacy. It's something very strong that you can control."[2]

Two Arms on a Quilt (1994) is a transitional piece between the quilt format and the anatomical fragments Beecher concentrated on in her 1995 Greg Kucera Gallery exhibition. With bottle caps as the wide border, Beecher summons up the skeletal arms and hands of dead quiltmakers in another memorial tribute. A small stone is inserted into the center of each of the 56 smaller squares at the center. These might symbolize the quiltmakers' "stone" foundation as a part of American folk art heritage.

Beecher has straddled a delicate line between references to cultural heritages and current events. *Guitar (for Kurt)* (1994) is one of a number of works by Seattle artists created in response to the tragic suicide of Nirvana rock group singer and guitarist Kurt Cobain. Coming a decade after *Homage to Sylvia Plath*, this work is more sculpturally adventurous, incorporating a real guitar which has been overlayered with a skeletal metal spine and pelvis.

On a more global level, Beecher's response to the fall of Communism and the end of the Cold War, *Red Flag* (1990) is a wry commentary on the prior merging of Communism and capitalism through a shared need for consumerism. The elaborately woven, cut-up Coca Cola cans form a beautifully rippling American flag that is faintly covered in one corner by a yellow hammer and sickle made of carpenter's tape measures. White stars of Old Glory are abruptly stapled around it. One of the artist's most compelling works, *Red Flag* epitomizes Beecher's dry humor and is also a tribute to a distant possible ancestor, Betsy Ross, the Boston seamstress who purportedly made the first American flag.

On a more materially complex note, *Stag* (1994/96) combines recycled metals on a carved and painted wooden background. This time, the accompanying plastic cigarette lighters are decorated with animals that have become product logos: Joe Camel, rabbits, bald eagles, etc. With no let-up in sight, Beecher is reminding us how, ever since Disney's *Bambi* and *Dumbo* films, Mother Nature can be sacrificed to pushing a product.

The male deer is an assaulted trophy head by now, literally composed out of dumpster garbage elements like coffee cans, rolling tobacco can labels, hubcaps, cigar tins, and even painted-tip cigarette butts. Disgust and pity come to the fore in this, one of Beecher's toughest pieces. More enraged than grieving, the tone of *Stag* may foretell an emerging *engagé* quality in the Seattle artist's work.

As in much of the best contemporary art today that favors the hand-made, material is the vehicle for meaning in Ross Palmer Beecher. As her skills at cutting, weaving, bending, punching and stapling togeth-er pieces of metal grow, her power over conveying meaning on com-plex and varied levels has increased. Allowing the found materials to speak of their humble origins does link her to folk art, to be sure; but her sense of color, design and stringent moral satire place her in a current vein, on a plane of art that criticizes American culture and myths while reverently mimicking and altering prior craft traditions.

SCULPTURAL HERITAGE AND SCULPTURAL IMPLICATIONS: TURNED WOOD OBJECTS IN THE WORNICK COLLECTION

(For my father, Arvid Kangas, 1918–2002,
logger, carver, turner, and sculptor of wood)

The fate of sculpture in the twentieth century has been so wrought with conflict, tension, liberation, and near extinction that it is almost dizzying to contemplate expanding sculpture's parameters yet again to include objects of wood made by turning them on a lathe. But why not? Everything else (including the kitchen sink; see Robert Gober [b. 1954]) has been allotted aesthetic status as sculpture, so why not turned wood? In order to justify conferring such a status on works in the Wornick collection, it is necessary to backtrack to the origins of twentieth-century sculpture, briefly scan precedents made of wood that have undisputed sculptural status, examine how they differ from turned-wood objects, and then fast-forward to the late twentieth century. Now, once again, the handmade object with the strong physical presence of natural crafts materials (wood, clay, glass, metals, and fiber) is being seen to embody, not only a rescue mission for sculpture, but perhaps a primary redefining quality: evidence of its making.

In the process, we may come to reappreciate humble qualities of construction, fabrication, and function as gauges of aesthetic power (so present in turned wood objects) and resolve issues that discomfort establishment curators, dealers, collectors and artists such as How can craft be art? What is the content or meaning of such art? Or How can we accommodate the new hybrid craft/art forms into the canon of twentieth-century art history? A cardinal characteristic of the post-modern period is an emphasis on scrutinizing art at the margins or fringes of the art world and society. Seen in this light, turned wood objects are definitely marginalized. Now is the time to move them toward the center, cast a critical light upon them, and set them in a new context: Modern and contemporary art.

Another question that arises in this context is, What is sculpture? To answer, we also need to remember how properties defining sculpture in the twentieth century alternately contracted and expanded any prevailing definition. Reacting to the monumental and commemorative status of works by nineteenth-century sculptors (Jean-Baptiste Carpeaux [1827–1875], François Rude [1784–1855], Antonio Canova [1757–1822]), modern artists radically shrank the size of sculpture

to the more personal and intimate scale of the pedestal. The nature
of the sculptural object next shifted to the use of found objects (Pablo
Picasso [1887–1973], Julio González [1876–1942]) and readymades
(Marcel Duchamp [1887–1968]). This contraction denigrated craft
and construction as defining properties of sculpture thus opening up
limitless potential on the one hand (a hardware-store snow shovel,
a galvanized-steel bottle rack) yet forsaking the technical skills that
prior generations had admired in sculpture of bronze, carved wood,
ceramic, or other materials requiring skill.

In this sense, early Modernism posited an anti-craft aesthetic that was
articulated most clearly by Swiss architect Le Corbusier (1887–1965) in
his 1925 book *The Decorative Art of Today* (English translation, Cambridge, Mass.: MIT Press, 1987). In this great paean to the superiority
of the machine, Corbusier launches an all-out attack on the decorative
and the handmade as "useless knickknacks," "bad taste," "disastrous,"
"Handicraft: Cult of Failures," and finally the dicta, "Modern decorative
art has no decoration," "Decoration is no longer possible," and "There
is no mystery in the crisis of decorative art; the miracle can occur of
an architecture that will be, the day when decorative art ceases to be."
Understandably, Corbusier was reacting against the prior 25 to 50
years when late 19th-century and early 20th-century movements such
as Arts and Crafts, Jugendstil, and Art Déco reigned along with producing artists such as Louis Comfort Tiffany (1848–1933), Emile Gallé
(1846–1904), and Peter Carl Fabergé (1848–1920). Great store was
placed upon the unique handmade decorative object. His broadside is
full of other attacks associating decoration and the instruction of craft
skills with "girls schools."

Nevertheless, it is important to note that wood survived Modernism's
machine aesthetic and Corbusier's attacks and continued throughout
the same period (and after, as we shall see) to attract the interest of
artists who developed its functional uses in furniture (Gerrit Rietveld
[1888–1964], Jean Dunand [1877–1942]) as well as in sculptural and
decorative objects, specifically (for our purposes) abstract sculpture.

There is a natural yet hitherto unnoted continuity between early
modernist or abstract sculpture and the turned wood object. The simple reductive properties of abstract wood sculpture—plane, volume,
mass, profile—also apply to the turned wood object and are supplemented by craft qualities common to works in the Wornick collection:
carving, construction, fabrication, and wood grain. Meaning and
content in 20th-century abstract wood sculpture (including turned
wood objects) revolve around issues of geometry, space, figurative
implications, color, horizontality and verticality. These are formal is-

sues, to be sure, but the meaning of much modern art is tied up with
such issues in lieu of psychological or compulsory ideological content.
Leaving aside the primacy and privilege of traditional bronze casting, then, many early modern sculptors turned to wood for its anti-
machine look and rustic appearance. It was a way of treating themes
of form and shape, line and mass, without the expense or elaborate
technical processes of bronze.

Thus, *King of Kings* (1937), for example, by Constantin Brancusi
(1876–1957), may be reassessed for its craft qualities: evidence of fabrication, cutting, carving, segmenting, and surface. Rough-hewn and
crudely hierarchic, *King of Kings* also may bear residual allusions
to Romanian folk art. In fact, the longer one looks at Brancusi in
this light, the more basic and earthy, the more crafty, *King of Kings*
becomes. With the sculpture bearing strong evidence of the human
hand, the tool marks become a new kind of surface decoration, the
evidence of the object's own making.

Nearly 60 years later, Joel Shapiro (b. 1941) undertook various wood-
block or four-by-four-inch lumber sculptures that reject *King of Kings'*
upright structure in favor of the frozen motion of extended limbs.
Eventually cast in bronze and more widely known in those versions,
Shapiro's figurative sculptures of wood provided an escape route for
him from Minimalism without sacrificing the formal austerity and
use of the serial unit, in this case, the four-by-four.

By contrast to Brancusi and Shapiro, *Cumulus* (1990) by William
Moore, adopts the former's segmented vertical structure without
recourse to the latter's stylized "arms" and "legs." Is *Cumulus* really
figurative at all then? Like *King of Kings*, it does share a vertical
segmented structure and, with its spun-copper top surface covering,
it could also be said to have a "head." Admittedly, at 14 inches high,
it does not compare in size to the nine-foot-high Brancusi but much
of the power of the turned wood object involves creating an intimate
rather than monumental object.

The division of sculptural volume became a central tenet of early
modern abstract sculpture. Often the sculpture was divided into the
separate modular parts later revived and admired by the Minimalists
of the 1960s and 1970s. In the aftermath of Cubism, however, European sculpture of the 1920s sought ways to reinvigorate the object or
have it reflect utopian ideals or universalizing qualities. Todd Hoyer's
Untitled [Vessel] (1994) withstands a comparison to *Construction of
Volume Relations* (1921) by Belgian artist and Piet Mondrian's (1872–
1944) De Stijl colleague Georges Vantongerloo (1886–1965). Ob-

sessed with mathematical approaches to art, Vantongerloo believed that this approach through the application of orderly systems could embody spiritual values basic to humanity. As a result, in works like *Construction of Volume Relations*, the mahogany slabs pile up into a vertical form that pushes outward into various planes in space. Its smooth surfaces are far different from those of Hoyer's vessel wherein the turning process on emery oak leaves jagged areas exposed beside the deeper cuts into the solid wood walls around an inner core.

Vantogerloo's stacking of the mahogany posited an extension by the object outward into space. With Hoyer's turning process, the tools cut into the wood, both altering the exterior surface into comparably segmented areas and protecting the inner void of the vessel form. No matter how lofty the rationale of the Belgian artist's sculpture (he was the author of two theoretical works) it is the blatant physicality of the mahogany that allows the work to retain its power today. Later in the century, it is the materiality of modernism that has survived, not necessarily its theories, utopian or otherwise.

If Brancusi's *King of Kings* sums up early approaches to the figure in modern wood sculpture, other artists like Jean Arp (1887–1966) borrowed aspects of the human body as the impetus for their wood sculptures. With his many works of painted wood, Arp occasionally let the grain and figured pattern of the wood show through, as in *Objects Arranged According to the Laws of Chance*, or *Navels* (1930). With only clear varnish as a surface treatment, Arp assembled a sculpture with figurative or anatomical allusions short of the full figure.

Similarly, although it may not seem likely at first glance, Vic Wood created a work that also alludes to the human form: two breasts. His *Untitled* [*Lidded Box*, 1987], shares Arp's mixture of flat and rounded forms. Wood's turned-wood object has latent functional purposes as well, but these are so unclear on first viewing that the Huon pine construction may operate equally for our purposes as an abstract sculpture. Whereas Arp's two-part title suggests both anatomical potential (navels) and purported random systems as a generative procedure ("law of chance"), Wood's sculpture functions on a highly abstracted plane. The properties of wood are what emerge most clearly nearly seventy years later. On Wood's lidded box, the bulging breastlike forms coexist in an undulating harmony reinforced by the light color of the pine and the gracefully turned and curved corners of each plane.

One of the great sculptors of the century to use wood, Henry Moore (1898–1986), made early smaller sculptures of wood that have often been overlooked in favor of his later monumental reclining figures in stone and bronze. Before World War II, the scale and size of Moore's wood sculptures remained intimate, pedestal size, and are far more conducive to human touch than would be the case once Moore attained heroic status as the greatest living British sculptor.

Moore's *Two Forms* (1934) employs a tropical hardwood, pynkado, as a material for a work that rejects the mathematical predictability of Vantongerloo's approach and presents instead an organic pretext that suggests the hollowed-out larger piece of wood "giving birth" to the adjacent smaller piece. The graining and cracking of the pynkado wood accentuate the growth or birth metaphor. With Moore and his contemporary Barbara Hepworth (1903–1975) stressing inner voids in sculpture (along with Russian sculptor Alexander Archipenko [1903–1975]), it is possible to see their work of this period anticipating by 60 years the inner vessel imagery of many of the turned wood object makers.

In addition, the bipartite composition used by both British artists finds an echo in two works in the Wornick collection, *Peeling Orb* (1987) by Hoyer and *Sculptural Vessel* (1979) by Mark Lindquist. Sharply distinct in their separate treatments of dual forms, Hoyer and Lindquist both use strategies that arise out of the turning process. *Peeling Orb*, centrally bisected by a curving mesquite wood wall, seems more about separation and movement than natal growth. The groove marks on the spherical shape in *Peeling Orb* remind the viewer of the lathe blade's actions whereas the surfaces of *Two Forms* are tranquil.

A second, upper form seems to emerge out of Lindquist's *Sculptural Vessel* yet, unlike the Moore, it is still bound to the original piece of wood. Sharing an inner void with the larger part of *Two Forms, Sculptural Vessel* exploits the burl figuration of white ash wood for its surface animation, sharpening an allusion to cell or fetal growth. Not dependent upon a matching oblong vase as is *Two Forms, Sculptural Vessel* declares its sculptural status more obliquely, less recognizably.

Over a decade later, Hepworth extended Moore's vessel-like voids farther into the puncture or the hole. In works like *Two Figures* (1947–48) or *Pelagos* (1946), Dame Barbara set up high surface contrasts between the elaborate graining of the elm wood (or plane wood or Spanish mahogany in other pieces) and the white-painted concave areas containing see-through penetrations.

Although eventually inspired by the transplantation of a machine aesthetic, Constructivism, into Britain by artists Naum Gabo (1890–

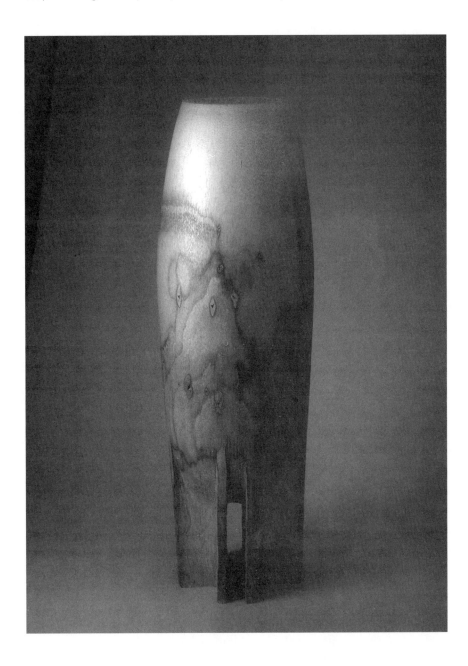

Howard Werner: *Untitled (Vessel)*, 1994, turned and carved palm wood,
42 1/4 x 13 7/8 x 13 7/8". The Wornick Collection, San Francisco.
Photo: M. Lee Fatherree

1977) and his brother Antoine Pevsner (1886–1962), both Hepworth and Moore could not escape their ties to British landscape, its forests, and natural forms. This, too, brings them closer to the earthiness and craft character of the turned wood object makers.

In an appropriate turnabout, *Pierced Geode* (1990) by Robyn Horn seems an indirect tribute to Hepworth. With *Pelagos* barely 15 inches high and *Pierced Geode* 12 inches high, the smaller size of both artists' works is another bond. Whereas both Moore and Hepworth moved their studios outdoors to accommodate large-scale national and corporate commissions, it could be argued that much of their finest work, like that of the turned wood sculptors, remains rooted in the smaller studio setting. The accessibility and approachability of their pedestal pieces allows for greater scrutiny and interaction on the part of the viewer in order to appreciate their craft properties. Their meaning lies in their making.

Pierced Geode is a bisected sphere that exposes, like a mineral geode or "thunder egg," the inner graining of the jarrah burl hardwood. At its center lies not a puncture but a concave hemisphere surrounded by a concentric cut-in circle. Instead of Hepworth's ubiquitous colored strings, Horn has affixed two ebony rods. On a formal level, they act as pure linear elements offsetting the cutting motion of the lathe. On another level, they represent map-like entry paths into the central void.

Isamu Noguchi (1904–1988), always sensitive to craft traditions, created important works in wood, stone, ceramics, metals and paper. In the same vein, function was never far away from a Noguchi sculpture. In *The Seeker* (1970), stone and wood combine in a table-like assemblage that elevates its upper wooden form to nearly sacred or altarlike status. Upholding the horizontal wood section, two lower "legs" may give figurative suggestions but they also summon up functional references. *The Seeker* finds analogies in two works in the Wornick collection, *Untitled [Vessel]* (1994) by Howard Werner, and *Zanthorean Offering Vessel* (1993) by Stephen Hughes. Both turned wood pieces share "legs" with *The Seeker*. The outer struts of Werner's turned and carved palm wood sculpture differ from the inner supports of *The Seeker*. Both works share a crude vision that is transposed into a hearty elegance by the fashioning of the materials in each. Hughes's *Zanthorean Offering Vessel* has a tripartite support of slim pine strands. With its charred appearance, it carries a stronger ritual flavor than *The Seeker*. At 15 ½ inches high, moreover, it summons up personal use rather than public ceremony but shares with the Noguchi a sense of indeterminate expectation of use.

Horizontal extension is carried to great extremes in *Vestigial Form* (1966) by Robert Maki (b. 1938) and in *Spoon From a Forgotten Ceremony* (1994) by Norm Sartorius. Worlds apart in terms of allusions to ritual use or secular, cerebral formal virtuosity, Sartorius and Maki nevertheless both address horizontal compositions. With Maki's laminated hemlock and Douglas fir lying directly on the floor, the pedestal is blatantly subverted and replaced with a frank acceptance of sculpture's undeniable debt to gravity. As the linear configuration claims the space around and above it, *Vestigial Form* is a remarkable technical tour de force, expanding the limits of what wood can do and how we expect sculpture to "behave."

Sartorius's double-handled object of pau ferro wood and ebony is equally forthright and yet, with its functional title and ambiguous ritual references, it looks backward to heritage and traditions rather than forward to unexpected forms for wood. Sartorius and Maki both emphasize how wood can deny mass or volume and also act as line or void. turning is the key operation for Sartorius; for Maki, it is laminating, drawing and cutting..

While Maki touches on illusion in the way he makes wood bend and wind in unexpected ways in *Vestigial Form*, Michelle Holzapfel takes illusion much farther in her *Scarf Bowl* (1992). In works like hers and Stephen Hughes's *Manta* (1991), the potential suppleness and malleability of wood are encountered head on and exploited to the limit. With ceramics normally considered the fountainhead of craft-material illusionism (see Marilyn Levine [b. 1935], Howard Kottler [1930–1989], Patti Warashina [b. 1939]), wood can also stake a claim for tour-de-force effects and the challenging of conventional reality.

It is worth remembering that the "folding" of wood, as we see in Holzapfel, goes back as far as 16th- and 17th-century English furniture with its elaborate "linen fold" creases on cabinet and drawer fronts. Designer-artisans like Grinling Gibbons (1648–1721) took such ornate illusionism to great heights. It became a machine convention by the mid-nineteenth century, frequently repeated in Victorian revivals of dark-stained Tudor and Stuart furniture styles. Holzapfel emphasizes the tactile quality of wood, however, forestalling a completely convincing illusion of cloth in *Scarf Bowl*. The striated groove marks remind us of the lathe, thereby reinforcing our wonder or disbelief at her accomplishment.

Manta is among the most graceful of examples in the Wornick collection. With the undulating curves around a central bowl cavity and absence of turning marks, illusion is used as a hallmark of further technical virtuosity through the concealment of fabrication traces. We know that *Manta* is stationary yet its edges appear in motion. *Manta* appears about to be airborne; *Scarf Bowl* is definitely earthbound.

In a series of works executed in British Columbia in the mid-1970s, Carl Andre (b. 1935) extended his floor-hugging sculptures of firebrick and lead into the realm of wood. Exhibited in New York, Seattle and elsewhere, these works acted like metaphorical compass points, pointers or directional signs in a basic and simple manner. *The Way East, South and West* (1975) uses cut blocks of western red cedar wood to embody their subdued approach to sculptural volume. Part of the power of such works today, however, lies in our apprehension of the graining, figuring and cut marks in the cedar.

A decade later, David Groth made his own group of turned wood bowls, the *Cock's Comb Oyster* series, and they bear a comparison to Andre's earlier endeavors. Cutting against the grain of the hard Oregon myrtlewood, Groth fractured the bowl form so that the 11 pointed tips surrounding it act separately in much the same way that Andre's red cedar sculpture-elements do. Instead of protecting or nestling the inner void, Groth pushes the wood outward and upward, exposing the center. The elaborately curving wood grain and figuring on the outer surface of *#2* (1984) sets up a tension with the threatening, jagged points of the segmented bowl wall. At barely nine inches high, #2 does not assert sculptural space in the same way as Andre's art but it carries a more accessible power, the kind of aesthetic encounter where one could hold the work in one's hand. Groth has added an expressionistic touch to Andre's reductive imagery by his aggressive carving. We admire the de-construction of the bowl form; for a work so small, it carries a near monumental impact when seen—and touched.

Finally, the concealment of inner spaced is shared by Martin Puryear (b. 1941) in his 1980 sculpture of basswood and cypress, *Thicket*, with two much smaller works in the Wornick collection by Ron Fleming, *Reeds in the Wind* (1988) and *Embrace* (1994). Far more Romantic and pastoral than *Thicket*, Fleming's turned wood objects interpolate a leaf or plant motif into the container form. With Fleming, there is a sense of precious mystery and enclosure in both works. For Puryear, the cut and assembled small planks of wood fit together like puzzle parts around a central core. The crisscrossing composition challenges our notion of how much wood is capable of: How can it bend? How can it be juxtaposed so effortlessly? With Fleming, turning has led to a baroque reconfiguration of the wood into leaf and reed forms. The spotting of the surface in *Reeds in the Wind* intensifies an outdoors atmosphere. The South African black ivory wood in *Embrace* is cut so that areas show through the rich shiny surface.

All three works depend on the mystery of concealment and enclosure for their aesthetic power. Puryear works from an additive, accretive position in the studio, preparing individual pieces of wood, which are then assembled into a complex whole. For the woodturners in the Wornick collection like Fleming, the studio procedures of turning and carving involve subtractive operations, chipping away at the original solid block.

As in all the other turned wood objects we have examined, the unraveling of process is part of the viewer's encounter and enjoyment of the artwork. More than that, however, the meaning of each work varies greatly, dependent not only on revelation of process but upon our final apprehension of form. Viewed both ways—process and result, beginning and end—the works by Ron Fleming, David Groth, Michelle Holzapfel, Robyn Horn, Todd Hoyer, Stephen Hughes, Mark Lindquist, William Moore, Norm Sartorius, Howard Werner, and Vic Wood all proclaim their object identity first, with their sculptural identity following only upon close examination and contemplation.

As usual with objects made of craft materials, the viewer must be willing to go along for the ride. With programmatic or ideological content absent, the viewer is free to indulge in poetic fantasies of nature and culture, heritage and tradition, which are embodies in these works of technical skill, beauty, and an expansion of Modernist abstract sculpture's reign far later into the 20th century than anyone would have imagined.

David Groth: *Untitled #2* (Cock's Comb Oyster Series), 1984, carved myrtlewood,
8 7/8 x 19 1/2 x 12 5/8". The Wornick Collection, San Francisco.
Photo: M. Lee Fatherree

DAVID GROTH

The art of David Groth is an amalgam of influences and inspirations that, when considered as a whole, reflects a sensibility at once formalist, pictorialist, ecologist and naturalist. Among the leading younger American artists using wood as a chosen sculptural material, David Groth emerges out of the 20th-century tradition of modernist abstract sculpture. Also, he is the son of the late Bruno Groth, a widely exhibited and collected sculptor whose own carved, hollowed wood sculptures were exhibited at the Brussels World's Fair in 1957. However, because he restricts his materials to myrtlewood logs he finds on the beach near his studio home in Trinidad, California, he is part or a strong naturalist tradition, too. Sensitive to the ecological balance of the environment, this dimension of his work takes on a postmodern aspect: saving trees is a political and social position and, as such, extends the meaning of his art beyond its original modernist context.

Born in California in 1950 and educated at Humboldt State University, Groth has experienced an evolution as an abstract sculptor that has occurred slowly with great thought and gradual material mastery. Although he has been associated with and included in exhibitions of contemporary American and international wood-turners, Groth is a direct carver, more so than ever with the sculptures in this exhibition (all of which were the result of studio undertakings in 2000). A surprising inspiration is Jackson Pollock, an artist who set the pace for direct involvement with materials, following them as they unfold before the artist's eyes.

Beginning with a stroll on the beach of the Pacific Ocean near home, Groth selects logs, branches and stumps of washed-up myrtlewood that interest him for their potential. While he once began each piece with sketches and drawings prior to cutting, for the last four years the artist has been addressing the wood openly without prior maquettes or plans. As the encounter proceeds, a chainsaw is used to rough out the form, shape and shell before pursuing a four-step finishing process.

After the chain-sawn piece is taken as far as the artist feels is appropriate, it is dried in a kiln. Smaller finishing tools like chisels and sandpaper are then employed to create a stronger profile for each sculpture, giving it an individual identity. This is an important phase because, with the same type of wood used for all the works, there could be a danger of all the pieces looking too similar. After the final satisfying form is found, a mixture of beeswax and mineral oil is applied thickly before the piece is returned to the kiln for 24 hours. After final curing, a coat of paste wax is applied over all the surfaces.

In North America, myrtlewood is indigenous only to the northern California and Oregon coasts. A hardwood in a land of evergreens, myrtlewood contains a great deal of variation from the root up through the trunk and branches. Depending upon the location, climate and soil quality, it can resemble black walnut, for example, with highly contrasting areas of yellow, brown, black and orange. Unlike most other woods, the fibers in myrtlewood are not parallel but interlocking, giving the wood great strength. The grains sometimes are straight, as in *Conversation*, or curving, as in *Mollusk*.

Given their pedestal size (14 to 49 inches high), the sculptures force the viewer to focus tightly on their remarkable surfaces, trailing the grain as it becomes convoluted throughout the sections connected as formal facets. This optical activity accounts for much of the pleasure for the viewer and is joined by a revelation of three-dimensional presence experienced in the round. Thus, *Magnus, Guardian* and *Maelstrom* revolve from one envisioned shape to another, rather than presenting as the front-and-back compositions common to much other abstract sculpture, Minimal art especially. Groth's sculptures retain the experience of uncovering the form within, constantly changing in ways not all that different from Michelangelo's revealing a human figure waiting within each piece of marble.

The early carved wood sculptures of Henry Moore and Barbara Hepworth were, unfortunately, left behind by both artists for the grander conversation of marble and bronze, but their wood sculptures still act as an entry point for the art of David Groth (along with the art of other wood artists, such as Robyn Horn). Although he was not one of Groth's teachers at Humboldt (where he taught), Melvin Schuler has made wood and, later, copper-sheathed wood sculptures that provide contextual examples for the younger artist. The thick-walled, simple forms in wood by Basque sculptor Eduardo Chillida are another historical precedent. Groth's sensibility is halfway between both artists, more complex than Schuler, less baroque or linear than Chillida.

With some of the titles alluding to nature (*Swan; Angelfish; Mollusk*), it might be tempting to read Groth's sculptures as veiled pictorial images drawn from nature. This can be helpful up to a point. However, titles are always more allusive than literal in Groth. The shell-like walls of *Mollusk* and *Mollusk #2* also operate as organically united curved and conical forms. This concentration draws us into the shape and surface, respecting the variety and individuality of each piece for its own sake, rather than gauging their closeness to a recognizable natural phenomenon.

Upright forms, as in *Guardian, Guardian #2* and *Griffin*, express a different formal authority, one slightly reminiscent of the human figure or even of a bird (especially, at 49 inches high, with *Griffin*). These works are less about a sheltered inner void than, say, *Maelstrom* or *Magnus*, and dramatically demonstrate the tensile strength of the myrtlewood fibers, reinforcing the handsome involuted display of the wood grain.

If pure form and ecology comprise the twin poles of, respectively, modern and postmodern meanings in Groth, other dimensions of content are possible, too. For example, with each piece conveying inward and outward formal dynamics, expansion and release operate as two general metaphors for all the sculptures. And works with bird titles like *Falcon* and *Fledgling* act as icons of the natural world, not that distant from the art of Morris Graves, a neighbor, friend and colleague long associated with birds as symbols of a fragile and gentle ecology.

One thing is certain: the art of David Groth is not about formal symmetry or static design. Dynamic in the extreme, its visual activity is an interplay of surface and profile. Omitting conventional color such as paint, glaze or enamel, Groth settles for the infinite variety of the glowing brown wood. In turn, this sets him a greater challenge by leading the viewer's eye to the edges of each piece. The combination of the outline and the surface is what ignites much of the optical pleasure for the viewer.

With this unusually strong body of work, David Groth has completed his initial dialogue with early 20th-century abstract sculpture. Fully in control of material, process, form and finish, an increased scale could be the next challenge on his horizon. Perhaps it is time for a longer stroll on the beach.

Jean Williams Cacicedo: *Tee Pee Coat: An Indian Dedication,* 1988, fulled woven wool, dye; piece, 52 x 59". Collection of Julie Schafler Dale, New York.
Photo: Barry Shapiro

JEAN WILLIAMS CACICEDO: EXPLORATIONS IN CLOTH

Jean William Cacicedo (b. 1948) spent her formative years as an art student in New York City and has lived in Berkeley, California since 1980. It is the combination of her experiences in New York, especially her exposure to great art in the city's museums, and her evolution as a fiber artist in the San Francisco Bay Area at a crucial time in the city's art scene that has led to her impressive achievements.

As Cacicedo once put it, she sees the garment as "a canvas to color and a sculpture to form."[1] Significantly, the fusion of painting and sculpture, as well as the adoption of the human body as a sculptural platform or pedestal, has provided alternatives to the art world avant-garde, especially at the time Cacicedo began as an artist.

Instead of calling up the fabricators and ordering the work construct- ed to her specifications (as did Minimal artists such as Carl Andre, Donald Judd, and Robert Morris), Cacicedo luxuriated in the person- ally handmade nature of her art. Her engagement in the process of creating the fabric—washing it, shrinking it, dyeing it—and then cutting, fitting, and covering it herself was a distinct departure from prevailing practice. Joined by other prominent American textile art- ists, including Sheila Hicks, Lia Cook, and Ana Lisa Hedstrom, Jean Cacicedo created a parallel, alternative art practice that is avant- garde in its own way, encompassing women's art, body sculpture, narrative content, and unexpected materials, yet still bears compari- son to modernist and postmodern advances within the art of the past century. Her hats, vests, coats, garments, collages, and drawings form their own seamless narrative of content, what critic Maria Porges called Cacicedo's "personal vocabulary of form and content."[2]

The use of the body as a container for art meanings goes back a long way. Whether the intricate makeup and adornment found in aborigi- nal cultures such as that of Papua New Guinea tribesmen or the cer- emonial tattoo or body painting of the Maori of New Zealand, prece- dents for using the body as a focus for art predate most of our notions of what constitutes art. In this sense, Cacicedo is a typical craft artist, in that she invokes a global heritage for her inspirations, not just the canonical legacy of Western European art. Extensively traveled, she has seen firsthand the craft and clothing traditions of Asia, Europe, and the United States.

Equally important, her studies at Pratt Institute in Brooklyn, New York, and her broad exposure to the collections of East Coast museums established an awareness of the different strategies that could be applied to conventional and unconventional materials and introduced her to benchmark artworks that suggested twentieth-century approaches to both the body and clothing as valid forms of high art.

Thus, Cacicedo draws from early twentieth-century costume and fashion design, such as Natalya Goncharova's and Alexander Benois's costumes for the Ballets Russes, which animate the dancers' bodies, and the hand-painted coats, hats, and dresses of the 1920s by Orphist artist Sonia Delaunay. Similarly, Man Ray's *Violon d'Ingres* (1924) is another example of how the human body can be the focus of art within the Western fine arts tradition. *Bed* (1955), by Robert Rauschenberg, was another influential work, in that it utilizes a tattered quilt covered with paint drips. Of more recent significance was *Felt Suit* (1978), by German artist Joseph Beuys. In this work, the artist uses autobiographical details, alluding to an incident in which he was wrapped in felt and animal fat by Russian peasants after his plane crashed during World War II. Felt, or fulled wool, became the chief material for Cacicedo. Seen in the light of such art, Cacicedo's work makes perfect sense, as she fast-forwards these projects into her world of American myths and the Far West, personal stories, and deepening symbols.

Following her pivotal move to San Francisco in 1970, after graduating from Pratt, Jean Cacicedo's earliest fabric or fiber pieces, such as *Helmet* (1970) and *Petal Vest* (1971), expanded on the notions of hat and vest, forcing the wearer to participate as both performance artist and spokesperson-art critic. The heavy brown crocheting and use of numerous different animal furs conspire to create an unusual object that may protect the wearer (like medieval chain-mail and armor headwear) but also becomes an object of curiosity, an adornment and a symbol of social rebellion.

Petal Vest may be more "wearable," but its dense mixture of black-and-white patterning and petal-like braiding and inserts anticipates New York Pattern and Decoration art by nearly a decade. True, Kim McConnell, Cynthia Carlson, Joyce Kozloff, and the other artists singled out by critic John Perreault[3] were involved mostly with painting. However, like Cacicedo, they chose alternate supports for their imagery, such as unstretched cloth and painted silk, tile, or wallpaper.

As much other art of the 1970s is currently being reevaluated, Cacicedo's *Fishing Vest* (1974), *Transformations* (1977), and *Carrot Top Kimono* (1978) must now be seen as important precedents in the reaction of contemporary art against the puritanical strictures of Minimal art. More important than reaction, though, is how these artworks carved out aesthetic territory of their own.

While living in Wyoming between 1971 and 1980, Cacicedo used the opportunity to explore new forms in cloth (adapted kimonos and Native American garments). She also experimented with dyeing techniques, materials including raffia, paper collage, and plastic mesh netting, and adapting and combining methods such as crocheting, gluing, and sewing.

Carrot Top Kimono and *Desert Kimono* (1982) are extravagantly decorated surfaces that evoke, respectively, a plotted-out vegetable garden complete with airborne crows, and a parched, pink desert. In these pieces and in subsequent works created after her 1980 move to Berkeley, the artist developed the extraordinarily vibrant palette for which she is noted today.

Cacicedo's real breakthrough, however, came with *Chaps: A Cowboy Dedication* (1982). It takes the crisscross-fence motif of cowboy country, adds elements of men's clothing (rider's chaps and a nod to long underwear), and creates a coat that envelops the wearer in a heavy, protective cloak to guard against Wyoming winters on the range. This wondrous work celebrates the life of the American cowboy.

The idea of continuous, wraparound imagery persisted in *Bird Coat* (1985), *Tail of Twins* (1990), *Coat of Arms*, and *Insight* (both 1994). *Tail of Twins* sets up an entire domestic-residential panorama complete with loyal dog and, according to the artist, a Balinese temple that, along with a legend about dogs, was the original inspiration for the piece.[4]

Black and white are again used as formal organizing principles, both for a reverse pattern on the coat's front and also in the signature checkered pattern lines. As Porges wrote, the black-and-white checks are present "to emphasize the distinction between areas of color and to define the outer boundaries of the coat."[5] Black and white carry symbolic significance for the artist, as in "yin/yang, good and evil."[6]

Coat of Arms has gloves fitted into the garment's sleeves, thus bringing even more of the wearer's body within its sphere. At its center is a silhouette of the artist's father fishing, a symbolic image of paternal protection that is reinforced throughout the rest of the garment. Guiding hands appear on the coat's lower edge.

Periodically, Cacicedo creates flat cloth-collage studies that use silhouettes of the female figure as a testing ground for new ideas. *For Sandra* (1997), *Red Hand* and *Yellow Hand* (both 1998) combine clamped-resist dyeing or sewn lines radiating around a central figure of felt cloth. More complex spatially, *Bed of Roses* and *The Conversation* (both 1998) adapt the diamond pattern of a quilt to, respectively, a nude figure with flowers, and a series of body parts (hands, lips, eyes) interspersed among the parallel lines associated with weaving patterns.

These, in turn, proved to be fruitful sources for *Reveal Handbag, Tattoo Handbag,* and *Transformation Handbag* (all 1999). The open-topped containers are surrogates for the human figure, complete with heads represented by handles and a deep décolletage "revealing" hot pink breasts. Here, Cacicedo differs from artists of the 1980s and 1990s, such as Lesley Dill, who view clothing forms as blank slates for poetry or as independent metaphors for the human body. Cacicedo's art is ignited and completed by the presence of the wearer or, as with the handbags, the carrier.

Three recent works, *Rain Coat* (1998), *Lotus Coat,* and *Hunting Coat* (both 2000) suggest an intensifying complexity of surface imagery and structure. The perforations in the gray areas above the black skyline in Rain Coat render the coat useless as real protection against rain and, instead, suggest a close affinity to what the wearer might (or might not) have on underneath by allowing us to glimpse it through the coat's holes. The artist's use of black and white is seen here at its most refined.

Lotus Coat sets out distinct areas of water lily imagery, not that different from the gridded sections in a Jennifer Bartlett painting. The dark colors suggest a murky pond, and the sleeves are autumnal orange and yellow. Large cuffs and a deep purple hat turn the body into a type of flower, emerging out of the dark green and blue areas.

Finally, *Hunting Coat*, inspired by the artist's father's hunting coat, includes a rich variety of symbols, such as targets, deer hooves, characteristic red-and-black plaid, and arrows. On an autobiographical level, it may be a "celebration of [her] father,"[7] but, in the long run, the imagery will remain self-evident, a meditation on the hunter and the hunted, a celebration of the color red: dangerous, sanguine, sexual, vibrant, and a warning to other hunters in the forest that a colleague is nearby.

Like all good sculpture, Jean Cacicedo's art must be experienced in three dimensions—front, side and back. Each area has significance, and, to be fully appreciated, each garment must be seen with a wearer. This quality of being rooted in the everyday nature of clothing is central. It is the transformation of the viewing experience and the wearing experience into art that gives Jean Cacicedo's accomplishments their unique beauty and importance.

RANDY SHULL

Randy Shull's painted, wall-mounted constructions represent a current culmination and triumph of his studio activities over the past decade. This award-winning North Carolina artist with roots in Illinois has traveled a considerable distance in his artistic evolution: from furniture to sculpture; from craft to art; from unconventional and marginalized influences to a fully individual and unique vision addressing contemporary art issues.

Instead of making furniture for use, he uses furniture as imagery and allusion. Chairs stand in as figurative symbols, set in the place where the figure would be were he or she present in each work. Poetic evocation of a humble, yet highly subjective, past is present in the recurrent chair image of the new works, along with reinforcing residues of the making process whether cutting, fashioning, painting or sanding. More akin to tributes to American craft than straightforward examples of it, Shull's work is notable for its unapologetic materiality, its brilliant color sense and its transformation of found objects from everyday life into constructions that are purely for aesthetic contemplation rather than practical use. It is the representation of use rather than his prior widely acclaimed adaptations of use through actual furniture that characterizes the current pieces.

Building on a variety of earlier influences that critics, curators and art historians have written about with great perception—folk furniture and vernacular art of the Caribbean, American South and Central Europe—Randy Shull approaches his studio undertakings as compressed and condensed encounters between such sources and his own deepening sensibility.

All the works in the 2000 Tercera Gallery exhibition share a centered, iconic composition that leads the eye to the assembly of found objects each piece honors. Dollhouse chairs, metal chocolate molds, and other assorted gatherings from second-hand, thrift and antique shops set up an atmosphere of remembrance and recovery that steers clear of nostalgia but still sticks with a warm, comforting memory of discarded functional objects which once had practical meaning associated with real work settings and childhood pastimes.

A consummate master of painted layers, Shull brings to each undertaking a mixture of intuition and plan. Within the repeated oval shapes (themselves recalling antique photo frames holding images of beloved family members), horizontal and vertical lines provide grid-, or lattice-like protection systems for the contained found objects.

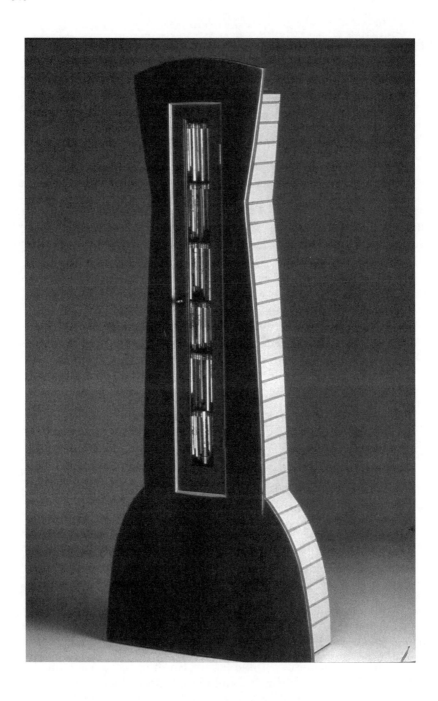

Randy Shull: *Butternut*, 1997, painted wood and pencils.
Mint Museum of Art + Design, 1998.6. Photo: Tercera Gallery

Sometimes resembling brick patterns, barrel struts, or even picket fence sticks, the painted backgrounds comprise an overlooked development for the 38-year-old artist: a concentration on abstract painting surfaces. Omitting the *objets trouvés* for a moment, each work qualifies as a self-contained abstract painting in the manner of Frank Stella, Brice Marden or Robert Ryman, for example. Shull's art thus exists in a variety of art worlds: contemporary abstract painting, assemblage sculptures, and the revival of handmade furniture.

But then, I have always felt that the repeated references to outsider art in his work have been overstated by Southern critics. Today the bulk of each construction has more to do with creating an interesting painting than with summoning up allusions to the quaint, peeling country furniture so beloved throughout the South. The colors that bleed through between the bands of red, brown, orange, green and blue are carefully chosen, far more intellectual and methodical than the purportedly intuitive choices critics have commented on. In fact, despite references to wall cabinets or containers, the elongated shapes with curving ends or blunted tops suggest the unendingly varied shape solutions of senior American abstract painter Ellsworth Kelly, for example. Could it be that all these years Randy Shull has been gradually becoming an abstract artist of the highest order?

Leaving that possibility aside, it is still necessary to examine the meaning of these works when taking into consideration the hallowed central niches and what they contain. *Ghost* seems nothing less than a crematorium with a Windsor-back wooden armchair as the entry tray for the coffin. The overall brick pattern and upper chimney shape assures us of such a darker reading. The eight metal duck-shaped candy molds in *Chocolate* are behind barred windows in a long horizontal, prison-like band. The confined treatment of animals could be one interpretation; the screened-off way we experience animals or nature in general might be another. The smaller birds in *Twin* are also set against rigid horizontal lines even though the doors they perch upon are hinged and open up to a shallow empty space behind them.

The central hinged doors in several of the new works are a link to Shull's earlier furniture but, this time around, they almost appear superfluous functional remnants, so overwhelmed by painterly intervention are the surrounding areas. *Family*'s six miniature chairs on the green door imply a coexistence of cultures within American society. Chinese, French, English and American chair styles are represented but all are covered in a uniform white. The vertically divided white and black trapezoidal panels around the green doors also make an oblique reference to biracial coexistence.

Finally, *Banjo* seems the most loaded with potential symbols and closest to the dark dream world assemblages of Joseph Cornell. A cowboy boot, a baseball bat, a miniature artist's model, and even a tiny blue rhinoceros are all crammed into a vertical niche behind an old-fashioned front door. The banjo shape of the title represents another shift (as in *Chocolate*) to two-part backdrops that complicate two-dimensional space. The only piece with a human head peering out, *Banjo* presents a man caught up in or, indeed, imprisoned by memory. The chicken on a child's toy block is beneath the toy cowboy boot, perhaps another reference to the domestication of nature or the confinement of living things.

Shull's world never scolds or taunts us despite its periodic interpolations of darker juxtapositions of elements. But the possibilities of bittersweet and ominous memory are there, along with a ravishing command of materials that draws our eye in and quietly urges us to contemplate content as we endlessly appreciate more purely optical pleasures.

PATTERNING THE PAST:
RACHEL BRUMER AND ISABEL KAHN

Two Seattle artists, Rachel Brumer and Isabel Kahn, create works of art that allude to cultural histories of Jews in the 20th century, yet both employ differing strategies of process, fabrication and multiple-image production that reinforce their subject matters, projecting them into a generalized realm not always dependent upon specific historical references.

Brumer, a quilt- and bookmaker, and Kahn, a painter with a printmaking background, both attempt to answer the question, "How can Jewish cultural and family histories be dealt with in the wake of the Holocaust?" Each artist has constructed a body of work that has multiple layers—heritage, family, self—and that has met with growing critical acclaim.[1],[2],[3],[4] They stand in the shadow of postwar thinkers like Theodor Adorno and Hannah Arendt who argued for the impossibility of art or poetry coping with or responding to the enormity of the Holocaust. Rejecting the argument that silence is the only moral response to such an overwhelming collective act of evil, both Kahn and Brumer have selected aspects of Jewish history to address.

In Brumer's case, French Jewish girls who were deported and killed are the inspiration for *Cover Them* (1997). For Kahn, the literary efflorescence among Yiddish poets in southern Russia before and after the Bolshevik Revolution acts as an impetus for a series of works like *Poets' Journey, Poets' Curtain* and *Poem Scroll* (all 1992). Such pieces by both artists present complex fields of figurative imagery concealed within grids and patterns, borders and fringes, pages and margins. By blurring, cropping, covering, clipping and altering the figures, Brumer and Kahn soften the violence often perpetrated against such real and legendary individuals.

In this sense, materials like cloth, fiber and paper are ideal palimpsests for the deeper dredging of historical meaning. The autonomy of the image, however, its iconic power free of cultural implication, comes first, and then participates in a narrative of facts, events of persecution, valiant heroics and, in some cases, vain resistance.

Nature is another important link between both artists, one that also is shared during and beyond any deeper preoccupations with treating social issues such as anti-Semitism and its consequences.

With Kahn, Mediterranean culture with its overlapping of Islamic and Jewish art, architecture and calligraphy, is a broad base for sub-

Isabel Kahn: *Poets' Song* (detail), 1992, relief inks on paper mounted on muslin, 21 1/2 x 274 x 4". Collection of the artist. Photo: Terry Reid

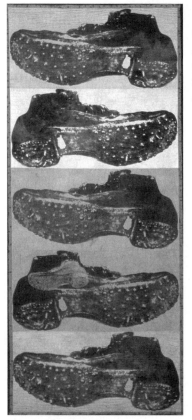

Rachel Brumer: *Fay Fuller's Boot,* 1998, cloth and photographic transfer, 104 x 14 x 1". Courtesy of the artist. Photo: Mark Frey

sequent visual references to pattern, color, and objects of meditation and devotion such as prayer shawls, prayer rugs, Torah scrolls and containers. Ferns, pine tree needles, irises, olive and laurel leaves all act as formal elements in Kahn's compositions, serving aesthetic purposes of spatial organization along with creating a nurturing, nestling environment, one protective of natural habitat and native animal species. Elk, birds, and deer populate a shimmering yet subdivided pictorial space that implies limitless boundaries through the conceit of wall- or pedestal-unfurlment, ceiling suspension, and tabletop scroll display. Although an accomplished painter with an extensive exhibitions record, Kahn's most interesting and successful works have been those that alter or violate the rectangle of traditional Western landscape art, the "window on the world." Instead, by either dispensing with the rectangle altogether or altering it and stretching it beyond recognition, Kahn forces us to re-opticalize the inherent image at the heart of each painting: a kneeling figure; a row of long-skirted dancers; a chain of black-hatted exiled poets. Thus, natural imagery in Kahn can still carry allusions to cultural history—acts of healing, cooking, dyeing and weaving—without sacrificing more current ecological or environmental meanings.

For Brumer, fabric or cloth, cut up, printed upon, or re-sewn into gridded tableaux, becomes the vehicle of remembrance. Recent works, like *Quire: Book of Findings* (2000) employ found natural plant specimens such as the leaves children might pick up on their way home from school. Elegiac of trodden-upon, urbanized plant life, the myriad leaves, blossoms and other formerly living materials are photographed by Brumer, their impressions set on high-contrast stiffened fabric. In the process of sewing and laminating them onto cloth backgrounds, their ghost images are re-united with the living material of the cloth.

No such re-energizing of dead matter is possible for the dedicatees of Brumer's *Cover Them*, the French Jewish schoolgirls mentioned in *French Children of the Holocaust* by Serge Klarsfeld. Brumer's quilts are each dedicated to a different little girl who never returned home. In *Arlette Montelmarcher, born 2/11/41* (2001), a tombstone rubbing text, "Beloved," is transferred to cloths that are sewn together. The 40 pieces of cloth act as baby blanket, marriage quilt and a shroud.

The grid format of *Arlette Montelmarcher, born 2/11/41* is used to more colorful effect in *I Know You Are. . . And What Am I?* (1994). Identity is symbolized by one silk-screened fingerprint within each of the 30 red, yellow, orange and brown quilt squares. Repetition of image-modules is a strong organizing strategy for Brumer, one that, when coupled with pre-existing quilt composition structures, can sometimes inhibit more imaginative placement.

Both artists have used alphabets to set up rhythmic patterns, allude to the narrative nature of language, and draw upon the Jewish legacy of writing that suggests traditions of sacred and secular knowledge, traditions that were endangered or destroyed by the Holocaust and by the Stalinist persecution in the Soviet Union after World War II. Kahn alters Hebrew letters (e.g., ayin, shin, tzadi, lamed) so that they resemble plant motifs surrounding her figures. Such letters also act as narrative clues to those who might recognize them as references to "meditation, reflection, transformation, humility and purpose."[5] Brumer does the opposite: sets up plant specimens in the stacked lines of *Quire: Book of Findings* so that they mimic, for example, the Islamic calligraphy prevalent in beautifully illustrated sacred texts.

Photography is also a key sharing point between the two but, again, with completely different results. In the *Satchel* series (1992), Kahn employs actual photographs of Yiddish writers (e.g., David Hofshteyn and Peretz Markish). Her *Library Table* (1992) uses an artist's model whom she dressed and photographed in peasant costume complete with lace shawl; the model holds Hebrew letters. Photography is both a studio tool and source of appropriation for her. "When I use a found photograph, I can alter it. When I take the photograph myself, I can construct the entire scene myself," Kahn noted.[6] In Brumer's case, *Fay Fuller's Boot* (1998) is a nine-foot-high banner of the repeated image of the mountain climbing boots used by the first woman to ascend Mt. Rainier in Washington State. Elsewhere, as in *Bread: Staple, 4th Removed* (1996), she uses rows of photographs of a single loaf of bread with crosshatched, gridded baker's marks atop each loaf. The 30 images summon up life-giving foodstuffs crucial for survival during the Holocaust.

Throughout *Cover Them*, Brumer's construction is deceptively crude and hurried-looking. She commented, "This is because the young women being honored didn't have the time to do such work properly, if at all. That's why the batting is often left exposed. As in the Exodus, things were rushed."[7]

Artwork by Brumer and Kahn seems to respectively assimilate and intensify Jewish imagery, and to move on toward other Mediterranean cultures. Heritage is upheld in both cases through the careful assembly process, retention of the human figure as image where appropriate, and through periodically somber palettes that suggest dark events, death, and brooding memories.

Using cloth and fiber-based papers, along with the attendant process-es of cutting, piece-assembly, and sewing or gluing, Rachel Brumer and Isabel Kahn have used the flexible topography of fiber art to transform images of remembrance into objects of powerful and lasting effect.

Keith Lewis: Sebastian (Imaginary Self-Portrait), 1999, sterling silver, 18-karat gold, 3 1/2 x 1 1/2 x 1 1/2". Collection of Susan and Bill Beech, Tiburon, California. Photo: Doug Yaple

KEITH LEWIS:
FROM PROPAGANDIST TO HUMANIST

Possibly the most controversial jewelry artist now working in the United States, Keith Lewis is undergoing a transition from propagandist to post-activist artist. Defiantly "out," queer, gay, male and all of the above, Lewis has spent the past decade or more dividing his time between teaching, lecturing and making art. That such a small body of work (roughly 40 objects) has generated such a raft of commentary and criticism underlines some key aspects of the American metals field: its poverty of other artists addressing unpopular subjects; the in-bred system of academic group shows; the nestling cocoon of protected free speech within the halls of tenured universities. The time has come to have a closer look at Lewis's art, compare it to his voluminous and revealing writings, and to judge it on critical terms rather than the artist's own stentorian and often hysterical intentional claims.

After teaching at Central Washington University in Ellensburg for six years, Professor Lewis attained tenure in 2000. Until then, a heavy load of committees and teaching only permitted four solo gallery exhibits (1988, 1993, 1995, 1999)—and 50 group shows, mostly on campuses with a few abroad.

Despite his sharing content with many contemporary painters and other sculptors, Lewis has never been written about in an art magazine. Instead, he has subsisted critically within the cozy craft world where commentary on his art has been shaped by his own extensive written and spoken statements of intent. Usually, the writers simply quote him rather than analyze his art. For so interesting and provocative an artist, this is a shame and a mistake. Controlling discourse is easier in the craft world because so few writers have ideas of their own. Lewis has supplied them all they need. To date, Lewis has essentially reviewed himself, and, as a result, carrying on a monologue of extreme claims with large doses of projected anger and guilt.

Is it even possible for us to step back and analyze such work objectively? So many red flags appear along with clanging alarm bells: gay sex, AIDS, explicit genitalia, self-absorption and oft-proclaimed guilt. Space does not permit a thorough meta-critical analysis of the reviews of his work, but it is worth setting Lewis in a historical context; repeating his intentions based upon his published and lectures; assessing published opinion; and, finally, noting how, most surprising of all, he has dropped propaganda art of late, reconciled with the heterosexual world, and fully embraced a broader definition of humanity and the decorative dimension.

Since CWU is the birthplace of Northwest Funk jewelry[1] and a haven for the discovery of found-object jewelry,[2] it is entirely appropriate that Lewis replaced Ken Cory (1943–1994) as jewelry professor at Ellensburg. Cory's work had a strong, if submerged, erotic character, too, but it grew out of a complex puzzle system that frequently concealed sex as much as it revealed it.

For Lewis, his position at CWU has allowed him a bully pulpit, especially when on the road. As he told an audience, "I live to lecture!"[3] AIDS activism preoccupied him long before he completed his graduate studies with Kathleen Browne at Kent State University in 1993. And although accompanied by slides of his work, the occasion of the numerous guest lectures became a launching pad for the artist's bold political positions. A few gems shared with undergraduate and graduate students include:

> The making of jewelry is a political act. I see it as propaganda. [There is] a cloying hetero-defined reality. . . . Their comfort . . . is my anxiety and outrage. These people won't stop until every shred of difference that distinguishes us . . . is obliterated. The heterosexist project depends heavily on the eradication of our history.[4]

Do the pins, brooches and necklaces hold up to this grandeur of intentional claims? Hardly. As early as 1988, the four golden tummies with "expanding" male genitals seemed amusing more than daring or angry. The headless cartoon figures of the early "self-portraits" with symbolic appurtenances (grim reaper scythe, as in *With Sharp Hair*, 1990) seem diminutive and dainty, especially when one notes the 24-karat gold plating.

How does an activist-artist deal with the essential paradox of jewelry: attractive body ornaments typically worn by women? After all, even though one writer called them "sculpture that happens to have a pin on the back,"[5] if no one wears them, they're not activated at all, let alone activist. Along these lines, by 1992 self-loathing became a central subject in Lewis's work, artfully and attractively done despite imagery of skin-gouging (*Just a Few Pricks*, 1992; *Peeling Off*, 1993; and *Well, Doug, It's 36 Now*, 1994). Expressed as AIDS survivor-guilt, self-loathing has been a powerful and effective position for Lewis as an artist. As he confessed to a group of students in Boston: "Why did the virus that killed him...hesitate to leap to me?[6] This joined a more troubling confession of guilt and possible bad faith: "How legitimate is this work? Does it prostitute the lives of the people that I called my friends? . . . I sell this stuff for money. . . . My project seems yet more callous and dishonest.[7]

Before that 2002 mea culpa, Lewis produced another dozen or so pins tracking the growth of AIDS among friends, dedicating memorial works to them, exhibiting in the sympathetic San Francisco Bay Area (site of his best reviews). Pride, rather than guilt, might be a more appropriate, if less opportune, emotion for the artist. Enhanced workmanship and potent animal surrogates (a rooster, a bear, a shrimp, an elk) make these among the best of the survivor-guilt series. *Bath Time* (1995), for example, uses a golden bear to satirize portly middle-aged gays at a steam bath (and virus-infection site), while *Salt Lick* (1996) adds real-diamond semen droplets to the gold-over-silver six-pack torso, enriching the artist's most explicit yet image of masturbation. Together, they take the notion of male brooches as icebreakers or conversation-starters to another extreme: art as the surrogate pick-up line in a bar. A Lewis pin on a man says, "Get closer and have a look." But could these outrageous ornaments ever really "encourage a change in societal attitudes," as one curator hoped?[8] Not likely. No more so than Judy Chicago's *Dinner Party* did or Andres Serrano's *Piss Christ*.

A sabbatical in 2001–2002 led to a significant breakthrough: the appearance of the female figure, the depiction of heterosexual intercourse, and the diminution of the artist's strident anti-straight rhetoric. Lewis's embrace of a broader humanism has enriched his work immeasurably. Now accepting the existence of the majority of the human race—women—Lewis is finally free to depict a wider range of anatomical parts. *Daisy Chain* (2000) anticipates the current, reconciliatory phase of his art. A silver and gold necklace with watch-crystal-size linked elements, each circle is filled with a different photographic image of the human anus, appropriated from available pornographic magazines. At least non-phallic in character (which is a refreshing change with Lewis), *Daisy Chain* also seems closer with its necklace structure to women's jewelry. It was followed by the paradoxical *Tool* necklace (2001) which uses intricate drawings of male and female genitalia interspersed with images of punning tools: pliers, screws, screwdrivers, vices and nails.

Similarly expansionist in spirit, *Boy and Girl Spread* (2001) introduces Limoges enamel technique in a series of his and hers rings, each displaying more appropriated porno images, in this case, low-angle views of male and female genitals seen from beneath the figures' bodies, a typical adult-movie camera-viewpoint.

Most promising of all, *Neckpiece for Zymrina* (2002) is an ingenious necklace of detachable pins, each with a different enameled image based on pornographic frescoes at Pompeii (where the artist traveled again during his sabbatical). Coming around to a more inclusive view of sex, one more comparable to Petronius's line from his *Satyricon*— "If it is human, I cannot reject it."—Lewis has matured from an angry propagandist to a poetic artist of high achievement. Still queer, the extravagantly beautiful gold filigree, the inset diamonds and pearls, and the comfortable wearability of Zymrina's necklace all move Lewis closer to a sexually integrated community, one in which straights and gays may coexist (as they did in Rome and Pompeii) with mutual respect and tolerance. Rejecting the sexual isolationism of his Act-up activist years, Lewis now embraces a more varied, caring population. Just as dividing lines between gays and straights in society as a whole are blurring of late, along with vanishing legal barriers and establishment religious prejudices, so has Lewis softened his stand by shifting to female imagery.

The AIDS pins were indeed, as one critic put it, "talismans that mark an angry reckoning of our nation's failure to engage this [AIDS] calamity."[9] However, *Daisy Chain, Boy and Girl Spread* and *Neckpiece for Zymrina* herald a new, post-activist Lewis, still involved with his precious "genderfuck" issues but now more open to sexual co-existence within a society still struggling, in this case, through its art, to create meaningful cultural artifacts.

NANCY WORDEN:
EXCAVATIONS

> It is most interesting just how important figuration, storytelling
> and the invention of a modern folk art have been in North American
> jewelry. . . Witty artists can use the commonplace and the cheap to
> wring emotions.
> —Helen W. Drutt English, *Jewelry of Our Time* (1995)

The art of Nancy Worden is both a part of a regional artistic identity—Pacific Northwest found-object jewelry—and an independent
aesthetic project of her own. While her earliest works were brooches
in the vein of her friend and teacher, Central Washington University
professor Ken Cory (1943–1994), her recent pieces take the form of
necklaces, seen most recently at Seattle's William Traver Gallery in
her solo exhibition, "Modern Artifacts." Never working serially, Worden conceives of each piece as an autonomous symbolic object. Elements serve dual purposes of ornament and meaning. Like her peers
in the area, many of whom come under the rubric "Ellensburg Funky"
(*Metalsmith*, Fall 1995), Worden has rejected precious materials
and abstract Euro-imagery in favor of objects that excavate popular
culture, American history, and current events. That she manages to
do so in necklaces of spectacular beauty that steer clear of ideology or
propaganda is a considerable achievement. Humor, social criticism,
and an endearing use of materials often available at the hardware
store or antique shop roots her work in American art and celebrates
the lives and circumstances of ordinary Americans.

Shockingly, Helen W. Drutt English omitted Worden from her epoch-making survey *Jewelry of Our Time: Art, Ornament and Obsession* (Rizzoli, 1995), while highlighting other West Coast Funksters
like Ramona Solberg, Laurie Hall, Ron Ho, Kiff Slemmons and Ken
Cory. At least a decade or more younger than the original Ellensburg
Funky group, Worden is achieving maturity a decade after Drutt's
book appeared. Perhaps a late bloomer, Worden now seems to have
been inspired by a clientele approaching middle age. Her ideal necklace wearer must be bold, confident, humorous and accomplished. Or
if she is not, wearing one of Worden's "modern artifacts" may render
her so.

With the death of Solberg in 2005 and the aging of the "Ellensburg
Funky" crowd, Worden stands to succeed her colleagues as its leader
as recognition by art critics, curators, and collectors of her art grows
and spreads beyond Seattle. Besides the use of found objects artfully
rearranged—coins, acrylic nail extensions, eyeglass lenses, hair curl-

Top: Nancy Worden:
Brigandine for Ishtar, 2005,
cut steel and glass, 21 1/2 x
14 x 4". Courtesy of William
Traver Gallery.
Photo: Rex Rystedt

Left: Nancy Worden:
Frozen Dreams, 2004, silver,
nickel and acrylic, 17 x 14 x
2 1/4". Courtesy of William
Traver Gallery.
Photo: Doug Yaple

ers—Worden reintroduces tighter, somewhat more technically complicated settings that draw her closer to jewelry precedents of the 1970s:
the electroforming of Stanley Lechtzin, the intricate clasps of Solberg,
the large-scale, sculptural presence of the Dutch jewelry masters of
the 1970s.

An artist in transition, Worden's work deserves a deeper analysis
than it has heretofore received. More American in content than her
globetrotting elders Ho and Solberg, Worden's art is often about the
expressions of minority cultures within the U.S. Worden has shifted
from the subjectivity and autobiography of her prior art ("My artwork
is a response to specific events in my life," she once said.) to a more
outward-looking, socially engaged and distanced feminism. Although
feminist ideologues told women in the 1970s that "the personal is the
political," this connection did not always lead to art of broader reference that could be enjoyed by men as well as women.

"Modern artifacts" may be triggered by the artist's social observations
of older women's delights and plights, but they proceed to become protective shields and conversation-starters that not every wearer can
handle. Wrapping a mass of metal, fur, plastic, glass, and even stones
and pebbles around one's neck requires chutzpah, positing a proud
and confident woman who not only needs the body (and back) to bring
it off, but one who can address audience comments and feedback.

Much more intense in person and in her writings than one would
suspect of the creator of such entertaining work, Worden wrote of
the origins of "Modern Artifacts" that "the quest for wholeness and
a voice is an initiation every adult woman must face as an antidote
to what our culture teaches us a 'nice' woman should or should not
do. These pieces incorporate small objects from the everyday lives of
women to build structures that are intended to empower the wearer."
Like magical talismans, Worden's necklaces have a visibly transformative power when adorning the wearer.

One of Solberg's prime contributions was the significance of the
clasp. It could be simple, complex, integrated, separate or detachable
entirely, but it became an important element of each neckpiece. In
Worden's case, the clasp's importance has continued into the second
half of each piece, how it appears on the wearer's back. Closer to armor while still acting as ornament, the new necklaces extend beyond
the neck and chest onto the back so that sculptural properties—volume, mass, profile— are reinforced and the overall meaning of each
work is better conveyed.

Transfer of Power (2005), for example, has an inner core of refash-
ioned, souvenir beaded Indian belts that continue down the back,

climaxing with a tuft of artificial hair. The tail of *Transfer of Power* slopes down from the shoulder. And *Ereshkigal's Hook* (2004) has 10 tufted leather balls set in electroformed copper descending from an eyeball-like clasp that echoes the inner core of the front.

The actual lead part of *The Leash* (2003) dangles a dog leash loop handle at the end of a long strand of pearls punctuated by thrift store fur. Here the back section can be activated either by the wearer or an assertive partner. Drutt spoke in *Jewelry of Our Time* of the fetish dimension in a lot of American jewelry and *The Leash* is as close as Worden comes to invoking ritual through a fetish-like object.

Women's quest for strength and fitness is gently satirized in *Lifting Weights* (2003), a perhaps overly complicated piece that sets weights in the form of small silver, lead, and gold weights on the wearer's shoulders. By slipping the necklace on, the wearer can work out while walking at the same time. She is projecting a commanding image. Ebony and ivory form the amusing links that echo barbell or weight-lifting machines.

Not for the faint of heart, then, Worden's necklaces balance adorn-ment with visible expressions of women's power. With much humbler materials like concrete and pebbles, as well as silver-cast ears, *The Good Omen* (2004) gets closer to the rougher, possibly more mascu-line look of Worden's latest works. Its stone fragments alternate with small ears attuned to hearing good omens. Symbolically "ears to the ground," *The Good Omen* is ignited by the contrasting femininity of the wearer. Like a site-related sculpture, its impact shifts depending upon the appearance of the wearer. The pebbles embedded in concrete are absurd surrogates for the expected gems or precious stones set in gold or silver. Worden is among the most extreme of the Ellensburg Funky group in her embrace of the street as an inspiration. By honor-ing pebbles, she privileges the mundane. It is her most "blue collar" collar to date.

Two final necklaces, *Frozen Dreams* (2004) and *Brigandine for Ishtar* (2005), offer opposite faces or sensibilities for the woman unafraid of making a spectacle of herself. One is transparent and airy; the other is opaque and brooding. With both works, Worden is expanding the province of jewelry's possibilities. Like her teacher at the University of Georgia, Gary Noffke, Worden's technical construction may be complicated but it gives an appearance of informality and American make-do or know-how. Not that they could be confused with high school jewelry projects (as in Laurie Hall), but construction is treated as what is necessary rather than what will impress with fussiness. As a result, the direct materiality of the work is immediately evident.

Taking the eyeglass form used so effectively in her earlier brooches (*Resolution to Lose*, 1992; *Mixed Messages*, 1993), *Frozen Dreams* aligns 50 polarized clear lenses on a silver chain. Each lens has slight cuts at one end to imitate Victorian glass engraving. In fact, the entire piece could also be seen as a riposte to Seattle's ubiquitous glass art scene. Within the chain is a larger glass pendant surrounded by chunkier glass and nickel-plated silver components. Two necklaces in one, *Frozen Dreams* is icy and tactile at the same time, evocative of historic and modern jewelry conventions simultaneously. One further element of parody comes to mind: diamonds. Flattened yet faceted by crude carving, each lens spoofs a precious part of a diamond necklace. In a sense regal and street-savvy, *Frozen Dreams* operates on many levels. Worden's excavations here are at their most complex pitch.

As this nation settles into an alarmingly protracted war abroad and stories of inadequate tank and body armor spread, they eerily recall the stories of shoddy rifles used in Vietnam that led to the deaths of hundreds of young men. Worden has created her own symbolic body armor for those she calls "the sons and daughters of Iraq," U.S. Army soldiers. *Brigandine for Ishtar* follows from *Ereshkigal's Hook;* both works refer to Babylonian mythology, the culture originated in what is present-day Iraq. The former was the goddess of love and war, who unwittingly brought about the death of her beloved. She was chastised by her sister, Ereshkigal, goddess of the underworld, and forced to remain in hell until rescued by a hermaphroditic beast.

Brigandine for Ishtar is one of Worden's most complex and symbolically layered works to date. Resembling armor for chest and back, it recalls bulletproof vests, medieval shields, and central Asian saddlebags drenched in beads. Possibly unisex as well in terms of wearability, *Brigandine* (the word alludes to an army subdivision) expands Worden's province of empowerment in the face of an increasingly powerless U.S.-led coalition force facing implacable foes in Iraq. Alluding as well to archaeological excavation sites and their precious loot, this work has a potent, current meaning that is sure to survive any contemporary conflict and act as one of the most important antiwar artworks to emerge from this misguided international conflict. Women may become empowered as soldiers as easily as men; they are also, for the first time, just as vulnerable. Seen in the context of Worden's milder necklaces and her earlier work that dealt with weight loss, for example, *Brigandine for Ishtar* may herald a new period of political seriousness, taking American art jewelry into a realm of international social consciousness. If so, Nancy Worden is sure to be on the front line.

Plate 1. Sherry Markovitz: *Chai*, 1993, glass beads and papier-mâché, 38 x 21 x 21". Becky and Jack Benaroya collection, Seattle, from "Breaking Barriers: Recent American Craft." Photo: Eduardo Calderón

Plate 2. Ken Price: *Untitled*, 1989, glazed ceramic, 3 1/2 x 5 1/2 x 2 1/2".
Courtesy of Charles Cowles Gallery, New York, from "The Myth of the Neglected
Ceramics Artist."

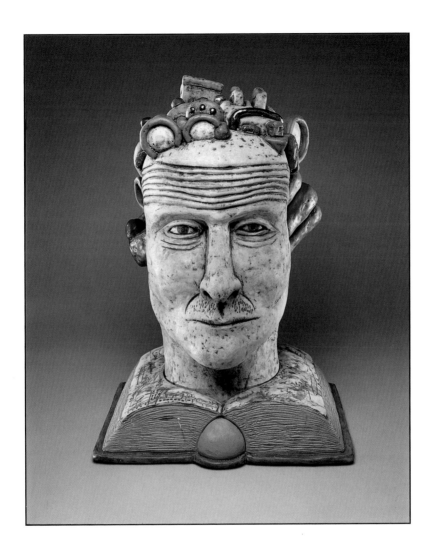

Plate 3. Allan Rosenbaum: *Tale*, 2002, earthenware, stains and glazes, 28 x 19 x 5". Courtesy of the artist, Richmond, Virginia, from "North American Ceramic Sculpture Now." Photo: Katherine Wetzel

Plate 4. Toots Zynsky: *Night Fire (Tierra del Fuego Series)*, 1989, fused glass filaments, 6 3/4 x 13 x 9". Stedelijk Museum, Amsterdam, from "Toots Zynsky: The Climate of Color." Photo: Courtesy of the artist, Providence, Rhode Island

Plate 5. Lynda Benglis: *Bratislava*, 1997, blown glass, add
dimensions. Novy Bor Glassworks, Czech Republic. Courtesy of
the artist, from "Metamorphosis: The Glass Sculptures of Lynda
Benglis." Photo: Fred Dorfman Projects, New York

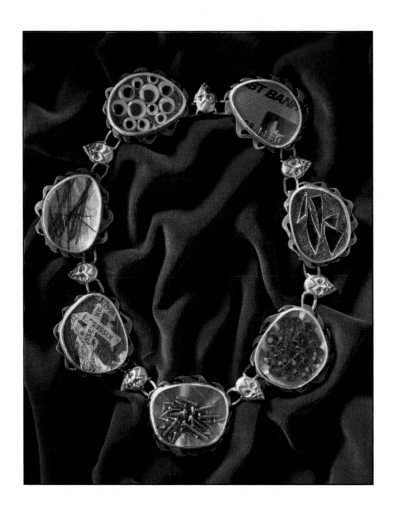

Plate 6. Nancy Worden: *Seven Deadly Sins*, 1994, silver, synthetic rubies, glass and found objects, 20 1/2 x 2 x 1/2". Courtesy of William Traver Gallery, from "Ellensburg Funky." Photo: Lynn Thompson

Plate 7. Todd Hoyer: *Peeling Orb*, 1987, turned mesquite
wood, 14 1/4 x 13 1/4 x 8". The Wornick Collection,
San Francisco, from "Sculptural Heritage and Sculptural
Implications: Turned Wood Objects in the Wornick
Collection."
Photo: M. Lee Fatherree

Plate 8. Dale Chihuly: *Untitled [Two Stacked Niijima Floats]*, 1991, blown glass with jimmies, 52 x 24 x 24". Courtesy of Chihuly Studio, Seattle, from "Dale Chihuly: Unfinished Odyssey." Photo: Claire Garoutte

PART V

TWO AMERICAN MASTERS

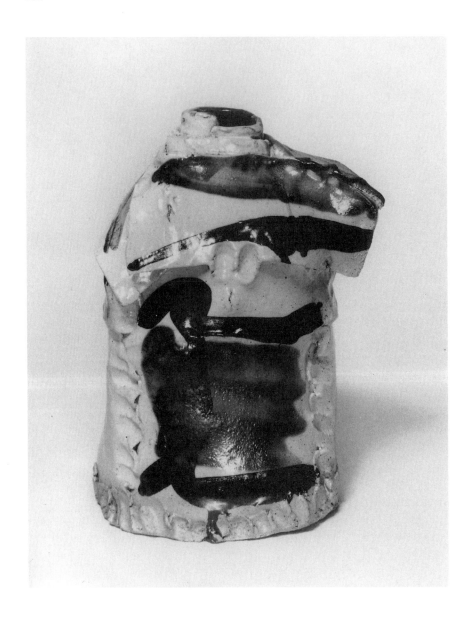

Rudy Autio: *Untitled*, 1962, stoneware with glazes, 15 x 7 x 4". American Craft Council Research and Education Dept. Photo: University of Washington Libraries, Special Collections

Rudy Autio: *Floor Vase,* 1964, hand-built stoneware, 48" h. Collection of Drs. R. Joseph and Elaine Monsen, Seattle. Photo: Dudley, Hardin and Yang

RUDY AUTIO:
MONTANA ARTIST

INTRODUCTION

In the art of Rudy Autio four essential elements merge: clay, modern
art, the natural environment, and Montana history. Along with many
other American artists who developed outside the nation's major
population centers, Rudy Autio is an artist whose career has contributed to a radical re-definition of regionalism.

Surveying American art of the past thirty years, in order to understand it as a whole, it becomes increasingly clear that one must
include ceramics. Rudy Autio has been the quiet man at the center of
the contemporary American ceramics movement that began in the art
departments of many universities after World War II. He is significant as a sensitive, supportive teacher, an articulate spokesman for
an emerging medium, and as an artist who has forged a personal way
of working with clay. Clay, more than painting or sculpture, had a
double tradition with which to contend: useful pottery such as vases
and bowls and non-useful items like figurines. Rudy Autio's art is
firmly rooted in Montana folk history, the rise of the contemporary
American ceramics movement, and the life of the artist in our times.
It relates as well to other, concurrent developments of world art.

Rudy Autio did not long remain a production potter, nor have his
achievements emerged out of virtuosity or technical mastery over the
glaze, the wheel, or the kiln. Rather, clay has served to express his
world view. Growing up in Montana, he was involved in one of the
centers of the new American ceramics in the latter half of the twentieth century, the Archie Bray Foundation.

In the first half of the century, before Autio's career began, ceramics
were primarily of a useful and decorative nature. After 1950, however, a different, and as it turns out, more significant, tradition of
twentieth-century clay arose, the sculptural or non-useful clay object.
Rudy Autio, to the degree that he makes sculptures that are nominal-
ly vessels or containers, is an artist caught between two ceramic conventions: useful pottery or ceramic fine art. He, perhaps more than
any other American ceramist, has used the container form as a point
of departure for a new art encompassing painting and sculpture.

No single exhibition or written statements, including this one, can
fully cover the depth and extent of Rudy Autio's oeuvre. Nonetheless,
his achievements have ranged across virtually every endeavor con-

fronting the modern artist: the figure, the object, the problems of form
and content, the challenge of public and corporate patronage, the
relationship of art and architecture, the conduct of an international
career, the frustrations and triumphs of full-time teaching, the master of line and color, the adaptation and assimilation of the greatest
artists of the century, and finally, the accumulation of these issues
into a body of work that resolutely stands on its own and offers the
viewer a completely individualistic vision of the world by which to his
or her own experience. This, after all, is the central function of art.

THE EARLY YEARS

To visit Butte, Montana, today is to witness the effects of the magnificent ravages of the Age of Copper in American history. Now the
mines have closed and the Anaconda Minerals Corporation, which
controlled the destinies of many Montana citizens, has withdrawn.
The huge Berkeley Pit, which gobbled up many miners' homes as it
chewed away at the eastern edge of the city, is a gaping hole, extending its life only as a tourist attraction. The legendary Metals Bank
and Trust Company, once repository of miners' salaries and the own-
ers' profits alike, is now the First Bank of Butte, part of a large bank-
ing conglomerate centered in Minneapolis. The Age of Copper has
passed, and with chapter in Montana history, a chapter Rudy Autio
has chronicled in art.

Eighty years ago, however, when Arne Rudolf Autio was born on October 8, 1926, at the Case Arms on Park Street, Butte was a bustling
center of world industry. Copper was kind and the miners and their
families its loyal and devoted subjects. Rudy's parents, Arne Autio
and Selma Wayrynen, had come from two Finnish towns, Pori and
Suomussalmi. Rudy was the third of three children, all of whom, like
their parents, spoke Finnish before English. These Finnish roots had
a great deal to do with the art that came later, and also prepared the
way for Autio's contribution at a continent's remove, as we shall see,
to another ceramic tradition in Finland.

In the 1920s and 1930s, Butte was alive with the buzz of industry and
commerce. The ore was extracted from the mines around the clock.
The thousands of inhabitants who worked in the mines came primarily from Europe: from Cornwall, from Finland, from Ireland or the
Slavic countries. They created a cosmopolitan community of working class people that continues to be proud of its varied ethnic backgrounds. They brought with them their churches as well, whether
Eastern Orthodox, Jewish, Roman Catholic, Methodist or Lutheran.

Growing up in Butte during the Great Depression, Rudy Autio saw
the Age of Copper first-hand and later contributed his own version—
through art—of both the old mining days and the presence of the
churches. His architectural projects of the 1950s and 1960s included
a bronze-and-copper mural of the history of mining in Butte for the
new Metals Bank and Trust Company building on Main Street. His
numerous clay low-relief murals of religious scenes for various Roman
Catholic, Methodist and Lutheran churches built in Montana after
1950 reflected the history of the miners' settlements in Butte and
Anaconda.

In 1946, Autio attended what was then known as Montana State
College (later to become Montana State University) at Bozeman.
Returning to Montana after a stint in the U.S. Navy, he enrolled at
M.S.C. under the G.I. Bill. It was there he met a teacher, Miss Frances Senska (herself fresh out of the WAVES), a fellow student, Peter
Voulkos (1924–2002), and his future wife, Lela Moniger. Miss Senska,
who became a leading figure in the rise of the Pacific Northwest crafts
and what museum curator T. Gervais Reed has called "The Montana
Style" in ceramics, offered no specific program or set of aesthetic dog-
ma in her design class. After her own undergraduate training in art
and graduate degree in home economics at the University of Iowa, she
had studied with three individuals who would later be seen as having
important impacts on the teaching of the decorative arts in the U.S.:
László Moholy-Nagy (1895–1946); Gyorgy Kepes (1906-add d. date),
and Maija Grotell (1899–1973). Grotell, another Finnish émigré,
taught at Cranbrook Academy of Art in Bloomfield Hills, Michigan.
The school building itself was designed by a Finnish architect, Eliel
Saarinen. Spending six weeks with Grotell in the summer of 1946,
Senska had witnessed the older artist's consummate control over
thrown stoneware forms and innovative surface decoration. Senska's
own work remained in this useful, decorative vein and subsequently
refined and expanded the range of patterns and motifs possible for
decorating the surfaces of studio-made pottery.

Earlier, during the summer of 1942, she had worked with the former
Bauhaus instructor Moholy-Nagy at the Illinois Institute of Design.
Students at the Bauhaus in pre-Nazi Germany were exposed to all
the arts and crafts through a set of design principles that carried no
hierarchical distinction between "fine" and "applied" arts. Balancing
Grotell's craftsmanlike devotion to one medium, clay, Moholy-Nagy
influenced Autio's most influential teacher, Frances Senska, with his
more flexible approach to art materials. Miss Grotell represented a
more conservative tradition of useful European—and Finnish—ce-

ramics: Moholy-Nagy, by contrast, was bringing an innovative approach to art instruction in the United States, one that would have a more far reaching effect on American art instruction—and on Rudy Autio. Moholy-Nagy elevated ideas over technique.

"Moholy's attitude toward new idea or media was 'Why not try it?,'" Miss Senska recounted in an interview at her home in Bozeman. "We would discuss and use a lot of different materials. It made sense because I was in the same boat."

Over a four-year period, Autio studied with Frances Senska at Montana State College. Besides Voulkos as a classmate, there was Rudy's future wife, Lela Moniger. Remembering the students who became towering figures in American sculptural ceramics, their former teacher recalled differences between the three friends.

"It's hard to speak of Rudy having an early style. He's always been a mature artist, sort of quiet, polite and curious. Rudy was a gentleman, Pete was so flamboyant, and Lela was so sharp that I think Rudy got a little left aside. He never had an arrogant inch."

"But stylistic evolution? I don't see it. Rudy started out 'grown up.' Pete ran through dozens of careers and styles in those days, but I don't think Rudy ever had to do that. . . . I think he was as great or greater."[1]

Graduating with a Bachelor of Science degree in 1950, Autio went on to Washington State University in Pullman, a small wheat-farming community in the state's extreme southeast corner. It was at this time that Autio came into closer contact with reproductions and photographs of vanguard European sculpture of the postwar era. During the next two years, he examined a variety of styles. Some works were linear and abstract, made of aluminum rods welded together and concentrated on industrial materials and machine-like forms, a tribute to the Constructivist tradition that began in central Europe with artists like Moholy-Nagy, Naum Gabo, and Antoine Pevsner. Others were figurative and faceted, using animals or humans or humans and animals together, more in the style of Marino Marini.

During the summer of 1951, midway through Autio's two years at W.S.U., he and Voulkos took jobs working at a brick factory, the Western Clay Company, in Helena, Montana. They had met the owner, Archie Bray, in the studio of Peter and Hank Meloy, also ceramic enthusiasts, the previous summer and needed jobs to help earn their graduate school tuition. This proved to be a highly fortuitous move. The original idea had been to work for Mr. Bray, as laborers, and fire their own ceramic creations in the large kilns alongside the bricks.

Archie Bray (1886–1953) had inherited the company from his father, a Cornish immigrant, in 1931. The rise of Montana ceramics at the Western Clay Company has been well chronicled by other writers.[2], [3] For our purposes, it is sufficient to note that Mr. Bray formed the Archie Bray Foundation in 1951 as a "non-profit educational corporation handling the business affairs of not only the pottery but eventually an entire art center."[4] While the other buildings Mr. Bray envisioned, such as a theatre and a concert hall, were never built, the Foundation did fulfill his dream of creating "a fine place to work for all who are seriously and sincerely interested in any branch of ceramic art." In the ensuing years, many potters of world stature came to Helena to work and help establish the pottery as a creative center.

The clay for the bricks came from Blossberg in the surrounding hills sixteen miles away. Though it was suitable for bricks and later used by some local ceramists (like Frances Senska), Autio soon began mixing his own stoneware clay because of technical difficulties he encountered with the Blossberg clay. His own mixture was a combination of half Kentucky ball clay and half Denver fire clay. Many years later Autio laconically commented, "Yes, we used to dig our own clays—until we found you could actually buy it in bags!"

A year later in 1952 when Voulkos returned from his graduate work at California College of Arts and Crafts and Autio had finished his Master of Fine Arts at Pullman, both continued their work as Western Clay Company laborers, but, at Mr. Bray's invitation, also stepped up their pottery production. The plates, dishes, and cups would be sold to provide income for the clay company and pay for the potters' living expenses. This worked for a while, but the two, along with another co-worker, Kelly Wong, became more interested in hand-building projects than in making production tableware.

The first non-brick objects made by Autio and Voulkos at Western Clay Company were jiggered planters, slipcast ashtrays, and dishes to be sold along with the building bricks. Autio also remembers making with Voulkos—and their wives Lela and Peggy—250 souvenir enamel-on-copper ashtrays for a convention at Yellowstone Park Lodge. It may have been experiences like this that turned Autio and Voulkos away from the tableware so prevalent at that time in American ceramics. Working during the day at the brickworks and late at night on his own art, Autio remembers using wire tools and bamboo sticks to carve clay. "We never talked about art [at this time]. We were more concerned with how to make things work,"[5] Autio added.

Voulkos moved permanently to California in 1954 to take a job at the Otis Art Institute in Los Angeles. He left behind Autio as artist-in-residence (until Rudy joined the Voulkoses for two months in 1956.) Just prior to Voulkos's departure, however, three important visitors came to Helena: Bernard Leach, Dr. Soetsue Yanagi, and Shoji Hamada. Because of Leach's subsequent influence on American vesselmaking, much has been made of the trio's visit to the Bray Foundation, and for good reasons.

Dr. Yanagi was a Zen Buddhist philosopher. Hamada was a potter who eventually founded his own museum in Japan. Leach, a complex and controversial figure, was, as Robert Sperry would later relate, "an Englishman who went to Japan to teach drawing and returned as a rather decent writer."[6] He was accompanying Hamada and Yanagi on their lecture tour throughout the United States and ended up as a self-appointed commentator on what he viewed as the sad state of American ceramics. "You," he said to Autio and Voulkos, "have no ceramic taproot." Considering he was addressing the two who would become the most important figures in the development of postwar sculptural ceramics, this was an unbelievably and unforgivably short-sighted comment. As Miss Senska put it, "I told him he was wrong. I said we had a global tradition [in America]. We came from all over the world." Additionally, as Autio pointed out in an interview, there was the strong tradition of Southwest Indian pottery.

Autio, reflecting on the trio's visit nearly thirty years later, put it this way:

> At the time, it provided a great deal of inspiration. It lifted our thinking up from one level to another. Hamada decorated so freely. But remember, we only had two weeks' contact. I think their significance may have been overstated. There were other Oriental influences as well. Hank Meloy was making his 'T'ang horses' and Pete and I were very interested in Kanjiro Kauai.

> Dr. Yanagi was the intellectual of the group; Hamada was the practitioner—he threw twenty or thirty pots while he was at Bray. And Leach was just the interpreter, more a scholar-potter.

Unlike the highly perfected forms of the time, Autio's clay shapes began to allow more of an informal or spontaneous shape to take hold. Some began on the wheel only to be completed by hand building. Others grew out of cut clay walls, which were assembled into stacked shapes similar to Northwest Indian totem shapes or the hierarchical forms of Montana's own native Americans. Always eschewing his own concern with technical mastery over the medium, Autio said,

> I let the material fly on its own. I don't try to impose excessive control on what the form will be. I think there's a kind of 'thusness' or Zen quality at work.

In addition to the Japanese visitors, Autio was becoming aware through art magazines,[7] of Picasso's adventurous ceramic activity at Vallauris, France. It is important to note that Picasso and Matisse were artists with a great deal more relevance to Autio than the Abstract Expressionists who were attaining ascendance in New York.

"We weren't even aware about Pollock, de Kooning, and the others," Autio recounted. Marini, Henry Moore, and Picasso, however, had a decisive influence on his early freestanding figurative sculpture (*Mother and Child, Family of Musicians*, c. 1952).

The summer of Leach's visit, another potter also arrived. Robert Sperry (1927–2001) stayed until December of that year when he left for the University of Washington in Seattle to work in the ceramics department with the Swiss designer, Paul Bonifas (1893–1967). It was at this time, for a short period, that three central figures of West Coast clay came together. All three would go on to head ceramics departments at university art schools. Voulkos's departure for Otis would have a tremendous impact on California ceramic art; Sperry's move to Seattle set in motion the flowering of ceramic art in Washington State over the next thirty years; Autio's tenure at Bray until 1956 (when he took over the ceramics department at the University of Montana) would lead to his series of architectural commissions. His architectural work would also create the seeds of all his later work: the use of the female figure, the perfection of incised surface decoration, and the highly individual way of throwing rolled-out slabs of clay together to form upright container shapes.

THE ARCHITECTURAL PROJECTS

"Mr. Bray would say to the architects or builders," Autio explained. "'Buy your brick here and I'll throw in a mural' or 'If you buy the brick here, I've got a kid who'll do a plaque.'" Thus it was that the young artist embarked upon a series of public commissions that can be seen throughout western Montana, and which, taken together, make up an impressive body of large-scale low-relief brick (and eventually metal and ceramic) murals. The mural subjects are sacred and secular; timeless and topical; universal and local. In the context of Autio's later sculptural work, they were important in the artist's development of carved and incised lines and in the development of public art throughout the U.S. during the 1950s and 1960s. They represented an important attempt at combining representational figuration with Modernist approaches to flat depiction and abstracted natural shapes in ceramic art.

Autio recalls that he may have gotten the idea of carved brick relief from F. Carlton Ball (1911–1992), whom he had met in the early 1950s. He has also referred to his earliest relief style as "Claremont Cubism," an allusion to the adapted Cubism of Millard Sheets, a teacher at Scripps College in Claremont, California.

Autio's first such project, and his only purely "Claremont Cubist" piece, was the Indian-motif mural on the exterior of the new Liberal Arts Hall at the University of Montana in 1952. His first major work, done around the time of his return from graduate school, the circular emblem is a distillation of the artist's interest in Montana Indian lore. The archer is a decorative medallion on a large scale, but not really integrated into the building's structure in the way his later projects would be. It seems stuck on as an architect's afterthought. It was also the last time Autio would make a mural of press-mold brick and glazed terra cotta.

The following year, 1953, Autio was given a project that offered him an opportunity to develop a modular motif for a long foyer at the Charles M. Russell Gallery. Autio constructed a repeated eight-tile module, alternating black and red, using stylized prehistoric petroglyphs incised into wet bricks. Ancient carved and scratched rock designs are prevalent at prehistoric Indian sites throughout eastern Montana. The Russell Gallery module is a significant work that represents the artist's first efforts at virtually abstract imagery, one that could still retain an identifiable or decipherable meaning. It was also Autio's initial use of the incised line on a flat surface that would become a hallmark of his later style. It also met the challenge of providing a dramatically appropriate exterior entry that could still express a young artist's own sensibility—even, in fact, in sympathy with Russell's Wild West imagery—but one that did not attempt to copy or compete with Russell's style.

That affinity between Russell and Autio—arguably Montana's two greatest artists—became more explicit in one project, the Lewis and Clark diorama executed for the Montana Historical Society in Helena. The realistic figures are fashioned from beeswax and other media and serve as the younger artist's most explicit venture into the area's history, i.e., the moment when the explorers concluded an important portion of their journey. Done to raise funds for the Bray Foundation (by this time in some difficulty after Mr. Bray's death), the diorama also has been remarked upon by a number of writers as being notable in that one of the figures in the expedition party bears a resemblance to Peter Voulkos.[8]

The Sermon on the Mount (1955), a large mural for Great Falls First United Methodist Church, contains the seeds of Autio's later style that would concentrate more on the incised clay line than on relief-carving. The figures, who are shown listening to Christ's sermon, are depicted in cut line rather than low relief. An unusual composition, the mural shows Christ from the back wearing a garment that Autio carved in long, swooping folds.

Autio returned to a historical and environmental theme the following year in his three reliefs of bulls and oxen for the Glacier County Library in Cut Bank.

His first commission from a Roman Catholic church was the *Fourteen Stations of the Cross* for St. Gabriel's parish in Chinook. here, the figures are carved relief, only a foot high with the corpus of Christ on a cross over four feet high. This was one of the few opportunities Autio had to work in a size that would later become more comfortable for him in his own studio work. The architectural projects were important to Autio, not necessarily as major aesthetic statements in and of themselves but as initial opportunities for him as a young, developing artist.

Suffer the Little Children Unto Me and *The Last Supper*, both done in 1957 for Lutheran churches in Butte and Anaconda respectively, are examples of the artist's growing control over the mural genre. His sense of narrative is more complex, his range of expressions necessarily more varied, and his densely peopled compositions more convincing than the space-filling devices of *The Sermon*. These are Autio's penultimate religious works and arguably his best architectural commissions. On the exterior of Gold Hill Lutheran Parish House in Butte, a forward-facing Christ embraces the upward-gazing children and yet seems to hover aloft at the same time. He is standing before what appear to be stylized evergreen trees in the background and is offset by brick inserts that are glazed deep blue. The entire vignette is in a cruciform shape and fits well into the peaked-roof shape of the Parish House's end wall.

In Anaconda, *The Last Supper* is both outdoors—under four entry skylights—and indoors in the First Lutheran Church's narthex. Here, Autio employed a variation of "Claremont Cubist" spatial foreshortening to great effect, and within a certain uniformity of style he has managed to individualize each of the Apostles present. Judas is on the far right looking away anxiously. Some of the Apostles are wearing prayer shawls; others are peering at Christ in wonder as if He has just told them that one of them would betray Him that night. The wine glass and pitcher before Christ are Picassoid in their attenuated geometric forms as is the small circular halo, which Autio placed above rather than behind His head.

The mural sustained some vandalism in 1973 but was repaired by the artist and is now enclosed in an extension of the narthex. This, at least, should insure its future safety and material integrity for some time. It is an important piece of American public art.

Two years later, in 1959, Autio returned to explicit historical themes in *Early Days in Last Chance Gulch*, which was commissioned by the then Union Bank and Trust Company (later Northwestern Bank) that is situated on Helena's main street, the original Last Chance Gulch. Over seventy feet long, the mural behind the tellers' cages includes prospectors, placer miners, claim-jumpers, freighters, "mountain men," Chinese "coolies," the ever-present "Eastern financier," and a burly Irishman in a bowler hat. Thus, without alluding to a specific historic event—unlike the Lewis and Clark diorama—Autio created a series of social and historical stereotypes that have great popular appeal.

The work is constructed of eighteen separate panels of fired and vitrified clay with a soft lead glaze. Autio overlapped the various tiles, however, and the effect is one of a continuous panorama. It is an instructive antidote to the detail and specificity of the Lewis and Clark diorama. During Autio's 1956 sojourn in California, where he came into contact with the Otis Art Institute clay group (then reeling from the arrival of Peter Voulkos), he also met sculptor John Mason who was also working in large-scale clay murals. Perhaps that meeting was the impetus for Autio's only completely abstract ceramic relief murals, done five years later for the Roland R. Renne Library at his alma mater, Montana State University in Bozeman. Embedded in the right side of the brick facade of the building they offer strong evidence of Autio's difficulty with fully abstract images; his mature work has always had its roots in the recognizable world. The many-faceted surfaces have an earthy rough look to them. One could possibly make a visual analogy to the surrounding Montana hills or valleys as an image source but in the overwhelming context of the four-story building, they stand as Autio's least successful architectural work. Whereas the religious and historical themes retain an artistic autonomy of their own within the overall architectural plan, this tends to blend in too well, to be easily forgotten or ignored by the thousands of students who have passed them by since their installation.

Autio's final religious commission was *Saint Anthony and Child* (1963) for Saint Anthony's Roman Catholic Church in Missoula. It is not by any means a summing up of this aspect of the artist's work, but it does comprise a competent detail for the exterior site of a brick church. Reviewing Autio's ecclesiastical commissions, one might say they are more significant within his development as an artist for keeping the figure alive, so to speak, than for making contributions to religious art per se. Autio, a nonbeliever but an obliging and cooperative Montana state artist, was called upon to perform a public service. To overvalue the aesthetic quality of these works because of their number and scale, however, would be to create an imbalance of judgment. As with the artist's secular architectural commissions, their importance lies in the opportunities they afforded the artist to develop a strong scratched or incised clay line.

Two final projects, *Mining in Butte* (1968) and *Nature and Ecology* (1971) round out Autio's architectural oeuvre. The former was executed in brazed steel and enameled copper. It is a remarkable example of how a public artwork can deal with specific industrial history and yet transcend such limitations of subject matter while standing as a Modernist work of art on its own grounds. His secret was the use of generalized abstract images.

The new Metals Bank and Trust Company building at Park and Main Streets (later renamed First Bank of Butte) actually contains two murals side by side that comprise *Mining in Butte*. The left-hand mural is over thirty feet long and is essentially a huge irregularly curved panel that reads as a stylized cross-section of the city of Butte in early days. Ore cars carrying the copper out of the mines are prominent as are the large gallows-frames that stood over the mineshafts. Elsewhere, plumes of smoke create a unifying, baroque line throughout the scene and lead from gallows-frame to shafts to waste dumps. Hard-hatted miners are caught in profile, mid-action, and surrounded by abstract shapes, suggesting industrial structures or houses.

On the right-hand side, another brazed steel and enamel copper panel over thirty feet long completes Autio's ambiguous narrative of the Montana copper industry—and, of course, of the town of his youth, Butte. It contains a cross-section of miners underground and uses sharp angles, curves, and half-circles to suggest sluice paths, shaft entries, and ore car tracks. A large cloud hangs beside the scene with spots of red, gold, and blue punctuating the bright metallic surfaces of both sections. Autio accomplished a feat many other artists would have found daunting and contradictory: how to treat a theme of industrial development, popular history, and serious environmental pollution for a corporate client without or giving into a predictably illustrational style. Once again, Autio's training provided for treat-

ing the theme with enough literal references to convey a story while
keeping it in a realm of nuance and ambiguous forms. Considering
that the mines are closed now, a specific chapter of Butte's history is
over, and the bank is no longer even locally owned, *Mining in Butte*
stands as more than an aesthetic evocation of an age gone by; it demonstrates the elusive and independent qualities of a style—Modernism—and how that style in the right hands can face and survive the
contradictory demands of public or corporate clients. Even so, Autio
wrote at the time,

> While a mining theme has been used, no effort has been made
> to represent the operational aspects of the copper industry. The
> primary intent of the sculpture is decorative, and should be enjoyed,
> it is my hope, for this reason alone

Autio's final ceramic mural, *Nature and Ecology* (1971), was installed
in the new Security State Bank of Polson, near Flathead Lake. This is
a large work that contains in seed-form the imagery that has dominated Autio's slab sculpture for the past decade (1973–1983). Bison,
deer, salmon, bears, Bighorn sheep, geese, and beavers are all present
beneath a stylized panorama of mountains, clouds, streams, and a
sunset over Flathead Lake. These are some of the animals that appear on the sides of the painted clay-slab sculptures Autio has subsequently made.

Nature and Ecology also uses a wide range of low-fire glazes that
anticipates the brighter colors Autio would employ toward the end of
the 1970s. Blue, green, red, and yellow balance brown, orange, and
black. In a town as small as Polson, the cultural impact of a piece this
large and of such high quality cannot be overestimated. The bank
regularly hosts exhibitions of local artists in its lobby and much of the
art, not surprisingly, are landscapes or reflect environmental themes.
The central position of the mural within the town doubly anchors *Nature and Ecology* within the community. The proximity of the artist's
summer home and the many happy years spent in the region come
together in this felicitous work. It is the capstone of Autio's public
architectural projects and a hymn to the Montana countryside with
its delicate balance of man, land, and animal.

SQUARING THE CIRCLE

Most of the pieces in Autio's 1983 retrospective at the University of
Montana dated from 1963–1983, Autio's most fertile period of work.
Discussion thus far, however, has centered on those works that were
a part of the artist's development but which were not necessarily a
part of the exhibition. This has been necessary for two reasons: first,

in order to chronicle the historical and biographical context of Autio's place in midcentury American ceramics; secondly, to document and analyze the architectural projects that prepared the way for the work which came later, but of necessity cannot travel with this exhibition and are visited by few people.

The themes of the female nude, the land, and animals did not emerge simultaneously or immediately; they were a gradual outgrowth of the artist's changing interests, his work on the various architectural jobs, and his idiosyncratic approach to surface decoration. An examination of some of the vessels reveals that at first they had no recognizable imagery on their surfaces (*Button Pot*, 1965). Other of the earlier pieces were not vessels at all, but attempts at freestanding animal shapes (*Angry Young Bird*, 1957; *Chicken and Egg*, 1956). Neither of these strains, however, was fully successful in resolving questions of form or content. They were also generally small in scale as was most of the freestanding work Autio did while at Bray (19511956).

After leaving the Foundation and moving on to the University of Montana, Autio's mature style emerged. Within a few years he hit upon what were to become the hallmark shape and image: the squar-ish slab vessel and the female form cut into its surface.

It is true, if one scoured the history of world ceramics, that precedents for the square-circle forms could be found. Japanese Igaware, for example, offers one such instance; certain of Peter Voulkos's pieces do also; Autio's production at this time (ca. 1960) also vaguely resembles some African pottery. And the Abstract Expressionist sculptor, Reuben Nakian (1897–1986), was making incised clay slabs too, often with a female nude form. More important, though, was the issue of expedi-ency. Autio's comments about the material "flying on its own" are more to the point than historical origins. Perhaps without knowing why, he began working in a mode that would afford the opportunity for easy construction and flat surfaces to decorate. At the same time, with grow-ing assurance and skill, Autio increased the size of his work.

Patti Warashina has spoken about the "front and back" aspect of Autio's vessels of the early 1960s and how impressed she was by that division of decorated surfaces. Rather than a continuous circular pat-tern (in the manner of Greek vases or Maija Grotell), they seemed to have distinct and opposite sides. This was sort of squaring the circle or flattening out the sphere, which became common to much Pacific Northwest ceramics of the period. It is nothing less than the observ-able process of rendering the clay object less functional. By rolling out the slab and then building it up around a hollow core, Autio created for himself a painter's canvas and gave the impression of shattering the vessel form itself—or disregarding its integrity.

Paul Soldner and Susanne Stephenson, among others, were doing this too, but, unlike Autio, they retained the vestigial container form in a more direct way; for Autio it became "residual" rather than "primary." A similar case could be made for Robert Sperry's dishes, which became increasingly flattened out into tablets—or *tabulae rasae*—for painterly decoration.

Why did this happen? Because none of the Northwest ceramists of the mid-century period trained as potters per se; they came to clay, as did Autio and Sperry, as sculptors or painters. This is another reason it makes more sense to discuss their work as a union of painting and sculpture instead of as consistent evolutions within the vessel tradition. This is why an investigation of the iconography of their work is a key to its deeper meaning.

After all, as Autio's work progressed at Missoula through the 1970s, there was no longer any need to keep up the illusion of the object being useful. It appears that what mattered to Autio was the union of exterior form and surface decoration, of painting and sculpture. The critic is concerned with the imagery of the surface decoration.

The issue of usefulness or function and the presence of the vessel has been paramount lately in the discussion of American ceramics. It is not at all an appropriate dimension in looking at the art of Rudy Autio. He has disregarded it himself both in his own comments and in the very appearance of his works. The slabs are rolled out and built up as a pretext for covering over with engobes, low-fire glazes, and the scratched, sensuous line. This has been a pretext for what Autio has called "painting with a trowel."

One can admire the spontaneity of construction, the rough edges, the thickness of wall, the inspired casualness, but, again, they are more a logical extension of an artist's drawings and a desire to create a painted, sculptural surface, than any devotion to a continuous tradition of container making. In this, Autio *is* the ceramic taproot Leach pined for; he is, along with a number of other West Coast artists, a taproot of contemporary clay sculpture.

THE FIGURE, THE BEAST, THE LAND, THE BIG SKY

Gretta Baltscheffskij, in *Savisepo*, the official journal of the Finnish china company, Arabia, asked Rudy Autio if the women and animals on his ceramic sculptures had any significance. "Not necessarily," he answered with typical modesty. "They exist for their own sake."

Nonetheless, they are the central images in his art of the past two decades. Existing "for their own sake," they also exist for the sake of the
individual viewer—and the critic: to appreciate, to ponder, to enjoy,
to interpret. They are symbols of humankind in the wilderness, the
interface between the feminine and the masculine, the intellectual
and the erotic.

They are that and more. On one level, they are surface-covering for
vessels; some might argue that they are only that—pottery decoration. That interpretation would consign their significance as art to the
historical relationship of surface design to pottery and, indeed, allusions could be found to earlier examples of simple, repeated, brightly
colored decoration in ceramics.

For example, the majolica Autio saw in 1963 during his Tiffany Fellowship in Italy. To uphold that view, though, would be to unduly diminish the aesthetic force of those images and to undercut criticism's
role in the New Ceramics. In the same way that one may examine an
heraldic plate or ceremonial tureen and posit a sociology of decoration, that is, an historical repository of designs reflecting a society,
so may one examine the many sculptures of Rudy Autio and draw
certain conclusions about the environment they were created in, the
society they reflect—and even the artist who made them.

What are the properties of Autio's hallmark sculptures? They are an
intertwining of the female figure, the animal or beast, and the hills of
Montana. Take the roughly twisted and formed slabs as an allusion to
the Montana hills. Take the Montana hills as a synecdoche of the entire Far West. The curves and slabs of Rudy Autio's sculptures are the
hills surrounding the towns of western Montana where he has spent
his life: Missoula, Bozeman, Helena, Polson. At first, in the earliest
Archie Bray work, there was even a literal link between the hills and
the art—the clay came from the hills around Helena. He soon turned
to using clay that could accentuate rough edges and sensuous forms
better than the clay from the actual hills. Thus, the shapes contain
the physicality of the female form and embody the lay of the land in
the foothills of the Rocky Mountains.

Floor Vase (1963) is one of the earliest examples of the female form
contained within the vessel shape—it even has a huge lid. The women
look Japanese. Autio's debt to Matisse's line drawings of women is a
possible source for these images, but *Floor Vase* is a strong demonstration of his interest in the Japanese printmaker, Shiro Munakata.
Voulkos had given Autio one of Munakata's woodcuts (which he still
cherishes today) and the sharp features and simple lines are defi-

nitely evident in Autio's transference of the female form to the sides of this large ceremonial-looking pot.

Frances Senska has pointed out how, rather than Japanese or French-Modernist, the features of the women on *Floor Vase* and the subsequent sculptures might be seen as Finnish given their high cheekbones and robust figures.

Be that as it may, *Floor Vase* gave way to the more unitary form of the untitled piece (1962–63), which was first shown at the 23rd Ceramic National sponsored by the Everson Museum of Art in Syracuse, New York. That piece has clearer links to Picasso than to Matisse. It recalls the Spanish artist's work at Vallauris, specifically *Lady in Mantilla* (1949) and Woman on *a Tile*, though both were done over ten years earlier. Although these works are not useful pottery, they depict the female form. Autio may also have gained a sense of the union between painting and sculpture from Picasso's clay pitchers of the period. While Picasso's work was mostly coil-built, cast, or thrown, Autio's work of this time is a combination of all. Many of the forms seem to have begun on the wheel and have been completed with the hand-built slab.

In 1962, the Autios visited the Seattle World's Fair, where the Montana artist saw his first examples of art by Willem de Kooning. The Dutch-born Abstract Expressionist's female figures (*Woman IV*, 1953) impressed the younger artist deeply as did the comparably expansive brushwork of the French-Canadian *automatiste*, Jean-Paul Riopelle (*Good Weather*, 1960). These two painters seem important for Autio's later development, just as some of the sculptures on view in the large international exhibition might be said to have confirmed a tendency in Autio's work up to this point.

Marino Marini's *Miracle I* and *Miracle II* (1958–60) were large abstract bronze sculptures at the World's Fair and very similar to Autio's unglazed, multi-faceted clay work of the late 1950s. Fritz Wotruba's tall stone *Two Figures* (1949–50) seemed to emerge slowly out of their carved form; the "unfinished" look of Autio's clay figures might be traceable back to Wotruba and, before that, to Michelangelo's "unfinished" slaves that the artist saw in the Florence Academy during his Tiffany travels. Much of the sculpture in curator Willem Sandberg's international wing of "Art Since 1950"[9] at Century 21 was a combination of heavily faceted forms and singular monumentality, such as the Argentine Sesostris Vitullo's wooden *Dead Christ* (1949) or Henry Moore's two-part *Reclining Figure* (1961). Thus, Autio's own version of international—and regional-Modernism developed gradu-

Rudy Autio: *Sculpture*, 1961, hand-built stoneware, 36 x 18 x 12".
American Craft Council Research and Education Dept. Photo:
University of Washington Libraries, Special Collections

ally, partly the result of his own inner direction and partly the result of the art he saw first-hand at this time.

Since then, Montana and the rest of the nation (and Finland) have witnessed the flourishing of Rudy Autio. From the voluptuous prostitutes of his youth in Butte (*Fallen Doves*) to the equally robust young lasses of Missoula who occasionally serve as his models (*Big Ellie*), Autio has blended memory and flesh into the figures of his art.

Some, like *Beauty and the Beast* (1980), have implied narrative. Others have alluded to historical events or western locales (*Victorville Ladies*). Still others have strong links to his painted and colored drawings—themselves worthy of an exhibition. The dozens of large drawings executed since early 1980 are another logical development in the artist's long-standing interest in line. They have come after the artist's mastery of the cut clay line, however, and their subject matter has most often revolved around a female figure with an attentive animal: dog, wolf, coyote, horse, elk, or cow.

It is in these recent pieces that the artist has moved into his current phase. Rodeo queens, bucking broncos—as in *Rodeo Covered Jar*—reclining or agitated nudes, all have come together as inhabitants of the world of Rudy Autio—and of the rich historical heritage and ecological beauty of the state of Montana.

The jumping cutthroat trout, the salmon, the blue skies of "Big Sky Country," these, too, comprise a part of this joyous body of work. In their collective presence, viewers are able to see clearly the obvious image-roots. They are affirmative, optimistic, and indelibly associated with a positive zest for living. Taking into consideration their particular context within the artist's evolution may add to that enjoyment. Encountering them as distinct art objects one at a time, walking around them to see the "front and back" of Rudy Autio, and then judging them for oneself will be the more significant procedures.

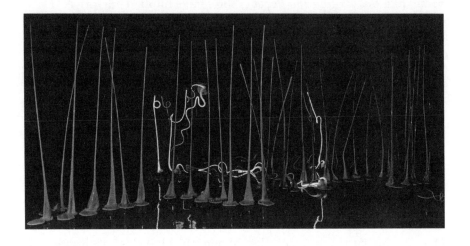

Dale Chihuly and James Carpenter: *Glass Environment*, 1971, blown glass and neon, dimensions variable. Collection of Museum Bellerive, Zürich, Switzerland. Photo: Chihuly Studios

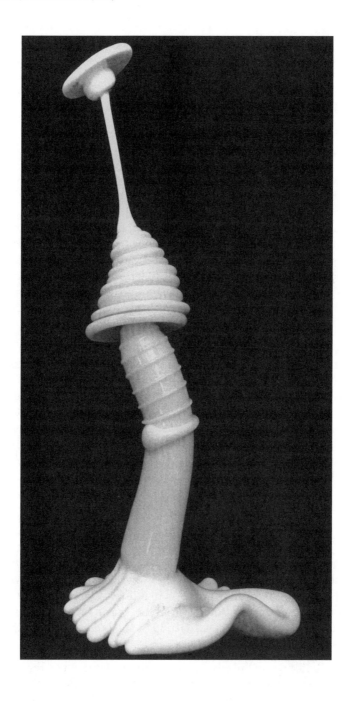

Dale Chihuly: *Untitled*, 1971, blown glass, 15 x 7 x 6".
Courtesy of Chihuly Studios. Photo: Bob Hanson

DALE CHIHULY:
UNFINISHED ODYSSEY

INTRODUCTION

As a child I did comb the beach for bits of colored glass.

—Dale Chihuly[1]

A child walks along a beach on Puget Sound as a northern sun sets behind the Olympic Mountains. He stops in his beachcombing to pick up and ponder a broken bit of glass, washed smooth by time and the ocean's activity. While he sits on the beach, his fingers caressing the fragment of glass with one hand, he scoops up a bunch of sand with the other hand and lets the sand run through his fingers. With the sky turning a brilliant orange above the water and the mountains, a memory is born linking the color of the sun, the shard of glass, and its origin, the sand.

Though we cannot document or record such an event in the life of America's greatest glassmaker, Dale Chihuly, it might have gone something like that. For Chihuly's art suggests the strongest affinity imaginable to glass' origins and its plastic and liquid powers. More than any other American artist, including Louis Comfort Tiffany, Chihuly has understood his chosen medium's inherent properties and extended their limits at every step in his long career. The sunset containing the entire color spectrum serves as a symbol for Chihuly's attitude to color: it is always an outgrowth of nature. As one of his mottoes has been "Follow nature," so in our search for the origins, development, and meaning of his art, it will be ours, too; to "follow nature" is to find Chihuly.

The art of Dale Chihuly is an art of transmission and innovation. It is he who unlocked the secrets of Venetian glass and brought them to the New World. It is he who used glass as a material to confront contemporary art developments on their own ground. It is he who elevated a craft's material properties to a level of art in a period when an established and institutionalized avant-garde favored concept over all else and feared craft's open attitude to the beauty of technique for its own sake.

As we shall discover, Chihuly has radically redefined the limits of how and what a contemporary artist can do. His work with a team, his dismissal of the unique masterpiece concept, his non-linear developments of styles, and his thorough reconstruction of the nature of color itself all require explanation.

Like the tiny bits of glass Chihuly made adhere to his vessels as "draw-ings", written commentary about Chihuly has also been numerous but in discrete pieces and chunks. What follows is an attempt to bring to-gether the best of those thoughts into a guide for the interested viewer. Added to that are connecting aids which seek to place Chihuly in the context of both art and craft for, like an increasing number of American creators, he is the product of both backgrounds. Indeed, he is among the major cultural figures of our age to merge both art and craft and, in so doing, attain appreciation in his own country, in Japan, and on the continent to which he is most indebted, Europe.

EARLY BACKGROUND:
A NORTHWEST DESIGNER CRAFTSMAN

Long before the night he experimented with a steel pipe attempting to blow into the melted glass he had heated in a kiln in the basement of a friend's home in Seattle, Dale Chihuly was in love with thread. Weav-ing is the key to understanding Chihuly's earliest use of glass. His efforts to recapture the satisfying linear quality of the weaving experi-ence drove him later to setting grids of glass threads onto heated glass cylinders. The results, done in collaboration with Kate Elliott, James Carpenter, and Italo Scanga at Pilchuck in 1974, were a combination of weaving's appearance and the innovation of drawing on glass.

Unlike glass, weaving is a solitary activity, meditative and plodding. As taught at the University of Washington architecture and interior design program, where Chihuly was a student (1959, 1963–65), it was presented with the utmost seriousness. Immersed in the same pro-gram that produced another great American craftsman, Jack Lenor Larsen, Chihuly studied the craft of weaving with Doris Brockway. Warren Hill and the late Hope Foote led the interior design program within the college of architecture and hammered into the young man from Tacoma a grasp of color which was at once architectural, contex-tual, and intuitive.

When one examines the woven room divider or window panels the young undergraduate student made, the color relationships are sys-tematic, professional, attractive—and unimaginative. It was while en-rolled in a "Design in Materials" class under Professor Steven Fuller that Chihuly first added bits of fused glass to the weavings he made on his own looms.

Chihuly benefited from the top-flight professionalism of the interiors program at the University of Washington in more ways than one. First, it strengthened and challenged his already innate color sense.

Next, it forced him to consider the art object in the context of the containing space or, put another way, it gave him an enduring sense for the site-relation of the art object which would strongly affect all his blown-glass environments. Most importantly, it made him aware, as it had for Larsen, of the entire history of design, the decorative arts, and their honorable heritage and relationships to the fine arts.

With the International Style riding high in Seattle architecture at the time (1959–1965), Chihuly caught the fever of the elegant functional design of interiors which, as was becoming the case in a growing number of Seattle buildings, mixed and matched the outside of the building to the inside.

All this philosophy was embodied in the Northwest Designer Craftsmen group, founded by, among others, Hope Foote and Warren Hill in 1955, in order to make available to architects and collectors appropriate high-quality work in ceramics, fiber, textile, glass, metals, jewelry, and wood.[2] Chihuly won an early award.

Building on his strong training and not yet considering himself an artist, Chihuly became the only student that year graduating in the class of 1965 to secure a position at the city's largest architectural firm, John Graham Associates. He got the job on the basis of winning a national competition for designing a master bedroom interior. Architects of the Space Needle, Seattle's residual symbol of the 1962 World's Fair, Graham Associates was large, corporate, and impersonal—like their buildings. At best, Chihuly's route there had been circuitous. He had interrupted his university education twice for extended sojourns in Europe and, within six months at Graham, left to concentrate on making stained glass.

It was at this time, 1961, in the basement of Fred Frey's little house on South Kenyon Street in the South Park area of Seattle, that Chihuly tentatively grabbed a steel pipe and blew into the glass he was melting for his weavings. Fortunately, he was hooked the minute the bubble appeared.

By 1966, after college, Europe and his first architectural job, there was really only one place to go to study glassblowing, short of getting a factory job: the University of Wisconsin in Madison. Harvey K. Littleton had set up a program there a few years before. Using the advances discovered by Dominick Labino (1910–1987) for melting glass at lower temperatures in 1962, Littleton virtually invented the American studio glass movement in a series of workshops at the Toledo Museum of Art.[3] Chihuly spent only one year in Madison (receiving a special dispensation for a one-year master's degree) but it was there that another fateful event occurred, his introduction to the team concept of blowing glass.

Although he spent much of the time with the painters, Andy Krantz, Michael Lawson, and Abe Rothblatt, it was Chihuly's work with fellow glass students, Fritz Dreisbach and Michael Whitley, who propelled him deeply and rapidly into the art of glassblowing. The three spent long hours and all their spare time working together in the hot shop. They met with Littleton only two mornings a week for sparse commentary and encouragement.

Within a month, according to Chihuly[4] he lost interest in the functional vessel shape, began exploring organic sculptural forms, and even tried neon for the first time. It was the height of the hippie era and Madison, Wisconsin, along with Ann Arbor, Michigan and Berkeley, California was one of the movement's nerve points. Experimentation on all fronts was encouraged and glass was, at this time, the newest and least institutionalized of craft materials being used in the U.S. The sky was the limit.

Leaving the Madison campus during the "summer of love", 1967, Chihuly accepted a teaching assistantship at the Rhode Island School of Design where he would spend, off and on, the next ten years. The chrysalis of the designer craftsman was about to fall off and be replaced by the butterfly wings of the classic sixties artist.

ON THE EAST COAST: AN ARTIST EMERGES

"Strange brew. . . . Girl, what's inside of you?"

—Cream

The late sixties and the entire decade of the 1970s were a period of intense growth, experimentation, and movement for Chihuly. The activities he undertook both looked backward to his heritage as a Northwest designer craftsman and forward to his new status as an environmental and conceptual sculptor using glass. His encounter with a freshman student at RISD, James Carpenter, and a visiting lecturer, artist Italo Scanga, would spur further undertakings in both directions.

When he arrived in Providence, Rhode Island, Chihuly had already begun exploring neon in Madison. In *First Neon Experiment* (1967), he added commercial neon tubing to a central blown sphere and hooked up a supply of argon gas. Illuminated in a darkened room, the piece had its popular-cultural analogy in the black-light environments of the hippies. In several subsequent pieces continued in Providence, the young artist combined more glass tubing with neon, argon, and mercury, all ignited for illumination by a high-frequency electronic coil. One such piece, *Form* (1968) was selected by curator Lee Nordness for the watershed exhibition at the Museum of Contemporary Crafts (now Museum of Arts and Design), *Objects, U.S.A.* (1970). These experimental works seem less than fully realized as art objects today but they represent the artist's finite explorations of the conductive power of glass and its relation to scientific research. The pale green tint of the tubing and the clinical appearance of the coil container would have been at home in Dr. Frankenstein's laboratory. Small in scale at 12 inches high, they were preparations for subsequent experiments on a much larger scale which Chihuly would undertake with Carpenter throughout the late 1960s and early 1970s.

Once in Providence, Chihuly set up a studio in a former mortuary off campus with extensive disused underground chambers. He made contact with a local neon technician, Bob Reed, who reminded him of neon's origins in the 1920s and its various gaseous properties. Soon, Chihuly was blowing nine-foot-long tubular forms and filling them with neon. The results were seen by very few people but they were an extension of Chihuly's growing mastery over site, environment, and the important role glass could play as a flexible sculptural element within such a context. For our purposes, they represented Chihuly's ongoing examination of natural forms and, because they were created in so flexible a material as glass, they were a parallel but critical activity in relation to the dominant strain of installation art in the 1970s: Minimal art.

With its geometric rigidity, repeated forms, and orderly presentation, Minimal art extended Modernism's chastened forms and resistance to representational allusions. True child of the sixties, Chihuly extended an organic, "flower power" imagery into his "glass forests" (done in collaboration with Carpenter), large upright blown forms in room-size settings; his smaller, neon-filled sculptures which exploited glass' power to form "blob" shapes connected to the thinnest possible flowing tubes; and into colored and white glass pieces which held an affinity to the West Coast "Funk art" sensibility.

"Funk art" grew out of the original hippie haven, San Francisco, and nearby Berkeley was the site of the definitive survey of such art, "Funk", organized by curator and critic Peter Selz at the University Art Museum in 1967.[5] Like much of the art on view in "Funk", Chihuly's freestanding pedestal sculptures of milky or black glass took on a decidedly erotic character. Several untitled works of 1971 pair ribbed phallic forms with conical openings either amusingly upright or in one case collapsed and at rest over the edge of a shiny stainless steel box.

These works are important because, among other things, they foretell
a comparable sublimated anatomical character in Chihuly's later *Sea
Forms*. Though ostensibly maritime in their allusions, *Sea Forms* are
undeniably sexual as well and reiterate another aspect of Chihuly's
ties to natural imagery. The flower blossom, after all, is the focus of
pollenization for a bee and, throughout his career, Chihuly has played
with these forms derived from nature. One tends to forget that "flower
power" was also called "love power" and that the atmosphere of the
sixties was strongly tied to a sexual revolution which emblemized the
flower as a symbol of fertility, sexual attraction, and natural ornament.
When one examines this period of Chihuly's work, the technical feats so
widely admired at the time must also be seen in the light of abstracted
petal, stems, tendrils, and stamens. Spectacularly upright with lambent floor-based petals, the "glass forests" are simultaneously male and
female and set a precedent for symbolic elements which would persist
on and off during the next 20 years.

James Carpenter's projects with Chihuly between 1969 and 1976
drew upon the latter's latent allegiances to the Northwest designer
craftsman aesthetic and Carpenter's affinity to design, and seventies
Process Art. With the company they formed in Providence in 1975,
J.C. Associates, both artists designed and executed a series of stained
glass windows for private clients and architectural interiors. Though
he worked at Graham Associates for barely six months, Chihuly
learned the architect's vocabulary well: blueprints, material availability, and cost estimates. In a series of tall doors, the two adapted
large blown rondel forms set into a leaded framework. They grew
out of Chihuly's admiration for circular and organic forms and were
complemented, however, with simpler, flatter pieces in which Chihuly's mastery of weaving patterns came in handy. Still other windows
adapted an irregular flagstone pattern which broke the regularity of
the warp-weft look and used softer, blush-like colors punctuated with
blue accents at the "flagstone's" intersections.

Two less utilitarian projects of Chihuly's and Carpenter's which
brought them art world attention and changed the face of American
studio glass were the installations, *20,000 Pounds of Neon and Ice*
and *Glass Environment* (both 1971). In *20,000 Pounds*, the artists
met Minimalism on its own ground, the repetitive block, but instead
of Carl Andre's soldier-like rows of cedar or stone, Chihuly and
Carpenter laid out large blocks of dry ice which, of course, gradually
melted but which were filled with red, yellow, blue, and green neon
gas. *Glass Environment* expanded the loopy free-standing or suspended blown elements and was originally shown at the Museum of

Contemporary Crafts before becoming permanently installed at the
Museum Bellerive in Zürich, Switzerland.

One other Chihuly-Carpenter collaboration worth mentioning was
the limited line of functional dishes, bowls, and vases they designed
and made for Steuben Glass, a subsidiary of Corning glass since 1918.
These works represent the other extreme of Chihuly's discourse on
glass, straightforward seemingly conservative glassware. At first, the
pieces seem perfect tributes to the Steuben tradition: clear, well pro-
portioned, and elegant. One might even find allusions to the forms, if
not the surfaces, of 19th-century American lead-cut crystal.

Designed and executed in 1973 and 1974, the Steuben series should
also be seen in the devilish context of Chihuly's blatant erotic blown
forms. Inspected more closely, the "historic" look of the Steuben
series gives way to outlandish figurative elements—pelvises, breasts,
nipples, triple-knobbed phalluses, and ovoid orifices, in all, suggestive
shapes. This raises them above the level of function and places them
on a plateau of high satire and spoof. Several of the pieces appear to
come in double, male and female, parts, each of which is amusingly
"inserted" into the other. The point is, whatever he touched, even traditional tableware, Chihuly left the imprint of his own style, his driving sensibility to "follow nature," wherever it might lead. Once again,
growth or, in this case, conception and intercourse, were the subjects.

CHIHULY IN VENICE: THE CODE IS BROKEN

Glass has been blown in Venice, Italy, since as early as 982 A.D. A
key part of the Serene Republic's foreign trade hegemony, the secrets
of particular Venetian processes were jealously guarded for centuries.
Renegade or exiled artisans were even sought out and, in some cases,
killed to keep them from divulging the formulas or methods related to
the collaborative fabrications in glass.

On a corresponding level, the European discovery of porcelain was literally locked up by Augustus the Strong, Elector of Saxony, at Meissen, Germany, when in 1715, alchemists matched the appropriate
high-firing temperature with the exact ratio of clay body and kaolin.
Perhaps to their surprise, they were immediately placed under house
arrest by the Elector's guard and remained comfortably imprisoned
for years so that the precious formula would not be leaked.

It is hard to imagine that the glassblowing process in Italy would still
be the subject of such closely guarded concern as late as 1968 but,
when Chihuly wrote over 200 Italian glass manufacturers inquiring about coming to work, he was met with stunned silence from all

except one, the Venini Factory on the island of Murano, across the lagoon from Venice.

Thus, in the midst of his stay in Providence and before his collaborations with young Carpenter, Chihuly returned to Venice, which he had first visited in 1962 as a student bumming around Europe.

As has been previously recounted,[6] Chihuly's Fulbright year at Venini was more one of close observations than his customarily prolific production. He found an ally in Ludovico Diaz de Santillana (1931–1989), the company's director who, like Chihuly, had an architectural background. Eventually, Chihuly made proposals for a large-scale architectural glass installation competition the firm was entering and also for a neon-filled spherical glass lamp. Neither was ever built nor put into production. More significantly for our purposes, it was the close teamwork Chihuly observed among the factory workers on Murano that influenced his subsequent work and, in turn, changed the face of American studio glass. As Karen S. Chambers has pointed out,

> Littleton made it possible for the artist to work directly with glass in the studio. Chihuly has provided another model for the American movement—teamwork, the traditional [Venetian] way of working with glass with each member assigned a specific task in preparing a piece to be finished by the master or gaffer.[7]

Although later series of Chihuly's would allude specifically to Venini production models and those of other 20th-century Italian maestri, the initial impact of Muranese procedures on Chihuly was more important than the objects being manufactured there. With typical American aplomb, Chihuly responded to a given standard by rebelling against it, or doing exactly the opposite. That is, the pride of the Italian teams was always their ability to reproduce exactly and repeatedly whatever the maestro or designer had planned. This is necessary in a production setting, of course, but to Chihuly it was superfluous when creating unique artworks. So, when he returned to America, it was the division of labor he incorporated into his studio process. Fortunately for the history of American crafts, this was precisely the information-sharing or technology transfer, if you will, which liberated American glass from the solitary, one-man, one-blow approach to the more elaborate and group-sensitive approach of the European system. (This crucial difference is discussed at greater length in the section below, "Process: The Question of Authorship"). Suffice it to say, Chihuly's *Italienischereise* was, like Goethe's, formative and influential in the extreme. It underscored a collaborative desire he already had and equipped him with personnel and management skills to instruct the individual members of any team he might assemble. Once back in

Providence where he was named head of the RISD glass department, the secret code of European artisan glass up to that point, simply the specific division of labor, had been broken for all time.

Reversing Goethe's journey on the map from Germany to Italy, Chihuly began in Italy and went north to Germany in the summer of 1969. On a pilgrimage of sorts, he sought out and met the leading Central European glass artists: Erwin Eisch in Germany and Jaroslava Brychtová and Stanislav Libenský in the Czechoslovakia.

As Chihuly began to instruct year after year of students and co-workers, the look of his glass and, in turn, that of his assistants' own work, radically changed. A more complicated and elaborate object was now possible. With several people involved, individual decorative elements could be prepared and applied at successive stages in the heating of the glass. Without realizing it, Chihuly's teams were touching on another aspect of contemporary art practice in the 1970s: performance art. Glass had come out of the arcane closet of Venice and onto the theatrical stage of America.

THE 360° DRAWING:
BLANKETS, CYLINDERS, & JAMES JOYCE'S *ULYSSES*

No matter how theatrical or experimental Chihuly's excursions were in the late 1960s and early 1970s, he still was drawn back to the precedent of weaving: flat, linear, and growing out of the thinnest of materials, thread. His admiration for all sorts of textiles continued unabated and settled, for a while, on Navajo blankets. It is not surprising that they were the subject of some of his flat-glass windows shown at RISD in 1977.

Much earlier in the decade, however, Chihuly, along with Italo Scanga and his assistant at the time, former student Kate Elliott (the first woman undergraduate glass major at the University of Wisconsin under Harvey K. Littleton) devised a way of literally applying the sense of thread or weaving to glass. It was a watershed development. Not only was it a way of bringing together his love of textiles with his love of glass, it freed him to pursue his other love, drawing.

As both Linda Norden and Karen S. Chambers[11] have explained, thin threads of glass were pulled from one of Chihuly's basic building blocks, colored Kugler rods, the pigmenting element for glassblowing. Thin threads of glass were laid out on the cold steel table or "marver," with a fresh and final layer of molten glass laid carefully on top of the "drawing" and then rolled, sometimes abstracting the drawing by twisting and turning the pipe with a large bubble.

Heretofore, imagery on glass had been mostly painted or created by a relief-casting system. What became known as the "glass pick-up" technique used real bits of glass as the drawing material. Thus, the image appeared a closer, material part of the glass, incorporated into rather than sitting up on the surface. The new method ignited Chihuly's imagination more than ever but it also made him more acutely dependent upon assistants. All this was a natural outgrowth of his lessons learned in Venice and, gradually, roles were assigned within the working process. One person would assemble the threads into a pattern previously described or drawn on paper by Chihuly; another would blow a cylinder shape; yet another would take the last gather and apply the "pick-up" to the heated bubble.

Seen in the context of the history of decorative arts, the innovation had important ramifications. Unlike glass, ceramics had employed linear frieze-like decoration as early as the Greeks' red-and-black vases and probably before. Glazes or a liquid clay called slip were painted directly on the pot and then fired. The drawing became an inextricable part of the pot. Over the centuries, this had led to a rich heritage of decorative iconography for ceramics which glass had never really attained. Images on glass had tended to be more difficult to apply, either by enameling, for example, engraving, or casting.

Within Chihuly's own Italo-American heritage, 16th-century Venetian milk glass plates were decorated with enamels and gold but the decoration always appeared to sit up on the surface rather than burned into it, as the "pick-up" technique allowed. As a result, pottery and porcelain decorations contained a far broader range of subjects than glass: religious images; regal portraiture; urban or rural scenery; and, by the 18th and 19th centuries, social and political satire. Chihuly's successful transposition of a flat image onto a circular or spherical form increased exponentially the possibilities for new kinds of glass decoration. In his hands and those of his team, such images became the 360-degree drawing.

Significantly, the earliest demonstrations were abstract, non-representational patterns based on Native American weaving, as well as those designed by Chihuly himself. With the growing assistance of Flora Mace, whom he met at a Utah workshop in 1975, the "blanket cylinders" proceeded rapidly. Again, unlike the controlled, fairly predictable patterning possible in ceramics decoration, the application of drawing to glass took on a different character, bent and distorted in appearance, depending upon the angle of the "pick-up" and the temperature of the glass. The effect is often of extended lines and illusionistic space. But more than simply coating or covering the cylinder's exterior, the "pick-ups" had a discrete presence of their own so that they really could emerge as subject matter to be contemplated and interpreted as art apart from any status as surface-covering design elements. This was a crucial advance, too, because another of Chihuly's contributions would be a growing respect for the interpretation of glass art in critical terms, beyond an appreciation of its various exquisite properties. Indeed, the luxurious technique would become part of the critical controversy surrounding glass.

The sculptural installations had demanded attention by virtue of their size, their startling appearance, and their unusual treatment of a medium associated with functional containers. By returning to the cylinder or container form, Chihuly took a calculated risk of being reconsigned to the camp of traditional functional craft artists. But with the introduction of drawing, the cylinder's form became less important than the nature of the external image it displayed. It was almost as if the "reading" of Chihuly's objects became more important than their shapes.

Once embarked on the new possibilities inherent in the "pick-up" technique, it was not that surprising that another colleague, Seaver Leslie, suggested a literary theme, James Joyce's 1922 novel *Ulysses*. Chihuly has been an ardent Hibernophile since his first visit to the Republic of Eire in 1969 when he spent the summer following his Fulbright year in Italy visiting Ireland. In many senses, Joyce's novel was an appropriate choice. Generally accorded the status as the greatest novel written in the English language in the 20th century, *Ulysses* is two tales in one. On one level, it is the story of one day, June 16, 1904, in the life of its main character, Leopold Bloom, wandering through Dublin and eventually meeting up with Stephen Dedalus, an angry young poet alienated from his family but drawn to Bloom as a father figure. On another level, it is a re-figuring of Homer's *Odyssey* legend of ancient Greece. The successful warrior and sea captain, Odysseus, wanders for years around the Mediterranean Sea after the Trojan War before returning to his home on the isle of Ithaca and to his faithful wife, Penelope.

As the novel has a circular, dawn to dusk to dawn, form, so the *Irish Cylinders* (1975) are also rounded in form. With simple colored line drawings adhering to opaque green glass, individual scenes from the novel's progressive chapters are applied to individual forms. Thus, the novel's opening chapter, set at Martello Tower, a disused fortress outside Dublin, is recorded by a drawing of the tower. Other cylinders commemorate Leopold Bloom in a bowler hat, busy Mabbot Street, scenes of horse-drawn carts in downtown Dublin, and several portraits of Joyce himself, including one of him, pen in hand, contemplating two female nudes beside a cross with his wife, Nora Barnacle, standing behind him. Sylvia Beach, Joyce's publisher, is the subject of another cylindrical portrait.

Without pressing a precise analogy between Joyce and Chihuly, (although both have completely international aesthetics and both suffered serious eye trouble) it is perhaps more apt to see Chihuly in relation to the Stephen Dedalus character or to Ulysses himself.

Young Dedalus, also the subject of Joyce's novel, *Portrait of the Artist as a Young Man* (1914), like Chihuly, found his artistic or poetic voice on the continent rather than at home. The name Dedalus strikes an appropriate chord as well. Another Greek mythic figure, Daedalus was the father of Icarus who flew too close to the sun wearing the waxen wings his father had fashioned for him. Daedalus is often seen as the mythic symbol for the artisan or craftsman using his talents to fashion the impossible and thereby daring or angering the gods. Chihuly's lifelong insistence upon never being content with the medium's constraints pushed him to the edge at every step of his career.

Ulysses, or Odysseus (to use the original Greek name), hero of the *Odyssey*, was sent on his mission by the gods after the triumph of the Trojan War. At every port or landing site, he faced a seemingly insuperable challenge such as the snake-haired Medusa, the Sirens, or the Cyclops, a one-eyed monster. Ever victorious, he is eventually rewarded and returns home.

The concept of the journey, the testing of the hero's mettle, is a timeless theme in world literature. It was Joyce's achievement to combine an ancient tale with a contemporary setting. Chihuly's and Leslie's undertaking (with Mace's help) brought forth another dimension to the Greek-turned-Irish story, its encapsulation in the form of glass. They, too, combined the Greek tradition of wrapping a narrative scene around the sides of a vessel but used a modern form, drawing on glass. Just as Joyce had extended the limits of the novel form and of language itself in *Ulysses*, so they adapted the episodic aspect of Bloom's 24-hour journey to the wrap-around circular character of the cylinder form. On a more somber note, like Ulysses during his dangerous journey, Chihuly and Leslie were about to face great danger and a fateful turning-point.

On January 16, 1976, Chihuly and Leslie were seriously injured in an automobile accident near Gloucester, England. Chihuly's injuries required 225 stitches, several operations, and cost him the sight in his left eye. Because the pupil became permanently dilated, he eventually chose to wear a black eye patch. This development impaired Chihuly's depth perception ability and, when he returned to working with a team at RISD and at the new Pilchuck Glass Center in Stanwood, Washington which he began in 1971, he chose to turn over the gaffer role, or that of master-blower, to a team member, at first in Providence, and later William Morris and Benjamin Moore in Stanwood in 1974. This is an arrangement he has continued to the present day with a long succession of valued co-workers.

Institutional recognition was growing steadily. When Henry Geldzahler (1935–1994) saw the first *Navajo Blanket Cylinders* (1974–75) in 1976, he purchased three for the Twentieth-Century Painting and Sculpture Department collection at the Metropolitan Museum of Art, New York. Charles Cowles, modern art curator at Seattle Art Museum, curated a three-person show of Chihuly, Carpenter and Scanga at the museum's Modern Art Pavilion in 1977–78. In addition, Michael Monroe, curator-in-charge of the Renwick Gallery, Smithsonian Institution, organized a further survey of the Blanket Cylinders and Pilchuck Baskets in Washington, D.C. during the same period.

THE PILCHUCK YEARS: BACK TO NATURE

Although he did not resign as the director of the RISD glass department until 1979, Chihuly was tugged back toward his native Pacific Northwest long before that. The summers of 1976, 1977, and 1978 were spent in Tacoma, recuperating at first in his mother's home, and then increasingly at Pilchuck, north of Seattle, where he embarked on a new series of work.

The saga of the Pilchuck Glass Center is long and complicated, worthy of a book in itself. Without going into great detail here, it is important to point out that the school was Chihuly's dream come true, along with that of the school's generous patrons, John Hauberg and Anne Gould Hauberg. Situated on a tree farm near Stanwood, Washington, the setting contained expansive views of the surrounding hills and mountains to the east and Puget Sound to the far west. By 1976, most of the buildings designed by architect Thomas Bosworth (who later became director as well) were completed. Based on Chihuly's vision of the best of two other schools, RISD and Haystack (with perhaps a bit of Penland thrown in), Pilchuck grew into something more: a unique sylvan environment for the making of art glass in all its forms and for the gathering together each summer of individuals from all over the world united in their exploration of the limits of the medium and the refinement of a craft. Not only did Pilchuck come to have a profound impact on the artistic climate of the entire region, especially Seattle, it provided a constant, stable setting for Chihuly's renewed enthusiasm after recovering from the accident.

It was during a 1977 visit to the Washington State Historical Society in Tacoma with Italo Scanga that the two saw dozens of coastal Salish-tribe bark-woven baskets stacked in piles for storage. Chihuly vaguely remembers seeing them this way when he haunted the museum as a child but it was his return visit with Scanga which ignited his imagination again and led him to his first significant body of work done with the new supervisory team arrangement. These were the *Pilchuck Baskets* (1977).

They differed from the earlier cylinders in a number of ways. First, from the beginning, they allowed the greater pull of gravity to move the blown form this way and that, away from the perfection of the cylinders. Often, the base was curved or irregular and unable to stand on its own. Echoing the woven forms of the cedar bark baskets, this series seemed to mark a quieter, more subtle approach to color and form, as Michael Monroe has suggested[12] perhaps in an attempt to equal the powerful understated simplicity of the ethnic originals without appropriating or copying their more ordered aspects. For instance, where a Salish basket might alternate light and dark banding around the entire basket, Chihuly applied only six or seven horizontal, parallel lines, only at the point of widest outer circumference. The colors were earth-toned, too, like the original peeled bark material but, executed in glass, color took on a luminescent transparency far removed from the matte opacity of the Indian baskets. Finally, for the first time, Chihuly began nesting the baskets within one another, another distant allusion to the way he and Scanga had seen them arranged at the Historical Society.

This proved to be a telling strategy for a number of reasons. It resembled a mini-environment all its own; it responded to Minimal art's repetitive module with a greater sense of imbalance and irregular form; and it allowed for a double historical allusion: the sense of how such baskets might have originally been stored and how such objects are often displayed in history museums—in groups.

A decade later, in the *Venetians*, Chihuly would return to the single autonomous *objet de verre* but, from the *Pilchuck Baskets* onward, his art took on a multiple, polyvalent character. The example of the display of baskets in Tacoma was not the only reason. The earlier neon-and-glass installations and the 1975 Artpark installations of colored plate glass also used multiple elements.

In 1979, Chihuly returned to Europe again, this time to Austria to make glass at the Lobmeyr factory in Baden. Besides Jeff Held and Michael Scheiner (who subsequently became a prominent glass sculptor in his own right and whom Chihuly had met in Providence), Chihuly brought three other men who would become key team members: Benjamin Moore, William Morris, and Richard Royal. While in Baden, the group worked on *Pilchuck Baskets* which were later shown in the Lobmeyr showroom in Vienna.

The following year, Chihuly decided that the time had come for him to work full-time as an artist rather than a teacher. As a result, he resigned his administrative posts at RISD, sold his first boathouse studio in Pawtuxent Cove, Rhode Island and (by 1982) moved back to Seattle.

No matter how far afield one travels, the native sons and daughters of the Pacific Northwest are always glad to return home. Perhaps it is the clean marine air, or the diffused daylight which makes color appear so pure, or the sense of timelessness in the old-growth forests. Added to his childhood memories of beachcombing bits of glass, all these elements no doubt played a role in bringing Chihuly back to Puget Sound. If the *Pilchuck Baskets* were cultural allusions, and homages to the region's earliest human inhabitants, the next series, *Sea Forms* (1980—), paid tribute to life forms of incomparably older origins, underwater organisms.

The meaning of the *Sea Forms* does not lie only in their resemblances to jellyfish or clamshells, though much of their immediate aesthetic appeal lies in our astonishment that the sense of liquid membranes is so effortlessly caught in the ribbed, optical-mold blown glass. Just as the sea creatures themselves rest below the water's surface, so the content of the *Sea Forms* is often submerged beneath their surface sheen and precarious sculptural positioning. They are Chihuly's impassioned response to the earth's growing ecological crisis. He has enlarged and accentuated the size of the original, often microscopic, sea creatures such as anemones or jellyfish in order to draw our attention to the fragile life forms the sea supports. As custodians of the environment, citizens of the Pacific Northwest states feel a proprietary sense toward preserving the environment. The combination of freshwater rivers and lakes and the saltwater bays, sounds, inlets, and oceans which touch on Oregon, Washington, and Alaska makes everyone aware of their interdependence.

In their extraordinary beauty, the *Sea Forms* dredge up from the deep not an approximation of the marine ecosystem but a parallel imagined world created by an artist. They attain a greater degree of reality because of their embroidered, imagined state. The whites and silvery greys are abstracted representations of oysters; the pinks and oranges are symbolic color codes for the jellyfish or swimming salmon, the blues and yellow-greens are allusions to the water or to seaweed.

With the *Sea Forms*, Chihuly raised the delicacy of glassblowing to new heights and, on the level of pure craft, the extraordinarily thin wall is their special contribution. On another level, however, they brought Chihuly back to nature again. This time, sea life became the subject. Whereas the work of the sixties had examined floral forms— another potent theme—the *Sea Forms* mark a period of inflating and collapsing forms which seem to breathe before our eyes. They continued the nesting composition begun with the baskets and, in this configuration, also took on the illusion of family groups. Over and over, the individual objects cuddle and nestle like a school of fish or an assembly of happy clams. The sense of unthreatened, contented innocence is an underlying part of the *Sea Forms*. In their largest assemblies, such as the Seattle Aquarium installation, they resemble self-contained colonies of sea life. When we see them in smaller groupings, they wave and waft in the air. As gravity appears less important underwater, so the *Sea Forms* defy earth-bound gravity, temporarily arrested in space, about to move on across the ocean floor.

There is at least some disagreement over the natural forms being abstracted. The title, *Sea Forms*, is countered by critic Linda Norden in her essay, "Dale Chihuly: Shell Forms,"[13] the first full-length published commentary on the series. She openly states her challenge to Chihuly's intentional statements and, as such, represents a breakthrough in critical commentary on the artist:

> . . . they are shells and, as such, imply protection and an earlier inhabitation by living forms—a loaded metaphor that again refers to process: fire no longer resides in the cool, translucent shapes. Yet Chihuly describes them as live creatures, moving in the odd way that only things underwater do, their endogenous forms and spiraling surfaces augmenting that liquid sense of asymmetrical movement.[14]

Whether shell or living creatures, the symbolic implications of the *Sea Forms* seem multifarious and sure to inspire further speculation. Whatever direction such criticism might take, it is essential to remember the regional context of this series, rooted in the artist's earliest memories of the beach and growing out of the natural world which shaped his earliest experiences, the inland sea of Puget Sound.

MACCHIA

It was Chihuly's close friend and mentor, Italo Scanga, who named the next series *Macchia*, from the Italian for spotted or speckled. The *Macchia* at first glance seem to draw their inspiration from geological rather than maritime sources although, paradoxically, they retain and expand the flowing, open wall shape of the *Sea Forms*. However, greater concern is given in the Macchia to the relationship between the inner and the outer walls. The inner walls, for example, are usually monochromatic with the exterior spotted in white "clouds" and speckled. Unusually large for blown forms, the *Macchia* advance the tradition of glassblowing in this and other ways.

One can see the extraordinary distance Chihuly has covered when comparing the manner and amount of color in the Macchia to the earlier baskets. The monochromatic body of the vessel was first used as a ground for the application of the drawing. By the time of the Macchia, the drawing and the ground seem to have merged into one.

Seen in the context of Modernism, Chihuly's tendency toward merging the "figure" into the ground rendered the surfaces flatter and, hence, more "modern." That is to say, if as critic Clement Greenberg held, modern painting was on an inevitable course toward accepting the inherent flatness of the medium—oil on canvas on wooden support—then Chihuly's surfaces, at least, seem to have been following a comparable trend during this period. There is no distinguishing separation between the variegated spots on the outside surfaces and their subliminal ground of color. Densely packed together, the marks also obviate any conventional sense of placement or composition. In this sense, too, they grow out of Greenberg's theory of "all-over" composition, first applied to Mark Tobey and Jackson Pollock. As Chihuly works in a combination of two- and three-dimensional surfaces, it is difficult to easily extrapolate or adapt pre-existing critical theories referring to painting or sculptural separately.

Nevertheless, the *Macchia* became Chihuly's boldest ventures to date. Their larger size, their intensified balancing of many colors, and their positioning in groups proposed a new context for appreciating glass. Seen in relation to 20th-century French glass, for example, (Lalique, Daum, Marinot), they are the exact opposite. The French masters prized an intimate, nearly tiny scale and a blurred, indeterminate sense of color.

As Chambers has pointed out, the link between the *Sea Forms* and the *Macchia* goes beyond their shared thin-wall forms; it is the appearance of watercolor painting on the Macchia which also relates

them to the maritime atmosphere of the *Sea Forms*. More explicitly painterly, however, glass is, according to Chambers, actually a
better carrier of color at its purest, purer than painting. She rejects
Greenberg's allegiance to what she calls "paint-on-canvas [as] a flat
representation of color" and seemingly out-Greenbergs Greenberg by
claiming that, in the *Macchia*,

> glass suspends color in air, a closer approximation of light, color at
> its most essential. Chihuly's *Macchia* accomplish what Color Field
> painters such as Morris Louis, Helen Frankenthaler, and others
> sought to do: to create a sensation of pure color.[15]

Robert Hobbs marshals the strongest case for the series' geological allusions. In a commentary for Chihuly's 1986 exhibition at the Musée
des Arts Decoratifs, Palais du Louvre, in Paris, Hobbs held that the
colors resembled rocks and stones: "Seen under bright light, they look
like nature caught on fire, nature in molten flux, nature in the process of being created."[16]

Thus, within one body of work, Chihuly gradually shifted from an
aqueous metaphor to one summoning up the elements at the heart
of many crafts, fire. Indeed, for the first time, the intensity of the colors—red, orange, brown, yellow—summon up the glassblower's oven
whereas, up to this time, the agonizing uncertainty of the "glory hole"
was covered over in virtuosic flurries. Now, the presence and partici-
patory role of heat is apparent in the elaborately curved rims or "lips"
as well as in the symbolic colors.

PERSIANS: EXCAVATED TREASURES

Chihuly moved closer toward an examination of the craft object as a
work of art in and of itself with his next series, the *Persians* (1986—).
In 1987, Chihuly had finally settled into his own first glass studio
where such forms could be explored in depth. While *Sea Forms* and
Macchia dealt with biomarine and geological subject matter, the subject matter of the *Persians* is a lost or dying civilization. In this sense,
they are closer to the *Pilchuck Baskets* which resuscitated Salish
coastal art. Searching for a source even earlier than Venice, Chihuly
turned to the appearance of Persian and Mesopotamian glass. The
vase, the bottle, the urn, the dish, and the "teardrop container" are
small-scale forms which, when assembled together, create an atmosphere of languishing, decadent culture.

An earlier historical precedent for a contemporary homage to an
earlier achievement was the Favrile work of Louis Comfort Tiffany
(1848–1933). Tiffany tried to capture the aged, iridescent quality of

glass when rescued from archaeological excavations. And, as Hobbs revealed when comparing Tiffany's Favrile to Chihuly's *Persians*, the latter emulated Near Eastern forms rather than their weathered surfaces.[18] In the case of Tiffany, the Favrile pieces which also, like Chihuly's, had narrow necks and fluted or flared lips, grew out of the 19th-century Romantic taste for "exotic" cultures like Turkey, Persia, or Lebanon. In fact, it is this comparable Romantic indulgence that places Chihuly in a direct confrontation with his only rival, Tiffany. Twentieth-century modernist rather than 19th-century historicist, however, Chihuly's approach has been abstracted, reductive, and stylized. The vestiges of Near Eastern original functional forms are present but distorted, exaggerated, inflated, or shrunken. What we witness is the action of the intense heat of the glass studio on the diminutive vessels.

In addition, we sense the weight of the ages, expressed by the pull of gravity, so that the conical minaret shapes or fluted towers seem survivors of a cataclysm or nuclear meltdown. This ravaged elegance is what firmly places them in the late 20th century.

With the first *Persians* small in scale and broodingly dark in color, the series developed into a larger scale with large fan or umbrella shapes as much as three or four feet in diameter. Color, too, shifted from the shimmering coppery hues to mixtures of orange and pink, navy blue and gold, Venetian red and lapis lazuli. The larger sets carried none of the historical allusions of the earliest sets wherein literally dozens of small objects would be placed on a tabletop, assembled into a mini-environment of mock-archaeological character.

Nevertheless, they seemed a cross or compromise between the *Sea Forms* and the *Macchia,* borrowing elements from each, such as spiral optical molding or speckled, mottled color. The achievement of the *Persians* is most clearly seen in the smallest pieces with their sinuous, vine-like twist-ons on their luxurious, reclining positions. One can easily imagine that Aladdin's genie in the lamp lived in one of these, awaiting his reawakening in the current century. Like the Persian epic poem, *One Thousand and One Nights*, the *Persians* summon up a variety of narrative implications because each small object has the sense of having belonged to a real individual, long gone and forgotten.

This kind of historical revivalism, which would reach its apogee in the *Venetians*, is an honorable and valid part of the crafts and decorative arts traditions which never suffered quite the same rupture of the avant-garde in painting and sculpture. To the contrary, the

seamless continuity of the decorative arts tradition has presented a
different challenge: to be free to borrow at will from earlier styles and
yet still make one's own art expressive of the current age, rather than
an historicist self-conscious copy. Chihuly achieves this in the *Per-*
sians by making the glass rich in spotting, patterning, striations, and
chromatic variety. He also drew from a fixed stock of Near Eastern
forms but modulated and "improved" upon them in each case, and
even inventing "new" ones. The imaginative content of the *Persians* is
instigated when one tries to recreate what the individual functions of
some of the forms might be. This aspect, the imaginary user's story,
and the interaction of color and form, complete the viewer's range of
aesthetic experiences of the pieces.

Thanks to Henry Geldzahler, the *Persians* were shown in Bridgehampton, New York in 1988 at the Dia Art Foundation. Critical
response was favorable yet also controversial. Roberta Smith, writing
in the *New York Times* (August 12, 1988) reviewed the Seattle artist
along with David Hockney and Robert Mapplethorpe raising the old
saw, "Is it art?" Smith epitomized an attitude prevalent in art circles
that holds beauty suspect, too differentiated from an establishment
avant-garde position that argues that aesthetic concerns are often
overridden by meaning related to challenging the status quo. Despite
their allusions to history, clearly articulated in the catalog essay by
Robert Hobbs, the *Persians* still challenged a status quo of Smith's:
great art is suspect if beautiful. Critic Rose Slivka anticipated (and
may have influenced) Smith's objections in her *East Hampton Star*
review when she asked of the *Persians*: "How beautiful can it be and
still be art? Can a thing be too beautiful?"[19]

VENETIANS: RETURN TO ORIGINS

The *Venetians* (1988—) brought the artist full circle, back to the city
of his artistic birthplace, Venice. A watershed in terms of critical
recognition and controversy, they also became the subject of the most
extensive written commentary Chihuly hitherto had received.

Before summarizing the appeal and potential content of the *Vene-*
tians, it is worth mentioning the evolution of Chihuly's working methods during the 1980s. Even though we have progressed through a discussion of nearly ten separate bodies of work, Chihuly's development,
as stated at the outset, is non-linear. That is, he has always exercised
the freedom to return to an earlier style of work at a later period in
time. This complicates things somewhat, if not for the present, perhaps for the future, and may present problems of dating though all
sets that leave the gallery or studio are signed and dated. Such an ap-

proach, moving freely backward and forward in time, should be seen as part of the artist's unfinished odyssey, his warm re-acquaintance with and refinement of an earlier body of work.

Sometimes, the results are a greater elaboration on the original, such as the large soft cylinders of the mid-1980s. When Chihuly re-encountered the cylinder form, he made them the new beneficiaries of both a more skilled application of drawing elements and of the *Macchia* spotting technique. The results were extravagant and gorgeous. It is not surprising that one of these works, *Cylinder* (1984), was selected to represent the artist in the landmark 1987 exhibition *The Eloquent Object*, organized by the Philbrook Museum of Art in Tulsa, Oklahoma. Other *Soft Cylinders* expanded the size of the *Baskets*, incorporated far more elaborate glass-thread drawings, and used a far wider spectrum of color than any of the earlier ones.

To return to the *Venetians*, this series first developed in four distinct phases: 1988, 1989, 1990 and 1991. It represents an important shift in Chihuly's art in a number of ways. It is true that the reverence for historical precedent of a specific character was first examined in the *Pilchuck Baskets* ande the *Persians* and that the *Venetians* must be seen in the light of those two series coming before. Breaking the habit of multiple-element installations examined in depth with the *Sea Forms* and *Macchia*, the Venetians mark a return to the work of art with a singular object identity. Furthermore, they mark a break with the drawing convention apotheosized in the *Soft Cylinders*. Instead, the linear element is an integral part of the vessel's form, playing the role of structural support, handle, or ornament. This aspect has undergone additional transformation in the course of the three distinct phases, first operating as functional element and then becoming part of an elaborately ornamented sculptural design that seems to work against function and in favor of an ameliorative or corrective kind of sculptural appurtenance surrounding the vase. Thus, within the *Venetians*, one may witness Chihuly's exploration of the entire spectrum of decorative arts' basic properties: from function to ornament to sculpture.

The evolution of the Venetians has been dealt with in depth in both published[20] and unpublished[21] commentary,[22] but it is necessary to recount briefly their origins before examining the startling array of critical responses to them. before examining the startling array of critical responses to them. Done initially with master Venetian glassblower Lino Tagliapietra, the groundwork was set in the summer of 1987 when maestro Tagliapietra visited Pilchuck as guest artist. At the time, he made a set of highly complicated latticino-type goblets for Chihuly and his bride, playwright and poet Sylvia Peto, as a wedding gift. Tagliapietra remarked that it would be nice to work together on something else and Chihuly rapidly responded by inviting him back for a collaboration the following summer.

During their honeymoon in (where else?) Venice in 1987, Chihuly and Peto were invited to view a private palazzo collection of Italian glass of the 1918–1939 period owned by the Carrero family. Chihuly was stunned by the extraordinary range of shapes, forms, and colors, some of which, in turn, obliquely echoed ancient Etruscan glass. When Tagliapietra returned to Seattle, Chihuly had built the first of two separate complete hot shops to work at in Seattle. Having immersed himself in a study of the Art Déco period of Italian glass before the maestro arrived, Chihuly was already primed for what proved to be a most remarkable and ongoing set of collaborations.

Without dwelling at length on all the historic examples that inspired the first phase, it is important to note *en passant* the precedents of Napoleone Martinuzzi (1892–1977), Ercole Barovier (1889–1974), Carlo Scarpa (1906–1978) and Vittorio Zecchin (1878–1947).[23] Their work provided some of the models for the first group of *Venetians* but what resulted is a far cry from the Fascist-period examples. Usually larger in size and brighter in color, the first phase (July, 1988) drew from certain devices of the originals—bubbly and "seedy" walls, acanthus leaf add-ons, multiple, tiered sets of handles—and retained a basic functional appearance.

The second phase (January and June, 1989) grew in extravagance and departed definitely from the Mussolini-era models by completely eschewing the smooth, machine-made appearance of the handmade originals. By this point, other historical models were brought to bear, as Chambers has noted:

> Starting with the tradition of Venetian glass, Chihuly has tuned into the entire decorative arts history with hints of Germanic glass, French art deco glass by Daum and Lalique, and even ceramics of the eighteenth and nineteenth centuries. His is creating works that do not merely appropriate that history but reinterpret it for the last part of the twentieth century[24]

In the tradition of modern composers like Igor Stravinsky who extrapolated from the Italian composer Pergolesi in his much more lively and bombastic ballet, *Pulcinella*, Chihuly is outlining with very bold strokes the art from which he first drew inspiration for the series. With a characteristic dynamic and spontaneous appearance, the Venetians in their second phase grew disorderly, garish, and spectacularly showy. Newly emboldened with true Italian swagger, they proclaimed their individual identities through hallmark decorative devices put to new use, their newfound status as sculpture.

The third phase (January and July, 1990) pushed the appearance of function even further into the background. It also included another Venetian maestro, Giuseppe "Pino" Signoretto. The acanthus leaves now filled the bowl instead of surrounding it. Leaves and vines grew into knotty tangles around the central core of the vase and over the opening, completely inhibiting the possibility of use. Abrupt, spiky appendages often in gold or silver leaf sprouted on the sides of the bowls or vases completed at the new facilities near Lake Union in Seattle.

The exuberance of the *Venetians* seems at distinct odds with their chaste and elegant originals. They overwhelm the residual upright forms and seem to express a luxurious entropic fantasy of nature gone wild, encroaching over the staid forms of the past. Placing the juxtaposition of old and new on a more specifically socio-political plane, Hobbs views the *Venetians* as Chihuly's critique of Italian glass of the interwar period. In fact, he sees it as a rescue operation for the "implicitly fascistic aesthetic that uses simple classical shapes as historical analogues for modern machinery's streamlined beauty."[25] In this sense, as before, Chihuly is using nature as a life-giving, ameliorating element that may not only save the planet but "reclaim even alien and resistant Art Déco forms. . . . These pieces present early Modernism as an antiquated style incapable of withstanding the life force assailing these pieces in the form of ribbonlike vines and leaves."[26] As we have followed Chihuly on his unfinished odyssey, we have, not surprisingly, found nature as the guiding force even so far, as Hobbs argues, to become the driving force in an international cultural dialogue Chihuly began 25 years ago at Venini (the site of much of the deco glass fabrication) and proceeded to follow up by undertaking the Venetians with Lino Tagliapietra.

For the time being, they bode well for the future because they suggest that a reverse influence has finally occurred. After the epoch-making event of Chihuly's retrieval and transmission of Italian teamwork methods onto American soil, he has been able to repay a debt to his Italian legacy in a way. What Chihuly and Tagliapietra brought back to the history of Italian glass, however, was an American exuberance and the transformative power of nature that grew out of Chihuly's crucial childhood experiences in the mountains and on the beaches of the Pacific Northwest. Like most authentic artistic events, it has been an internal dialogue conducted, at first, through the subjective medium of the drawings but, as the *Venetians* develop, they take on a public character that seems to foreshadow a new phase, a new series, as yet unnamed.

With bravura technique, strident and garish color sense, and a residual debt to the past finally repaid, Chihuly seems poised for his greatest period of work. It is a part of his greatness that no one, not even his closest admirers, can possibly guess what form it might take.

PUTTI: THE FIGURE EMERGES

> I don't know where the idea of the *Putti* came from.
>
> —Dale Chihuly[27]

Once the figure appeared in Chihuly's art, an entire realm of potential narrative and additional aesthetic meaning also emerged. Begun in 1990 in collaboration with another Italian, Pino Signoretto (whom Chihuly had brought over from Venice to teach at Pilchuck), the *Putti* became appurtenances of the vessels in the *Venetians*. While both men were at the summer school in Stanwood, Washington, Chihuly was asked to give a demonstration with Signoretto. The results were a series of small cherubs, baby angels, or cupid figures (*putti* in Italian) which startled many. Over the next four years, the small, usually gold-leafed figures traveled onto the artist's subsequent series: *Ikebana* (1990—), *Pilchuck Stumps* (1992—) and *Chandeliers* (1992—). Not that they constitute a series of their own, but the addition of the figures, sometimes singly, sometimes paired or in groups, jolted the *Venetians* into a world of storybook events and adventures. Perched on the rim of a vase, they toyed with scale, reinforcing the oversize nature of the vases by contrast and turning the surfaces into landscape-like arenas where the figures could roam.

Small at first, startlingly comic and unexpected, the cherubs populated the vases and bolstered the increasingly complex nature of the *Venetians* after 1990. Eventually, with Signoretto's return visits in 1991 and 1992, and with the gradual making of the figures by resident team members like Martin Blank at Chihuly's next studio on Lake Union, the "Boathouse," they became larger and larger ranging up to actual infant size.

Chihuly was inspired by Signoretto (whom he calls "one of the great glass sculptors of Venice") and he recalls the sense of excitement that the possibility of incorporating the figure into other glassworks gave him:

> Then we started putting them on sea creatures and dolphins and starfish and clamshells, and doing stories with the putti. . . . I like doing things for kids and I see them, in many ways, as being for children.[28]

Not only that, they provided a return to a state of childhood innocence for the artist that could not be obtained otherwise. Like the toys or dolls British psychoanalysts call "transitional objects,"[29] the *Putti* become both fantasy projections for the artist's imagination and surrogates for his re-entry into the child's innocent relation to the magic of the natural world. Chihuly continued his odyssey but, with the advent of the *Putti*, it became an interior one. The *Putti* are "transitional" in reverse. Instead of helping the baby orient itself to the larger world away from Mother, they provide Chihuly with a manufactured regression to the carefree infantile state.

As the viewer contemplates the *Putti* tableaux—stumps, landscapes, swamps, seaside settings—he or she is also able to join in the fun and fantasy the artist has created. Though they may have been triggered by the specific skills of a visiting artist, Chihuly expanded and adapted Signoretto's technical ability by "finding a new home" for the immigrant cherubs, far away from the painted ceilings of the Tiepolos of Venice or their stagy positioning in Italian Baroque art, closer to a far more complex and perhaps confusing world, the artist's mind: Chihulyland.

As they progressed, the glass babies, rendered divine or comically "sacred" by the gold leaf, entered into darker and more threatening worlds as well. Entangled by snake-like vines, caught on rusting stumps, stranded in the "forest" of a massive glass chandelier, the cherubs woke up to their late 20th-century world: conflict and danger, mixed with bright color and glamour. The residual infantilism of the image gave way to one of arrested development. Literally out on a limb in some of the *Ikebana* arrangements, the *Putti* matured beyond their initial frolic and themselves became parts of the hotshop team, hard-working team members, present for the maestro's bidding.

Are they, as some have suggested, self-portraits? Some even have eye patches. With their wild ringlets of hair, their pudgy baby fat, and animated hand gestures, they might be so interpreted. But more importantly, they act as symbolic surrogates for the artist's channeled narrations. Although he has said:

> I'd like to write the stories myself but I probably wouldn't be able to. ... Writing is too painful for me.[30]

the artist has nonetheless created intuitive narrative of innocence and danger (the danger of growing up) without recourse to conventional plot, text, or writing. Part of their significance lies in the artist's strong visual storytelling powers heretofore suppressed or unacted upon. With the entry of the *Putti*, Chihuly can now extend subjective memory into the circumscribed drama of the cherub on the vase or stump or chandelier. Far more than technically dazzling add-ons, these figures enriched the levels of meaning possible in the artist's world immeasurably.

IKEBANA: GILDING THE LILY

While in Japan, an Ikebana master approached Chihuly and requested permission to create a flower arrangement using one of his pieces. The artist immediately agreed but also came up with the idea of making his own flowers to insert into vases. Pliable and (re)movable, the resulting *Ikebana* series (1990—) touched on a number of interests the artist had long pursued.

First, his love of flowers dating back to childhood experiences in his mother's rhododendron garden in Tacoma came to the fore. To not only admire flowers but to be able to make them! That was a challenge not to be missed. Earlier, in the Sheraton Seattle Hotel lobby installation (*Flower Forms #2*, 1986), tall white floral blooms and tendrils make up an entire encased environment. With the *Ikebana*, however, the artist could go beyond the mottled whites of the Sheraton work, explore color with the stem-and-bloom configuration, and further incorporate nature into the sculpture.

Considering Chihuly's earliest works often dealt with natural organisms, and the *Putti* represent man's intervention in nature, these works offered the artist an opportunity to meet God on his own terms: create natural-looking growth forms within the manmade vessel. In fact, the flowers overpowered each vase and became, once underway, the container forms became much simpler if not plain.

The wildly linear stem, the erratic twining of the leaf, the open form of the bloom, all these require a compositional anchor of greater simplicity. The gourd form, beloved by Chinese and Islamic artists as symbols of fecundity, was a logical choice. Bulging and pregnant-looking with its double or triple-bulb rings, the *Ikebana* vase-supports also reinforce the sense of life bursting forth in the bloom above. Now dependent on color and meandering line, the *Ikebana* vases seem especially close to the artist's expanding repertoire of paintings and drawings of the early 1990s. With the crew able to match the master's desires for wandering or arching stems, each combination in the series cuts into the space above, lifting the glass out of the self-contained energy field of the *Venetians*, into an area of organic growth that pushes at the limits of what glass can do.

Eventually, the stems grew up to five feet in length and found their way into several installations (e.g., *Ikebana Wall* at Union Station in

Tacoma and Bellevue Ikebana, a 1990 installation for *Masterworks: Pacific Northwest Arts and Crafts Now*, at the Bellevue Art Museum in Bellevue, Washington). Removed from their containers after Bellevue, the objects took on new life in greater numbers, emulating an arbor of wildly entangled growth, standing in again as metaphors for the gardens that increasingly preoccupy Chihuly. Begun as responses to the simplest and most austere model, the Japanese flower arrangement, the *Ikebana* were rapidly Americanized, adapted to a faster, brighter world, but still retained a whiff of their Asian predecessor.

NIIJIMA FLOATS: PAN-PACIFIC GLASS

> And I remember as a kid, walking along the beach and running into these Japanese fishing floats.[31]

Living at the edge of the Pacific Ocean, Chihuly has developed strong ties to Asian communities interested in glass in Japan, Taiwan, Hawaii and Australia. These travels, an additional, fruitful extension of his unfinished odyssey, have had positive impacts on his art. They link him to cultures, like the Chinese and Japanese, that not only have no discriminating boundaries between art and craft, but share heritages that frequently elevate functional objects of porcelain, for example, above painting and sculpture. As an American craftsman who is also an unquestioned fine artist, Chihuly is paradigmatic of the global, completely multicultural nature of the crafts in general. With his art not dependent on specific ideological references in order to make a point, Chihuly's audiences have expanded into Asia though exhibitions and workshops.

A turning point came in October 1989 when the artist visited a small glassblowing center on Niijima Island in Tokyo Bay. After returning to Seattle, the team responded to Chihuly's desire to create very large blown-glass spheres. Because they reminded him of the washed-up fishing floats he had seen on Puget Sound, and because of the experience of recently being in Japan, they were named *Niijima Floats* (1991—).

Among the largest objects ever blown in glass, the individual balls can grow up to 40 inches in diameter and 50 to 100 inches in circumference. With each ball weighing between 50 and 60 pounds, the teamwork perfected was crucial. During the height of activity in December, 1991, each ball was planned with a particular color or colors in mind. Once the glass was heated and blown a number of times, it became too heavy for the blowpipe to be comfortably rolled on the stand. In order to accommodate the new weight and its attendant difficulties, Chihuly devised a new tool, the first new glassblowing implement to be invented in decades within the centuries-old tradition of glassblowing. It is comprised of four pairs of metal rollers, two pairs set nearest the blower, and two pairs at the other end of the table. Between trips to the oven, the pipe holding the glass can now rest between both sets of rollers and be more easily turned during the blowing that expands the form.

When maximum desired size was achieved and the ball no longer able to be reinserted into the oven or "glory hole" to keep it hot and pliable, a daring "anatomical" effect was undertaken. The side opposite the blow-pip was heated with a propane torch and the gaffer inhaled sharply on the pipe, creating an indentation or "dimple" where the glass had been locally heated.

Speckled, mottled, or gold- and silver-leafed, the *Floats* became an extension of the artist's earlier work in installation art chronicled in both a catalogue and exhibition at the Seattle Art Museum.[32] Emphasizing the fragility and weight of glass to another extreme, they have been displayed in multiple groupings by the artist in New York[33] and, in a turnabout that sent floats back to the Far East, at the Honolulu Academy of Art where they were shown in a series of garden courtyards.

After the first blows in October, November and December, 1991, the balls were stacked snowman-style in a manner that briefly perpetuated the figurative dimension possible with the *Putti*. Chihuly soon abandoned this strategy, however, preferring to position them directly on the ground. The low-to-the-ground effect created the artist's most restrained and hermetic body of work to date. Often presented in a darkly lit and mysterious setting, as at the Seattle Art Museu, and at the Corning Museum of Glass, the *Niijima Floats* seem minimal but not Minimalist. They copy the repetitive-module element of much Minimalist art but do not parallel the regulated positioning of Donald Judd (1928–1994) or Carl Andre, favoring instead a seemingly random placement that echoed their locations on the beaches of Puget Sound.

Seen in isolation, a *Niijima Float* is not only a float, it is a symbol of the world, a globe to be mapped by the "jimmies," or broken bits of colored glass that adhere by heat. With many of the *Floats* acquiring greater and greater individuality, it is worth examining their single-object status as well as their role in larger installations. After all, the installations have always followed from the development of individual series and each series has begun with just one piece.

Confetti Float (1992) is perhaps the largest of all with a yellow-white
ground and an uneven but seemingly random distribution of surface
"jimmies." It stands on its own as a glowing presence and reminds us
that, once a museum installation is dismantled, the fate of the elements
is often uncertain and not necessarily tied to future combinations.

PILCHUCK STUMPS: INTO THE FOREST

Just as the characters in Belgian playwright Maurice Maeterlinck's
(1862–1949) play, *Pelléas et Melisande* (1892) wander into a dark
forest that changes their lives forever, so the invitation to design sets
for a 1993 production of the 1906 opera of the same name by Claude
Debussy (1862–1918) offered Chihuly a challenge that would transform his vision of glass in a number of ways.

Seattle Opera general director Speight Jenkins approached the artist
in 1992 because he saw an affinity between the mood of Debussy's opera and the look of Chihuly's art: often photographed against a dark
background, decoratively charged, and redolent of sparkling color,
irregularly forms and organic in structure.

Debussy's music, now lush and surging in sound, now frail and
swooning, became the constant background while Chihuly was working on the project. Technical director Robert Schaub and lighting designer Neil Peter Jampolis saw that Chihuly's glass sculptures could
be captured in fiberglass and, as Chihuly suggested, the forest scenes
could be built with iridescent mylar sheeting. With five acts and
fifteen separate scene changes, the impact was startling, beautiful
and controversial. International press reaction ranged from enthusiastic to enraged. With all performances sold out, the undertaking on a
theatrical level was a smash success.

Most of the sets adapted the artist's floral glass forms but, in the forest scenes (Act I, Scene I), tall tree forms built of columned mylar (Radiance Paper manufactured them in California) ascended to the stage
ceiling. These were first tried out at the Seattle Art Museum exhibition in the summer of 1992 and were met with great enthusiasm by
the public and the Seattle Opera parties involved.

At the same time, as a spinoff of the set designs, the artist came up
with the idea of smaller, tree-like forms, *Pilchuck Stumps* (1992–).
Initially exhibited at the Seattle Art Museum near the mock-up of Act
One, Scene One, the *Pilchuck Stumps* grew out of the opera designs, a
collaboration described by Donald Kuspit as the "apotheosis of theatre and ecology."[34] They are significant in a number of ways. From
a technical standpoint, they were the first of Chihuly's works blown

into specially built wooden molds that formed the exterior "bark" of each piece. Earlier series, like the *Sea Forms*, had used optical molds to give each blown form its sea-organism "spine" or bone system, but the *Stumps* employ more complex molds that create the basic form as well.

The colored Kugler rods are selected, heated and blown. Before placing in the mold, some of the Stumps have silver leaf adhered to them. When placed in the mold, the silver leaf reduces—and creates color— from its interaction with the inner sides of the mold and bits of cork and newspaper present. Upon removal, the mold-blown form is then sprayed with a titanium-oxide mixture that provides the iridescent "frosting" of each piece before placement in the annealing oven.

Although they grew out of the multiple-element placement of the trees in the opera sets, the *Pilchuck Stumps* are really a return to pedestal sculpture. Exhibited individually, they return the viewer's focus to the unitary object. More intimate in size than the *Floats*, they also continue the ecological theme—"Follow nature"—prevalent in the artist's work from the beginning. Chihuly is reclaiming the forests of the Pacific Northwest in the *Pilchuck Stumps*.

Originally a tree farm owned by Weyerhaeuser executive John H. Hauberg, Pilchuck Glass School's founding patron, the Pilchuck site itself was spared from clear-cutting only by the formation of the School in 1971. By returning to the basic element of the forest—the stump that decays and acts as fertile mulch bed for new seedlings— the artist is retrieving a form with latent potential for growth even though it resembles, on first glance, something dead and discarded. Both alive and dead, then, the *Stumps* symbolize the entire cycle of modern forests: growth, death, reseeding, harvesting, and planting, and so on.

With their bizarre iridescent sheen, they echo Tiffany's Favrile glass, the first American art glass to employ iridescent fuming. Inspired by archaeological glass uncovered at Near East sites, Tiffany's Favrile attempted to recapture the aged surface of excavated glass. Similarly, Chihuly is heightening the sense of decayed bark, accentuating it with a toxic glow that summons up radioactivity, a more possible influence on eccentric life form development one hundred years after Tiffany.

CHANDELIERS: LUX ETERNA

> I was in Barcelona recently, and I was in a restaurant and there sat an extraordinary chandelier over a table. And I had been thinking

about chandeliers and then, lo and behold, here was a chandelier
that was hung in such a way that it was no longer a chandelier and
it inspired me to want to come back and make a chandelier.[35]

Chihuly's experience in the restaurant in Barcelona, capital of the
Spanish autonomous region of Catalonia, was a fitting beginning to
his latest series. With its heritage of Art Nouveau architecture by Antoní Gaudí (1852–1926) and others, Barcelona has long been a model
for artists seeking fusions of art and architecture. Such expressions
were also vibrantly colorful and ornate, much like Chihuly's own sensibility. Indeed, the exterior of Casa Mila by Gaudí is completely covered with iridescent-glazed ceramic tiles that react as mirrors to the
sun and sky during the day. In its glassiness, it resembles the kind
of architecture Chihuly may someday undertake: fanciful, eccentric,
illusionistic and organic.

Although some of the later chandeliers are illuminated from within
by neon elements, the earliest ones, like *Seattle Art Museum Chandelier* (1992), have exterior light sources. They are like the Barcelona
restaurant lamp, "chandelier[s]. . . that [are] no longer chandelier[s]."
The clustering composition of individual blown elements alludes to
natural forms as well such as beehives, bundles of fruit like bananas,
and clumps of moss. The *Seattle Art Museum Chandelier* began on
an even more nurturing note: breast forms. Comprised of over 500
transparent and opaque yellow elongated blown spheres, the chandelier is bursting with life, extending down from the ceiling, its entire
collective form one large breast made up of many smaller ones. With
a large black granite sheet beneath it, the sculpture posits potential
breakage and containment simultaneously. At over eight feet tall, the
work offered another solution for attaining large scale in glass. This
time, however, instead of the floor being covered with multiple, dis-
tributed elements à la Niijima, the suspended symbolic light source
challenges our expectations of gravity, tension and fragility.

As the series develops, other individual blown forms evolve into a
variety of shapes. *Honolulu Academy of Arts Chandelier* (1992) introduced a hornet shape for each element, pointed, swirling forms of
bright yellow that point outward and cumulatively suggest a swarm
of bees. Appended beneath it is a single blue *Ikebana* stem. *Char-
treuse Chandelier* (1993) adapted striated leaf forms, also clustered,
massing into a sphere and, again, suspended from above. *Red Putti
Chandelier* (1994) uses red hornet forms with an inverted *putto*
beneath, as if a child or cherub is escaping the angry swarm. *Polychrome and Gold Hornet Chandelier* (1993) breaks the monochrome
pattern and hangs dozens of transparent-color shapes above a looping

amethyst floral stem. Others, like *Yellow and Red Chili Pepper Chandelier* (1994), mimic a familiar display of dried chili peppers, mixing shapes of both chilies and more elongated variants.

In an unusual departure for the 1994 Artfair in Seattle, the artist assembled for a Northwest art dealer, *Cadmium Red Niijima Float Chandelier*. Here, a huge blazing red float—like a bloody eyeball—is surrounded by elongated tentacles resembling the muscle structure of the eye socket. Among the most violent and disturbing of all Chihuly's works, this chandelier acts more as a suspended autonomous sculpture installation than as a light source. As usual, one series is begun and, thanks to the advantage of being able to explore it at length and in depth with the hotshop crew, it leads to many other unexpected areas.

Ikebana Chandelier (1992), for example, uses a fabricated inner steel strut to affix numerous floral stems of mostly primary colors. The flowers appear caught in the vertical gridded form (a twisted arbor?) and simultaneously escaping from it. Even more bizarre, *Putti Chandelier* (1993) executed for an exhibition at the Detroit Institute of Arts, reintroduced the artist's surrogate, the golden *putti*. With dramatic gilded dark-blue floral stems, the suspended sculpture operates horizontally, reinforcing a sense of journey, event and narrative for the small golden figures. Caught and entangled in the complex linear pattern, they disturb more than delight and emphasize once again how the artist's attitude toward nature is always mediated by an awareness of our fragile, potentially lethal, industrial environment. Set in Detroit, the blending of such elements had special reference. *Blue Chandelier with Putti* (1994) is a companion piece accentuating the grotesque linear forms, adding clustered areas that "capture" the *putti* and undercutting the earliest chandeliers' qualities of volume and mass.

Large-scale private and corporate commissions for the chandeliers, such as those for Microsoft, Inc. of Redmond, Washington, and for a former Microsoft executive in Mercer Island, Washington, vary the swarming configuration and use more dispersed compositions. They are another way the artist has challenged inherent limits traditionally associated with glass: gravity and breakability. Each chandelier conveys the threat of damage and collapse, yet each remains vibrantly alive and intact. Barely functional in the strictest sense, they emerge out of a European tradition of elaborate architectural chandeliers in Italy, Austria, France and Germany wherein the spectacular nature of the purported lighting fixture is a pretense for the celebration of public places like the reception area in an opera house.

In this sense, the *Blue Chandelier* (1994) at Union Station in Tacoma, Washington is among the artist's most successful undertakings. Suspended at the exact midpoint in the train station's former waiting room, the 2,750 elements are widest at the top, descending to a single point 30 feet below. Viewed from a distance, the chandelier seems a pyramidal mass. Up close, the viewer realizes that the chandelier is essentially flat, two-sided, with the dark blue elements creating a "wall" that occupies space but does not assemble it into a massive volume. More so than the other chandeliers, the Union Station chandelier interacts with its container space, occupies a planar sliver of space, and acts as an emblematic form in an area once dedicated to mass transportation.

So far as this goes, the chandeliers have moved from ceremonial light source to icon or symbol of the purpose of a chandelier: to announce status, display spectacular artisanship, and, for Chihuly, operate on a subjective level of meaning.

PROCESS: THE QUESTION OF AUTHORSHIP

> Now no longer the master of the team, Chihuly's role is that of a choreographer who maps out the moves for his dancers.
>
> —Henry Geldzahler[36]

Teamwork has long been a part of the craft tradition. Since the technical process is often complicated and laborious, requiring highly skilled practitioners, it makes sense that an artist might work with assistants. In his case, Chihuly is fairly typical of many contemporary artists, including those not working in craft materials, who use assistants or artisans to create part or all of their work. No one questions the authorship of sculptures by Alice Aycock, Louise Bourgeois, Jeff Koons, Robert Morris, or Dennis Oppenheim, all of whom "job out" their art, so why should Chihuly come under any scrutiny? Could there be a double standard, one for "fine arts" and another for "craft artists"?

The fact of the matter is, Dale Chihuly has been more open about admitting such collaborations, even though he was warned against being so forthright early on in his career. This openness grew out of his work as a teacher, a role he unofficially continued at Pilchuck, while artistic director, and out of the circumstances following his accident when it became obvious, due to his impaired depth perception, that his hands-on role would be revised to that of constant observer in charge of all decisions on the spot.

A closer look at this genesis, however, reveals that, not only was Chihuly involved in teams and collaboration before the 1976 accident, but that the arrangement has been responsible in large part for his extraordinary achievements in glass which, if executed alone, simply would not have been possible. This goes back to our earlier discussion of how Chihuly became the transmitter of Euro-Venetian working concepts, namely, the division-of-labor method he observed at Venini and brought back to the U.S., thereby breaking the nearly 1000-year-old code of secrecy surrounding the design and manufacture of Italian glass.

Stepping outside of the decorative arts tradition for a moment, it is worth remembering that many of the leading Western artists throughout history also worked in close collaboration with a staff of assistants who, in some cases, worked directly on the object in question. Michelangelo did not paint the Sistine Chapel all by himself, regardless of our image of a sweating Charlton Heston in "The Agony and The Ecstasy". Furthermore, as Svetlana Alpers has pointed out,[37] that hallowed icon of 17th-century Dutch painting, Rembrandt van Rijn, had assistants working around the clock on commissions. It is true that this is part of what has created the problem of authorship in Rembrandt scholarship but evidence of authenticity in Rembrandt today is based on microscopic analysis of matching canvas samples to those known to have emerged from Rembrandt's Amsterdam studio-home, not on exclusively attempting to determine a characteristic identity of brushwork. In any case, Chihuly is the only person to sign his work and it is only signed and dated when it leaves the studio for the gallery.

All the same, one should distinguish the nature of Chihuly's different collaborations over the years for they do not all fall into the same category. He has spoken about how his first taste of teamwork at the University of Wisconsin with Fritz Dreisbach and Michael Whitley opened his eyes to the extraordinary possibilities afforded by the team approach.[38] His extensive projects with James Carpenter have been discussed above. Authorship was shared or individually assigned based on an agreement at the time between the two artists. J.C. Associates, their company in Providence for the stained glass commissions (1974–76) was the focus for their commercial and corporate jobs. The dry-ice-and-neon environments were assigned to Chihuly.

On the *Irish Cylinders*, Seaver Leslie and Flora Mace co-signed the pieces with Chihuly because Leslie did the drawings and Mace transferred them to a form that could be applied to glass.

With the closer dependence on a master blower or gaffer after the accident, Chihuly began to assemble and train a number of young craftsmen, several of whom have gone on to substantial careers of their own. This genealogy is worthy of a study all its own because the question of Chihuly's influence is an important issue for the history of studio glass in the final quarter of our century but also for that of European glass, considering his extensive travels and blowing demonstrations in France, Germany, Italy, Czechoslovakia, and Japan, to name a few. Briefly, however, the better-known Chihuly team members who have separate, established careers are Benjamin Moore, Flora Mace and Joey Kirkpatrick, William Morris, Charles Parriott, Richard Royal, Martin Blank, and Preston Singletary. In addition, Robbie Miller, Paul Cunningham, Pat Davidson and Bryan Rubino played important team roles. Space does not permit an examination of the question, "Is there a Chihuly tradition?" That must remain the focus for a different exhibition or study. Suffice it to say, each of the team members above has a markedly different and individual style from Chihuly's although certain similarities and attitudes could be found. When working with Chihuly, their own identities are subordinated to his.

The designer and artisan relationship with Lino Tagliapietra is in a class by itself. In this case, a remarkably simpatico arrangement arose with mutual respect on both sides. Chihuly does not hover around maestro Tagliapietra while he is working but, rather, continues to prepare drawings for the crew to execute in glass, planning in advance size, color choice, and the specific character of each piece. Chihuly responds to Tagliapietra's growing enthusiasm at each blowing session, altering and revising expectations depending upon the outcome. After the morning blow, for example, relaxing over lunch or grappa, the two discuss the recently completed work and then might examine together the cooled-down pieces from an earlier day's blow in order to decide together which pieces will be kept, which might be destroyed, and which might undergo yet another step such as sandblasting a surface.

COLOR

> The team can do many things without me but it starts with color and that is where I'm needed. Color is very important.
>
> —Dale Chihuly to Dagmar Sinz[39]

As Chihuly told Dagmar Sinz in an interview in Paris, color is the crucial aspect of the process where he must be centrally involved. Along with form, size and scale, it is among the most important aspects of the team's interrelation with him. Before examining how color operates in Chihuly, one should compare his use of it to that of other glass artists. In a way, it is an East Coast versus West Coast issue. The older tradition of American studio glass, arising out of the achievement of Chihuly's first glass teacher, Harvey K. Littleton, prizes clarity and absence of color, or sparing, select use of it. The man who developed the studio blowing system along with Littleton, Dominick Labino, also has a restrained attitude toward color. The transparency of glass, its light-transmitting quality, is foremost to both artists. And seen in the continuum of 19th-century American glass, the admiration for clear, lead-cut crystal, so dear to the Victorians, the citizens of America's Gilded Age, is also of paramount importance to the East Coast glass establishment.

In Chihuly's case, however, a different 19th-century model comes to mind: Louis Comfort Tiffany. There was something prescient about Chihuly's winning a 1967 Tiffany Foundation Fellowship for never was there an artist working in glass who shared more with Tiffany than Chihuly. Prolific, innovative, capable of supporting large workshops of artisans, and subject to huge popularity and acclaim both at home and abroad, Tiffany and Chihuly share an appreciation for the exotic, as the discussion above of the *Persians* makes clear. But clarity, lucidity, and transparency are not hallmarks of Tiffany glass. Rather, as a 1990 exhibition in Washington, D.C. at the Renwick Gallery made evident,[40] Tiffany's goal was an approximation of the powers of paint—executed in glass. This is close to Chihuly's intentions. Not content with limiting his palette to the pale lucidity of some glass, Chihuly has seized on the entire spectrum ranging from the contrasting and complementary combinations of the early work to the bold, garish combinations of the later work. After all, one period's "good taste" in color is another's anathema. Chihuly subverts period taste in color by embracing it all and subordinating it to only one thing: the desired expression or mood of the individual piece. As he once said, "I never met a color I didn't like."

The pastel pinks and blues of the *Sea Forms* come closest to the East Coast sensibility in glass. In between those works and the *Venetians*, the somber browns, red, and golds of the *Persians* evoke the chromatic sense of Oriental carpets, for example. Perhaps the widest range of all colors occurred within individual *Macchia* where the inner wall would be one solid color, the outer wall would be a spotted mix against a contrasting ground, and the linear "lip wrap" at the wall's upper edge would be a thin punctuating color somewhat salient to all the rest. All such decisions are Chihuly's alone.

On another level, the unsystematic nature of Chihuly's decision-making about color must be stressed. His is not an art arising from

Purism, the Bauhaus, the Institute of Design, or Cranbrook Academy of Art, all bastions of orderly, function-subordinated attitudes toward color. More to the point, it is the very subjective and spontaneous appearance of color in Chihuly which secures its status as art instead of as design. Declarative of their own objecthood, Chihuly's glass works command attention by virtue of their idiosyncratic expression of color. This places him in the expressionist wing of 20th-century art, closer to the overheated emotion of the Fauves as well as much eighties art but rescued from any gloom-and-doom by uplifting, elastic forms.

Seen within another critical matrix, Greenbergian modernism, we have discussed above how Chambers contends that Chihuly surpasses Color Field painters in his ability to embody color in a medium better suited than oil and canvas to a purer transmission of color's central property, light.

I concur, but would like to suggest how, as sculpture, Chihuly's *objets de verre* do not at all conform to the generally two-dimensional criteria Greenberg praised in sculptors like David Smith and Anthony Caro.[41] The experience of color in sculpture, something Greenberg deemed superfluous for the most part, must be seen in all three dimensions in order to fully appreciate Chihuly. Indeed, it is this inextricability of color and sculptural form which brings us to an examination of our next aspect of Chihuly's work.

FORM AND FUNCTION

> In the beginning, my interests were primarily sculptural. I wasn't interested in the vessel form at all.
>
> —Dale Chihuly[42]

Even if one accepts Chihuly's statement above at face value, it is still necessary to trace the role of form in his oeuvre back farther, before "in the beginning." As we have seen in our discussion of color, it leads to the two-dimensional surface he first encountered in weaving. True, textiles are not totally flat. They have texture and raised surfaces occasionally. But in addition to the sculptural properties Chihuly's art has attained over the years, it is necessary to retain in our memories the precedent of his mastery over the two-dimensional surface in order to understand the transposition of the drawing onto the curved cylinders. In this context, Chihuly's attitude toward form is tempered by an a priori dedication to drawing; his sculptures are mixtures of two-dimensional and three-dimensional activities. This qualifies his statement above and should help us when trying to delineate the role of form and function in his work.

First of all, to what does "form" refer? It is the manipulation of the given object in space in all three dimensions. "Shape," often confused with form, is the linear outline of form and can often occur in two dimensions as well. Shape is a contributor and participant in Chihuly's forms but it is subordinate to their overall form.

Again, the character of form in Chihuly is expressive, expressionistic, irregular, asymmetrical, figurative, and gravity-defying as opposed to limited, ordered, planned, earthbound, idealistic, and utopian. Given this dichotomy, however, one must review briefly the two major influences on Chihuly's attitude toward form: the 1950s architectural sensibility of the Northwest Designer Craftsman group attained through his education at the University of Washington interiors program, and the 1960s "anything goes" aesthetic prevalent in Madison, Wisconsin and, later, Providence, Rhode Island. It would be a mistake to preclude one for the other although the latter seems to have become the more dominant. Chihuly's success at binding color to form is a result of his strict architectural interiors training and his obsession with surface design through weaving. His success at making form become color grows out of his liberated, sixties attitude when the sense of possibilities in life and art seemed limitless and the confidence of the youth culture fed a sense of freedom to experiment continuously and, in his case, confront the unknown or untried.

More specifically, other writers have gone into greater detail about form in Chihuly. Norden reminds us that the influence of Northwest Coast basketry on Chihuly's form took two aspects. First, the woven construction of the ethnic baskets influenced Chihuly to create vessels in which "form and surface decoration developed simultaneously.[43] Alluding to Chihuly's viewing of the stacked baskets and how their display and storage tended to weigh them down visually, she suggested how "their disfigured shapes gave greater play to gravity."[44] Thus, surface decoration and irregular, asymmetrical forms are always inextricably intertwined in Chihuly.

Hobbs draws attention to the openings of the vases and how important a part of the overall form they play in, for example, the *Persians*. Indeed, part of the achievement of the Persians is in their extraordinary diversity of openings. Calling them "orifices," Hobbs sees their initial inspiration in Near Eastern historical examples such as rosewater bottles and teardrop containers but notes how, in Chihuly, the originals are stretched out of recognition with "wondrous elasticity."[45]

Form plays the most important role in determining subject matter and content in Chihuly. The lambent fluidity of the blown form of the

1960s not only expressed a languid, hedonistic culture, it resembled flowers mutated into solid glass. Twenty years later, the blossom motif has recurred in some of the *Venetians* winding its way around the central vase form, setting up a tension, as Hobbs proposed, between the smooth machine-like forms of the Fascist Déco inspirations and the overpowering qualities of natural growth. I might add that the floral or blossom motif also introduces the erotic element at each stop along the way. Thus, formal components initially tied to the level of ornament in blown glass take on a character of their own contributing significantly to our interpretation and appreciation of Chihuly's art.

Composition becomes a part of form's role in Chihuly when one contemplates the multi-form aspect of the sets. We have seen how the baskets unlocked an entirely new way of forming for Chihuly but they also affected the work's visual composition. Seen in groups, the overall form of a set is the most open, least controlled aspect of form partly because the individual elements are changeable and subject to spontaneous rearrangement. This has been obviated in the large installations such as the Rainbow Room at Rockefeller Center where final positioning must be predetermined and agreed upon. Nevertheless, Chihuly has been known to completely reblow and reinstall an installation even once it has been dedicated. This fluid attitude toward composition reveals a restless, dissatisfied approach to form. It is exactly what gives the works their dynamic appearance.

Though their appearance is what has generated the bulk of critical interpretation of his work, Chihuly's own explanation of how those forms emerge is more basic:

> All the forms we've invented are based on the ability of the molten glass to be blown and manipulated in a very natural manner[46]

Seen in the context of craft, it could not be any other way. That said, it still seems that, working under the taskmaster of molten glass, Chihuly has remained ever the devilish student, eager to break rules, find limits and extend them, do things that people never imagined glass could do. As form expands in Chihuly, it must be viewed as the triumph of the blower over the material, not fighting it but training it to do the master's bidding.

Function plays a lesser role but also deserves clarification. Living in a philistine society as we do, usefulness takes on a dominating dimension that seems applied to every aspect of American life. Within the national community of American studio craft artists, there is no consensus as to the status of function either; half seem to have enshrined it and the other half left it behind some time ago. Much of craft's appeal to the American public still lies in the pragmatic, useful part of a hand-fashioned object. Yet art has always skirted and avoided usefulness, unless one subscribes to the tired and unconvincing notion that "to decorate a space" is also a possible function. Extended that far, function in craft loses the force of its original meaning of helpfulness on an everyday basis.

Where does this leave Chihuly? As he has claimed, sculptural properties were always more important to him than functional appearance and, indeed, it was not until ten years into his career that he made functional-appearing art objects at all, the *Pilchuck Baskets*.

Before that, however, his period of collaboration with Carpenter led to an examination of function *inter alia*. The twenty to thirty separate cups, bowls, dishes and vases which Chihuly and Carpenter created for Steuben in 1975 are only one aspect of their fruitful collaboration but they also represent a high-water mark for beautifully and amusingly imaginative functional glass objects. As analyzed above, their figurative and erotic sculptural properties seem to predominate in retrospect, especially when seen in the context of all Chihuly's art, but taken separately, they propose that strictly useful objects can also take on subtly sculptural aspects without forsaking the necessarily plain design required of objects for everyday use.

Henry Geldzahler does not shy away from confronting the function of "use" of a Chihuly sculpture. He reminds us that:

> The blurring of art categories is one of the bequests of the radicalism of the 1960s that these artists [Kenneth Price, Peter Voulkos, Wendell Castle, and Dale Chihuly] have effected and benefited from. Old distinctions between 'fine' and 'decorative' art, between the 'uselessness' of high art and the 'usefulness' of furniture, vessels, and porcelain, no longer have meaning for us.[47]

As to a Chihuly sculpture's "use":

> It locates the magic and alchemy inherent in molten glass, in gorgeous and permanent materiality. His work stands for change in constancy, highlights on surfaces of permanent fluidity. . . . One may put oranges or limes in his 'baskets' or dried flowers in his 'cylinders', but one can also use a Picasso to cover a hole in a wall.[48]

While it is soothing to accept Geldzahler's analysis disposing of the art vs. craft debate, my fear is that, in our rush to honor the best of craft as art, we might play down or re-denigrate craft's older and equally honorable status as function. Chihuly is a crossover artist, one who began with a traditional craft material, glass, and used it to different, but not higher, aesthetic ends. His Steuben commission must rank with equal seriousness and success to his later vessels and sculptures. Just because the usefulness of the more highly artificed objects gradually became evacuated does not cancel out his, or anyone's, residual debt to the functional heritage common to the entire tradition of craft and the decorative arts.

My own first experience with Dale Chihuly's work grew out of early exhibitions in Seattle at the Foster/White Gallery. Shortly thereafter, however, another more telling encounter occurred. In the city's artist quarter, Belltown (also known as the Denny Regrade area), a group of artists which included Heather Ramsay, Randy Eriksen, Sheila Klein, and Buster Simpson held an annual rummage sale called the "urban yard sale." Most of the group lived in adjacent large storefront spaces and managed to accumulate numerous items including work from fellow artists.

It was at one of the "urban yard sales" that I found my own Chihuly, a small pale-orange cylinder or basket with horizontal, brighter-orange banding. Barely seven inches high, it sat amid a clutter of cast-off fabric, pottery, and houseplants. The price was five dollars. Probably a gift of the artist to one of the yard-sale participants who had worked at Pilchuck, it found a far more appreciative home in my small studio apartment on Capitol Hill.

Since then, it has been my pleasure and privilege to watch Chihuly's art develop and thrive. Far from the subtlety of the little orange basket, it now boldly declares its position on an international stage. Seen within the context of contemporary American art, it can be compared to the exotic-garish wing of American painting and sculpture of the 1970s and 1980s. Painters Rodney Ripps and Frank Faulkner create lush metallic surfaces on their canvasses; sculptors John Torreano and Lynda Benglis allude to jewels and gemstones in their wall-affixed objects. All these artists, including Chihuly, reject the puritanical austerity of the Minimalists as well as the slick cynicism of the consumer-critique artists like Haim Steinbach, Jeff Koons, and Ashley Bickerton. Instead, they favor the tactile, the constructed, and the crafted as pathways to a different consciousness: the sanctity of the handmade object writ large to provoke the viewer into an awareness of the art object on its own material terms.

Less primarily conceptual, they present the artwork as a sensuous visual experience and reject the Baudrillardian notion of the phantom double, or simulacrum. Indeed, the aggressive physicality of Chihuly's art is the best argument yet against the neurasthenic vitiation of art's power put forth by many continental theorists.

CONCLUSION

Unbeholden to the photo-reproduction for its existence, regardless of Chihuly's obsession with photography, the experience of his art insists upon an immediate physical encounter between viewer and object for its impact. Empirical and experiential, the art of Dale Chihuly returns contemporary sculpture to a more primal viewing experience. Instead of pondering its meaning first, his glass communicates its material status immediately. As the viewer takes in the elaborate technique, the object's meaning is released gradually. As the discussion above has affirmed, the character of that meaning might take on many forms but they are inescapable bound up with the nature of the glass medium.

This is a bitter pill for many critics to swallow, so alien is it to mainstream critical theories of the past that stress the primacy of concept over objecthood. It is well worth pondering, then, because much recent contemporary sculpture has failed to have a life beyond its interpreters, failed to attain adequate visual liveliness to survive a barrage of commentary.

To the contrary, the vigorous status of Chihuly's art calls for a different kind of commentary, one that pays equal court to process as well as meaning, to craft as well as content. And, indeed, the best writing on the artist does this.

Finally, in order to fully appreciate Chihuly, one must descend from Parnassus, step back in time, and remember the curious child on the beach. The sunset, the broken bits of glass, the fishing floats, and the sand are the talismans of memory that triggered the spectacular achievements later in life. Like Ulysses, Chihuly's journey began by the sea, agent of travel and discovery. As it continues in mid-life, Chihuly's odyssey is open-ended, unfinished. It will be his task, as it was Ulysses's, to balance the inner need for constant discovery against the clamor, the acclaim and the uncertainties of legend.

ENDNOTES

PART I: ON THE CRAFTS
STORYTELLING IN AMERICAN CRAFT 1750–1950
(Essay from *Storytelling in Twentieth-Century American Craft*, organized by Craft Alliance, St. Louis, at Washington University Gallery of Art, St. Louis, Missouri, June 18-August 15, 1993)

[1] Robert Graves, *The Greek Myths: 1*. London: Penguin Books, 1955, 194–195.

[2] Susan Gray Detweiler, *George Washington's Chinaware*. New York: Harry N. Abrams, 1982.

[3] John B. Judis, *Grand Illusion: Critics and Champions of the American Century*. New York: Farrar, Straus & Giroux, 1992.

[4] John Spargo, *Early American Pottery and China*. Garden City, NY: Garden City Publishing Co., Inc., 1926, 284–285.

[5] Garth Clark, *American Ceramics: 1876 to the Present. Revised Edition*. London: Booth-Clibborn Editions, 1979, 12–13.

[6] Frances Weitzenhoffer, *The Havemeyers: Impressionism Comes to America*. New York: Harry N. Abrams, Inc., 1986.

[7] Barbara A. Davis, *Edward S. Curtis: The Life and Times of a Shadow Catcher*. San Francisco: Chronicle Books, 1985, 39.

[8] Wendy Kaplan, *The Art that is Life: The Arts & Crafts Movement in American 1875–1920*. Boston: Museum of Fine Arts, 1987, 142–143.

[9] Ibid., 191–192.

[10] Joan Marter, et al. *Design in America: The Cranbrook Vision 1925–1950*. Detroit: Detroit Institute of Arts, 1986, 184.

[11] Sidney Waugh, "The Bowl of American Legends," interview transcript in Corning Museum of Glass Archives.

[12] Ibid.

[13] Op. cit.

[14] Viktor Schreckengost, conversation with the author, August 28, 1992.

[15] Edwin S. Scheier, conversation with the author, September 1, 1992.

THE EMBODIMENT OF INGENUITY
(*American Craft*, August/September 1987)

[1] "Craft Today: Poetry of the Physical," is currently at the Laguna Art Museum, Laguna Beach, California (August 7-October 4), and will travel to Phoenix, Milwaukee, Louisville and Richmond through 1988. "In Pursuit of Beauty: Americans and the Aesthetic Movement" was shown at the Metropolitan Museum of Art, New York (October 23–1986-January 11, 1987). "The Machine Age in America 1918–1941," which opened at the Brooklyn Museum (October 15, 1986-February 16, 1987), is now at the Los Angeles County Museum of Art (August 16-October 18) and will end its tour at the High Museum of Art, Atlanta (December 1, 1987-February 14, 1988).

[2] Rob Barnard, "Craft in a Muddle," *New Art Examiner*, February 1987, 24–27.

[3] John Bentley Mays, "Comment," *American Craft*, December 1985-January 1986, 38–39.

[4] Kenneth Baker, remarks at critics' panel, American Craft Council conference, "Art/Culture/Future," June 6, 1986, Oakland, California. Neal Benezra, "But Is It Art?", *The New York Times*, October 19, 1986.

[5] Robert Hughes, "A Cool Eye on Hot Art," address at University of Washington, Seattle, February 4, 1987.

[6] I am indebted here to Donald Kuspit for his informal suggestion of the artifact category. Conversation with the author, New York City, October 24, 1986.

PACIFIC NORTHWEST CRAFTS IN THE 1950S
(in Barbara Johns, ed. *Jet Dreams: Art of the Fifties in the Northwest*. Seattle: University of Washington Press, 1995, pp. 81–95.)

[1] Tom Folk, "Frances Senska: Studio Potter," *American Ceramics* 8:2 (1990); 34–39.

[2] Thelma Lehmann, "Bonifas Became Ceramist to Prove Important Point," *Seattle Times*, July 21, 1957.

[3] Jane Van Cleve, *3934 Corbett: Fifty Years of Contemporary Crafts* (Portland, Ore.: The Contemporary Crafts Association, 1986).

[4] Dave DePew, "The Archie Bray Foundation," Ceramics Monthly (May 1972): 18–23. Also see Frances Senska, "Pottery in a Brickyard," *American Craft* (February/March 1982).

[5] Senska, "Pottery in a Brickyard."

[6] Frances Senska and Diane Douglas, *The Legacy of the Archie Bray Foundation* (Helena, MT: The Archie Bray Foundation for the Ceramic Arts, 1993).

[7] Maynard Tischler, et al., *James and Nan McKinnell: A Retrospective Exhibition* (Denver, CO: University of Denver, 1993).

[8] Margery R. Phillips, "For Art's Sake," *Seattle Times*, May 10, 1959.

[9] Robert Sperry, conversation with the author, January 21, 1994.

[10] LaMar Harrington, *Ceramics in the Pacific Northwest: A History*. (Seattle: University of Washington Press, in association with the Henry Art Gallery, 1979).

[11] Russell E. Day, "Art in Contemporary Living," *Washington Education* (April 1962).

[12] *Northwest Designer Craftsmen* (Seattle: Northwest Designer Craftsmen, 1976), pp. 84–85.

[13] Dorothy Brant Brazier, "Jewelry 'Builder' to Put on Show," *Seattle Times*, October 3, 1958.

[14] Scott Landis, *Leroy Setziol: Retrospective Exhibition* (Eugene: University of Oregon Museum of Art, 1991).

[15] Colin Graham, *Philip McCracken* (Seattle: University of Washington press and Tacoma Art Museum, 1980), 40.

[16] Nancy Helvy, "Hobby Now Big Business," *Seattle Post-Intelligencer*, October 21, 1958.

[17] Russell Edwin Day, "Experiments in Glass and Colored Light," (M.F.A. thesis, University of Washington, 1957).

[18] Ibid.

BREAKING BARRIERS: RECENT AMERICAN CRAFT
(Essay for *Breaking Barriers: Recent American Craft*. New York: American Craft Museum, 1995)

[1] Janet Kardon, et al. *Explorations: The Aesthetic of Excess*. New York: American Craft Museum, 1990, 10.

[2] It is important to note that humbler functional forms—pots, jewelry, tumblers, knives, etc.—are still being produced today in the United States by artists of great skill and creativity, but their devotion to basic functional form is not in question here.

[3] Linda Johnson Dougherty, "Joyce J. Scott," *Art Papers*, September, 1993, 56.

[4] Carol Ferring Shipley, "Jane Sauer: St. Louis Art Museum," *New Art Examiner*, September, 1988.

THE REMATERIALIZATION OF THE ART OBJECT
(*Sculpture*, July/August 1996)

[1] Lucy R. Lippard and John Chandler, "The Dematerialization of Art," *Art International*, February, 1968, 31.

[2] Ibid.

[3] Lucy R. Lippard, *Six Years: The dematerialization of the art object from 1966 to 1972*...New York: Praeger, 1973.

[4] Ibid.

[5] Ibid.

[6] Ibid.

[7] Harold Rosenberg, "The De-Aestheticization of Art," *The New Yorker*, January 24, 1970.

[8] Lippard, *Six Years*.

[9] Peter Plagens, "Seattle," *Artforum*, November, 1969.

[10] Donald Kuspit, "Craft in Art, Art as Craft," *New Art Examiner*, April, 1996, 14–19, 53.

[11] Lucy R. Lippard, in Leach, et al., *Michael Lucero Sculpture 1976–1995*. New York: Hudson Hills Press, 1995, 37–47.

[12] Lippard, *Six Years*.

THE MYTH OF THE NEGLECTED CERAMICS ARTIST
*(Adapted from a talk given at "Tangents: Ceramics and Beyond," March 16, 2004 at Henry Hope School of Fine Arts, Indiana University, Bloomington, Indiana)
(*Ceramics Monthly*, October, 2004)

[1] Mary L. Alexander, "The Week in Art Circles," Cincinnati Enquirer, May 8, 1949.

[2] John Canaday, "Artists and Materials: Potters and Painters May Yet Meet on Common Ground," *New York Times*, November 20, 1960.

[3] Rose Slivka, "New Ceramic Presence," *Craft Horizons*, No. 4, 1961.

[4] William J. Homer, "Carl Walters, Ceramic Sculptor," *Art in America*, Fall, 1956.

[5] Dore Ashton, "Art: 'New Talent' Display at Museum: Peter Voulkos Work Shown at Modern," *New York Times*, tk.

[6] John Coplans, "Abstract Expressionist Ceramics," *Artforum*, November, 1966.

[7] Peter Selz, *Funk*. Berkeley, CA: University Art Museum, Berkeley, 1967.

[8] Alfred Frankenstein, "The ceramic sculpture of Robert Arneson: Transforming craft into art," *ARTnews*, January, 1967.

[9] Prudence Carlson, "New York: Daisy Youngblood at Willard," *Art in America*, February, 1980.

[10] Donald Kuspit, "Elemental Realities," *Art in America*, January, 1981.

[11] Hilton Kramer, "Ceramic Sculpture and the Taste of California," *New York Times*, December 20, 1981.

[12] John Perreault, "Fear of Clay," *Artforum*, April, 1982.

PART II: CERAMICS
TOWARD A BICAMERAL ESTHETIC OF CLAY
(*American Ceramics*, Vol. 1, No. 1, Winter 1982)

[1] Clement Greenberg, "The Status of Clay," Transactions of the Ceramics Symposium 1979 (Los Angeles: Institute for Ceramic History, 1980).

[2] Graham Marks, "An Open Letter to the *New York Times*," The Shards Newsletter: Review of Published Resources in the Ceramics Arts 1, no. 1 (Spring 1980). A letter protesting Vivian Raynor's review of the Brookfield Craft Center in the *New York Times*, July 22, 1979.

ROBERT SPERRY: PLANETARY CLAY
(*American Craft*, December 1981/January 1982)

AMERICAN FIGURATIVE CERAMICS
(Reprinted from Robert Bell, ed. "American Figurative Ceramics" in *Perth International Crafts Triennial*. Perth, Australia: Art Gallery of Western Australia, 1989.)

SHATTERED SELF: NORTHWEST FIGURATIVE CERAMICS
(*American Craft*, August/September, 1986)

HOWARD KOTTLER
(American Ceramics, 6/2, 1990)

PATTERN RE-EXAMINED IN AMERICAN CERAMICS
(Surface Design Journal, Vol. 15, No. 1, 1990)
[1] Barbara Perry, ed. *American Ceramics / The Collection of Everson Museum of Art.*
New York: Rizzoli, 1989.
[2] Rose Slivka, "The New Ceramic Presence," *Craft Horizons*, July-August, 1961.
[3] Jeff Perrone, "Approaching the Decorative," *Artforum*, December, 1976.
[4] Donald Kuspit, "Betraying the Feminist Intention," *Artsmagazine*, November, 1979.

RICHARD FAIRBANKS: TURNING POINT
(From Richard Fairbanks, American Potter. Seattle: University of Washington
Press, 1993; 32–38)
[1] Richard Fairbanks, unpublished letter to Carolyn Price Dyer, December 5, 1959.
[2] Marianne Aav, *Kyllikki Salmenhaara 1915–1981.* Helsinki: Museum of Applied Arts,
1986, unpaginated.
[4] James Egbert, telephone conversation with the author, April 8, 1992.
[5] Ibid.
[6] Ibid.
[7] Richard Fairbanks, unpublished letter to Carolyn Price Dyer, February 13, 1960.
[8] Richard Fairbanks, unpublished Helsinki Journal, 1959–1960.
[9] A razorblade, placed by someone or inadvertently dropped in her special batch of
clay, cut her finger while throwing. It caused a persistent infection under the nail that
lasted for many years. It is not known who placed the sharp metal in the clay but, as
James Egbert has stated, an atmosphere of jealousy and rivalry pervaded the eighth
floor artist studios at Arabia.
[10] Dixie Parker-Fairbanks, telephone conversation with the author, April 2, 1992.
[11] William Tyner, telephone conversation with the author, April 9, 1992.

JIM LEEDY: PREHISTORIC MODERN
(American Craft, June/July, 1990)
[1] Revered today by the Japanese as a contemporary raku master, Leedy completed a
major public art mural for Himeji City in 1987. It was dedicated on March 21, 1990.
[2] Jim Leedy, conversation with the author, January 28, 1990.
[3] Rose Slivka, *Peter Voulkos: A Dialogue with Clay.* Boston: New York Graphic Society,
1978.
[4] See my *Rudy Autio: A Retrospective.* Missoula, Montana: University of Montana,
1983, 18.
[5] Jim Leedy, conversation with the author, November 11, 1989.
[6] Jim Leedy, "News & Retrospect," *Ceramics Monthly*, May 1981, 70.
[7] Rudy Autio, "News & Retrospect," *Ceramics Monthly*, December 1981, 91.
[8] Donald Hoffmann, "Sometimes the beauty is obscure," *Kansas City Star*, January 8,
1994.
[9] Michael Cadieux, "New Ceramic Sculpture by Jim Leedy," unpublished manuscript,
part of which appeared in "News & Retrospect," *Ceramics Monthly*, May 1982.
[10] Ibid., 3.

RICK DILLINGHAM AND THE REPARATIVE DRIVE
(American Ceramics, 8/4, 1990)
[1] Adrian Stokes, *The Image in Form.* Harmondsworth, UK: Penguin Books, 1972, 120.
[2] Elaine Levin, *The History of American Ceramics: 1607 to the Present.* New York:
Harry N. Abrams, Inc., Publishers, 1988.
[3] Garth Clark, *American Ceramics: 1876 to the Present.* London: Booth-Clibborn Edi-

tions, 1987.

4 Levin, 256.

5 Clark, 261–262.

6 Deborah Phillips, "Artist's ceramics show influences of the ages," *The New Mexican*, February 24, 1984, 18.

7 Jan Adlmann, *Rick Dillingham*. Santa Fe, New Mexico: Linda Durham Gallery, 1990.

8 Rick Dillingham, interview with the author, May 1, 1990.

9 Hanna Segal, "Art and the Inner World," [London] *Times Literary Supplement*, July 18, 1975, 800.

10 Ibid.

MICHAEL LUCERO DISCOVERS AMERICA
(*Sculpture*, July/August 1992)

1 Carter Ratcliff, *Michael Lucero*. New York: ACA Contemporary Gallery, 1988.

2 Ursula Ilse-Neumann, "Michael Lucero," in Janet Kardon, ed. *The Aesthetic of Excess*. New York: American Craft Museum, 1990, 32–35.

3 See my "Howard Kottler," *American Ceramics*, Vol. 6, No. 2, 1987, 16–23.

4 Robert J. Charleston, ed. *World Ceramics: An Illustrated History*. New York: Crescent Books, 1990, 313.

VIOLA FREY'S FAMILY PLOT
(*Sculpture*, May-June, 1994)

1 D. W. Winnicott, "The Concept of Trauma in Relation to the Development of the Individual within the Family," in *Psychoanalytical Explorations / D. W. Winnicott*, eds. Claire Winnicott, Ray Shepherd and Madeleine Davis (Cambridge, Mass: Harvard University Press, 1989), 131.

2 Thomas Albright, "Mythmaker Art—Humor and Fantasy," *San Francisco Chronicle*, August 8, 1981.

3 Jan Butterfield, "Viola Frey: The Figure Is Always There," in *Viola Frey: Paintings / Sculptures / Drawings* (San Francisco: Quay Gallery, 1983).

4 Jeff Kelley, "Viola Frey," *American Ceramics*, Vol. 3, No. 4, (1984).

5 Susan C. Larsen, *Viola Frey: Monumental Figures 1978–1987*. (Los Angeles: Asher-Faure, 1988).

6 Ibid.

7 Cheryl White, "The Company of Strangers," *Artweek*, December 19, 1987.

8 Ibid.

9 Winnicott, "The Concept of Trauma."

10 D. W. Winnicott, "The Fate of the Transitional Object," in *Psychoanalytical Explorations*, 54.

11 Ibid.

12 Peter Fuller, *Art and Psychoanalysis* (London: Writers and Readers Publishing Cooperative, 1980).

13 Larsen, *Viola Frey*.

14 Bill Berkson, "Viola Frey: Rena Bransten Gallery," *Artforum* (March 1988).

15 D. W. Winnicott, "The Child in the Family Group," in Home is Where We Start From, eds. Clare Winnicott, Ray Shepherd, and Madeleine Davis (New York: W. W. Norton & Co.), 1986), 140.

DOUG JECK: MONUMENTS TO UNCERTAINTY
(American Ceramics, Fall 1995)

1 Catherine Fox, "Clay figures come to life at Connell," *Atlanta Journal and Constitution*, January 25, 1991, E-2.

2 David Ribar, "Doug Jeck...," *Artpapers*, November/December, 1992, 46.

3 Hank Lazer, "Beauties and Beasts: Issues of Aesthetics," *Artpapers*, September/

October, 1992.
[4] Greg Burkman, "Severed Art," *The Stranger*, April 18–25, 1995.

RYOJI KOIE: NEW CONTEXTS
(From *Ryoji Koie*. Seattle: Bryan Ohno Editions and University of Washington Press, 2000)

LAWSON OYEKAN: ORIGIN AND EXILE
(*CRART*, Winter 2005)

PICASSO'S CERAMICS: A LIFELONG INTEREST
(*Ceramics Monthly*, February, 1999)

NORTH AMERICAN CERAMIC SCULPTURE NOW
[1] See my "American Ceramic Sculpture in Crisis," in *International Ceramic Symposium Shigaraki '91*. Shigaraki, Japan: Ceramic World Shigaraki '91 Executive Committee, 33–39.
[2] See my *Jim Leedy: Artist Across Boundaries*. Kansas City: Kansas City Art Institute and University of Washington Press, 2000.
[3] Garth Clark, *American Ceramics 1876 to the Present*. London: Booth-Clibborn Editions, 1987.
[4] Elaine Levin, *The History of American Ceramics*. New York: Abrams, 1988.
[5] Jonathan Fineberg, "Humor at the Frontier of the Self," in *Robert Arneson: Self-Reflections*. San Francisco: San Francisco Museum of Modern Art, 1997, 10–22.
[6] Signe Mayfield and Daniel Rosenfeld. *Big Idea: The Maquettes of Robert Arneson*. Palo Alto, California: Palo Alto Art Center, 2002.
[7] Ken Johnson, "Annabeth Rosen," *New York Times*, March 28, 2003.
[8] Levin, 158.
[9] Mike McGee and Larry Reid, *Charles Krafft's Villa Delirium*. Santa Ana, California: Grand Central Press, 2002.
[10] Cydney Payton and Mary Barringer, *North American Legacies: life in general*. Boulder, Colorado: Boulder Museum of Contemporary Art, 2000.
[11] Paul Bourassa, *Léopold Foulem: Phantasses et soucoupes*. Ville St-Laurent, Québec (Canada): Musée d'art Saint-Laurent, 2000.
[12] Mark Richard Leach, et al. *Michael Lucero: Sculpture 1976–1995*. New York: Hudson Hills Press, 1995.

PART III: GLASS

AMERICAN STUDIO GLASS SINCE 1945: FROM COLD WAR TO HOT SHOP
(*Glass & Art*, No. 11, 1995)

GLASS AS ELEMENT: FIVE ARTISTS
Previously unpublished, 1981
BUSTER SIMPSON: THROWAWAY GLASS
(*GLASS*, No. 47, 1992)

TOOTS ZYNSKY: THE CLIMATE OF COLOR
Previously unpublished, 1997
[1] Mary Blume, "Breaking Point: Free-Form Adventures With Glass," *International Herald-Tribune*, December 3–4, 1994.
[2] Jean-Claude Bester, "Toots Zynsky," *La Revue de la Céramique et du Verre*, January, 1995.
[3] Shawn Waggoner, "My Full Name is Mary Ann Toots Zynsky....," *Glass Art*, July/

August, 1989.
4 Ibid.
5 Toots Zynsky, conversation with the author, June 7, 1997.
6 Bester, see no. 2.
7 Jean-Claude Billaud, in *Toots Zynsky*. Paris: Clara Scremini, 1989.

WILLIAM MORRIS: PALEOGLASS
(*GLASS*, No. 55, Spring 1994)
1 Adolph Gottlieb, Mark Rothko, and Barnett Newman. Letter to the Editor, *The New York Times*, June 13, 1943.
2 Robert C. Hobbs, et al. *Abstract Expressionism: The Formative Years*. New York: Whitney Museum of American Art, 1978.
3 Roger Downey, "Sacred bone yard," *Seattle Weekly*, October 2, 1992.
4 Ron Glowen, "Northwest feeling alive in works of these artists," *The Herald*, December 21, 1990.
5 Ben Marks, "William Morris: Brendan Walter Gallery, Santa Monica, California," *New Work*, Fall, 1988.
6 Patterson Sims, et al. *William Morris: Glass Art and Artifact*. Seattle: University of Washington Press, 1989.
7 Henry Geldzahler, "The Stubborn Voice From Within," in *William Morris: Glass Art and Artifact*. Seattle: University of Washington Press, 1989.
8 Narcissus Quagliata, in *William Morris: Glass Art and Artifact*. Seattle: University of Washington Press, 1989.
9 Marija Gimbutas, *The Civilization of the Goddess: The World of Old Europe*. San Francisco: Harper San Francisco, 1991.
10 Downey, see no. 3.
11 Holland Cotter, "Glass Sculptors whose work transcends craft," *The New York Times*, June 18, 1993.

THERMAN STATOM: INSTALLING SPACE
(*GLASS* #65, Winter, 1996)
1 Rose Slivka, *Four Leaders in Glass*. Los Angeles: Craft and Folk Art Museum, 1980.
2 Therman Statom, conversation with the author, September 12, 1996.

GINNY RUFFNER'S INSTALLATIONS: CONTAINING SPACE
(*GLASS*, No. 83, Summer 2001)

METAMORPHOSIS: GLASS SCULTURES BY LYNDA BENGLIS
(*GLASS* #82, Spring, 2001)
1 Robert Pincus-Witten, "Lynda Benglis: The Frozen Gesture," *Artforum*, November, 1974.
2 Carter Ratcliff, "The Fate of a Gesture: Lynda Benglis," in *The Fate of a Gesture: Jackson Pollock and Postwar American Art*. New York: Farrar, Straus and Giroux, 1999.
3 Erica-Lynn Huberty, "Intensity of Form and Surface: an Interview with Lynda Benglis," *Sculpture*, July/August, 2000.
4 Interview with the author, Bryan Ohno Gallery, Seattle, October 12, 2000.
5 Surprisingly, one of the most extensive commentaries on Benglis's controversial ad is in an essay on Scott Burton by Pincus-Witten, reprinted in his *Postminimalism into Maximalism: American Art 1966–86*. Ann Arbor, MI: UMI Research Press, 1987, 214–215.
6 Interview with the author.
7 Ibid.
8 Ibid.

DANIEL CLAYMAN: THE OBJECT IS THE IMAGE
(*GLASS, No.* 75, Summer, 1999)

GLASS IN PUBLIC ART TODAY: PRESERVATION, RENOVATION, INNOVATION
(*Public Art Review*, Spring-Summer, 2001)

PAUL MARIONI: THE VISITOR
(*GLASS*, No. 74, Spring, 1999)

ROBERT KEHLMANN: ASPECTS OF MEANING
(*GLASS*, No. 63, Fall 1996)
[1] Susanne K. Frantz and William Warmus, *Robert Kehlmann / Painting with Glass / A Retrospective*. Moraga, CA: Hearts Art Gallery, Saint Mary's College of California, 1996.
[2] Conversation with the author, June 17, 1996.
[3] Letter to the author, June 16, 1996.
[4] Robert Kehlmann, "An Interview with Clement Greenberg," *Glass Art Society Journal*, 1984–85, 31.
[5] Clement Greenberg, letter to Robert Kehlmann, July 6, 1984.

MARVIN LIPOFSKY: CONCEALING THE VOID
(*GLASS*, No. 68, Fall 1997)
[1] Shawn Waggoner, "The Natural Form of Glass: Marvin Lipofsky," *Glass Art*, May/June, 1997.
[2] Maria Porges, "Marvin Lipofsky: Artist and Educator," *Neues Glas / New Glass*, 4/91.
[3] Cheryl White, "Marvin Lipofsky: Roving Ambassador of Glass," *American Craft*, October/November, 1991.
[4] Robert Kehlmann, "An Interview with Marvin Lipofsky," *Glass Art Society Journal*, 1983–84.
[5] Peter Selz, *Funk*. Berkeley, CA: University Art Museum, 1967.

FEMCLUSTER: A NEW PARADIGM
(*GLASS*, No. 80, Fall 2000)

ROBERT WILLSON: IMAGE-MAKER
(Introduction from *Robert Willson: Image-maker*. San Antonio, Texas: Pace-Willson Foundation in association with University of Washington Press, 2002)
[1] *Robert Willson: Sculpture in Glass,* prod. Multi-Media Associates for the New Orleans Museum of Art, , 1990, videocassette.
[2] Pino Signoretto, interview with the author, Venice, March 9, 2001.
[3] Robert Willson, *Texas, Venice and the Glass Sculpture Era—Notes* (San Antonio: Tejas Art Press, 1981), "Venice and Solid Glass Sculpture," unpaginated section.
[4] Thomas McEvilley, "Doctor, Lawyer, Indian Chief: 'Primitivism in 20th-Century Art,'" *Artforum*, November 1984, pp. 54–61.
[5] Serge Guilbaut, *How New York Stole the Idea of Modern Art: Abstract Expressionism, Freedom, and the Cold War* (Chicago: University of Chicago Press, 1983).
[6] Paolo Rizzi, "The Color of Venice," in *A Story in Glass: Robert Willson* (Venice, Italy: Edizioni in Castello, 1984), p. 26.

VISION QUEST: NATIVE AMERICAN GLASS
(*GLASS* #95, Summer, 2005)

BENJAMIN MOORE: THE TRANSLATOR
(*GLASS* #97, Winter 2005)

PART IV: WOOD, FIBER AND METALS
LEROY SETZIOL: SYSTEM AND SYMBOL
(*American Craft*, April/May, 1992)
[1] Unless otherwise noted, all artist's quotations are from an interview with the author in Eugene, Oregon on October 28, 1991.
[2] Available from University of Oregon Museum of Art, Eugene, Oregon 97403, $29.00 postpaid.

BRIAN GLADWELL: TWELVE WORKS
(*Brian Gladwell: Twelve Works.* Saskatoon, Saskatchewan: Mendel Art Gallery, 1993)
[1] Helen Marzolf, *Brian Gladwell: Furniture*. Regina, Saskatchewan: Dunlop Art Gallery, 1987.
[2] Marzolf, *Gladwell*, 1987.
[3] Marzolf, *Gladwell*, 1987.
[4] Marzolf, *Gladwell*, 1987.
[5] W. P. Morgan, *In Place: Craft From Saskatchewan*. Saskatoon, Saskatchewan: Saskatchewan Craft Council, 1991, 7.
[6] Elly Danica, "Brian Gladwell," *The Craft Factor*, Vol. II, No. 1, Spring, 1986, 11.
[7] Franklyn Heisler, *Tables Turned: Aspects of Furniture as Visual Art*. Banff, Alberta: Whyte Museum of the Canadian Rockies, 1987, 1.
[8] Brian Gladwell, *Beyond the Object*. Saskatoon, Saskatchewan: Saskatchewan Crafts Council, 1987, 3.
[9] Morgan, *In Place*, 14.

ALBERT PALEY: ORGANIC FORM
(*Sculpture*, May, 1999)

LIA COOK: ARIADNE IN BERKELEY
(*Lia Cook: Material Illusions*. Oakland, CA: The Oakland Museum of California, 1995)
[1] Robert Graves, *The Greek Myths: Volume One*. Harmondsworth, Middlesex (England): Penguin Books, 1955, 339
[2] "Stilisti de oggi/Lia Cook/Tessuti come opere dell'arte," *Jacquard*, June, 1990, 14–15.
[3] Esperienze Diddatiche, "Il corso sulle tecniche dei Tessuti operati, Fondaztione Arte della Seta Lisio," *Jacquard*, September, 1990.
[4] Lia Cook, "Ed Rossbach: Educator," in Ann Pollard Howe and Rebecca A. T. Stevens, eds. *Ed Rossbach*. Asheville, NC: Lark Books and The Textile Museum, 1990, 100.
[5] Rémy Prin, *Lia Cook: Identités textiles no. 2*. Beauvais [France]: National Gallery of Tapestry and Textile Art, 1983.
[6] Nancy A. Corwin, *Lia Cook*. Washington, DC: National Academy of Sciences, 1990.
[7] Lia Cook, unpublished statement for panel, "Materiality and Content," Women's Caucus for the Arts, Chicago, 1992.
[8] Catherine Lynn, "Surface Ornament: Wallpapers, Carpets, Textiles, and Embroidery," in Doreen Bolger Burke et al., *In Pursuit of Beauty: Americans and the Aesthetic Movement*. New York: The Metropolitan Museum of Art and Rizzoli International, 1986, 92.
[9] See no. 7.

THE AGE OF SOLBERG
(*Metalsmith*, Vol. 15, No. 1, Winter 1995)
[1] Cindy Cetlin, "Art, Artifact and the Jewelry of Ramona Solberg," *Metalsmith*, Summer 1985, 14–16.
[2] Carolyn Benesh, "I'm sort of the Henry Ford of jewelry," *Ornament*, Vol. 13, No. 1, 1989, 58–63.
[3] Ramona Solberg, conversation with the author, July 12, 1994.
[4] Spencer Moseley, "The Necklaces of Ramona Solberg," *Craft Horizons*, June, 1973,

20–24.
[5] Ibid.
[6] See no. 3.
[7] See no. 1.
[8] See no. 2.
[9] Rose Slivka, *The Object as Poet*. Washington, DC: Smithsonian Institution Press, 1977.
[10] Kiff Slemmons, letter to the author, July 20, 1994.
[11] Ibid.
[12] Sylvia S. J. Kennedy, "Ron Ho's Transformations: Found Objects into Jewelry," *Ornament*, Vol. 11, No. 4, 1986.
[13] Ron Ho, conversation with the author, July 8, 1994.
[14] Laurie Hall, conversation with the author, July 18, 1994, Seattle.
[15] Ibid.

ELLENSBURG FUNKY
(*Metalsmith*, Vol. 15, No. 3, Fall 1995)
[1] Peter Selz, "Notes on Funk," in Selz, *Art in a Turbulent Era*. Ann Arbor, MI: UMI Research Press, 1985, 325–330.
[2] Ibid.
[3] Nancy Worden, interview with the author, April 9, 1994.
[4] For example, R. E. Beans, Art Detective, Mike Holmes, Gary Green, Jimmy Jet, Charlie King, Marty Lovens, Jeanette Papadopolous, and Larry Reid.
[5] Donald Paul Tompkins, "Crafts, the High Arts, and Education." Dissertation for Doctorate of Education degree, Columbia University Teachers College, New York, 1973.
[6] Michael Dunas, "Ken Cory and the Pencil Brothers," Metalsmith, Vol. 8, No. 2, Spring, 1988, 14–21.
[7] "It's like sticking your finger down the throat of the material to see what comes up." This final line of the article was itself a paraphrase of a description by Harold Paris in "Sweet Land of Funk," *Art in America*, March-April, 1967.
[8] Worden interview.
[9] Ed Wicklander, interview with the author, May 28, 1994.

ROSS PALMER BEECHER: EXPLORING AMERICAN MYTHS
(*Metalsmith*, Spring, 1996)
[1] Interview with the author, 1995.
[2] Ibid.

SCULPTURAL HERITAGE AND SCULPTURAL IMPLICATIONS: TURNED WOOD OBJECTS IN THE WORNICK COLLECTION
(Reprinted from *Expressions in Wood: Turned Wood Objects in the Wornick Collection*. Oakland, California: The Oakland Museum of California, 1997)
DAVID GROTH
(From *David Groth*. Eureka, CA: Morris Graves Museum of Art, 2001)

JEAN WILLIAMS CACICEDO: EXPLORATIONS IN CLOTH
(*Jean Williams Cacicedo: Explorations in Cloth*. San Francisco: Museum of Craft and Folk Art, 2000)
[1] Jean Williams Cacicedo, interview with the author, March 10, 2000.
[2] Maria Porges, "Coat Tales," *American Craft*, October/November 1989, 46.
[3] John Perreault, "Pattern Painting," *Artforum*, September 1977.
[4] Cacicedo, interview with the author, March 10, 2000.
[5] Porges, see no. 2.
[6] Cacicedo, interview with the author, March 10, 2000.

[7] Ibid.

RANDY SHULL
(*Randy Shull*. San Francisco: Tercera Gallery, 2000)

PATTERNING THE PAST: RACHEL BRUMER AND ISABEL KAHN
(*Surface Design Journal*, Winter 2003)
[1] Cherry Haisten, "Profile: Rachel Brumer: Taking Notes from Philip Glass," *Fiberarts*, November/December, 1996.
[2] Rock Hushka and Tara Reddy, *Documents Northwest: Sewn*. Seattle: Seattle Art Museum, 2001, unpaginated.
[3] Robin Updike, "Isabel Kahn: Women in community," *Seattle Times*, December 7, 1995, p. G30.
[4] Diane Tepfer, *From Her Studio to Geneva*. Washington, D.C.: U.S. Department of State, Art in Embassies Program, 2001, unpaginated.
[5] Isabel Kahn, interview with the author, August 5, 2001.
[6] Ibid.
[7] Rachel Brumer, interview with the author, August 2, 2001.

KEITH LEWIS: FROM PROPAGANDIST TO HUMANIST
(*Metalsmith*, Winter 2004)
[1] See my "Ellensburg Funky," *Metalsmith*, Fall 1995, Vol. 15, No. 4, 14–21.
[2] See my "The Age of Solberg," *Metalsmith*, Winter 1995, Vol. 15, No. 1, 24–29.
[3] Keith Lewis, "Body Politic," unpublished lecture notes, delivered University of Wisconsin—Green Bay, April, 1999.
[4] Ibid.
[5] Chiori Santiago, "Keith Lewis Undercover," *Metalsmith*, Summer 2000, 46.
[6] Keith Lewis, "Embodied: Flesh, Memory and Longing," unpublished lecture notes, delivered in Boston, Massachusetts, September 2002.
[7] Ibid.
[8] Barbara Tannenbaum, *Her Story/His Story: Jewelry and Sculpture by Kathleen Browne and Keith Lewis*. Akron, OH: Akron Art Museum, 1994.
[9] Santiago, "Keith Lewis Undercover."

NANCY WORDEN: EXCAVATIONS
(*Metalsmith*, Spring 2006)

PART V: TWO AMERICAN MASTERS

RUDY AUTIO: MONTANA ARTIST
(*Rudy Autio--Retrospective*. Missoula, Montana: University of Montana, 1983)
[1] Frances Senska, interview with the author, August 5, 1982, Bozeman, Montana.
[2] Dave DePew, "The Archie Bray Foundation," *Ceramics Monthly*, May, 1972, 18–23.
[3] Frances Senska, "Pottery in a Brickyard," *American Craft*, February/March, 1982.
[4] Dave DePew, see no. 1.
[5] Rudy Autio, interview with the author, August 3, 1982, Missoula, Montana.
[6] Robert Sperry, interview with the author, September 9, 1982, Seattle.
[7] "Potters of Vallauris," *Ceramics Monthly*, April, 1954.
[8] Gene Kleinsmith, *Clay's the Way*. Victorville, California: Victor Valley College, 1978.
[9] Sam Hunter and Willem Sandberg, *Art Since 1950*. Seattle: Century 21, Inc., 1962.
[1] Frances Senska, interview with the author, August 5, 1982, Bozeman, Montana.
[2] Dave DePew, "The Archie Bray Foundation," *Ceramics Monthly*, May, 1972, 18–23.
[3] Frances Senska, "Pottery in a Brickyard," *American Craft*, February/March, 1982.
[4] Dave DePew, see no. 1.

[5] Rudy Autio, interview with the author, August 3, 1982, Missoula, Montana.

[6] Robert Sperry, interview with the author, September 9, 1982, Seattle.

[7] "Potters of Vallauris," *Ceramics Monthly*, April, 1954.

[8] Gene Kleinsmith, *Clay's the Way*. Victorville, California: Victor Valley College, 1978.

[9] Sam Hunter and Willem Sandberg, *Art Since 1950*. Seattle: Century 21, Inc., 1962.

DALE CHIHULY: UNFINISHED ODYSSEY
Previously unpublished, 1995

[1] Dale Chihuly, "On the Road," in *Chihuly: Color, Glass and Form*. Tokyo, Japan: Kodansha International, Ltd., 1986, 15.

[2] LaMar Harrington, *Northwest Designer Craftsmen*. Bellevue, WA: Bellevue Art Museum, 1990.

[3] Chloe Zerwick, *A Short History of Glass*. Corning, NY: The Corning Museum of Glass, 1980, 88.

[4] Dale Chihuly, interview with the author, September 8, 1990, Seattle.

[5] Peter Selz, *Funk*. Berkeley, CA: University Art Museum, 1967.

[6]Linda Norden, "Introduction," in *Dale Chihuly Glass*. Pawtuxent Cove, RI: Dale Chihuly, Publisher, 1982..

[7] Karen S. Chambers, "The Man Who Made Glassblowing a Fine Art," *The World & I*, November, 1987, 246–250.

[11] Karen S. Chambers, "Mission: Impossible," in *Chihuly / A Decade of Glass*. Bellevue, WA: Bellevue Art Museum, 1984, 11–22.

[12] Michael W. Monroe, "Drawing in the Third Dimension," in *Chihuly: Color, Glass, and Form*. Tokyo, Japan: Kodansha International, Ltd., 1986, 36–37.

[13] Linda Norden, "Dale Chihuly: Shell Forms," *Artsmagazine*, June, 1981, 150–157.

[14] Ibid.

[15] Karen S. Chambers, "A Description of Dale Chihuly's Series," unpublished manuscript, 1989.

[16] Robert Hobbs, "Chihuly's Macchia," in *Dale Chihuly: Objets de verre*. Paris, France: Musée des arts decoratifs, Palais de Louvre, 1986, unpaginated.

[18] Robert Hobbs, "Dale Chihuly's *Persians*: Acts of Survival," in *Chihuly / Persians*. Bridgehampton, NY: Dia Art Foundation, 1988, 8.

[19] Rose C. S. Slivka, "From the Studio," *East Hampton Star*, August 4, 1988.

[20] Robert Hobbs, "Chihuly's *Venetians*," unpublished manuscript, 1989.

[21] Matthew Kangas, "Dale Chihuly: Return to Origins," *GLASS*, No. 39, 1990, 18–27.

[22] Ron Glowen, *Venetians / Dale Chihuly*. Altadena, CA: Twin Palms Publishers, 1989, unpaginated.

[23] William Warmus, "The Venetians," in *The Venetians: Modern Glass 1919–1990*. New York: Muriel Karasik Gallery, 1989, 5–9.

[24] Chambers, see no. 15.

[25] Hobbs, see no. 20.

[26] Ibid.

[27] Dale Chihuly, unpublished transcript, 1993.

[28] Ibid.

[29] D. W. Winnicott, "The Fate of the Transitional Object," in Clare Winnicott, et al., eds. *Psychoanalytical Explorations / D. W. Winnicott*. Cambridge, MA: Harvard University Press, 54.

[30] Chihuly, see no. 27.

[31] Ibid.

[32] Patterson Sims, *Dale Chihuly / Installation 1964–1990*. Seattle, WA: Seattle Art Museum, 1992.

[33] See my "Dale Chihuly: Gifts from the Sea," in *Dale Chihuly*. New York: American Craft Museum, 1991.

[34] Kuspit, see no. 6.

[35] Chihuly, see no. 27.

[36] Henry Geldzahler, in *Dale Chihuly Japan 1990*. Tokyo, Japan: Japan Institute of Arts and Crafts, 1990, unpaginated.

[37] Svetlana Alpers, *Rembrandt's Enterprise*. Chicago: University of Chicago Press, 1988.

[38] See no. 4.

[39] Dagmar Sinz, "A Talk with Dale Chihuly," *Neues Glas / New Glass*, January/March, 1987, 17.

[40] Alistair Duncan, et al., *Masterworks of Louis Comfort Tiffany*. New York: Harry N. Abrams, Inc., 1989.

[41] Clement Greenberg, "Recentness of Sculpture" in *American Sculpture of the Sixties*. Maurice Tuchman, ed. Los Angeles, CA: Los Angeles County Museum of Art, 1967, 24–26.

[42] See no. 4.

[43] See no. 10.

[44] Linda Norden, *Chihuly: Baskets*. Seattle: Portland Press, 1994.

[45] Robert Hobbs, *Chihuly Persians*. Bridgehampton, NY: Dia Art Foundation, 1986.

[46] See no. 16.

[47] See no. 4.

[48] Henry Geldzahler, "Foreword," in *Chihuly: Color, Glass and Form*. Tokyo, Japan: Kodansha International, Ltd., 1986, 10–12.

ABOUT THE AUTHOR

Matthew Kangas read English literature at Manchester University with David Pirie and C. B. Cox before returning to the U.S. and completing his B. A. at Reed College. In 1972, he returned to England where he completed an M.A. at Oxford University, studying there with John Bayley, Francis Warner and J. D. Fleeman. After working briefly in art book publishing in New York, he returned to his native Seattle, Washington and began writing about art and craft. Now the author of eleven books and a contributor to numerous magazines including *Art in America, Sculpture* and *Glass*, he has received many awards including those from the National Endowment for the Arts, the Manufacturers Hanover/*Art World* prize for distinguished newspaper art criticism, and the Everson Medal for his contributions to American ceramics. He has an honorary appointment to the aesthetic education research laboratory at Shanghai Teachers University. In 2003, he was named commissioner for North America at the Second World Ceramic Biennale in Icheon, Korea. A collection, *epicenter: Essays on North American Art* (Midmarch Arts), was published in 2004.

CREDITS

PART I: ON THE CRAFTS

STORYTELLING IN AMERICAN CRAFT 1750–1950
(Reprinted from *Storytelling in Twentieth-Century American Craft*, with Lloyd E. Herman. St. Louis: Craft Alliance and University of Washington Press, 1993)

THE EMBODIMENT OF INGENUITY
(*American Craft*, August/September 1987)

PACIFIC NORTHWEST CRAFTS IN THE 1950S
(Reprinted from Barbara Johns, ed. *Jet Dreams: Art of the Fifties in the Northwest*. Seattle: University of Washington Press, 1995, 81–95)

BREAKING BARRIERS: RECENT AMERICAN CRAFT
(*Breaking Barriers: Recent American Craft*. New York: American Craft Museum, 1995)

THE REMATERIALIZATION OF THE ART OBJECT
(*Sculpture*, July/August 1996)

THE MYTH OF THE NEGLECTED CERAMICS ARTIST
(Adapted from a lecture given at "Tangents: Ceramics and Beyond," March 16, 2004 at Henry Hope School of Fine Arts, Indiana University, Bloomington, Indiana; *Ceramics Monthly*, October, 2004)

PART II: CERAMICS

TOWARD A BICAMERAL ESTHETIC OF CLAY
(*American Ceramics*, Vol. 1, No. 1, Winter 1982)

ROBERT SPERRY: PLANETARY CLAY
(*American Craft*, December 1981/January 1982)

AMERICAN FIGURATIVE CERAMICS
(Reprinted from Robert Bell, ed., *Perth International Crafts Triennial*. Perth, Australia: Art Gallery of Western Australia, 1989)

SHATTERED SELF: NORTHWEST FIGURATIVE CERAMICS
(*American Craft*, August/September, 1986)

HOWARD KOTTLER
(*American Ceramics*, Vol. 6, No. 2, 1990)

PATTERN RE-EXAMINED IN AMERICAN CERAMICS
(*Surface Design Journal*, Vol. 15, No. 1, 1990)

RICHARD FAIRBANKS: TURNING POINT
(Excerpted from Richard Fairbanks, American Potter. Seattle: University of Washington Press, 1993; 32–38)

JIM LEEDY: PREHISTORIC MODERN
(*American Craft*, June/July, 1990)

RICK DILLINGHAM AND THE REPARATIVE DRIVE
(*American Ceramics*, Vol. 8, No. 4, 1990)

MICHAEL LUCERO DISCOVERS AMERICA
(*Sculpture*, July/August 1992)

VIOLA FREY'S FAMILY PLOT
(*Sculpture*, May-June, 1994)

DOUG JECK: MONUMENTS TO UNCERTAINTY
(*American Ceramics*, Vol. 12, No. 1, 1995)

RYOJI KOIE: NEW CONTEXTS
(*Ryoji Koie*. Seattle: Bryan Ohno Editions and University of Washington Press, 2000)

LAWSON OYEKAN: ORIGIN AND EXILE
(*CRART*, Winter 2005)

PICASSO'S CERAMICS: A LIFELONG INTEREST
(*Ceramics Monthly*, February, 1999)

NORTH AMERICAN CERAMIC SCULPTURE NOW
(Reprinted from *Now & Now: World Contemporary Ceramics*. Icheon, Korea: 2nd
World Ceramic Biennale 2003, 2003, 12–73)

PART III: GLASS

AMERICAN STUDIO GLASS SINCE 1945: FROM COLD WAR TO HOT SHOP
(*Glass & Art*, No. 11, 1995)

GLASS AS ELEMENT: FIVE ARTISTS
Previously unpublished, 1981

BUSTER SIMPSON: THROWAWAY GLASS
(*GLASS* #47, Spring 1992)

TOOTS ZYNSKY: THE CLIMATE OF COLOR
Previously unpublished, 1997

WILLIAM MORRIS: PALEOGLASS
(*GLASS* #55, Spring 1994)

THERMAN STATOM: INSTALLING SPACE
(*GLASS* #65, Winter 1996)

GINNY RUFFNER'S INSTALLATIONS: CONTAINING SPACE
(*GLASS* #83, Summer 2001)

METAMORPHOSIS: GLASS SCULTURES BY LYNDA BENGLIS
(*GLASS* #82, Spring 2001)

DANIEL CLAYMAN: THE OBJECT IS THE IMAGE
(*GLASS* #75, Summer 1999)

GLASS IN PUBLIC ART TODAY: PRESERVATION, RENOVATION, INNOVATION
(*Public Art Review*, Spring-Summer 2001)

PAUL MARIONI: THE VISITOR
(*GLASS* #74, Spring 1999)

ROBERT KEHLMANN: ASPECTS OF MEANING
(*GLASS* #63, Fall 1996)

MARVIN LIPOFSKY: CONCEALING THE VOID
(*GLASS* #68, Fall 1997)

FEMCLUSTER: A NEW PARADIGM
("A New Paradigm," *GLASS* #80, Fall 2000)

ROBERT WILLSON: IMAGE-MAKER
(Introduction from *Robert Willson: Image-maker*. San Antonio, Texas: Pace-Willson
Foundation in association with University of Washington Press, 2002)

VISION QUEST: NATIVE AMERICAN GLASS
(*GLASS* #95, Summer 2005)

BENJAMIN MOORE: THE TRANSLATOR
(*GLASS* #97, Winter 2005)

PART IV: WOOD, FIBER AND METALS

LEROY SETZIOL: SYSTEM AND SYMBOL
(*American Craft*, April/May, 1992)

BRIAN GLADWELL: TWELVE WORKS
(*Brian Gladwell: Twelve Works.* Saskatoon, Saskatchewan, Canada:
Mendel Art Gallery, 1993)

ALBERT PALEY: ORGANIC FORM
(*Sculpture*, May, 1999)

LIA COOK: ARIADNE IN BERKELEY
(*Lia Cook: Material Illusions.* Oakland, CA: The Oakland Museum of California, 1995)

THE AGE OF SOLBERG
(*Metalsmith*, Vol. 15, No. 1, Winter 1995)

ELLENSBURG FUNKY
(*Metalsmith*, Vol. 15, No. 3, Fall 1995)

ROSS PALMER BEECHER: EXPLORING AMERICAN MYTHS
(*Metalsmith*, Spring 1996)

SCULPTURAL HERITAGE AND SCULPTURAL IMPLICATIONS: TURNED WOOD
OBJECTS IN THE WORNICK COLLECTION
(Reprinted from *Expressions in Wood: Turned Wood Objects in the Wornick Collection.*
Oakland, California: The Oakland Museum of California, 1997)

DAVID GROTH
(*David Groth.* Eureka, CA: Morris Graves Museum of Art, 2001)

JEAN WILLIAMS CACICEDO: EXPLORATIONS IN CLOTH
(*Jean Williams Cacicedo: Explorations in Cloth.* San Francisco: Museum of Craft and
Folk Art, 2000)

RANDY SHULL
(*Randy Shull.* San Francisco: Tercera Gallery, 2000)

PATTERNING THE PAST: RACHEL BRUMER AND ISABEL KAHN
(*Surface Design Journal*, Winter 2003)

KEITH LEWIS: FROM PROPAGANDIST TO HUMANIST
(*Metalsmith*, Winter 2004)

NANCY WORDEN: EXCAVATIONS
(*Metalsmith*, No. 26, Vol. 1, Spring 2006)

PART V: TWO AMERICAN MASTERS

RUDY AUTIO: MONTANA ARTIST
(*Rudy Autio--Retrospective.* Missoula, Montana: University of Montana, 1983)

DALE CHIHULY: UNFINISHED ODYSSEY
Previously unpublished, 1995

INDEX